ENGLAND'S HERITAGE

ENGLISH HERITAGE

ENGLAND'S HERITAGE

DERRY BRABBS

FOR ENGLISH HERITAGE:
DAVID MILES, CHIEF ARCHAEOLOGIST
VAL HORSLER, HEAD OF PUBLICATIONS

CASSELL&CO

First published in the United Kingdom in 2001
by Cassell & Co, in association with English Heritage

Text copyright © Derry Brabbs, 2001;
chapters 12 and 13 © English Heritage, 2001
Design and layout copyright © Cassell & Co, 2001

Distributed in the United States of America by
Sterling Publishing Co., Inc.
387 Park Avenue South
New York
NY 10016-8810

A CIP catalogue record for this book is available from the British Library.
ISBN 0304 355992

Editor Catherine Bradley

Design Director David Rowley
Designer Ken Wilson
Art Editor Austin Taylor
Indexer Drusilla Calvert

Typeset in Monotype Spectrum
Printed and bound in Italy by Printer Trento S.r.l.

Cassell & Co
Wellington House
125 Strand
London
WC2R OBB

'MAN IS A HISTORY-MAKING CREATURE WHO CAN NEITHER REPEAT HIS PAST NOR LEAVE IT BEHIND.'

W H AUDEN
FROM 'D H LAWRENCE', *The Dyer's Hand*, 1963

CONTENTS

INTRODUCTION
ENGLAND'S PAST: A LIVING LEGACY

ENGLAND'S ARCHITECTURAL HERITAGE is amongst the richest in the world, and preparing this book has been a pleasure and a privilege. It has involved travelling across the length and breadth of what is still a remarkably diverse nation, with strong regional identities influenced by the varied terrain. I have photographed beautiful, extraordinary and evocative buildings and monuments from both the remote and relatively recent past: Neolithic sites and grand country houses, parish churches and Roman villas, medieval castles and industrial mills. Some are well known attractions, others more idiosyncratic choices – vernacular, local buildings reflecting the character of their immediate surroundings. Whether urban or rural, the physical legacy of the past is everywhere, continuing to dominate the national landscape and to

illustrate the diverse influences that have shaped the modern age.

Many of England's historic buildings have been adapted and modified over the centuries, reflecting different uses and fashions in their architectural fabric. Such complex, highly individual structures illustrate the essential continuity that has accommodated England's social and political changes over the last millennium. Norman churches, for example, were imposed on existing Saxon foundations, and strategic defences such as Dover Castle and several of the Saxon Shore forts were redeveloped around an original core. The pattern of streets in modern towns and cities frequently follows the layout of Roman roads, and many prosperous Tudor manor houses grew out of medieval fortified homes. Current schemes of urban regeneration and dockland conversion are merely the latest expression of a practice that has existed for centuries. Informed exploration of these intricate layers has provided archaeologists with fascinating insights into how our ancestors conducted their lives.

The distinctive landscape of England is also an evolving legacy which contains the seeds of a surprisingly remote past. Crop marks, visible through aerial photography, have revealed the shape of early settlements that were concealed for centuries. We now know that many field boundaries

1 A detail from the stone pulpitum in York Minster. The screen was completed *c*.1461 and portrays kings of England from William I to Henry VI.
2 The Welsh Marches was a volatile region from prehistoric to late medieval times, subject to raids and border disputes. Ancient hillforts and ruined castles still dominate its beautiful land-scape.
3 The view from Sutton Bank, Thirsk, North Yorkshire, looking across the rich agricultural land of the Vale of York. England's fertile soil and good grazing land were the core of its prosperity for centuries.

2

are extremely old, dating back to medieval or even prehistoric times, although the buildings around them may have moved or disappeared. More sophisticated analysis of soil and vegetation can challenge our perceptions of the past, exposing the sites of 'ploughed out' buildings or new evidence of agricultural activity. Modern archaeological techniques enable us to trace the individual history of a hay meadow, pasture land or cultivated garden, extracting valuable information about the past generations who worked or tended it.

The land and buildings of England were intimately linked for centuries. Regional materials were used in churches, houses, cathedrals, bridges and the structures of local industries such as forges and mills. Elegant market towns and country mansions articulated the confidence of their eras in stone, timber, slate and brick, expressing a communal identity through a variety of architectural styles. Technological advances in the 19th century were to transform industrial regions with innovative constructions of cast iron and steel, but a nostalgia for rural tradition found expression in the Gothic inspiration of wealthy manufacturers' retreats.

England's heritage is a complex tapestry, woven from many overlapping strands. This book is

consequently structured through themes, rather than chronological sequence, to consider how conquest and war, religion and education, industrialization and trade have influenced England's fortunes across the centuries. With the assistance of the expertise and unique archives of English Heritage, I have sought to celebrate the depth and vitality of an endlessly fascinating past.

3

CHAPTER

1

The population of England has a complex genetic
inheritance, reflecting the different peoples who have traded and
settled there over the centuries. Relatively little is known about the
diverse Neolithic communities who constructed the megaliths, henges
and barrows across prehistoric Britain, but the Celtic society that emerged
before the Roman Conquest is more clearly defined. Many Britains today
consider themselves to be of Celtic descent, although the contribution of
Angles and Saxons, Jutes and Vikings, Romans and Normans also shaped
England's genetic legacy. A subtle blend of cultures and languages
is apparent in regional architecture, place names and dialects.
Modern scientific techniques, allowing new exploration
of DNA distribution, have yet to reveal the
full diversity of this intriguing
national heritage.

WHO ARE THE
'ENGLISH'?

A DIVERSE LEGACY

The dramatic megaliths of prehistoric Britain — barrows, henges, stone circles and standing stones — are a well known, intriguing inheritance from the distant past. Other, more subtle influences on the landscape provide evidence of early peoples' farming and technology, while hillforts bear witness to the turbulent millennium before the Roman Conquest. Centuries after the withdrawal of the Roman legions, the physical impact of their rule remains in England's cities, roads and fortifications. Often concealed by later settlements, they provide the foundations of our modern civic society.

THE INFLUENCE OF SUCCESSIVE Ice Ages on Britain's landscape and climate was enormous. Mountains, rivers and valleys came and went, while changes in sea level meant that the country was alternately attached to the European landmass and severed from it. Swampy flatlands now under the North Sea encouraged seasonal migration of animals from northern Germany and Scandinavia, and the small groups of hunters who pursued them became the first, temporary settlers of Britain. Many of the sites these nomadic hunter-gatherers inhabited were later buried in sand and gravel brought down by glaciers. Significantly, the remains of the earliest known hominid in Britain, Boxgrove Man (thought to have lived around half a million years ago), were recently excavated from a gravel quarry in West Sussex.

During the early Mesolithic period, which began around 8000 BC, the British Isles were still joined to mainland Europe by marshy land bridges. Over time, the landscape in Britain changed from treeless tundra into a dense woodland of pine, birch and alder. At a lakeside camp near Star Carr in North Yorkshire, dating from Mesolithic times, evidence has been found of tree felling, providing both shelter and platforms over the water's edge, and, significantly, the skeleton of a dog tamed for use in hunting — fleet-footed animals required new hunting techniques. Deer, elk and wild pig bones were found at Star Carr, as were shells; the consistency in antler growth indicates that the site was only used for part of the year.

There is a fine dividing line between managing the land and farming, and some Mesolithic people are now believed to have cleared areas of woodland and grown selective plants. Indigenous animals may also have been managed. However, farming in its more accepted sense — sowing and harvesting crops, breeding domesticated animals and adapting the landscape — developed in Britain before 4000 BC (the beginning of the Neolithic era), probably spreading across Europe from the Near East. Whether new farming techniques were necessarily linked to an influx of Neolithic people is unclear, but these new arrivals did bring prehistoric varieties of cereal, goats and sheep. They were able to produce stone tools on a larger scale and establish more permanent settlements.

The organization and strategic thought needed in farming were also required to create the stone circles, henges, standing stones and barrows found across the British Isles. In England, Wiltshire is especially rich in Neolithic sites and monuments, including the Windmill Hill settlement, the West Kennet Long Barrow, Silbury Hill, Avebury and Stonehenge. Modern carbon dating techniques have enabled archaeologists to assess when the megaliths were built and to show that they were not single, unitary structures. Rather like castles and cathedrals, the sites today reflect the consequences of many centuries of use, adaptation, destruction and renovation, clouding the original purpose. The archaeologist Catherine Hills and others have noted that, given the close distribution of monuments, they may have symbolized territorial possession; ancestral bones in barrows may have reinforced land ownership claims.

Whether religious or secular, the importance of such megaliths to their communities is self-evident. Both  Avebury and Stonehenge have avenues leading into their circles, indicating a processional aspect to the ceremonies and rituals held within. In some respects Avebury is the more perplexing of the two, not least because it is linked to another site over 1.5 km (1 mile) away, known as The Sanctuary, by the clearly defined double line of standing stones of West Kennet

1 Archaeologists estimate
that the stone circle at
Avebury, one of many
Neolithic megaliths in
Wiltshire, was built
c.2500 BC. Unusually, a
wider perimeter encloses
two smaller circles.
2 This aerial view of Avebury
shows the henge monu-
ment within the wider
landscape. It emphasizes the
sheer size and scale of the
surrounding earthworks.

2

1

1, 2 Five massive trilithons
form the inner core of
Stonehenge, the third and
final phase of which began
around 2100 BC. The lintels
on top of the upright sarsen
stones were fixed in place
using a complex system of
mortice and tenon joints.
The artist's impression
(right) gives an insight into
how Stonehenge might
have appeared c.4,000 years
ago. The outer sarsen and

inner bluestone circles
enclose the central
horseshoe of five trilithons.
3 Castlerigg Circle near
Keswick, Cumbria, is a
Neolithic circle thought to
thought to pre-date Stonehenge. Although few of the
33 stones in the slightly
elongated circle exceed
1.5 m (5 ft) in height, the
dramatic surroundings
compensate for any lack
of stature.

2

Avenue. Avebury's 11.5-ha (28.5-acre) site consists of
one large ring of standing stones, within which are two
smaller groups, all three encompassed within bank and
ditch earthworks. The distance from the ditch's base to
the bank's summit measures up to 15 m (50 ft) in places.
Dug from almost solid white chalk, it must have been
dazzling in sunshine.

The stones erected within Avebury's henge were
dragged from neighbouring downland. Many stones
weighed up to 20 tonnes, rising to around 60 tonnes in
some cases. Unlike Stonehenge's great sarsens, those at
Avebury remained undressed, in their natural form.

Ergonomic experts have calculated that to excavate
and transport the stones would have taken a staggering
1.5 million man hours. Discipline and teamwork would
have been essential, as well as links with other communities – whether peaceful or aggressive – to supplement
local labour. Avebury is estimated to have been built
around the middle of the third millennium BC, midway
between the first two of Stonehenge's three phases of
construction. Phase one produced a basic henge, an
arena used for some 500 years before being temporarily
abandoned. Later stages, leading to the creation of
the stone circles within the henge, coincided with the
arrival of a new group of settlers from Europe around
2200 BC. The Beaker people, about whom
we know very little, were named after the
distinctive earthenware drinking vessels
found in many of their burial sites.

The extent and significance of new settlers at this time has recently been questioned by archaeologists, aware that metal
– and indeed the 'beakers' themselves –
had also entered the country through
cross-Channel trading routes. Also uncertain is the relationship of Bronze Age
immigrants with the existing population.
Existing monuments and megaliths were
still used and, in the case of Stonehenge,
significantly adapted around 2100 BC.
Some 80 bluestone pillars were imported

with the intention of creating two concentric circles
within the henge. Incredibly, the bluestone must have
been transported 386 km (240 miles) from the Preseli
Mountains in South Wales. One can only speculate what
perceived powers bluestone held to make its inclusion
in Stonehenge so important.

It was during the erection of the bluestone circles
that the famous astronomical link was created, aligning
the site's entrance with the rising sun at the summer
solstice. Massive lintelled sarsen stones were set in a continuous circle around the site, with another horseshoe
formation inside. The huge stones, up to 9 m (30 ft) high,
were dragged a distance of 32 km (20 miles) from the
downs, and those around the perimeter laboriously
dressed to a smooth finish by constant pounding with
stone hammers. Remarkably, the stones were deliberately tapered near the top to ensure they appeared
vertical to the naked eye – an optical device used 1,700
years later on the pillars of the Parthenon.

The new arrivals' skills in woodcraft and construction
are proved by the 'Dover Boat', dated to 1300 BC and
uncovered during excavations in the south-coast port.
Providing cross-Channel transport for settlers or traders,
it is over 9 m (30 ft) in length and made from long single
pieces of oak, jointed in places. Side planks were stitched

3

1 A substantial stone wall encircled the Bronze Age settlement of Grimspound on Dartmoor, Devon, and the 1.6 ha (4-acre) site originally contained at least 20 separate dwellings. A stream was diverted to pass within the protective corral, and traces of stone beds and hearths can still be detected amongst the ruined huts.

2, 3 An area of deeply pitted landscape around Thetford in Norfolk marks the site of Grimes Graves. The indentations were caused by collapsed or filled-in shafts that formed part of a Neolithic flint mine. The illustration shows how an individual pit may have looked in use.

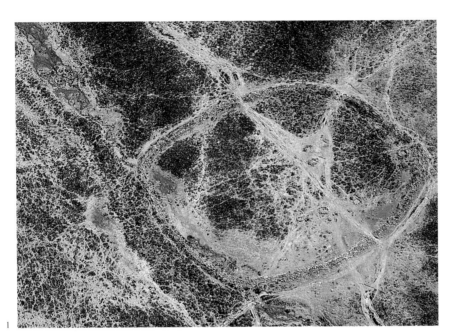

1

to the base with yew withies, and moss forced tightly into joints and seams made the vessel watertight.

Metal's integration into everyday life took place gradually, and natural resources such as flint were still relied upon heavily. Prized for its durability and hard cutting edges, flint was only found in certain parts of the country and extensively mined where it occurred. An area of strangely pitted landscape near Thetford in Norfolk, known as Grimes Graves, was in fact a Neolithic flint mine. The 300 or more indentations are filled-in pit shafts, each laboriously excavated to a depth of around 9 m (30 ft) using rudimentary tools fashioned from antlers and ox shoulder blades. Oil lamps provided illumination. The raw material was fashioned on site into axes, arrowheads and scrapers for cleaning animal skins.

In the millennium before the Roman Conquest of Britain, a new emphasis seems to have been placed on fortifications. Impressive hillforts such as Maiden Castle in Dorset and South Cadbury in Somerset dominated the landscape, and even single farms had banked and ditched enclosures. Celts from western Europe provided

a further prehistoric influx into Britain; a collection of tribes from Alpine regions, they were famed for their skills in battle, farming and the working of iron. Known as 'Keltoi' by the Greeks and 'Celtae' by the Romans, they were to have a lasting effect on Britain's landscape, population and way of life. Recent interpretations of DNA carried out by University College, London reveal clear genetic links between the modern Irish and Welsh and inhabitants of the Basque country. This common heritage, a few centuries removed, can be extended to the Britons of England and Scotland before the arrival of Romans, Vikings and Anglo-Saxons.

The legacy of the Celtic language survives in modern Welsh, a direct descendant of the Celtic speech once used in much of Britain. Cornish, an ancient language currently enjoying a revival, is a related form of Gaelic, but curiously Basque is of non Indo-European origin. The Celtic style of art, distinguished by flowing, dynamic motifs in curvilinear designs reminiscent of waves or plant tendrils, has also endured. The Romans may have regarded the Celts as barbaric, but artefacts, weapons and jewellery of the period reveal a society able to produce metalwork of great beauty. Intricately worked gold torcs, carved bronze mirrors and lavishly decorated and burnished armour display designs and motifs still admired and copied today.

As Celtic infiltration from Gaul became more pronounced, around 500 BC, individual tribes sought to establish their own territories in Britain. Different tribal regions and settlements, the equivalent of our counties and shires, were apparent by the first Roman expedition to Britain. The two most successful tribes were the Trinovantes and Catuvellauni, who dominated

3

the southeast during the 1st century AD under King Cunobelinus (Shakespeare's Cymbeline). The site of their capital, Camulodunum, 3 km (2 miles) southwest of Colchester, was immense – 280 ha (700 acres), now visible as crop marks from the air.

Although individualistic, the Celts had a well established hierarchy with a tribal chieftain at its pinnacle. An aristocratic warrior class was supplemented by the farmers, augmented by slaves taken in battle. Some hillforts were merely the defensive strongholds of tribal chiefs, but the larger ones – such as Maiden Castle and Hambledon Hill in Dorset – have revealed evidence of self-contained villages existing within the ramparts. Farming and agriculture were transformed by the Celts,

who established patterns of small fields that could be ploughed in a day by ox-drawn ploughs. Crop rotation ensured more productive land, while greater numbers of sheep provided wool for both trading and clothing. The study of Iron Age farming methods at Butser in Hampshire, an innovative site of 'experimental archaeology', has included the cultivation of ancient crops and the rearing of animals close to prehistoric breeds, such as Soay sheep and Dexter cows. Butser appears to confirm that sufficient food could have been produced by a farmer class to support a hierarchy of warriors.

Trading links with other European tribes had existed long before Julius Caesar's two expeditions in 55 and 54 BC, but connections expanded considerably during the decades prior to Claudius' invasion in AD 43. Exports of tin, copper, lead and metalwork were traded for pottery, wine, olives and other luxury goods. However, Roman writers frequently refer to the remoteness of Britain. In his *Annals*, Tacitus laments the wreck of a Roman fleet in the North Sea in AD 16, citing the survivors' reports of 'terrible hurricanes' and a belief that it was 'more stormy than any other sea in the world'.

When the Romans finally did invade Britain, the conquest was a protracted, often bloody campaign, which did not permanently subjugate many northern and western regions. In population terms, the influx was only a small minority, recruited from all over the empire to serve in its army or administration. Italians were complemented by Germans, Gauls, Spaniards, Africans and Syrians; the traders who followed the conquest were even more diverse.

2

1 A Roman coin depicting the head of Constantine, first Christian emperor, who was crowned in York in AD 306.

2 This small votive shrine to the goddess Venus was discovered during excavations at the Roman city of Wroxeter near Shrewsbury.

3 Remains of the 2nd-century municipal baths and exercise hall at Wroxeter. The fourth largest town in Roman Britain, Wroxeter was first established as a cavalry fort, housing some 6,000 men and several hundred horses.

4 An aerial view of Richborough Roman fort clearly showing its stages of expansion from ceremonial entry port and township to one of the major forts of the Saxon Shore.

Efficient government and a powerful army encouraged the tribal upper classes, especially in the centre and south, to adapt to Roman rule, emulating their country villas, mosaics, fashions and aspirations. As the graft became more established, governors such as Agricola organized visits to Rome for chieftains' sons and daughters to further the Roman influence.

Celtic Britain was not an urbanized society and, although there were regional tribal capitals, such as Camulodunum, towns in the accepted sense did not exist. Under the Romans other tribal centres were rebuilt or adapted to establish *civitas* (regional administrative capitals throughout the province which included Exeter, Cirencester, Canterbury and Winchester). Many smaller towns were created on the site of forts, their Roman origins surviving in names ending in -chester, signifying a fortress. One characteristic strategy in the province was the development of *coloniae*, for example Lincoln, Gloucester and Colchester. Deliberately filled with retired soldiers, these sites demonstrated the benefits of Roman life and kept a useful source of experienced troops on hand. In time, forts built to quell native unrest became seen as defensive structures for citizens of the Roman province.

Some Roman towns were not inhabited and developed by subsequent peoples. This left places such as Wroxeter and Silchester as archaeological sites to assist our knowledge of how such towns functioned. Wroxeter was bisected by Watling Street, one of the Romans' main arterial roads that ran diagonally northwest through the heart of Britain. It was an important route, linking the main coastal port of Richborough with Wales. Roman towns were usually constructed with a grid pattern of streets, surrounded by a defensive gated wall and dominated by the central forum. Other public buildings included amphitheatres, temples and impressive basilicas; the one in Silchester was magnificent, with elaborate Corinthian columns and marble from Purbeck and the Mediterranean.

Prominent amongst the ruins of Wroxeter are the remains of the public bath house complex, one of the most important features of any town and the focus of much social life. Those bath houses were the equivalent of modern-

day leisure centres, containing exercise halls in addition to the traditional sequence of cold, warm and hot pools.

Despite its apparent invincibility, the empire was coming apart at the seams. Domestic and international pressures were mounting and resources overstretched. The policy of containment, symbolized by Hadrian's Wall in Northumberland, was a reduction of Roman expansionist hopes, despite the magnificence of the wall's 112-km (70-mile) structure. In reality, Britannia's land and coastal borders were under increasing threat from Scots and Picts in the north and Saxons from their German homelands. In AD 367, simultaneous attacks by both sets of enemies proved too much for the reduced Roman forces. Secluded country villas were easy prey and only reinforcements from Rome drove the Saxons back. That respite was merely temporary, as by the end of the 4th century, Germans had invaded Gaul leaving Rome's most northerly province almost cut off.

Although many Roman buildings have disappeared under more recent structures, the empire's legacy survives in England's towns and cities, and the network of roads between them. Inland waterways enabled the efficient movement of goods, and advanced farming methods improved the land's productivity. Many species of fruit and vegetables were introduced in Roman times, including peas, broad beans, celery and cherries. Christianity, laws and civic administration, even if abandoned under subsequent occupation, all resurfaced to provide a framework for later societies.

During the centuries of Roman rule, few who settled permanently in Britannia were Italians. Many of the legionaries and auxiliaries were in fact Romanized Gauls, and so much of the Celtic stock prevailed. After the Roman departure, however, new arrivals from Scandinavia and Germany made an impact on England's genetic inheritance that has lasted to the present day.

THE BEGINNINGS OF ENGLAND

THE WITHDRAWAL OF THE ROMAN LEGIONS LEFT BRITAIN VULNERABLE, AND SOON THE EAST OF THE COUNTRY WAS EXPERIENCING AN INFLUX OF ANGLES, JUTES AND SAXONS. THE POLITICAL FORTUNES OF THE MAJOR SAXON KINGDOMS, SUCH AS NORTHUMBRIA, MERCIA AND WESSEX, WAXED AND WANED IN THE 8TH CENTURY WITH THE QUALITY OF THEIR LEADERS, TO BE FOLLOWED BY VIKING RAIDS THAT DOMINATED THE 9TH AND 10TH CENTURIES. INITIALLY, SUCH INCURSIONS WERE CHECKED BY ALFRED AND AN ENGLISH KINGDOM WAS CREATED. THE PROSPEROUS SAXON CULTURE WAS TO BE OVERWHELMED, HOWEVER, FIRST BY THE DANES AND THEN THE NORMANS.

THE INCREASE OF ANGLO SAXON POWER in Britain was not a single, orchestrated event. Frequent raids had been carried out by Germanic tribes long before the Roman withdrawal; the huge square forts of the Saxon Shore defences, from Brancaster near the Wash to Portchester close to Portsmouth, represent a response to the north-eastern threat. Although archaeological evidence of burning and bodies is notoriously hard to assess, changes in buildings and burials in eastern Britain do indicate an influx from the Netherlands, Germany and Denmark, filling the void left by the retreating legions.

By 410, the last serving legionary had departed. Britannia was released from all allegiances to Rome but in turn left relatively defenceless. How long the Roman way of life lasted, and in what circumstances, is difficult to ascertain. Coins were in less frequent circulation, with no soldiers to be paid or government to collect taxes, and pottery ceased to be mass produced or imported so widely from abroad. The fate of Roman towns proved unpredictable; some were abandoned earlier than anticipated, and others partly rebuilt on the same site. Wroxeter's large basilica, for example, demolished in the early 4th century, was replaced first by small wooden buildings and then by several larger edifices, including a splendid timber house with two storeys and classical porticos. Several Iron Age hillforts, such as South Cadbury, were re-occupied – testimony, as at Wroxeter, to someone in authority able to organize building works. In the west, a Romanized existence may have endured for a few more centuries; the east, by contrast, was experiencing Saxon settlement and a more turbulent transition.

For many peasant Romano-Britons, the arrival of Angles, Jutes and Saxons may not have made much difference to their lives. Some would have been enslaved, others ruled by a new lord or chieftain, but the daily grind of extracting a living from the land continued. Sites in the more remote west, such as Carn Euny and Chysauster, seem to have reverted relatively easily to a pre-conquest way of life. Those with most to fear were the wealthier and educated classes, and indications of rapid departure have been suggested by the discovery of buried silver and valuables close to remote country villas. The apocalyptic account of Gildas, a monk writing in Wales in the 6th century, presents a chaotic picture of burning towns and butchered inhabitants. Historians have been somewhat sceptical of Gildas' polemical view of events, but as the new arrivals swept inland from eastern landing sites, some Britons, possibly including the legendary King Arthur, mounted determined resistance. According to Gildas, the British victory over the Saxons at Mons Badonicus (Mount Badon) was particularly important.

In addition to subduing dissenting regions of Britain, 5th-century Saxon tribes fought one another for territorial supremacy. Many settlers quickly colonized eastern regions, settling in small groups of three or four families to form a farming hamlet, such as the village recently discovered and excavated at West Stow in Suffolk. Buried and preserved by shifting sand, the site has provided large quantities of tools, domestic implements, animal bones and pottery. A full complement of farm animals has been identified, which, together with cereals and other crops, would have ensured agricultural self-sufficiency.

1

1 St Paul's monastery in Jarrow, Tyne & Wear, was home to the Venerable Bede, one of the greatest scholars of the early Christian church and author of many important sources of pre-conquest English history. The chancel of the present parish church dates back to the 7th century. Parts of the monastic complex were built using recycled Roman stone.

2 West Stow Anglo-Saxon village has been reconstructed on the basis of detailed archaeological evidence and was thought to have been occupied between AD 450–650. Established by the banks of the river Lark, it was typical of many around East Anglia during a prolific period of settlement that followed the Romans' withdrawal from Britain.

21

Who are the 'English'?

2

A large, hall-type building at the heart of the enclosure provided the village's meeting place – a focus for the poems and songs so important to an illiterate society. West Stow also contains reconstructions of sunken pits grouped around the main hall, a recurrent feature of Saxon settlements. It is not known whether these were subterranean dwellings or were simply cellars under more substantial, ground-level timber buildings – basic forms of peasant dwelling which may nonetheless have been elaborately decorated and carved.

By around 600, the Saxon heptarchy of kingdoms (Kent, Wessex, Essex, Mercia, Northumbria, East Anglia and Sussex) was well established. The southwest and

Wales still remained under British control. There seems to have been some continuity in field systems and estate boundaries from Roman times or earlier, indicating that at least part of the landscape was simply adopted by the new settlers (or worked by the original population for new masters). Local tribal distribution, reflected in regional and county names – Essex, Sussex and Wessex; East Anglia, Suffolk and Norfolk – may have provided a stronger identity than British or Celtic, Angle or Saxon as the population merged. The strongest ties in Anglo-Saxon society were to kin, or community, and to individual lords rather than inherited position (one reason why Saxon dynasties were swift to wax and wane).

The kingdom of Northumbria was dominant in the heptarchy during the 7th century and became a religious and cultural centre. The magnificent Lindisfarne Gospels were produced there, artistic successors to the elaborately cast metal goods found at Sutton Hoo. A Northumbrian monk, the Venerable Bede, provided an evocative and detailed account (factually questionable on occasion) of England's beginnings in his celebrated *Historia ecclesiastica gentis Anglorum.* Bede's masterpiece was written at St Paul's monastery in Jarrow on the south bank of the River Tyne and completed in 731. The church still stands, its grime-blackened stones flanked by surprisingly substantial remains of the monastic complex. The moving atmosphere of the site is oddly enhanced by a bleak backdrop of industrial estates.

Mercia eventually emerged as the richest and most powerful region; its most famous king, Offa, ruled for 40 years from 757 to 796. During his reign, it is likely that Offa controlled greater resources than any ruler in Britain

since the Romans. By the latter part of the 8th century, literacy was becoming more widespread, enabling better administration of taxation and trade. Increased wealth served to strengthen the king's authority, which in the late 780s led to the building of Offa's Dyke. This vast earthwork linked the north and south coasts of Wales and was designed, at least in part, to subdue the Welsh tribes troubling Mercia's western border. A remarkable structure, the dyke consisted of a ditch and bank up to 2.5 m (8¼ ft) in height, reinforced by wooden palisades; it ran in a virtually straight line between the River Severn and the Dee estuary. It may well have been effective in keeping the Welsh at bay, enabling Offa to revive the country's Roman legacy with his magnificent palace at Tamworth, basilica at Brixworth, Christian baptism and beautiful coinage. Despite all this, the eventual balance of Saxon power in the century was to transfer to the rival kingdom of Wessex, which had control of the port of

1 Lindisfarne was the first landfall made by Viking longships in 793. The sacking of its monastery heralded a sustained period of looting and desecration of churches and religious houses within reach of England's eastern seaboard.

2 A replica of the dedication stone in Bede's church of St Paul at Jarrow, dated 681. The monastery was founded by St Benedict Biscop, a Northumbrian nobleman who had earlier endowed a similar foundation at nearby Sunderland.

3 Part of a Viking grave marker discovered on Lindisfarne and dating from around 900. The front carving depicts a group of heavily armed warriors, and the back features a cross among heavenly bodies.

4 The powerful 7th-century king of Mercia erected Offa's Dyke as a defensive barrier against marauding Welsh tribes. The dyke runs the full length of Wales, a distance of some 257 km (160 miles).

Southampton and ready access to the southwest's valuable mineral deposits.

Over the next century, Viking raids were to prove a greater threat to England's stability than tussles between Mercia and Wessex. Displaying extraordinary seamanship, the Vikings crossed the treacherous North Sea in their longships – shallow-draughted boats capable of carrying up to 200 warriors. Their initial landfall was in 793, when they raided the monastery at Lindisfarne, off the Northumbrian coast. The monk Alcuin of York was horrified at such desecration, writing of 'the Church of St Cuthbert spattered with the blood of the priests of God'; it established a pattern for many 'hit and run' attacks on rich and vulnerable religious houses.

Viking was a generic term applied to all Scandinavians. In fact, those from Denmark generally concentrated their efforts on England's eastern seaboard, and Norwegians attacked the Western Isles and Ireland. As raids intensified in the 9th century, much of England was under threat and regional rulers attempted to buy off invaders with 'protection money', referred to as Danegeld. The tactic sometimes worked, but on occasions Vikings took the money and raided anyway. The motives for these repeated assaults on England were not simply plunder; there was also a domestic agenda. It had become difficult to sustain a growing population on the limited agricultural resources of mountainous or cramped lands, and so the Vikings sought new places to farm and settle.

Those intentions were brought to fruition in 865 with the arrival of the 'great army' from Denmark, a massive invasion force that rapidly conquered and colonized much of eastern and central England. York, one of the early casualties, was soon settled by the Vikings, who called it Jorvik. The city became the Viking capital of Northumbria and, through river links to the sea, a key trading centre. In 1976, the York Archaeological Trust discovered extensive remains of Jorvik beneath the central Coppergate district. Excellent conditions for preservation made it an invaluable find, offering insights into a Viking city's layout, commerce and way of life.

4

Relentless Danish progress across England continued more or less unopposed until checked by Alfred king of Wessex. Minor skirmishes took place in 871, but the Danes withdrew to deal with troubles further north, returning to Wessex in 878. Caught off guard by the first attack, Alfred sought refuge in the almost impenetrable marshy wastes of Athelney. He emerged months later to inflict a crushing defeat on the Danes at the battle of Edington, near Warminster on Salisbury Plain.

In a pact known as the peace of Wedmore, the Danish leader Guthrum agreed to withdraw all Danish forces and settlement to the north of Watling Street, effectively dividing the country diagonally. Within that northern sector, Danish law, customs and language would prevail. The legacy of that division lives on in the names of towns and villages, and indeed in dialect, throughout the north of England. Places ending in -by

1 An illuminated letter 'F' containing King Alfred from the *Liber Regum Antiquorum Regum*, *c*.1321. More manuscripts survive from the Middle Ages than any other artefact. Their production was originally the preserve of monasteries, later supplemented by secular scribes.

2 One of the earliest surviving detailed maps of England, Scotland and Wales by English historian Matthew Paris, dating from *c*.1250. Although understandably deficient in terms of geographical accuracy, it presents a picture of a united England that had changed little since the 10th century in terms of counties, cities and towns.

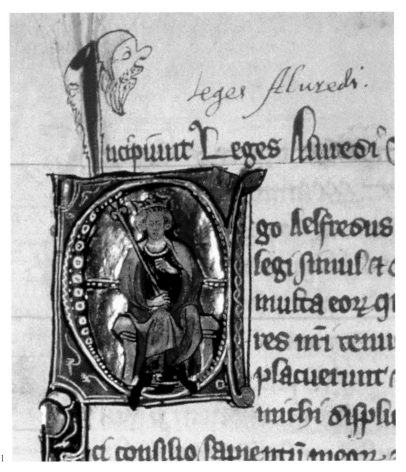

1

signified an inhabited area of any kind; -thorpe also indicates a small settlement. Those names ending in either -with or -thwaite originally meant a settlement created from the clearing of woodland.

Alfred also made a significant contribution to England's cultural heritage. He learned Latin and translated several major works from that language into Old English, including Bede's *Ecclesiastical History of the English People*. Alfred also instigated the compilation of the *Anglo-Saxon Chronicle*. Begun in the 9th century and continuing under different hands until the 12th, it traced England's history from the Roman invasion to 1154.

Alfred established schools for the sons of noblemen, actively encouraging the dissemination of knowledge, and codified new laws, designed to make courts, rather than private vengeance, the appropriate way to settle disputes. Treason was also made an offence for the first time under English law.

By the time Alfred died in 899 he had ensured greater security for Wessex through the establishment of fortified towns, or *burhs*, such as Wareham in Dorset or Wallingford near Oxford. London also regained the commercial importance it had enjoyed in Roman times. The creation of *burhs* was carried on by Alfred's son and daughter, and a concerted campaign extended Wessex power as far as the Humber. The crowning of Edgar the Peaceful in Bath Abbey in 973 symbolized the creation of a united kingdom of England. Weak though it was in places, the new administration was able to impose a uniform royal coinage on England and reap the benefits of growing prosperity. Edgar's successor was his 12-year-old son, Edward, who was soon murdered and replaced by his younger brother, Aethelred the Unready. Aethelred's reign, which began in 979, saw the launch of further attacks by the Vikings, and this time the prize at stake was nothing less than the 'kingdom of the English'.

The Scandinavian onslaught came mainly from King Swein of Denmark and his son, Cnut. Despite efforts to repel the invaders, resistance collapsed and Aethelred fled to Normandy in 1013. Cnut assumed the English throne, returning garrison troops to Denmark and increasing England's trading position. On Cnut's death, Aethelred's son, Edward the Confessor, became king. He reigned until 1066 – a pivotal date that saw the defeat of Saxon rule and irrevocably changed the face of England.

CHAPTER

2

The landscape of England has been moulded by centuries of human activity. The archaeological sites, settlements and buildings that people the countryside have over time given a separate personality to the different regions of England. The varieties of soil, stone and wood have given texture and colour to buildings and the geological upheavals of earlier ice ages have thrown up mountain ranges and deep valleys, smooth downland, fertile plains and marshy coastlines. The successive waves of settlers and invaders have added Iron Age forts, Roman cities and medieval castles. Ruined abbeys, great country houses and humble half-timbered cottages, together with meandering field patterns, lush meadows and towering chalk cliffs, are the enduring visual symbols of what we think of as Quintessential England.

QUINTESSENTIAL ENGLAND

LANDSCAPES OF
THE WEST

THE SOUTHWESTERN COUNTIES OF ENGLAND HAVE A COMPLEX HISTORY THAT IS REFLECTED IN THEIR MONUMENTS AND SCENERY. FROM THE ANCIENT SAXON KINGDOM OF WESSEX TO THE GRANITE CLIFFS OF LAND'S END, THE REGION'S LINKS WITH THE PAST ARE MANIFESTED IN DIVERSE HILLFORTS, BURIAL MOUNDS, STONE CIRCLES AND CROMLECHS, ALTHOUGH EXTRACTION OF MINERALS, STONE AND PEAT HAS ALSO SCULPTED THE TERRAIN. THE CHANGING LANDSCAPE, FROM SMOOTH TURF TO BLEAK MOORLAND, IS PART OF THE SOUTHWEST'S CHARM, AS IS THE ELEGANT ARCHITECTURE OF ITS PROSPEROUS HISTORIC TOWNS.

ONCE FORMING the ancient Celtic kingdom of Dumnonia, Cornwall and Devon are dominated by the ocean. The contrast between their two coastlines is remarkable: the north, lined with rugged cliffs and dramatic headlands, offers few havens for shipping and its exposed trees cower in the face of fierce Atlantic gales; the more benign southern coast, facing the English Channel, is punctuated by deep-water inlets and drowned valleys. Densely wooded creeks penetrate far inland, providing useful refuges for the smugglers traditionally associated with the region.

The West Penwith peninsula, a stark moorland area ending in the sheer granite cliffs of Land's End, is the most westerly point of England. Some 5 km (3 miles) north of Penzance is the ruins of Chysauster, one of the best preserved Iron Age villages in England, which until recently was surrounded by a historic honeycomb pattern of tiny fields.

For thousands of years people have exploited the peninsula's natural resources, tin-mining and fishing being the two dominant industries. Neolithic settlers were the first to extract tin, using the primitive method of 'streaming', a process in which surface materials were washed away to expose the heavier ores beneath. Copper was also discovered locally and the two metals were later alloyed to produce bronze, from which weapons and jewellery were made. Inventive metal-workers among the later Bronze Age peoples began to create more durable implements such as ploughs. This innovation, coupled with more sophisticated agricultural techniques, made it possible to clear even the most inhospitable ground for farming at a surprisingly early date. Dartmoor, for example, is still divided into field systems by stony banks or walls, locally known as 'reaves', that run directly across the terrain. At one time the reaves were assumed to be medieval in origin, but more recently they have been associated with Bronze Age settlements on the moor, which offer evidence of cattle and sheep farming as well as the cultivation of beans and grains.

The Romans also engaged in tin-mining in the area, but its boom time began with deep-shaft mining in the 18th century, when Newcomen's beam-engines made it possible to drain flood waters from the workings. Over 650 beam-engines worked in Cornwall alone during the 1850s when the county became one of the leading tin and copper producers in the world. Devon Great Consols, exporters of top-grade copper ore from their 'Mine of Mines', created a major port on the River Tamar, Morwhellham Quay, to service the shipments. Cheaper imports and exhausted seams ultimately brought about the collapse of the industry, leaving the countless ruined engine houses on moors and clifftops as evocative reminders of more prosperous times. The underground legacy of the industry is even more dramatic, with hundreds of miles of hand-hewn tunnels and pit shafts traversing the landscape.

The southwest peninsula is rich in natural harbours; fishing villages such as Boscastle in Cornwall are well protected by cliffs on either side, requiring only a small additional breakwater to keep moored ships secure. Sadly, many villages are now in decline; nets once used to catch the greatly prized herring and pilchards have become heritage items as dwindling fish stocks and changes in demand combine to limit the industry's viability. Vast seasonal shoals of pilchard were once eagerly awaited, their arrival offshore signalled by special lookouts known as 'huers' (from the French verb *huer*, meaning 'to shout'). The huers' watchtowers can still be found

1

2

standing on some stretches of coast. With the arrival of the railway in Cornwall in the mid-19th century came decades of prosperity for local fishermen, who were able to transport fresh fish much further afield than had been previously possible. The lucrative marketplaces of London were a particular prize.

One of the few local industries not in decline (other than tourism) is the extraction of china clay for use in the manufacture of pottery and paper. The process has been conducted in a broadly similar way for over 200 years following its discovery c.1755 by a Plymouth Quaker, William Cookworthy, in the granite of St Austell's Hensbarrow Downs. The chalky white powder is formed by the decomposition of feldspar within the rock, and can be extracted through a combination of

3

water pressure, purification and a spell in settling pits. Steam power transformed the china clay industry in the late 19th century, and works such as those at St Austell were modernized in 1880 to satisfy increased demand. Over time, the mining process has resulted in the accumulation of huge gleaming white spoil heaps of sand and quartz which give the whole area a lunar aspect. Greater environmental awareness by modern producers

has reduced the impact of new spoil deposits by reseeding. The innovative Eden Project was opened on one redundant site early in 2001, creating glorious botanical gardens within a series of vast geodesic domes.

The expansion of the Great Western Railway network in the 19th century rendered the remote West Country more accessible for tourists as well as business. It introduced some exotic architecture as well, such as the Royal Albert Bridge of the River Tamar at Saltash, designed by Brunel. The novelist Thomas Hardy described the pre-railway countryside of Wessex with a frequently elegiac note, aware that the landscape and the rural life it supported were to disappear forever in favour of mechanized production. Although much of Dorset's countryside is still used for grazing sheep, just as it was at Hardy's death in 1928, the gorse- and heather-clad heathland he once described as 'untameable' has certainly diminished significantly. Fortunately some of the largest surviving tracts have been designated nature reserves to preserve the habitat for species dependent on its flora. Examples include the glorious Silver-studded Blue butterfly, dragonflies and damselflies, birds such as the elusive Dartford Warbler, and all six species of British reptile.

The unique countryside of the Somerset Levels and Moors is created by the flood plains of five rivers that flow into the Bristol Channel near Bridgwater. Much of the area is below sea level and so prone to flooding during high winter tides, a seasonal cycle resulting in an area of rich meadows, criss-crossed by willow-lined drainage ditches known as 'rhines'. Withies (willow shoots) for basket-making are grown in these ditches at West Sedge Moor, one of the most original landscapes in the area. The Somerset Levels have been designated an Environmentally

PRECEDING PAGES
The coastguard and others
at Newlyn, Cornwall,
photographed in 1907
collecting fresh water
supplies. Newlyn was, and
remains, the county's
largest fishing port.

1 Gold Hill, Shaftesbury,
Dorset, is one of the few
remaining cobbled streets in
southern England. Its row
of 17th-century cottages
faces the site of a nunnery
in which King Alfred's
daughter, Ethelgiva, was
once abbess.

2 The sea has carved the
natural arch of Durdle
Door out of the local
Purbeck limestone at
Lulworth Cove in Dorset.

3 Peat cutting during the 19th
century at Shapwick in the
Somerset Levels. The airy,
domed stacks were called
'ruckles' and when dry, the
peat was burnt as fuel.

4 Both its geography and its
underlying geology
contribute to the unique
countryside of the Somerset
Levels, making it one of
England's most precious
wildlife habitats.

4

Sensitive Area in order to accommodate the diverse needs of conservationists and local farmers.

One area that straddles the River Brue is renowned for its peat moors, formed to a depth of up to 7 m (23 ft) by thousands of years of rotting vegetation. Before the railways enabled coal to become a relatively cheap nationwide commodity, peat was cut, dried and used for fuel. Traditionally, the laborious process was carried out by hand, cutting the water-sodden peat into bricks and arranging them in large airy stacks until thoroughly dry. Today, machines effortlessly scoop peat from the ground, after which it is dried and packed in bags for distribution to the nation's gardeners.

The particular composition of peat – a high acid content and lack of oxygen – contributes to the preservation of organic materials within it. Archaeologists have found wooden trackways buried in peat on the Levels. Dendrochronology (a method of dating wood) has confirmed that these routes are between five and six thousand years old. The trackways provide important evidence of early farming practice. The hurdles from which they were constructed came from coppiced hazel trees, indicating Neolithic advance planning and woodland management. Dung beetles have also been found in the peat, and this suggests that cattle were herded along the tracks, presumably being driven to new pastures. Traces of ancient lakeside settlements have been found submerged in the peat, including boats and tools.

One of the region's most historic settlements is Bath, now acknowledged as the most complete and best preserved Georgian city in Britain. The hot natural spring upon which it is founded has shaped the city's fortunes across the centuries; even today its unpleasant-tasting, sulphurous waters continue to fascinate visitors. Originally a sacred Celtic site, Bath was expanded by Roman architects into an internationally renowned complex of temples and baths. It bore the name Aquae Sulis after the Celtic deity Sul, to whom the waters were dedicated (although the Roman goddess Minerva was also nominally installed there and honoured with

1 The King's Spring is a decorative drinking fountain located within the Pump Room in Bath, whose tea rooms once formed the social hub of the 18th-century spa community. The Pump Room overlooks the King's Bath, a reservoir built around Bath's main spring by the Romans to create a sufficient head of water to feed their bath complex.

2 The impressive lead-lined Great Bath, at the heart of the Roman baths, is 21 m (70 ft) long and fed by water at a constant temperature of 46°C (116°F).

3 Built between 1769 and 1774, the Pulteney Bridge was Robert Adam's sole, but magnificent, contribution to the architecture of Georgian Bath.

a temple). The curative powers of the waters fused with the normal social function of baths in a Roman town to create a popular centre of commerce, healing and religion. Today, part of the temple precinct has been excavated and is visible under the Pump Room; the Great Bath, surrounded by Roman columns, is also on display.

In AD 973 the Anglo-Saxon abbey at Bath was the site of the crowning of Edgar, the first king of all England. The Normans tore down the church and built a massive cathedral in its place, but this proved too costly for

the monks to maintain. By the end of the 15th century it was in ruins, but in 1499 a magnificent new building – the last great medieval church in England – was begun by Bishop Oliver King.

Bath's prosperity continued through the 16th and 17th centuries, but it was not until Dr William Oliver built the Mineral Water Hospital there in 1740 that the city's potential as a spa resort was recognized. Architect John Wood was one of the most important influences in shaping the city. Collaborating with landowners and speculative builders, he and his son, also John Wood, worked in the fashionable Palladian style to create a sophisticated balance and poise in the most elaborate patterns of streets. They used national as well as classi-cal references: the Circus, England's first circular street, draws upon both Stonehenge and the Colosseum. The Royal Crescent, built between 1767 and 1774 by the younger John Wood, was another of the resort's best addresses. The splendour of Bath's porches, doorways, columns and windows shows how the select spa attracted some of the most wealthy families in the country. In contrast to the terraces of nearby Bristol, the mews in Bath's smart terraces were concealed at the rear to avoid disrupting the well-orchestrated façades.

Bath accommodates its diverse layers of history well; even the railway and canal manage to contribute to the elegance of a bustling provincial town. Classical and neoclassical influences are everywhere in its buildings; Queen Square, the Pump Room and the Assembly Rooms provide attractive focal points. Another architectural landmark is Robert Adam's Pulteney Bridge, lined with shops in possible emulation of Florence's historic Ponte Vecchio.

3

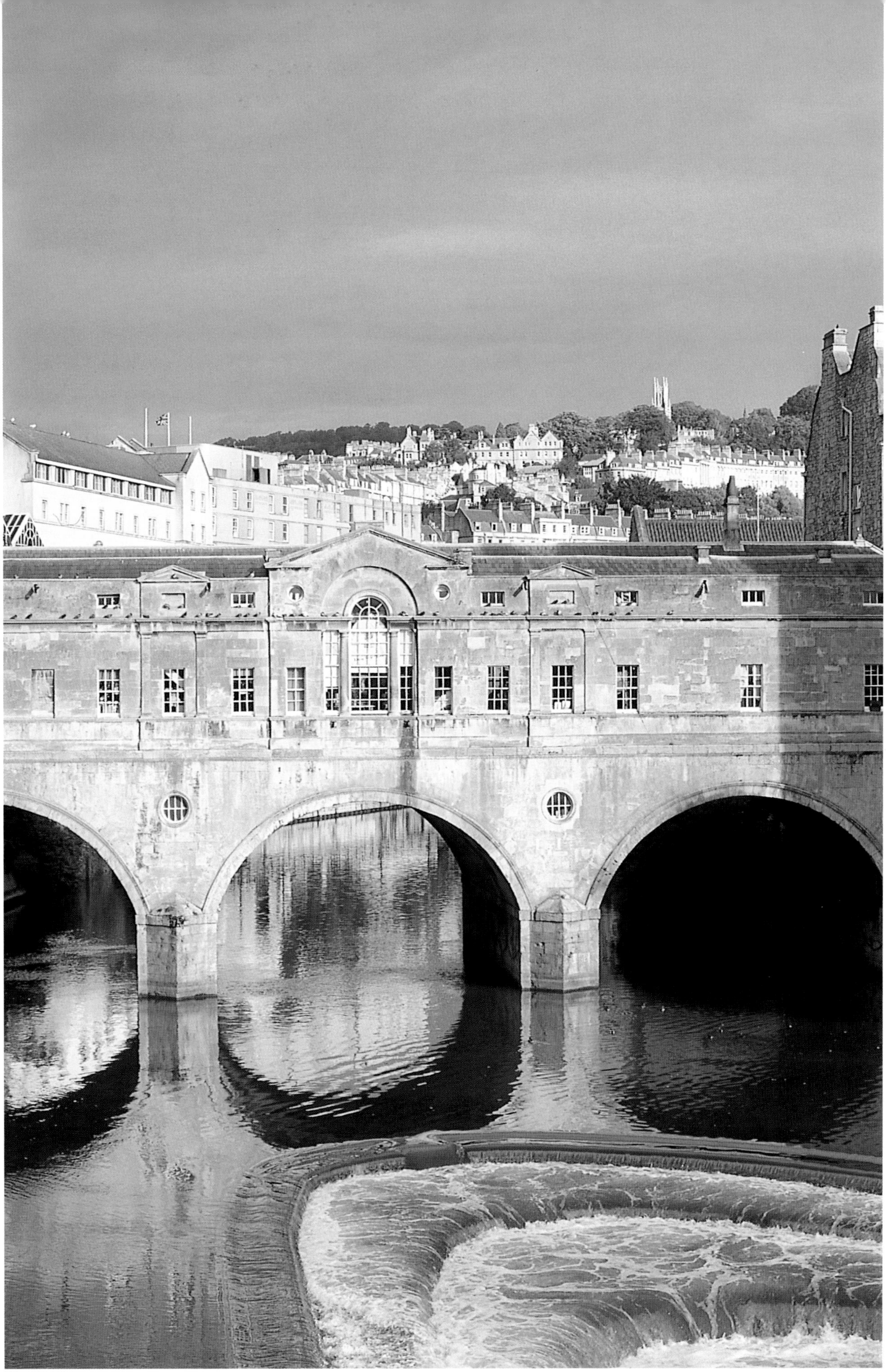

THE POWERHOUSE
OF ENGLAND

With its thriving agriculture and industries, the southeast has long been one of the richest areas of the country. Its proximity to continental Europe has meant that many of the changes that shaped England – the advent of Christianity, the Norman Conquest – began here, gradually extending their influence to more remote regions. For centuries Kentish farms have provided fruit and vegetables for the markets of nearby London, as well as hops for the city-dwellers' beer. The growth of medieval London was also fuelled by iron produced in an area between the North and South Downs known as the Weald.

The white cliffs of Dover have long been regarded as the gateway to England. Impressive as they are, the searing white chalk cliffs of Sussex– unencumbered by the ugly sprawl of cross-Channel docks and freight terminals – are in many ways a more attractive spectacle. The chalk ridge of the South Downs ends abruptly at the undulating line of cliffs known as the Seven Sisters, culminating in the formidable Beachy Head, 163 m (535 ft) in height.

The cliffs are remarkable for their sheer vertical drops – the consequence of coastal erosion. They originally extended substantially further south, but over time the sea has undercut the cliff base and, because of the chalks' vertical joints, huge chunks collapse periodically on to the shore where the chalk is rapidly destroyed by the water's pounding. The undulations in between the pinnacles of the Seven Sisters are the remains of long-disappeared river valleys whose waters have sunk underground through the highly permeable chalk. Beachy

1

Head has recently suffered two monumental rock falls, highlighting the vulnerability of the chalk cliffs to prolonged periods of heavy rain.

Beachy Head has long acted as a visual navigation aid. A little to the east of the landmark lie the flat shingle beaches on which William of Normandy landed in 1066, before marching a few miles inland to meet Harold Godwinson's army at what is now called Battle. Visible miles out to sea, the cliffs also offer a good defensive lookout point. The great bare whale back of the South Downs is England's doorstep; elevated and a short distance inland, it contains sites such as Firle Beacon, dating from the time when England was threatened by the Spanish Armada. A great line of beacons stretched along the south coast, to be lit at the first sighting of the enemy fleet.

In an apparent contradiction, the Downs are actually uplands, their name originally deriving from the Old English word 'dun', meaning hill. Chalk downland is typified by springy turf, deep, dry valleys and occasional beech copses on hill summits. Where those do occur, it is often indicative of an ancient hillfort as the Downs were heavily settled from prehistoric times. Both Neolithic and Bronze Age peoples found an environment in which they could readily survive. The earliest settlers benefited from the large numbers of flints produced within areas of chalk, and for most of history the Downs were pasture for sheep that were able to flourish on soils too thin for regular cultivation. In more recent years, partly because of subsidies during World War II aimed at much-needed increased food production, refined techniques and specially developed fertilizers have helped to make the land more viable. The vast shimmering fields of wheat and barley that now carpet much of the South Downs as harvest approaches are therefore a contrast to the sheep-dotted pastureland of the past.

A contemporary concern is that even though the Downs have been accorded the status of an Environmentally Sensitive Area and are designated an Area of Outstanding Natural Beauty, they are 'ring-fenced' by agricultural land. It is possible that the artificial fertilizers still used in much of England's agriculture create a chemical wind draft, affecting the habitats of the rare species of flora and fauna that thrive on downland. Butterflies known to be at risk include the Chalkhill Blue and Adonis, whilst orchids such as the Early Spider and Burnt Tip are now confined to only a few sites.

Despite being known as the 'Garden of England', it is hops and the circular oast house, rather than fruit orchards, that bring a distinctive character to Kent. The

1 The Seven Sisters mark the
dramatic end to the South
Downs. Their gentle undu-
lations roll up towards the
great bastion of Beachy
Head, one of the south
coast's highest cliffs.
2 Reclaimed land on the
South Downs near the
Devil's Dyke. Extensive
20th-century agriculture
resulted in the loss of many
natural habitats of rare
species of flora and fauna.

1 Oast houses at Herstmonceux, East Sussex. These brick-built kilns, used for drying hops, are a familiar site within the traditional brewing counties of the southeast. They were fuelled by charcoal well into the 20th century.

2 The process of hop picking at Northiam, East Sussex. Originally grown as herbs, hops became an essential ingredient in the brewing process when beer was introduced to England during the 15th century.

3 The dense broad-leaf woodland of the Weald was a vital source of charcoal for the region's iron industry which flourished during the medieval and Tudor periods.

1

decided to make beer for the English troops and civil servants in India. To help the beer survive its long journey, it was made with double the normal quantity of hops. The result was clear and light with a distinctive hop flavour. It proceeded to gain widespread acclaim as India Pale Ale.

Before mechanization, the picking of hops was a labour-intensive exercise. Kent's proximity to London resulted in a huge seasonal workforce descending on the hop fields for a working summer holiday. For many families from the slums of London's East End, the annual pilgrimage to Kent would be their only escape from the drudgery of city life. Conditions were not idyllic and the work was hard, although some employers established temporary housing for the pickers. Hops were collected in baskets and a picker's daily quota recorded by tally sticks or tokens.

Wood was used to fire the oast house kilns during the 16th and 17th centuries; later it was replaced by charcoal. Approximately 1 ton of hops required 100 sacks of charcoal to complete the drying process. To make the charcoal, a shallow circle measuring up to 7.5 m (25 ft)

useful properties of hops are contained within the acids, oils and resins of the cone-like flower, the female part of which is harvested and dried in the oast houses. Hops are spread across a floor, located roughly halfway up the oast house, beneath which fires are lit to generate hot air. The white cowls at the top of each oast house turn with the wind, aiding and controlling the flow of warm air circulating over the hops. When dried, hops are cooled and compressed into sacks for transportation to the brewery.

Hopped beer was introduced to England by Flemish weavers in the 15th century, but it took a long time to become established due to continued support for the traditional drink, known as 'gruited' ale. Gruit was the mixture of plants, herbs and spices added to ale as a flavouring agent; many vested interests lay behind its production and use. The superior preservative qualities of hopped beer were gradually recognized until most households were producing homebrew. During the industrial revolution, dark porter began to replace beer as the preferred working-class beverage.

The foundations of the lighter, 'hoppier', uniquely English beers were laid when one enterprising brewer, deprived of export markets by the Napoleonic Wars,

2

1 Charcoal burners standing by a finished 'clamp', in which the wood is stacked around a central core, covered with earth and vegetation and left to burn for up to three days.

2 Biddenden, Kent, was once an important centre of the cloth trade. Its broad main street, lined with timber-framed houses, dates from the 15th century.

3 Canterbury Cathedral dominates the medieval city and surrounding countryside. Its most prominent feature is the central tower, Bell Harry, built at the end of the 15th century in Perpendicular style by John Wastell.

4 Mercery Lane is Canterbury's most atmospheric street, leading to Christ Church Gate through overhanging medieval houses.

in diameter was scooped from the ground, and within that area lengths of coppice wood were stacked around a central triangular flue. The wood intended for charcoal was then stacked vertically against that inner core, the whole construction finally being thatched with vegetation and covered with earth. The heap was fired from the top by dropping live charcoal embers down the central hole, which was then sealed. The slow burning process was regulated by small holes made in the earth skin. When the charcoal was ready, the fire was put out with water and the heap broken apart and sorted. The next kiln would have been under simultaneous preparation, ensuring an almost continual process. Charcoal burners and their families lived on site, setting up rudimentary dwellings of wood and turf for the duration of their stay in that particular area. Although not necessarily labour-intensive, charcoal production required constant supervision during the three days it took for each kiln to burn through.

Charcoal was also heavily in demand to fire the Weald's blast furnaces when that heavily wooded area, sandwiched between the North and South Downs, was England's major iron-producing region. Consumption was high: it is estimated that for every tonne of iron, 2

tonnes of charcoal would be required. Looking across the green expanses of the Weald from a South Downs hill-fort, it is difficult to imagine that such a rural scene was once a prosperous industrial area bustling with ironworks.

The Weald's rich ore deposits had been identified and exploited by both Celts and Romans, but the industry's most productive period occurred during the 15th and 16th centuries. As the demand for iron increased in the Middle Ages, bigger blast furnaces were introduced during the middle of the 15th century. Molten iron ran out of the base of the furnace and was collected in sand moulds; the resulting ingots could then be re-heated and cast into whatever shapes were required. One of the prime uses was to make guns and cannonballs as well as domestic products such as firebacks, gravestones and crosses. The manufacture of iron impacted directly upon the landscape, as water-generated bellows were needed to produce the powerful draughts of air needed for the combustion process. Streams were accordingly diverted and dammed to form a series of ponds from which water was fed down on to the wheel powering the bellows. Known as hammer ponds, many of these pools still exist in most areas of the Weald. Often they are the only evidence of a once great industry.

The city of Canterbury stands on a site that had been occupied for around 350 years when the Romans arrived there in AD 43. They found a settlement of the

Belgae tribe at a key crossing point of the River Stour and turned it into their encampment fortress of Durovernum. In 597 St Augustine was sent to England to convert the Anglo-Saxons to Christianity. He settled in Canterbury and today the city's long grey cathedral, the focal point of Anglicans around the world, dominates the skyline. The earliest parts of the current church date back to the Norman era. In 1170 Thomas Becket was murdered in the cathedral, and for centuries afterwards his shrine at Canterbury was the destination of pilgrims.

Long stretches of Canterbury's walls remain intact, partially encircling the city's medieval core. Built on Roman foundations during the 13th and 14th centuries, the walls originally contained seven gates; Westgate is the only survivor. Both that gate and the austere semicircular bastions that regularly punctuate the walls serve as a reminder that even sacred places such as Canterbury required defensive structures to guard against their enemies, both domestic and foreign.

Many of the ancient buildings in Canterbury are linked to religious foundations. Some, such as the black and white timber-framed houses lining the Stour's banks by King's Bridge, are a legacy of religious persecution abroad. The extra light from their disproportionately large windows was required by the Huguenot weavers who settled there after fleeing France following the revocation of the Edict of Nantes by Louis XIV in 1685. Originally signed by Henry IV in 1598, the edict granted religious freedom to the Protestant Huguenots and Louis' action was viewed with great concern.

One of Canterbury's most intriguing aspects is the view up towards the cathedral, past the overhanging houses along the narrow confines of Mercery Lane. The mid-ground is filled with the magnificently decorated Christ Church Gate, and the cathedral's pinnacled towers rise behind. It is a powerful dramatic irony that the gate was commissioned by Henry VII to celebrate his eldest son's marriage to Catherine of Aragon in 1501. When Prince Arthur died the following year, his brother not only married Catherine himself, but as the monarch Henry VIII proceeded to dissolve the English monasteries approximately 30 years later.

4

THE FERTILE FLATLANDS

WITH ITS EXPANSIVE SHORELINE AND NETWORK OF RIVERS, DYKES AND CANALS, WATER IS THE DOMINANT FEATURE OF EAST ANGLIA. FOR THOUSANDS OF YEARS PEOPLE IN THE FENS HAVE SOUGHT TO TAME THE WATERS AND RECLAIM THE LAND. THE BATTLE AGAINST FLOODS AND EROSION IS CONSTANT, BUT THE PRIZE IS WORTH THE STRUGGLE — THIS IS SOME OF THE RICHEST AGRICULTURAL LAND IN THE COUNTRY. THE ARCHITECTURE, TOO, IS DIFFERENT HERE. HISTORICALLY, A LACK OF LOCAL STONE AND SLATE LED TO A VERNACULAR DOMINATED BY OTHER BUILDING TECHNIQUES SUCH AS THATCHING.

THAT PART OF ENGLAND's eastern coastline that extends from Essex's winding tidal creeks and iridescent mudflats to the bleak windswept Humber Estuary is engaged in a permanent struggle for survival against the relentless onslaught of the North Sea. Few sections of that eastern seaboard have cliffs, and even where they do occur a geological composition of sand and clay renders them vulnerable to rapid erosion.

The history of Dunwich offers ample evidence of the ocean's immense powers of attrition. Located between the Suffolk towns of Aldeburgh and Southwold, Dunwich was a Roman settlement and subsequently a flourishing medieval port. It had been the seat of the first Christian bishop of East Anglia, Felix of Burgundy,

but in 1326 a violent storm swept away 400 houses and three of the town's nine churches. This pattern of destruction and erosion resulted in the last church collapsing during the 20th century. The town now exists only as a scattering of masonry on the seabed. The sea continues to eat away at the cliff, in places losing as much as 7 m (23 ft) of land a year.

Around the northern tip of East Anglia, the sea's action has created a completely different coastal environment: the salt marshes, sandbanks and spits that make

up the shoreline harbour one of England's most important natural bird sanctuaries. The area around Blakeney Point has been established by a combination of offshore currents and waves approaching the shore at an angle. That action shifts vast quantities of sand, silt and shingle parallel to the coast, depositing it in places to form a curving spit. Finer sediments build up behind the spit, creating mudflats and marshes. As they get higher and are exposed for longer with each tide, grasses and other plants take root and trap the mud. Broad salt marshes built up to high tide level in this way can be reclaimed as land by building dykes, like those around the Wash on Norfolk's border with Lincolnshire.

The recent discovery of a Bronze Age ceremonial timber circle at Holme next the Sea, to the west of Blakeney, illustrates well just how impermanent sections of the coast can be. Christened 'Seahenge', the 4,000-year-old site had been preserved by freshwater peat and then covered by marine sands. Its existence was discovered after prolonged storms washed the protective covering away. It was rumoured that local people were fully aware of the circle's presence long before the historians and archaeologists came to examine the timbers. After all, that stretch of coastline had suffered such turbulent conditions before, and those familiar with the tidal patterns in north Norfolk would have known that the site would shortly be buried again under a new coating of sand.

The tabletop-flat agricultural lands that radiate inland from the Wash are collectively referred to as the Fens, but true fenland has all but disappeared from the East Anglian landscape. To appreciate the appearance of the region before it was artificially drained, it is useful to visit the National Trust site of Wicken Fen in Cambridgeshire. The untamed, watery wilderness of reeds, grasses and trees supports a myriad of wildlife, plants and flowers – unlike the seemingly endless acres of hedges and treeless cultivated land that surround Wicken's precious 240 ha (600 acres).

1 The coastal town of Aldeburgh in Suffolk assumed the role of a major medieval fishing and shipbuilding port when its prosperous neighbour Slaughden was partially destroyed by the sea. Sir Francis Drake's ship, the *Pelican* (later renamed the *Golden Hind*) was built at the Aldeburgh shipyard.

2 Norfolk's northern coastline is one of the most atmospheric in England, an area of sand, shingle and salt marshes. At high tide, the sea sweeps through innumerable salt-marsh channels, which become glistening muddy creeks at low tide. They provide a rich feeding ground for the waders and sea birds that thrive there.

2

1 Before being drained by Dutch engineers during the 17th century, the Fens were watery wastelands. Now, the flat fields, with their distinctive black earth, are some of England's most fertile regions.

2 A photograph showing the weaving of eel traps from reeds grown along the rivers and drainage channels of the Fens. They yielded a rich eel harvest.

3 Both the Cambridgeshire Fens and the Norfolk marshes were once dotted with windmills similar to this one at Hornsey, near Great Yarmouth. The mills were used as drainage pumps to prevent flooding until the advent of steam power in the 19th century.

When prehistoric people first settled the area, they adapted their hunter-gatherer lifestyle to cope with the marshland environment. Natural resources such as reeds were managed. Those who inhabited the fens became adept at boatbuilding, eel fishing, wildfowling, weaving reed baskets and constructing dwellings from alder. They also grew crops on the rich peat deposits.

Recent excavations at Flag Fen near Peterborough revealed a 1-ha (2½-acre) prehistoric wooden platform built to stand in shallow water. Timbers preserved by waterlogging revealed the framework of a substantial rectangular building, including a doorway complete with wooden threshold and a plank floor. The discovery is particularly interesting in East Anglia where relatively few hillforts have survived – earth and timber constructions are vulnerable to the plough in an arable area. The defensive potential of this raised site, which dates from approximately 800 BC, suggests that not all was peaceful in the region even before incoming Celtic tribes had established themselves and begun territorial disputes.

Two such tribes closely associated with the southeast were the Trinovantes and the Catuvellauni, who were ruled during the early 1st century AD by Cunobelinus. This king exerted a major influence over the area from his fortified base at Camulodunum, 3 km (2 miles) southwest of Colchester. In around AD 10 this would have been a very impressive structure, consisting of a series of strategic earthworks, an enclosure surrounded by a ditch, trackways, dykes and even a temple precinct; in function it almost anticipated a Roman town, or *oppidum*. Cunobelinus even had his own coinage, issued in bronze and silver from Camulodunum and Verulamium (St Albans). After the Roman invasion in AD 43, a victorious Emperor Claudius visited Camulodunum to receive the submission and allegiance of 11 British kings in a magnificent official ceremony complete with elephants.

Some of the Fens' oldest remaining settlements were built on isolated outcrops of Jurassic boulder clay that literally formed islands amidst the morass. The most notable is Ely. Originally the site of a 7th-century monastery founded by St Etheldreda, Ely became the base for the legendary Hereward the Wake during his ultimately fruitless campaigns against the Normans. After the suppression of resistance in the Fens, the Normans developed the old monastic site into one of England's finest cathedrals. Its silhouette dominates the low-lying countryside for miles around.

Recognizing the agricultural potential of the fertile fenland soil, the Romans were the first to make a serious drainage attempt, digging open channels and raising causeways above the treacherous swamp. Traces of their endeavours can be seen around Waterbeach, north of Cambridge, where the Car Dyke was one of the channels dug to alleviate flooding. However, a concerted programme of drainage only began in the 17th century.

After the dissolution of the monasteries the 1st earl of Bedford made gigantic gains, including estates from Thorney and Whittlesey abbeys situated to the east of

2

Peterborough in the heart of the Fens. The three main fenland rivers, the Welland, Nene and Great Ouse, drained into the Wash, but as the terrain was so flat each river was sluggish and prone to tidal backflow. In 1630, the 4th earl and a group of speculators enlisted the services of a Dutch engineer, Cornelius Vermuyden, to devise a workable drainage system. In addition to creating rich pasture for cattle, the scheme was also intended to produce land for the successful cultivation of flax, enabling English cloth manufacturers to compete on equal terms with their northern European rivals. Vermuyden's scheme involved the cutting of wide drainage canals to straighten out the wayward rivers and then sluice them against tidal encroachment. His two greatest drains, the Old and New Bedford Rivers, are respectively 21 m (70 ft) and 30 m (100 ft) in width and run parallel to each other between Earith and Denver. They served to bypass completely a long meandering section of the Great Ouse.

Unfortunately, as the drains became increasingly effective, the spongy peat dried out and began to shrink. The problem was exacerbated by the fact that the land immediately bordering the Wash was composed of silt and not prone to shrinkage. As the level of the peat was lowered still further, to below that of the channels, natural gravitational draining became impossible – the water was literally expected to flow uphill.

To rectify the problem, hundreds of pumping windmills were installed to draw water from the sunken fields and into the main drainage channels. Surplus water from these was discharged into rivers at low tide. When the tide turned, sluice gates were shut to prevent the waters flowing back. The same process has continued to operate over the centuries. Early in the 19th century, steam replaced the windmills, to be succeeded in turn by diesel and electricity. One surviving beam pumping engine, built in 1831 and now preserved as a working museum piece in Stretham, was able to lift water 365 cm (12 ft) into a dike at the rate of 124 tons per minute.

In 1884 concerns were voiced at the progressive loss of such a valuable natural resource as peat. To provide some kind of barometer, a huge metal measuring post was driven deep into the peat at Holme village. Its top, originally level with the land surface, now protrudes

1

about 4 m (13 ft) above the surface – an alarming loss of the richest soil in England. Fortunately for the future of the Fens, government and conservation agencies are working together to preserve as much original fenland as possible; they are also seeking to arrest the decline in the quality of agricultural land within the region.

Because so much of its land is artificially reclaimed, East Anglia lacks much appropriate building stone for walls or roofs. Other locally sourced materials are used wherever possible. Flint, rubble, timber and clay often provide the walls, with thatch being one of the most common types of roofing. Despite the fact that it is now an expensive operation, both in terms of the raw material and in skilled craftsmen to lay it, thatching is currently undergoing something of a renaissance.

Norfolk reeds are acknowledged to be the supreme natural material for thatch, and in reasonable weather conditions a reed roof might last between 60 and 80 years. Other sources, such as straw, will probably only survive half that time, especially in the more western counties where rainfall is greater than in East Anglia.

Some reeds are harvested naturally, but most are grown commercially in fenland beds, such as those on the marshy fringes of the Norfolk Broads. Forming some 320 km (200 miles) of navigable inland waterways, the Broads are flooded medieval peat workings and have recently been accorded National Park status.

The growing and harvesting cycle of Norfolk reeds begins and ends in spring. Reeds ready for harvesting are cut, exposing the new growth beneath. The beds of new shoots are artificially flooded and completely submerged for two weeks, then drained and allowed to grow to maturity through the summer. The reeds grow to around 180 cm (6 ft) long and are allowed to dry out naturally through the winter before being cut in the spring, when they are ready for use.

Techniques vary from region to region, and different thatchers have their own individual styles, but the principle behind a perfect thatched roof is universal. One of the great benefits of using thatch for old vernacular buildings is that it can be adapted to any shape and moulded to fit walls that have become irregular with age. Working from the bottom up, bundles of thatch, known as 'yealms', are pinned to the roof battens using horizontal hazel rods, and secured in place with thinner hazel ties and pegs. Further layers are gradually added, each overlapping the one below and rising up to the top of the roof. More yealms are folded and fixed to the roof's apex, their ends often trimmed into fancy shapes and patterns. Just as medieval stonemasons often left their marks on a piece of work, some thatchers can be identified by their signatures in the patterns.

Further inland, the ancient city of Lincoln dominates the flat surrounding agricultural countryside.

2

1 Unlike many other rural crafts, thatching still flourishes in those regions where it is a common roofing material. Straw is frequently used, but Norfolk reed thatch is the most durable.

2 Purton Green is one of the many 'lost', or deserted, villages of Suffolk. This rare example of a mid-13th-century hall is its only surviving building. Standing alone on the site of an ancient road, the house was rescued and restored by the Landmark Trust.

3 Little Hall is just one of the 300 or more Listed Buildings in Lavenham, one of Suffolk's most prosperous medieval wool towns.

3

1

1 One of England's oldest houses still in use, the Jew's House in Lincoln dates back to 1170. It is one of very few stone domestic buildings dating from that period.

2 Lincoln's High Bridge spans the River Witham and is the oldest example in England of houses constructed on a bridge. Parts of the structure date from the 12th century.

3 Alfred Lord Tennyson (1809–92) was born at Somersby in the Lincolnshire Wolds and was adopted as 'Lincoln's poet'. His memorial statue was erected in Minster Yard in 1905.

4 A wonderful blend of architectural styles and building materials can be seen in Lincoln's Michaelgate, which runs parallel with Steep Hill.

The Romans were not the first to appreciate its strategic position, perched high on the edge of a limestone ridge, pierced by the River Witham. The settlement named Lindum that was established by the 9th Legion in AD 48, near to the junction of Ermine Street and the Fosse Way, adapted the remains of an existing Celtic hillfort. The original northern gate of the Roman town exists as Newport Arch. It is the only surviving such example in England still used by traffic.

Despite the importance of its visible Roman roots, Lincoln has an essentially medieval atmosphere. It is dominated by the cathedral's three towers, the central one of which rises to an imposing 83 m (272 ft). Facing the cathedral's elaborately carved west front, an almost equally dramatic castle has developed from the Norman fortress at its core. Built soon after the conquest, the Norman castle is set in the southwest corner of the original Roman settlement and incorporates redundant walls and earth banks into its construction.

During the Middle Ages, Lincoln gradually expanded on to the plain immediately below. Upper and lower segments are linked by steep cobbled thoroughfares, the main one of which is appropriately named Steep Hill. Before that last strenuous section is reached, the road passes through what was originally Lincoln's Jewish enclave, the largest in England outside London. The Normans were instrumental in encouraging Jews to settle in England's major towns and cities to help finance trade (a situation which bred envy and intolerance, and which led to the massacre of 150 Jews at the castle in York in 1189). A remarkable surviving example of domestic architecture from the period is the Jew's House, dating from around 1170 and one of the oldest inhabited buildings in the country. Its longevity stems from being built entirely of stone, a rarity in a period when most domestic buildings were made of timber.

Lincoln is in close proximity to Sherwood Forest, hideout of the legendary outlaw Robin Hood. Stories recount how Robin was clothed in 'Lincoln Green' and such a woollen cloth was in reality exported from medieval Lincoln. The fabric was a type of loden, similar to that worn today in parts of Germany and Austria. Together with other manufactured goods, the fabric was exported from the city by barge, using a canal dug by the Romans. The canal connected the rivers Witham and Trent, forming a vital trading link with significant impact upon Lincoln's enduring wealth and status.

THE HEART OF ENGLAND

For many the centre of the country, with its rich and varied landscape sprinkled with mansions, villages and towns, is the sometimes elusive core of England. The region has managed to retain its rural feel, in the face of agricultural reforms that left much of its population looking for a source of income other than the land. To the west, the border with Wales is dotted with fortifications, evidence that this apparently tranquil area has been the site of countless conflicts and incursions through the ages.

THE COTSWOLD VILLAGES are often considered to represent the very core of England – a contemporary illusion of rural life. The beautiful landscape is located mainly in Gloucestershire, on the highest and widest part of a belt of Jurassic oolitic limestone that extends diagonally across England from the northeast coast of Yorkshire to Dorset. Laid down over 150 million years ago, the rock is composed of minute, tightly cemented spheres of calcium carbonate, creating a hard, fine-grained stone that is easily sawn. Shades of colour can vary substantially within the belt of limestone, providing a palette ranging from pale cream to a dark ochre. The mellow, honey-coloured stone characteristic of Cotswold villages is quarried locally and used for buildings throughout the region.

A distinctive feature of Cotswold villages is their limestone slate roofs, and the production of 'frosted' slates was a thriving local industry by the early 17th century. Stonesfield, 6 km (4 miles) west of Woodstock, was one of only two sites well known for their production; the limestone was first extracted through adits, or passages dug into the hillside, but later it was mined from galleries only 1.5 m (5 ft) in height. At Stonesfield, agricultural labourers dug out the stone between

1

2

October and February — welcome seasonal work, for all the cramped and difficult conditions. The slabs were copiously watered and left exposed for a series of frosty nights, after which hammer blows could divide it into separate slates along the 'veins'. The slates were widely used, from the roofs of Oxford colleges to agricultural buildings such as the Abbey Farm at Enstone, built by the monks of Wintercombe as early as 1382.

Limestone allows water to permeate rapidly, resulting in upland areas with few springs or streams. Those that do occur are often seasonal, reflected in names such as Winterbourne Monkton, near Marlborough. The resulting tough, springy grass is ideal terrain for sheep grazing. Anglo-Saxon settlers first recognized the region's potential as sheep-rearing country, from which the name Cotswolds derives: 'cots' is a Saxon word meaning 'sheepfold', while 'wold' refers to an expanse of high, open land. The economic importance of sheep is apparent throughout the region.

One of the Cotswold's most elegant towns is Chipping Campden, whose golden houses and attractive civic buildings reflect the prosperity generated by the medieval wool trade. Fleeces were brought from surrounding districts to the Woolstapler's Hall where they were purchased by merchants who made huge profits exporting the wool.

Other regions lying at the core of England include Herefordshire, Worcestershire and the Midlands Plain. They still possess many elements associated with the traditional English countryside: gently undulating pastures and agricultural land; mosaics of fields bordered by tree-lined hedgerows, presided over by farmhouses of varying size and grandeur. That landscape was largely created by the process of enclosure, which occurred at intervals between the 16th and 19th centuries. The age-old system of strip farming,

whereby peasants cultivated narrow strips of land allocated to them in three large fields, was gradually phased out as landowners consolidated their holdings. The large fields were enclosed, as ultimately was ancient common land. In the 18th and 19th centuries the need to feed an ever-increasing urban population resulted in Parliamentary acts sanctioning widespread enclosure and the reshaping of the agricultural landscape. Millions of acres previously unsuitable for cultivation were added to the agricultural pot by crop rotation and better husbandry. The 'ridge and furrow' effect, caused by the action of the plough on the narrow strips and still evident in fields today, is a visible reminder of the strip-farming tradition.

3

In many parts of the countryside, enclosures caused great poverty, homelessness and rural depopulation. Labourers unable to afford the newly imposed rents or considered surplus to requirements were simply evicted from the land. Low agricultural wages, especially in the fluctuations of the Napoleonic Wars, drove many from the countryside into the growing urban conurbations of the Black Country, Lancashire, South Wales and London. The more fortunate became tenant farmers, but yeomen

1 Horse-drawn and steam-powered farm implements and machinery gradually mechanized harvesting as the 19th century progressed. However, horses still provided most of the motive power on farms.

2 The Oxfordshire town of Bampton has held horse fairs since the reign of Edward I. The fair, which takes place each August, is now more of a social event.

3 The Long Mynd near Church Stretton in Shropshire offered excellent hilltop defences close to the England-Wales border. Sheep also grazed the hills, and the region's association with the wool trade is reflected in village names such as Cardington and Woolstaston.

1

farmers continued to migrate to the towns. Rural industries also established themselves there, reducing the self-sufficiency of village communities.

An example of what the English countryside looked like before enclosure can be found at Laxton in Nottinghamshire. Although a modified strip method is still practised elsewhere, Laxton retains a unique manorial form of government similar to that which prevailed in medieval times. A body known as the Court Leet enjoys a legal status which permits the levying of fines against anyone abusing prevailing manorial laws. Its functions include the appointment of a jury to inspect the fallow field drilled with wheat for the coming year. Any farmer found to have ploughed more than his share by encroaching on another's land may be reported to the court and if appropriate subjected to a fine.

The difficulty of living off the land in England has resulted in dramatic changes to the landscape. As the industry strives for ever-increasing efficiency, many farmers have grubbed out miles of ancient hedgerows. Larger fields are more efficient in a new arable age of high-technology 'prairie' farming, but conservationists argue that the eradication of hedgerows

is causing irreparable damage to wildlife habitats, as well as altering the historic countryside. Some special conservation areas have now been created within farm boundaries to preserve threatened species of national flora and fauna.

Mechanization changed farming practice relatively slowly; tractors did not become commonplace on farms until well into the 20th century. Traditional ploughs and harrows, the two main implements essential to preparation of land prior to seeding, were heavy and cumbersome, needing large teams of oxen to drag them across heavy soils, and all other operations were carried on with hand tools and manual labour for centuries. In 1701 Jethro Tull invented a horse-drawn seed drill, alleviating the time-consuming method of sowing by hand. During the later part of the 18th century, agriculture benefited from new industrial technology, including the first iron plough share. Steam, used to power threshing and winnowing machines, also played a vital role in making harvesting more efficient. None of those advances were self-propelled, however, and the horse – especially heavy horse breeds such as the Percheron, Suffolk Punch and

2

the great Shire horse – has continued to be the farmer's indispensable aide.

Although local horse fairs have largely died out, they were once regular features of the rural calendar. In the heart of the Cotswolds, Stow-on-the-Wold held bi-annual horse fairs in May and October; these events originated as sheep fairs but became the sole province of horses when demand for wool declined. Horses were valuable commodities, requiring constant care and attention if they were to work effectively. Traditionally, they were given the protection of lucky charms that were attached to their harnesses, following the Celtic veneration of nature spirits of both good and evil intent.

Further west, the irregular landscape of Shropshire's hills and valleys contains many hillforts, earthworks and Norman castles. The region endured centuries of turbulence as disputed border territory; long before the arrival of the Romans, the Celtic Cornovii tribe had established a network of forts whose outlines are still prominent on almost every Shropshire hilltop. It was from those bastions that Caratacus and the Welsh tribes battled against the advancing Roman legions.

One of the most dramatic natural features of the Shropshire hills is the Long Mynd, from the Welsh word myndd meaning mountain. It consists of a range of hills 9.6 km (6 miles) in length and rising to 518 m (1,700 ft), located roughly midway between Shrewsbury and Ludlow. In addition to the surviving traces of prehistoric hilltop defences, an ancient track called the Port Way runs along the entire length of the ridge. The whole range is penetrated by deep-cut valleys, referred to locally as 'batches', which once provided ideal terrain for waging guerrilla warfare against an enemy unfamiliar with the terrain. The uneasy frontier zone between England and Wales was occupied by a collection of Anglo-Norman barons, earls and bishops, each ruling individual mini-states from the safety of well-fortified strongholds. Goodrich, Clun and Wigmore were all

1 One of the most dramatic
views of the Wye valley is
from the vantage point of
Symonds Yat. The 'yat', Old
English for 'gate', was once
a pass through Iron Age
fortifications.
2 Rush punts at Fisher Row,
Oxford. Rushes were tra-
ditionally strewn over stone
floors in medieval houses,
a custom still celebrated in
some English towns and
villages through processional
rush-bearing ceremonies.

3 Ludlow, a prosperous
market town in the Welsh
border region, has been an
important commercial
centre since medieval times.
Its wealth is reflected in the
substantial merchants'
houses that gather around
the central square and
butter cross.

border castles established in the aftermath of the
Norman Conquest, but despite these formidable structures the Welsh were hard to subdue. For a considerable
time after the conquest, Norman territorial acquisitions
were largely restricted to the lowland areas either side
of Offa's Dyke, and the area retained some vestiges of
autonomy. The Earldom Palatine of Shrewsbury,
together with those of Chester and Durham, were at
the end of the 11th century the only three counties not
directly governed by the Norman monarch's officers.

The River Wye rises on the barren slopes of
Plynlimon, close to the source of the region's other
great river, the Severn. The Wye crosses both rough terrain and pastoral landscapes before joining the Severn
estuary by the border town of Chepstow. One of the
Wye's most spectacular sections is its passage through a
wooded limestone gorge, and the summit of Symond's
Yat offers dramatic river views as the Wye loops in an
almost complete circle around the bluff, 122 m (400 ft)
in height. When Offa was building his defensive ditch
between Mercia and Wales in modern Herefordshire, the
river must have presented itself as an obvious natural
barrier. By continuing the famous earthwork east of the
Wye, he enabled defenders to have a clear sighting of
intruders attempting to cross its leisurely loops.

One of the most impressive of the original 32 Welsh
border fortresses is Ludlow, which developed in

2

medieval times into a prosperous local market town.
Built on a strategic site overlooking the River Teme,
the red sandstone castle was begun by Roger de Lacy
in 1085. It subsequently developed into a fortified royal
palace under the ownership of the powerful Mortimer
family. Roger Mortimer was instrumental in bringing
about the demise of Edward II, and the castle has other
unhappy royal associations. It was from there that
Edward IV's sons were removed to the Tower for 'safe
keeping' by their uncle, later Richard III, and Henry
VIII's elder brother, Prince Arthur, died in the castle
shortly after his marriage to Catherine of Aragon.

Ludlow was a planned town which grew up from the
castle's east side. Its architecture consists of a glorious
collection of buildings from medieval, Tudor, Stuart
and Georgian periods, all dwarfed by the massive perpendicular-style tower of the parish church. Of the town's
original seven gates, only Broadgate has survived;
beyond its narrow archway, Broad Street climbs steeply
up to Ludlow's classically-designed butter cross in the
heart of the market square. Timber-framed buildings
and old coaching inns remain important features of
this prosperous town, set on an important coaching
network. The two most famous are the Angel and the
Feathers, the latter widely acknowledged to be one
of the finest timber-framed buildings in England.

3

COASTS, MOORS & VALLEYS

ENGLAND'S LARGEST COUNTY, YORKSHIRE IS BOUNDED TO THE SOUTH BY THE HUMBER, TO THE NORTH BY THE TEES, AND EXTENDS EAST-WEST FROM THE NORTH SEA TO THE PENNINE HILLS. THE CITY OF YORK HAS BEEN A REGIONAL CAPITAL SINCE ROMAN TIMES; ITS STRATEGIC IMPORTANCE WAS RECOGNIZED BY SUBSEQUENT SETTLERS, INCLUDING THE VIKINGS AND THE NORMANS. THE DISTINCTIVE TERRAIN OF THE NORTHEAST, ESPECIALLY ITS MOORS AND DALES, IS PERHAPS THE REGION'S GREATEST ASSET. CRISS-CROSSED BY DRY-STONE WALLS AND DOTTED WITH SHEEP, IT IS AN OLD LANDSCAPE, CHARACTERIZED BY SPLENDID ISOLATION.

A S AN ISLAND RACE, the English have always relied upon the sea as a source of food, a medium for transportation and a natural defensive barrier. The waters have also had a major impact on the climate and landscape, most evidently but not exclusively in coastal regions. England's long North Sea coastline, for example, facing directly towards Scandinavia, receives winter winds and weather patterns from the Arctic Circle beyond, resulting in freezing temperatures across the area. The physical impact of the sea is immense; the Holderness region of East Yorkshire, for example, is particularly geologically susceptible to erosion, with the consequence that great chunks of its post-glacial boulder clay shoreline are destroyed at an alarming rate. Roads which once led to thriving local farms and settlements now terminate abruptly in jagged, severed strips of tarmac, their original destinations obliterated from the map.

The sea has traditionally been an economic asset, and fishing is still a source of employment in the northeast, although not on the scale of previous centuries. The North Sea is notoriously treacherous (stories of wrecks are legion), especially in winter when an easterly gale from above the Norwegian fjords can lash the sea into a maelstrom. Despite the benefits of modern technology on board ships, it is difficult not to admire the courage of those making their living from the sea.

England's east coast north of the Wash is comparatively exposed, with relatively few natural harbours. Havens for boats generally occur where rivers and streams flow into the sea. From the vast Humber Estuary northwards, villages and towns have developed around almost every sheltered cove and inlet able to support some form of fishing. Even in places where no landing facilities exist, brightly painted traditional fishing boats called 'cobles' still line the beaches. The

cobles have a high bow to fend off high seas and their keels are reinforced to prevent damage whilst being hauled in and out of the water across abrasive shingle.

Unfortunately, like many other industries that once sustained the nation's economy, fishing is now in decline. Once great ports such as Grimsby are now largely redundant, although a Fishing Heritage Museum offers a poignant reminder of an era when landing stages and quayside markets were alive with noise and commercial activity. A combination of depleted fish stocks and the development of giant freezer ships has radically changed the nature of the industry, and the great trawler fleets that once dominated the North Sea are things of the past. However, fishing on a smaller scale is very much alive in historic towns such as Whitby and Scarborough on the North Yorkshire coast. There is still a demand for high-quality, freshly caught fish and shellfish by discerning restaurateurs, a niche market offering a lifeline to family businesses that have fished the inshore waters of England for generations.

Harbours are a focus for the fishing communities in these small towns. The River Esk runs through the centre of Whitby and has carved out a sheltered anchorage

set well back from the sea. The harbour is still dominated by the gaunt ruins of Whitby Abbey, a medieval foundation on the site of St Hilda's 7th-century monastery. The abbey brought historic influence and importance to the town. It was the venue for a synod in 664 which proved to be a decisive event in the re-introduction of Christianity to England.

Shipbuilding still thrives on local river banks, turning out both fishing and leisure craft, although its scale is much reduced from the days when Captain James Cook's exploration vessel, the *Endeavour*, was built in the yards. The town was also important for commercial enterprise. Although well known as a whaling port, it

1

PRECEDING PAGES

1 The tiny North Yorkshire fishing village of Robin Hood's Bay perches precariously on a shrinking coastline. Elaborate sea walls have been erected to prevent further erosion.

2 The Old Harbour at Scarborough still provides a haven for fishing vessels, although the town now derives more income from tourism than the sea.

1 Helmsley is a small market town on the fringes of the North York Moors and close to Rievaulx Abbey, whose Cistercian monks were renowned sheep farmers.

2 Solid stone barns are a distinctive feature of the Yorkshire Dales.

3 Swaledale epitomizes the character of the Dales. Rich pastures flank the river, gradually giving way to summer grazing on the hills.

was the lucrative transportation of coal from the Tyne that transformed Whitby from a flourishing fishing village into one of England's leading 18th-century ports.

Whitby's southerly neighbour, Scarborough, has an even more diverse past. Its relative proximity to inland areas, especially York, served to make Scarborough more accessible than other coastal settlements. The Romans used its clifftop as a vantage point for a signal station during the 4th century, and an imposing Norman castle also took advantage of Scarborough's strategic location. The town itself has successfully blended fishing with tourism for centuries since becoming established as a spa. The beneficial properties of its natural springs (complemented by its famously robust sea breezes) were discovered as long ago as 1626.

The North York Moors National Park encompasses areas of coastline, but its main attractions are the miles of unbroken heather-clad moorland radiating westwards from the sea. Even though the moors do not exceed an altitude of around 450 m (1,500 ft), their perceived height is greater due to the extreme flatness of the surrounding land. That contrast is particularly marked along the park's northern and western edges, where escarpments plunge down almost vertically to the agricultural plains below. The magnificent views northwards across a dizzying patchwork of fields are counterpointed by the vast chemical refineries of Teesside, a jarring juxtaposition of nature and industry.

2

Few areas of England contain as many relics of past settlements as the moors of North Yorkshire. There is a substantial legacy of prehistoric inhabitants – barrows, cairns and dykes are found scattered everywhere – and a curiously large number of standing crosses. The precise function of these is unknown, but they are significant features

in the landscape and are likely to have been for religious or territorial purpose, perhaps marking boundaries or trackways. Some are formal stone crosses, others come in a variety of shapes and sizes, often with extraordinary names such as Old and Young Ralph, Old Margery, Lilla and Fat Betty. Some crosses are engraved with curious, indecipherable markings, but others clearly indicate the names of villages, even though they stand isolated in the middle of heather and bracken.

Modern roads are scarce amidst the more remote areas, but many ancient tracks still exist. The moors were traversed by several north-south drovers' roads, used for centuries by cattlemen and traders en route to lucrative southern markets. Old drovers' milestones were often phonetically spelt in local dialect: one leading to Kirby Moorside, for example, is inscribed with the words 'This Kerby Rad'. Other long forgotten tracks date back to the times when the Yorkshire Moors, in common with several other northern upland areas, were predominately grazed by huge flocks of sheep owned by powerful monasteries.

Yorkshire has a large concentration of monastic ruins, the most impressive of which were founded by the Cistercian Order. The monks' desire for isolation led to the establishment of monasteries in more remote parts of the countryside, often corresponding to areas suited to sheep rearing. The early Cistercian communities introduced a new vitality into the production and sale of English wool. They developed commercial sheep farming for domestic and overseas wool markets on a much larger scale than had been practised before, and until around 1300 were the most influential producers of wool.

One notable Cistercian foundation within the boundaries of the national park was Rievaulx Abbey,

1

which owned land in excess of 2,400 ha (6,000 acres) spread throughout the moors. The most significant monastic sheep farmers of medieval times, however, were the monks of Fountains Abbey. Based on the fringes of the Yorkshire Dales, the abbey acquired vast estates through patronage, spreading west to the Lake District and north towards Teesside. Those outlying farms, known as 'granges', were managed by lay brothers on behalf of the monks; modern farms containing the name 'grange' are legacies of that period of prosperity. A familiar feature of the Yorkshire Dales from medieval times are the 'green lanes', broad tracks flanked by gleaming limestone walls down which sheep would be driven from the high fells at times of lambing and shearing. Mastiles Lane, which links the Yorkshire communities of Malham and Kilnsey, is one of the most famous surviving examples of that period.

Sheep rearing is still the mainstay of many hill farms in the Dales, following a pattern that has changed relatively little over the centuries. The unfenced open high country may be grazed by several farmers, each having a specified quota of grazing animals, with the better pasture lower down the slopes fenced off and in private ownership. The best land is on the valley floor where hay is produced to provide winter feed. Lambs born in the shelter of the valleys are moved back up to the hills in late spring, the whole flock being brought down again for shearing during the summer before being returned to the high pastures. They are then moved progressively lower down the fell sides as autumn and winter approach. Lambs and older ewes are subsequently sold off to lowland farmers for fattening and breeding respectively. Although cattle may now feature more prominently in the agriculture of the Dales, the sight of a farmer and his dogs rounding up hundreds of reluctant sheep from the open fells remains one of the countryside's great spectacles.

Dry-stone walls are essentially a phenomenon on those northern and western uplands where the poor growth potential of hedging plants is offset by an abundance of available stone. The monks were responsible for building some of the earliest walls in the Dales, but

1 The North York Moors terminate abruptly in a steep escarpment overlooking the rich agricultural plain of the Vale of York. Views from the top of Sutton Bank reveal how land enclosures shaped the farmed landscape. Smaller field patterns have probably remained unchanged for centuries.

2 Swinnergill Mine is located in a desolate valley high above Gunnerside in Swaledale. Its grim surroundings show the harsh existence endured by lead miners of the 18th and 19th centuries.

3 The Old Gang lead smelting complex near Low Row, Swaledale. Locally mined coal or peat fired the furnaces and water from the nearby fast running stream powered the bellows.

3

2

most of those in existence today are more recent, dating back to the enclosures of the late 18th and early 19th centuries. The pattern of dry-stone walls soaring up near vertical fell sides and disappearing over the distant skyline is a feature of the Dales. It represents a vast undertaking by the landowners who commissioned them and the skilled craftsmen responsible for their production. The numbers of practitioners of this art dwindled during the 20th century, but today is experiencing something of a renaissance. The skill lies in creating two gently tapering 'skins' which gradually converge towards the wall's summit. An experienced exponent of dry-stone walling will never reject a stone once it has been picked from the pile, knowing that it will always slot in somewhere. Each larger stone is pinned with smaller ones to hold it firm. If properly constructed a wall will last indefinitely as there is no mortar to degrade over time or weaken joints. The open nature of the construction also enables a wall to withstand high winds.

Unfortunately, there are parts of the Dales and other upland regions where walls are in urgent need of restoration. The fragile economics of 21st-century hill farming leave little leeway, and barbed wire has become the only viable option for many hard-pressed farmers.

The natural mineral resources beneath the surface of remote upland areas has attracted attention since prehistoric times. Iron and lead were the most commonly mined. Limited extraction by Bronze and Iron Age peoples, followed by the Romans, escalated during the

1. Askrigg in Wensleydale prospered through various local industries, including clockmaking, lead mining and textiles. The village's wealth was reflected in the Perpendicular-style church of St Oswald, the largest in the Dale. The village also profited from local road improvements; the Richmond to Lancaster turnpike opened in 1751.

2. Countless layers of history are encompassed within York's city walls. They remain almost unbroken for 4.8 km (3 miles), still pierced by four of its original medieval gateways.

3. York Minster was constructed over a period of 250 years between 1220 and 1470. Over half of England's surviving medieval stained glass is contained within its impressive windows.

1

medieval period under monastic enterprise. Lead mined during the 12th century, for example, was exported for use on French and Italian abbeys and cathedral roofs.

Demand for lead grew significantly during the 17th century, resulting in a near Klondyke-style 'rush' in the Dales and northern Pennines where the greatest concentrations of the metal were located. Much of Swaledale's mining heritage is concealed in minor valleys in the Gunnerside and Arkengarthdale areas, resulting in landscapes of 'Jekyll and Hyde' character. The pastoral aspects of Swaledale, with its barns, cottages and brightly coloured hay meadows, are juxtaposed with scenes of desolation off the beaten track.

Adits and levels were employed in later mining activity, but earlier, more primitive methods involved the use of water power. Streams, known as 'hushes', were dammed to build up a head of water, released in turn to cascade down the fell side, tearing away vegetation and subsoil to expose veins of lead beneath. When the Swaledale industry was at its peak, around 5,000 tons of lead were produced annually. During the 19th century, however, the best veins became exhausted and cheaper metal imported from Europe took over. Some mining families stayed in the Dales and Pennines as farmers, but others left to work in the Durham coalfields.

Both the Dales and Moors national parks have long been used as valuable sources of stone. A belt of hard sandstone quarried not far from the coast provided the stone for Whitby's Benedictine abbey. A particularly prized source, it also contributed in later centuries to the construction of Covent Garden Market, Waterloo Bridge and parts of the Houses of Parliament.

In direct contrast to the sandstones of the Yorkshire Moors, the Dales is very much limestone country. The gleaming white stone was thrust to the surface by massive upheavals in the earth's crust millions of years ago. Modified by glacial action, it created the vast limestone pavements and cliffs characteristic of this region of Yorkshire. The limestone has featured in buildings, but more recently has been extensively quarried and crushed for road building.

The present settlement pattern of the Yorkshire Dales resulted from successive waves of colonization by Angles, Danes and Norsemen from the 7th to 11th centuries. The first two groups moved up the Pennine valleys from the east, settling on the valley floors and lower pastures where they kept livestock and cultivated the land. Several Dales villages have large greens at their heart, a legacy of times when livestock was corralled for safety from raiders, both local and from further afield. The Norse influx arrived in the region from the west, and the influences of the Scandinavian languages are reflected in the titles of natural features such as beck, crag, tarn, rigg, gill and mere. Norse farmers introduced a pattern of grazing to the higher fells, using summer pastures with shepherds' huts known as shielings. The names of Wensleydale villages such as Appersett and Countersett derive from the use of these locations.

The diverse and evocative names given to York – Eboracum, Eoforwic and Jorvik – reflect the city's long and complex history. Its streets and buildings bear the traces of the different peoples who have lived there since the Romans first established their fortress of Eboracum

2

on the banks of the River Ouse. The city subsequently became capital of the Saxon province of Deira, and was later transformed into an important trading centre by the Danes. The giant conical Norman motte supporting Clifford's Tower dates from the conquest and the repressive policies adopted by England's new masters.

Many of the attractive buildings in York today date from the medieval period when it was an important and prosperous town. Elegant additions from Stuart and Georgian times complement the timbered buildings, such as those in the famous street called The Shambles. This narrow thoroughfare is artificially darkened by overhanging gabled houses whose upper storeys almost touch. Originally the butcher's quarter, it runs parallel to the cobbled market square. Today it is given over to art galleries, antiquarian bookshops and diverse shops dispensing anything other than fresh meat.

3

The city's walls remain virtually intact and extend for some 5 km (3 miles), pierced by the medieval gateways of Micklegate Bar, Bootham Bar, Monk Bar and Walmgate. Of those four barbicans, Bootham is the only one occupying the same site as an original Roman gateway, one which led onto the Via Principalis (now known as Petergate). As was the custom in London and other walled cities, the fortified gates were not only used as entry portals to the city, but were also a grim civic noticeboard, displaying the heads of those executed for treason or lesser crimes. Following the battle of Wakefield in 1460, during the Wars of the Roses, Queen Margaret placed the severed head of Richard duke of York on one of the gates, having first mockingly adorned it with a paper crown.

As an archbishopric, York is surpassed in rank only by Canterbury within the Church of England. Entirely in keeping with its rank, the Minster is one of England's finest churches, constructed over an extended two centuries from 1220. It houses the largest collection of original medieval stained glass in the country.

FORESTS & UPLANDS

STRETCHING FROM THE SCOTTISH BORDERS TO THE MANUFACTURING CITIES OF LANCASHIRE, ENGLAND'S NORTHWESTERN COUNTIES ARE REGIONS OF DRAMATIC CONTRAST. EXPOSED MOORLAND AND THE RUGGED FELLS OF THE LAKE DISTRICT ARE COUNTERBALANCED BY DEEP VALLEYS, WITH THE FAST FLOWING STREAMS THAT POWERED THE COUNTRY'S EARLY TEXTILE MILLS. DIFFICULT TO ACCESS FOR SEVERAL CENTURIES, THE REMOTE REGION ATTRACTED MONASTERIES AND RELIGIOUS FOUNDATIONS WHOSE FARMING SKILLS BROUGHT NEW WEALTH TO THE AREA. THE MARCH OF PROGRESS IS CLEARLY EVIDENT IN THIS VARIED LANDSCAPE; RUINED ABBEYS AND CASTLES ARE JUXTAPOSED WITH HISTORIC INDUSTRIAL BUILDINGS, ONCE THE SOURCE OF NATIONAL PROSPERITY AND INFLUENCE.

THE PENNINE HILLS form the natural backbone of England, extending from Derbyshire to Northumberland and cutting through the heart of many of the country's major industrial centres. The water power their steep gradients offered, followed by steam power, drove the engines of iron and steel works and textile mills, resulting in the 19th-century boom cities of Manchester (known as 'Cottonopolis'), Rochdale and Bolton, together with Liverpool, their associated port. Foundations of the previous century were transformed by developments in manufacturing techniques and the movement to large-scale mechanized production. Some of England's most famous engine manufacturers were based in the region, where they created the vast wheels, boilers and pistons that drove the industrial age.

Nevertheless, grandiose factory architecture and magnificent machines could not disguise the squalor of urban living conditions at the beginning of the 19th century. For many who laboured in the cotton mills around Manchester and the furnaces and foundries of Sheffield, Derbyshire's Peak District was the nearest open countryside for recreation. Most landowners guarded their sporting rights, however, and allowed access to just 500 ha (1,200 acres) of the 60,000 ha (150,000 acres) between those two major towns. As long ago as 1884, attempts were made to introduce a Parliamentary bill to secure easier access to those tracts of countryside, but it did not succeed. A strong protest movement resulted in the creation of 10 national parks between 1951 and 1957, the second of which was the Lake District.

Geological upheaval over millions of years created the Lakeland mountains as layers of rock, buckling under pressure from the earth's crust, and twisted from

the horizontal to near vertical. Subsequent surface erosion revealed rocks from various geological ages in juxtaposition, accounting for the diverse characteristics of individual mountains. Such a variety lies at the heart of the Lake District landscape: jagged volcanic rocks of England's highest mountain, Scafell Pike, complement the smoother slates of such rounded peaks as Skiddaw, 914 m (3,000 ft) in height. Most of the lakes themselves resulted from glacial action during the Ice Ages. U-shaped valleys, gouged out by the advancing ice, carried great piles of boulders and other rock debris before them. When the ice retreated, those moraines formed natural dams, trapping waters fed into the valleys by mountain streams and rivers. Even here, however, human influence is in evidence; some stretches of water within the national park are man-made reservoirs supplying the urban conurbations of the northwest.

Despite its harsh environment, exploitation of the mountains' resources began in prehistoric times. Significant examples of a Neolithic 'axe factory' have been located near the summit of Pike O' Stickle in the Lake District; its distinctive grey-green volcanic rock is thought to have been highly prized by the axe makers and their clients. Examples from that source have been found in locations all over England, as far south as Hampshire, highlighting the value of such commodities in an established trading society. Minerals were extracted from the later Middle Ages onwards, progressing to the establishment of major iron-smelting furnaces during the 18th century. Copper mining was also developed on a large if localized scale, the focus of activity during the 19th century being around Coniston (which at the height of the boom allegedly resembled an American frontier town during the Gold Rush).

1

Now a gentle lakeside tourist resort, the spoil heaps and engineering debris from Coniston's earlier incarnation litter the fells above.

Slate quarrying is still a viable business in some areas due to an upsurge in demand. A characteristic feature of the Victorian terraces and villas of Keswick, Lakeland slate is now too expensive for general house construction, but the distinctive grey-green stone is prized for cladding and ornamental use. Small disused quarries are a recurring feature of the Lake District landscape.

Timber was sourced from the gradual clearance of the vast native forests to create farmland. Medieval industries relied heavily on wood, whether as charcoal to use in iron smelting (page 40) or in the form of bark, stripped from trees and used in tanning. Cistercian monks from Furness Abbey, to the southwest of the Lake District, managed considerable areas of coppicing. Although most are now overgrown, it is still possible to see traces of the charcoal burners' circular pitsteads.

Lake District timber has a wider industrial application too. Its woods were one of the main providers of bobbins for the textile factories of Lancashire and Yorkshire. Numerous mills, such as Stott Park Bobbin Mill,

were established *in situ*. Later, a number of imposing country houses scattered through the district were converted from those original mills.

During the last 70 years, a policy of afforestation in upland areas has led to considerable conflict between conservationists and the Forestry Commission, a legacy of World War I when roughly one-fifth of private woodlands were felled to maintain supplies of timber to coal mines supplying the iron and steel industry.

The Forestry Commission, set up in 1919, was charged with increasing the supply of native timber. Many areas of virgin countryside were ploughed up and planted with conifers, especially the sitka spruce. This species, imported from British Columbia, adapted well to poor quality upland soils, but its vast, dark green plantations had a dramatic effect on wildlife. Trees were so tightly packed that no daylight could penetrate the year-round foliage, nor could plantlife survive in the artificial darkness. During recent years, conifers have been more sparsely planted and mixed with broad-leaf trees. When the conifers are harvested, a new deciduous woodland will be established, allowing rapid regeneration of the natural flora and fauna.

The remoteness of the Lake District region, and the unique nature of its landscape, have resulted in specialist farming of local breeds such as Herdwick sheep. Wiry and able to survive life on the fells, such animals were valuable resources which may often have been the target of border raids – a frequent occurrence in the region for centuries. Towns and villages bore the brunt of bitterly disputed territorial claims on either side of the Anglo-Scottish border. Large-scale incursions happened from time to time during the turbulent medieval period, but those living close to the border experienced frequent

2

3

1

harassment by renegade groups. Even the Act of Union in 1707 did not entirely curtail the practice.

Bands of raiders regularly mounted attacks on churches, monasteries and farmsteads. Religious houses in particular were virtually defenceless and made easy targets. Lanercost Priory near Brampton in Cumbria, for example, suffered repeatedly from raids in the 13th and 14th centuries – one carried out by the famous William Wallace. Although the majority of such raids were fairly localized, there were occasions when larger Scottish raiding parties penetrated some considerable distance south into England, leaving a trail of devastation in their wake.

Many landowners, tired of such constant harassment, added square fortified towers to their farmsteads to protect their family, servants and livestock. Those buildings were known as 'pele' or 'peel' towers, from the Middle English 'pel', meaning a 'stake' or 'palisade'. Their remains still scatter the border landscape today. More affluent landowners constructed towers with up to four storeys, permanently stocked with food and provisions in case of trouble. Cattle and other livestock could be driven into the tower's ground floor, while the family sheltered above. Few of the pele towers could withstand a determined siege, but, as many border raids were opportunistic, even a moderate obstacle might send raiders away in search of easier plunder.

As the first line of defence against invading forces, or as strongholds from which to dominate a native population, border towns have always played key roles in a nation's history. Standing on one of the main routes from Scotland to England, Carlisle's castle has borne the brunt of many attacks and sieges during its long history. The Romans established a major garrison, known as Luguvalium, in what is now Carlisle, to the south of where Hadrian's Wall met the Solway Firth. This fortified base was an important staging post for legionaries bound for tours of duty on the wall's western sectors. The principal town of the border region, it is believed to have become one of Britannia's five provincial capitals in AD 369. Indications are that it endured well after the

first Saxon invasions in the southeast. Roman buildings were rebuilt, roads and an aqueduct kept operational, and urban life maintained till well after AD 400. Bede, the historian, describes an established Christian community in the 7th century, and the early Saxon church of St Clement (8th–10th century) integrates elements of an earlier Roman building. It has also been argued that local Romano-British warlords have provided a basis for the Arthurian legends, and that Carlisle may be a contender for a northern Camelot.

Having conquered England, the Normans showed little enthusiasm for venturing much further north, but were nevertheless vigilant in protecting their new

2

1 Fortified pele towers, such as this example at Kentmere Hall in Cumbria, were common defensive features on farms near the Scottish border, subject to frequent incursions and raids.

2 These heavily studded oak doors guarding Carlisle Castle's outer gatehouse have probably been in place since the 16th century.

3, 4 The Chester Rows represent an exceptional piece of medieval urban building. Continuous ranges of first-floor arcades or galleries are reached by stairways from street level. Chester's strategic location made it prosperous in medieval and Roman times, when it became a military base for campaigns.

territories from intruders. Trouble on the border brought William II to Carlisle in 1092; he erected a basic motte castle to secure the area and encourage people to re-establish their community. Some 30 years later, Henry I provided money for the building of a stone castle and town fortifications; his original Norman keep is at the heart of the extended castle which exists today. Ironically, the early stages were completed by a Scottish king, David I, when the northern counties fell into Scottish hands during Stephen's reign in England (1135–54). Only in 1157, following Henry II's accession to the throne three years earlier, were Carlisle and the border regions regained.

The castle has been repeatedly extended over the centuries to keep pace with changing armaments and warfare. This was particularly the case during the reign of Henry VIII and at the outbreak of the Civil War in 1642, when substantial artillery batteries were added.

At the other end of the north-west region, Chester was also an important Roman site. One of two major Roman fortresses established to maintain security along the Welsh border, it is now among the richest cities in England for archaeological and architectural treasures. The original Roman walls remain virtually intact, augmented during the Middle Ages by towers and city gates, and excavations have also revealed the largest amphitheatre in England, capable of seating 7,000 spectators. The arena would have doubled as a training and drill centre for the 20th Legion, who were stationed there and formed part of the force mustered

3

4

by governor Suetonius to end Boudicca's revolt.

Impressive though the Roman remains may be, it is the legacy of Chester's medieval prosperity as a port and trading centre that make it unique. The city's distinctive galleried streets, known as 'The Rows', were certainly in existence during the 14th century; they still run along the entire length of Eastgate Street, containing shops both at ground level and along a first-floor balustraded walkway. This tier can be reached only by flights of external steps from the road.

The city's fortunes declined drastically during the 16th and 17th centuries when the River Dee silted up. Chester was marooned inland and later subjected to a two-month siege in the Civil War. Its eventual surrender, fortunately for its historic buildings, was the result of starvation rather than cannon fire.

MARKETS, FAIRS & GUILDS

A TRADITIONAL INGREDIENT OF MOST ENGLISH TOWNS, MARKETS HAVE SUSTAINED THE NATION'S ECONOMY SINCE PRE-MEDIEVAL TIMES. OF VARYING SIZE AND SELLING VERY DIVERSE PRODUCE, THEY HAD A SOCIAL AS WELL AS COMMERCIAL FUNCTION, WHICH THE LOCAL SQUARES AND MARKET BUILDINGS NATURALLY FULFILLED. CERTAIN MARKETS, LINKED TO THE FEAST DAYS OF THE CHURCH, EVOLVED INTO SOME OF THE GREAT FAIRS THAT SHAPED THE ENGLISH CALENDAR FOR CENTURIES. GUILDS, ANOTHER KEY ELEMENT OF ENGLISH LIFE, ALSO HAD CONNECTIONS WITH THE CHURCH AND SOUGHT TO MAINTAIN CONTROLS OVER ALL KINDS OF WORK AND PRODUCE, AND THE TRAINING OF APPRENTICES.

MARKET TOWNS were an important focus of England's rural communities from early medieval times, not least for the opportunities to obtain hard currency that they offered to labourers and peasants, who survived largely on barter. The markets themselves were important economic assets and correspondingly regularized; none could become a regular fixture unless it had approval from the crown, and around 1,000 charters were granted between the early 13th and mid-14th centuries. Although most English market towns evolved from existing villages, others arose from casual market sites which in turn became permanent settlements. Market Harborough in Leicestershire developed during the 11th century from traders who established an occasional market by the ford in the River Welland. By 1203 the assembly had become sufficiently well established to warrant the levy of market dues by the exchequer and the town continued to expand around the marketplace.

In the Middle Ages markets were identified by a cross. In its simplest form this consisted of a basic stone shaft and cross mounted on top of a polygonal set of steps. Designed to remind people of their moral obligations and provide a toll-collecting point, crosses gradually evolved into more complex covered structures. These served as shelters in times of bad weather and provided shade in summer months to preserve the butter and other dairy products sold by farmers' wives; many are still referred to as 'butter crosses'.

The location of markets within a town was important and many towns owe their street layout to the medieval market site. On a small scale, particularly if linked to the church calendar, markets might take place in the churchyard, in the porch and on occasions in the nave by paying tolls to the clergy for the privilege. In larger markets, wooden stalls became established on permanent pitches, eventually to be replaced by shops of brick or stone. During the later Middle Ages, those streets became the province of particular merchandise, reflected in modern names such as Bread Street, Cornmarket and Butcher's Row. A successful market became a valuable source of income for a town and rights to hold one were granted in perpetuity to lords of the manor or religious houses who, for reasons of convenience or profit, established markets outside their gates. In towns such as Richmond in North Yorkshire, Kimbolton in Cambridgeshire and Ludlow in Shropshire, the markets were set up directly outside the castle gates to enable the local lord to regulate proceedings more easily. His officers were responsible not only for collecting rent from stall-holders but also for the discovery and apprehension of cheats and swindlers. Anyone found to have contravened market laws in terms of weights, measures or other deceptions could be tried at 'Courts of Pie Powder'. The strange phrase was derived from the French *pieds poudres*, or 'dusty feet'. It is probably a reference to the pedlars who formed the majority of people brought before the court and tried, with the mayor acting as

PRECEDING PAGES

1 Wymondham's octagonal half-timbered market cross was erected around 1618. Symbols associated with wood-turning, the town's staple industry, are carved onto its pillars and beams.

2 Covent Garden market was once a teeming mass of carts and porters. The porters originally used baskets instead of barrows.

1 Elegant Georgian buildings and a mighty Norman fortress surround Richmond's cobbled market square. At its heart is the Obelisk, a 10.6-metre (65-ft) high pillar erected in 1771 to replace an older cross.

2 *Frost Fair on the Thames, 1683–84* by Abraham D. Houdins. The frozen river was crowded with stalls, carriages and activities of all kinds.

judge and a jury of other traders. Such courts probably convened at the local inn. Unsurprisingly, a disproportionate number of inns and hotels exist around market squares, providing refreshments for stallholders and their clientele.

Livestock markets played an equally important role in some parts of the country, not only for buying and selling meat but also for upgrading breeding stock. In the 18th century enclosures both increased land productivity and extended interest in specialist methods of stock breeding, such as those practised by Thomas Coke on his estate at Holkham in Norfolk. As the results were displayed in local markets, more farmers were encouraged to experiment themselves. Trade in wheat also increased in the 19th century to meet the needs of fast-growing cities, and separate covered corn exchanges were established close to existing markets. Many of

them were built by private companies, often in ebulliently classical architectural styles. Markets were also sometimes accommodated under civic buildings, as at Abingdon in Oxfordshire. Its small, elegant town hall was built in the 17th century by Christopher Kempton, an architect colleague of Sir Christopher Wren. The building's bold scale and harmonious proportions reflect Wren's influence, but also contribute to an efficient and practical design. The tall, open arcades beneath the main hall were not purely decorative; they provided space for market stalls and associated activity.

One of the finest surviving buildings of the 18th-century textile industry is Piece Hall in Halifax, West Yorkshire. It was not intended for large-scale producers, but instead offered a marketplace for the region's domestic weavers to sell their pieces of cloth on to merchants and manufacturers. The two-storey, colonnaded Piece Hall enclosed a large courtyard and contained over 300 separate rooms for the weavers to display their wares.

Fairs of various sizes have also existed in England for centuries. They began as wholesale trade markets, enabling shopkeepers and smaller traders to stock up in bulk on a wide variety of goods. Fairs also required royal assent, and by the early 15th century about 40 were taking place annually. The fairs often lasted for days or weeks, attracting itinerant entertainers and other amusements. In time, this aspect became almost as important as the business dealings themselves.

One of the country's most famous events was Bartholomew Fair, held near Smithfield in London on the saint's feast day of 24 August. The charter for what became the main cloth fair in England was granted by Henry I in the early 12th century, and it quickly achieved such a reputation that people would travel for days on foot or horseback to attend. The

fair was still thriving in the 16th century, by which time it had developed into one of London's most riotous carnivals and public holidays. A similar change of emphasis took place at other fairs across the country, resulting in many becoming venues for entertainment rather than markets. The large fair traditionally held on Angel Hill at Bury St Edmunds developed into one of the great events on the social calendar, supported by balls, dinners and socializing at the nearby assembly rooms.

No royal charters were needed to sanction the spontaneous fairs that occurred when the River Thames froze solid on at least four occasions between the 17th and 19th centuries. During one of the later 'great freezes' in 1789, which extended from Putney to Rotherhithe, contemporary accounts mention the roasting of an ox on the ice – a somewhat perilous way of earning a few shillings. The practice does not appear to have been uncommon, however. The diarist John Evelyn described how so many stalls were erected on the frozen Thames between December 1683 and February 1684 that parts of the river almost resembled a small town: 'the Thames before London was planted with bothes in formal streetes, as in a Citty, or Continual faire, all sorts of Trades & shops furnished, & full of Commodities, even to a Printing presse, where the People & ladys tooke a

fansy to have their names Printed … on the Thames … There was likewise Bull-baiting, Horse and Coach races, Puppet-plays & interludes, Cookes & Tipling, & lewder places.'

London was also the location of some of the country's most important, more conventional markets. Animals and produce were brought from all over the country, the range of fresh food increasing as transport improved. Cheapside, the largest, had existed since late Anglo-Saxon times, originally divided into Eastcheap and Westcheap (the latter being the main food market selling mostly local produce). Wares were spread out on trestle tables or in baskets from dawn or 6am in winter until late afternoon, and bells were rung to warn traders that the market was about to open or close. Within the city walls, allotments and gardens provided copious quantities of vegetables and herbs, and the countryside surrounding London supplied the city with meat, dairy produce and wheat for bread.

As London expanded in the 11th century, the city's narrow streets became increasingly congested and the new livestock market at Smithfield began to take over Eastcheap's role. Established as the main provider of the capital's meat, Smithfield continued to expand in response to a rapid population increase – by 1725

1

Londoners were eating 60,000 cattle, 70,000 sheep and 240,000 pigs each year. To meet these demands, livestock was driven to the capital from all points of the country, resting in rich Islington pasture for fattening-up before being slaughtered. Smithfield is today housed in a magnificent, cathedral-like structure designed for the City Corporation and finished in 1868.

Fish was the staple diet of Londoners in the Middle Ages. It was cheap and plentiful, and, even more importantly, meat eating was forbidden on religious grounds on as many as 150 days of each year. Billingsgate, which grew up around a wharf built by the Romans, has been London's wholesale fish market since Saxon times, trading from a riverside location near London Bridge until 1982, when it moved to the Isle of Dogs. During the early medieval period it was also a major wholesale market for coal and corn, and all three commodities were landed by boat in vast quantities. Unsurprisingly, given the bustle of traders, porters and fishmongers, the market was held to be the noisiest in London, with a speciality in abusive language. Most notorious were the women who cleaned fish by the quayside.

2

Inigo Jones created an elegant Italianate piazza for the 4th earl of Bedford in the 16th century. It transformed the original convent garden owned, prior to the dissolution, by the monks of Westminster Abbey. This tradition was revived when the 5th earl secured a charter from Charles II to hold a horticultural market there; it thrived and in time overwhelmed the residential aspect of the district. By 1800 the market was able to draw upon 6,000 ha (15,000 acres) of market gardens within a 16-km (10-mile) radius; produce was brought in by night to reach the market by daybreak. During the strawberry season, literally hundreds of women were hired to carry the fragile fruit to Covent Garden lest it should be bruised and squashed on a cart.

The market at Covent Garden was one of London's great institutions, but its rapid expansion was adding to the disorder of an already notorious area. In 1813 and 1828 acts of Parliament were passed to try to regulate it. The second act prompted James Fowler to erect the famous piazza buildings in 1829–30, which were soon filled with colourful produce and characters. As railways increased the volume of produce, surrounding streets were subsumed into the site until the original convent garden covered approximately 12 ha (30 acres).

Guilds were also an important aspect of English commercial life. They were essentially medieval trade associations, formed to provide mutual aid and protection, and divided into merchant or craft guilds. The merchants' guild was the first to be established, seeking to protect its members' trading rights against interference from feudal lords. As the merchants often strove to exclude artisans and craftworkers from their ranks, craft guilds developed in turn during the 12th and 13th centuries. The associations became closely involved in

regulating and protecting their commercial activities, both in local and long-distance trade. They controlled the distribution of food, cloth and other staple goods, often achieving monopolies within local business. At the same time, their members sought to establish good trading practice, setting accepted standards of quality and seeking to maintain stable prices.

As guilds became increasingly prosperous, their buildings became more magnificent. Today guildhalls represent some of the finest surviving medieval architecture in English towns and cities. Many were used as town halls for several years, and some continue to house civic authorities.

Craft and merchant guilds would often control different areas of a particular industry. The merchant guild in a town dominated by the wool trade, for example,

1 Chequered flintwork adorns the elaborate facade of the Trinity Guildhall in King's Lynn, Norfolk. Built in 1421, the lavish guildhall celebrates the town's status as an important medieval port.

2 The coat of arms of the Merchant Adventurers outside their medieval hall in York. The guild controlled the northern cloth trade and traded with the Low Countries and northern Europe.

3 The half-timbered Cutlers' Guildhall at Thaxted in Essex was built early in the 15th century. It was restored and used as a grammar school between the 18th and the 19th centuries.

3

1

would oversee the purchase of fleeces and raw wool and the subsequent sale of the processed fibre. Craft guilds would control the actual carding, dyeing and weaving. Essentially hierarchical bodies, guilds were composed of masters at the head, supported by the journeymen and young apprentices. An apprentice was assigned to a master who would educate the boy, feed and clothe him and pass on the skills and techniques of his trade. The apprentice would receive very low wages, if any at all, but after a period of between five and nine years he could expect to be elevated to the rank of journeyman. Eventually, if he could afford to set up his own business,

2

a journeyman could seek to become a master himself. The apprenticeship system within manual trades lasted long after the guilds themselves had ceased to exist and was only gradually phased out during the 20th century.

In an era with no social security, many guilds provided a support network for their members, particularly those involved in different trades. Journeyman masons, for example, were often required to travel considerable distances on foot with heavy tools to their next job. Fellow workmen might contribute to a communal fund to provide a new arrival with an advance on his wages. It was also not uncommon for them to buy the tools of an ill or retiring mason at an artificially inflated price. Founded in 1492, the Worshipful Company of Masons sought to control the quality and integrity of building work by operating a long and difficult training period. Only after seven years' apprenticeship and a period as a journeyman could a mason aspire to master status.

Many guilds were strongly based on religion and individual organizations were often associated with a particular patron saint. Local guilds might maintain and support a chapel within their parish church. They were also instrumental in the funding and establishing of schools and almshouses, such as the Merchant Taylors' and Haberdashers' schools. St Paul's School in London is

1, 2 Participants in the annual
Swan Upping ceremony
photographed in 1895. The
event has taken place on the
River Thames since the 13th
century. All swans on the
Thames belong to either the
Queen or the two City
livery companies, the
vintners or dyers. The
ceremony is designed to
catch, identify and mark
new cygnets.

3 The headquarters of the
Vintners Livery Company
on the northern bank of the
Thames opposite the reconstruction of Shakespeare's
Globe. The vintners were
one of the 12 'great com-
panies' established when an
order of precedence was
established during the reign
of Henry VIII.

another famous establishment for which the Mercers'
Company assumed responsibility.

Craft guilds were sometimes known as 'mysteries'
after the Latin *ministerium*, meaning occupation. The
name was also given to the religious plays traditionally
presented by the guilds at the festival of Corpus Christi
(11 days after Whitsun) in many towns across England.
These mystery plays are still performed in some places
today, and they reveal some intriguing associations
between guild and narrative theme. The Mystery Plays
of York, for example, follow in the tradition of the medieval shipwrights, who performed The Building of Noah's
Ark, and the goldsmiths' version of the Arrival of the
Three Kings.

Livery companies, named after the distinctive dress of
their members, were London trade guilds incorporated
by royal charter. Edward III granted the first charters
during the 14th century and most were established by
the 17th century. Liverymen were the controlling elite
of their trades. They set the appropriate standards, regulated apprenticeship conditions and had the sole right
to confer on members the freedom
of the city (a necessary prerequisite
to the practice of any trade). Livery
companies today still exercise their
right to elect the office, now a
purely ceremonial one, of the lord
mayor of London. The 12 most
prominent livery companies are
collectively known as the 'great
companies' – a roll call that
includes the mercers, grocers,
drapers, merchant taylors, haberdashers and vintners.

Representatives from two of
London's livery companies, the
dyers and vintners, still join the
keeper of the royal swans for a
historic annual ceremony known
as Swan Upping which takes place
on the River Thames between

Sunbury Lock and Abingdon Bridge. According to tradition, all swans on the River Thames belong to either the
crown or one of the two livery companies (although on
occasion the sovereign has given permission to others
to keep the birds). The swans are identified by nicks
made on their beaks with sharp knives. The dyers' swans
are identified with one nick on the beak, the vintners
with two. Only the royal swans remain unmarked – any
new arrivals thus automatically become crown property.

The Swan Upping ceremony has not changed for
centuries. Two skiffs from each of the three swan owners
are rowed down the river, trapping families of birds by
the bank. The cob and pen (male and female) have their
beaks examined and any new cygnets are marked by
their owners accordingly. In the past it was a serious
business as these were valuable birds, prized delicacies
at the banquet table. During the reign of Elizabeth I,
the penalty for driving away swans or stealing eggs was
a year's imprisonment, while anyone caught near the
river in possession of a suspicious-looking hook was
liable to a substantial fine.

3

HERALDRY & PAGEANTRY

THE HERALDIC DEVICES OF ENGLAND ARE CLOSELY LINKED WITH SOME OF ITS OLDEST FAMILIES, BUILDINGS AND TRADITIONS. ONCE A PRACTICAL IDENTIFICATION IN COMBAT, INSIGNIA BECAME INCREASINGLY COMPLEX IN MEDIEVAL TIMES, AND DESIGNS AND COLOURS WERE STRICTLY CONTROLLED. COATS OF ARMS WERE A KEY ELEMENT OF THE TRAPPINGS OF JOUSTS AND TOURNAMENTS, AND OF THE COLOURFUL NATIONAL PAGEANTRY THROUGH WHICH THE POWER OF DYNASTIES AND STATE WAS DISPLAYED. CEREMONIAL WAS NOT ONLY THE PROVINCE OF THE RICH, HOWEVER, AND A VARIETY OF RURAL PARADES AND SHOWS CELEBRATED EVENTS OF THE AGRICULTURAL YEAR.

THE CRUSADES of the 11th, 12th and 13th centuries had a major influence on medieval warfare, not least in consolidating the need for knights to carry armorial bearings, a practice with earlier origins. Composed of warriors from all over Europe, the Christian forces converging on Jerusalem needed to be able to recognize their own compatriots; language alone could prove a problem to those not proficient in Latin or French. Different coloured signs of the cross were consequently adopted as badges of national identity. One such heraldic badge to survive from the crusades and be in practical use today is the emblem of the St John's Ambulance. This voluntary organization is descended from the Order of the Hospital of St John of Jerusalem. Its monks not only healed sick pilgrims but also, as brother knights, defended the frontiers of Christian states.

In the later Middle Ages, when knights became even more heavily armed and faces were fully covered by helmet visors, heraldic decoration was essential. By the 14th century, painted shields were complemented by surcoats embroidered with insignia and worn over coats of chainmail. These were often highly ornamental, such as the magnificent emblazoned surcoat, helmet, sword, shield and gauntlets worn by Edward the Black Prince in battles at Crécy, Poitiers and Najéra, and now suspended above his tomb in Canterbury Cathedral.

The complex insignia brought on to medieval battlefields significantly altered the role of the herald in conflict. Previously little more than a neutral servant-messenger, heralds became responsible for monitoring the course of battle and, in conjunction with their opposite numbers, assessing the eventual outcome. They required an in-depth knowledge of

colours and designs, acquired from research at parades and gatherings, supplemented by copious records. One of a herald's more unpleasant tasks was to identify the dead from his own side after the battle – often a difficult task if the body was mutilated and had been stripped of armour and surcoat. The unfortunate herald required to identify the earl of Shrewsbury at the battle of Castillon in 1453 could do so only by a pronounced gap in the earl's teeth. When knights were captured and ransomed rather than killed – a common practice during the Hundred Years War, of which Castillon was the final battle – their heraldic insignia were often removed and accompanied the demand for money as proof of the captive's identity.

Towards the end of the 15th century, further developments in weaponry and armour meant there was little room for personal heraldic display. Nobles and their retainers fought instead under banners and standards decorated with the holder's arms – rather as the Roman legions had done, under the powerful symbol of the eagle. Although such a device provided a useful rallying point for soldiers separated from their comrades, it also acted as a beacon for an enemy. Nevertheless, the use of regimental banners continued for centuries of conflict. The tattered relics proudly displayed in regimental chapels and museums bear the scars of relatively recent battles in France and Flanders, reminding us of the lives lost in defence of the banners.

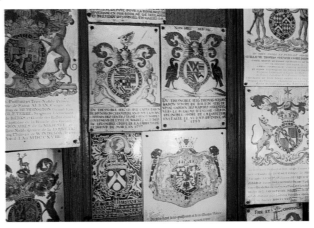

The use of a surcoat for displaying one's personal insignia led to the generic term 'coat of arms' to describe insignia no matter on what, or where, it might be displayed. Coats of arms are not the sole prerogative of the nobility or military, but can be owned by companies, civic bodies and even clergy. If they do not

1 Plaques displaying the coats of arms of Knights of the Garter in St George's Chapel, Windsor Castle. Founded by Edward III in 1348, the Order of the Garter was a chivalric foundation based upon the Arthurian legends. It originally consisted of 26 knights including Edward III's son, Edward the Black Prince.

2 St George's Chapel, Windsor Castle, is one of the finest examples of the Perpendicular style in England. It was built at the instigation of Edward IV to serve as a royal mausoleum and to add splendour to the annual ceremonies of the Order of the Garter.

2

1 A page from a French illustrated manuscript depicting departure to the Third Crusade (1189–92). Heraldry was first employed during the Crusades as a means of identification where uniformity of armour and language differences made swift recognition difficult.

2 Illustrations to heraldic trappings from a 14th-century manuscript. Tournaments of jousting were colourful spectacles with competing knights resplendent in coats of arms; by the 14th century they had become a form of staged entertainment.

relate to family history, arms can contain any elements pertinent to the bearer; a town council, for example, might feature a landmark in its history. Those relating to lineage and family alliances have significantly stricter controls, drawing on a set of rules compiled in medieval times. A formal body was established to determine what were acceptable colours and designs, and to compile an accurate register to avoid duplication. Even the language of heraldry is complex; or and argent are clearly gold and silver, but terms such as gules, meaning red, and tenne, a form of orange, are less apparent.

For centuries the English royal arms included territories over which the monarch claimed to rule, as well as those in his or her actual possession. The arms of the Black Prince, for example, bore the French fleurs de lys as well as the gold lion adopted by all Norman and Plantaganet kings since the conquest. His arms merely reflected those adopted by his father Edward III in 1337, the fleurs de lys emphasizing the king's claim to the French throne through his mother, Isabella of France. Subsequent monarchs retained the basic royal arms of lions and fleurs de lys in a quartered design until James I added the red lion of Scotland and a gold harp to denote sovereignty over Ireland. The implicit claim over the French throne was not removed from the royal arms until 1801 during the reign of George III.

The use of emblems on coats of arms extended far beyond identification in combat. They became the equivalent of signatures when incorporated into a seal, varying from a single shield motif to a detailed engraving of a knight galloping on horseback. It was also common practice to have one's family motto inscribed round the seal's edge. Coats of arms were also set into buildings as a physical embodiment of dynastic lineage and power. Wroxton Abbey in Oxfordshire, an attractive Jacobean house, bears the coat of arms of its owner, Sir William

Pope earl of Downes, complete with earl's coronet. The historical provenance of a building can be revealed by an unexpected coat of arms, as in the royal arms in the southeast corner of Sherborne Abbey in Dorset. Originally the 14th-century chapel of St Mary le Bow, it was divided from the church in 1560 and converted into a house for the headmaster of Sherborne School – an establishment refounded by Edward VI after the dissolution of a monastic institution. Now used as a baptistry, it retains a curiously domestic aspect, counterpointed by the bold colonnettes around the royal arms.

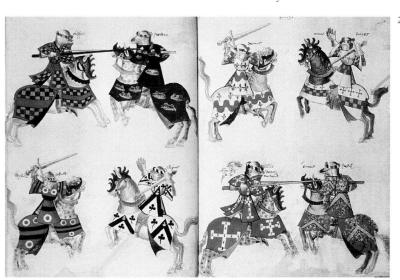

2

Knights possessed arms of both war and peace, the latter worn and displayed at stylized military contests such as jousts and tournaments. Jousts generally took place between two combatants, while formal tournaments involved groups of knights, but each provided invaluable training in the weapons handling and horsemanship essential for real warfare. From the late 13th century onwards, blunted weapons were used at these entertainments, and 'arms of peace' were a logical extension of the theme. One of the best known examples is the white fleurs de lys on a black background sported by the Black Prince. Tournaments enabled a knight to display

1 The Yeomen of the Guard
was a corps founded by
Henry VII in 1485 to act as
the sovereign's bodyguard.
Commonly referred to as
'beefeaters', their duties are
now mostly ceremonial,
reflecting their traditional
role as wardens of the
Tower of London.

2 *The State Opening of Parliament,
1855* by Eugene-Louis Lami.
Flanked by Yeomen of the

Guard and other dignitaries,
the procession is both
colourful spectacle and
solemn ritual, which
comments upon many
aspects of England's
Parliamentary tradition.

3 A portrait of Elizabeth I
attired in coronation robes
c.1559. Throughout her
reign, Elizabeth's sense of
theatre elevated her to the
status of glittering icon.

his chivalry and skill to an appreciative audience, providing the chance to increase one's individual prestige. Chivalry was an important ingredient of the displays; more than politeness, its codes were interwoven with the Christian allegiance of a knight, explicit in Edward III's Order of the Garter based at St George's Chapel, Windsor. The helm and sword of a garter knight, required by definition to be of noble birth and irreproachable honour, were hung above his personal stall in the chapel. They signified his enduring commitment to the defence of the church.

Tournaments were not by any means solemn affairs, however. They were sources of entertainment as well as military training, expanding over time into colourful social events held at weddings, baptisms and festivals. On occasion an aspect of pantomime could creep into proceedings, such as the comic bout held at Smithfield in 1343 (during the early stages of the Hundred Years War). Participating knights dressed up as a pope and 12 cardinals and challenged all comers to battle in a mocking jibe at Pope Clement VI, whose election had signalled a marked pro-French shift in papal policies.

The taste for spectacle was not confined to a courtly elite, however; both processions and pageants were used to entertain and bring political messages to a much wider audience. During the Middle Ages, a pageant consisted of a part or scene of a play, usually performed in public arenas such as market squares or in front of

churches. Each scene from the play would be acted by a different group of players with a movable stage or platform, enabling the same tableau to be presented in alternative locations. Pageants generally followed themes of religion or national pride and they were a curiously spellbinding form of theatre. More elaborate preparations, staging and costumes went into the spectacular pageants presented to monarchs, for example as they were carried round London on the traditional coronation eve procession.

This celebration of a monarch's impending coronation was an important, carefully orchestrated event. Although the monarch was not in any real physical danger from the crowds, their response, or lack of it, could set the mood for the following day. The procession of Elizabeth I was particularly magnificent, reflecting her political awareness of the power of display. She exhibited all the powers of showmanship characteristic of her reign, riding on an open litter swathed in gold and white satin, playing to the crowd and making animated response to the five elaborate pageants that had been staged in her honour. These, not surprisingly, represented historical themes. One showed how even as Elizabeth of York had brought the Wars of the Roses to an end through her marriage to Henry VII, so another Elizabeth would bring peace to a strife-torn England. The final play was a complex but dramatic affair, depicting Elizabeth as the biblical Deborah, the prophetess responsible for rescuing Israel from Jabin. Even a date palm was improbably imported to simulate the Israeli desert.

For the coronation itself Elizabeth took centre stage. She walked from Westminster Hall dressed in crimson Parliament robes, changing into gold and silver garments before entering Westminster Abbey. Resplendent in gold from head to foot, she presented an awe-inspiring, almost

1 *Arrival of Queen Victoria at the
   House of Lords* by George
   Baxter. The young queen,
   illuminated by symbolic
   sunlight, is surrounded by
   all the pomp and ceremony
   of the state opening of
   Parliament.
2 A team of Morris dancers,
   representing a rustic
   tradition of pageantry,
   perform in the market place
   at Richmond, North
   Yorkshire.

3 The Cotswold Town of
   Chipping Campden is one
   of many English towns and
   villages that have maintained the centuries old
   tradition of May fairs and
   floral festivals. This
   photograph, from 1903,
   illustrates its floral parade.

iconic figure, seated on St Edward's chair in Westminster Abbey to receive the ornaments of investiture. Fanfares of trumpets sounded to acknowledge each one of the three crowns placed on her head in succession. Solemn ceremonial was blended with carefully crafted spectacle.

The Lord Mayor's Show is an enduring example of itinerate pomp, demonstrating London's pride in its history and status as a centre of world commerce. The parade from the Guildhall to the Royal Courts of Justice is one of the most elaborate staged in the capital, complete with the gilded lord mayor's coach. Dating from the mid-18th century and painted by the Florentine artist Giovanni Cipriani, it is accompanied by an impressive array of liveried pikemen and musketeers. The coach is in fact a relatively recent addition; when the show was first instigated, some 600 years ago, it was a waterborne procession. London's river was used for ceremony far more in past centuries, including royal progresses and pageants, and the traditional role of the River Thames is remembered in the historic office of barge master.

The most colourful and important event of the parliamentary year is the state opening of Parliament, when the monarch reads the speech prepared for him or her by the government of the day, setting out its legislative agenda for the coming session. The occasion is filled with ritual; many of its traditions can be traced back to 1536, when the Act of Union brought Wales into Parliament's range. The ceremony is organized by the earl marshal, the duke of Norfolk. Before the royal procession sets out, a detachment of the Yeomen of the Guard searches the cellars of the Palace of Westminster, making sure there is no repetition

of the Gunpowder Plot of 1605. As the monarch arrives, the vice chamberlain, a government whip, is kidnapped and held hostage at Buckingham Palace to guarantee the safe return of the sovereign – a reminder that terms between crown and Parliament have not always been cordial. The monarch is met by the lord great chamberlain and led to the robing room to put on the imperial state crown and parliamentary robe. As he or she enters

2

the House of Lords, they are preceded by the earl marshal and lord great chamberlain, who walk backwards as a mark of respect. Once the monarch is seated, Black Rod – an officer of the House of Lords and of the Order of the Garter – is ordered to summon the members of the House of Commons. As he approaches the door to the Commons it is slammed in his face; he has to knock three times before being allowed entry. Once the Lords, the Commons and the monarch are gathered in one place, the royal address begins.

Pageants, parades and dances were also a strong tradition in country towns and villages; several still take place today in streets and market squares, albeit often in a modified form. Many English festivals are linked to the rural calendar and the rituals of the farming year; May Day activities, for example, derive from a pagan celebration of fertility at the beginning of summer. Events differ in tone and character from region to region; the West Country, for example, is associated with grotesque hobby horses, snapping and cavorting their way through the streets of Padstow and Minehead. Probably the most traditional May Day sight is that of children dancing around a brightly coloured maypole erected on the village green. Originally a tree would have been felled early in the morning, its branches lopped and then hung with garlands of flowers to form the centrepiece of the communal display. Mobile pageants on themed floats decked with flowers form colourful processional preludes to the crowning of a May Queen in many rural areas. The Cotswold town of Chipping Campden still holds the the Scuttlebrooke Wake and Robert Dover's Games – sporting activities begun as a personal protest against Puritanism in 1604 and continued until 1852, when

they were condemned as 'too rowdy' by Victorian authorities and suppressed. That tradition has been restored and the games are followed by the Spring Fair, a colourful carnival of flowers and the crowning of the Scuttlebrooke Queen.

Although ostensibly a celebration of hunting rights in Needwood Forest, the Abbots Bromley Horn Dance also has overtones of an ancient fertility ritual. In a folk dance that is unique to the occasion, 12 men from the Staffordshire village make their way from the church out to surrounding farms, bearing ancient sets of deer antlers on their shoulders. The Derbyshire custom of 'dressing the wells' has been traced to the medieval period, but it may also have associations with fertility, or the Celtic veneration of springs. As the practice came under Christian influence, wells were blessed and the decorations adopted religious themes. Once simple floral wreaths were placed by the wells, but the 'dressing' has now evolved into an art form. Each village pursues a specific pictorial theme and the floral tableaux around each well are made up of thousands of individual petals.

3

CHAPTER

3

The Iron Age earthworks, Roman walls and Norman mottes
are mute testimony to the shifting tides of invasion, conquest
and battle which swept through England over the centuries. Probably
the most eloquent testimony to a warlike past are the thousands
of stone castles, most roofless and with shattered walls, which are such
a feature of the English countryside. Built initially to subdue and
subsequently used as a centre for administration and the law as well
as for defence in times of war or border raids, they nevertheless
on the whole met violent ends. The straight roads which march
through the English countryside are as much a product
of warfare as trade. The need for Roman legions to move
swiftly about their domains prompted the network
of trunk roads which are still in use today.

INVASION, CONQUEST & WAR

A PROVINCE OF ROME

The relationship between Celtic Britain and the Roman empire developed long before Claudius' formal conquest in AD 43. Trading links existed and many Celtic kings, especially those in the southeast, were responsive to Roman influence. Strategic colonization after the conquest sought to give tribal chieftains a limited involvement in the new administration — a policy that disastrously failed with the Iceni on the occasion of Boudicca's revolt. Over the centuries a Roman lifestyle and culture were more widely adopted and integrated into the social fabric. England's landscape was transformed by the roads, forts and villas that bound the province, architecturally and politically, to the vast and powerful Roman empire.

In the first century AD, Britain lay at the extreme west of the Roman empire's borders. It was viewed by many in the empire as a remote, barbaric place, although the Belgae tribes dominating the south of the country, including the powerful Catuvellauni, came from the Gallia Belgica region of Gaul. Strong trading connections were maintained with Gaul, well established as a profitable Roman province; the Belgae were renowned metalworkers of gold, silver, bronze and iron as well as efficient farmers who cleared much of Britain's wooded southeast for agricultural use.

The first two Roman incursions were led by Julius Caesar in 55 and 54 BC. His intention was not to set up a formal administration, but to enhance his political reputation in Rome through military prowess, slaves and tribute. The first attempt barely moved inland from the Straits of Dover, but the following year a larger force fought several battles to cross the Thames and reach Hertfordshire. Although inconclusive, Caesar's expedition did achieve the surrender of Cassivellaunus, chief of the Catuvellauni, allowing Caesar to return to Rome in triumph.

During the following decades, trade and cultural links with the Roman empire increased, strengthening Roman influence at the courts of Celtic kings. Internecine disputes between rival Celtic chiefs resulted in requests to Rome for support, particularly against the Catuvellauni. Having recently been declared emperor, Claudius recognized an ideal opportunity to stamp his authority on the throne, as well as remove the potential threat posed by Gaul's volatile neighbour. Raw materials, particularly grain, timber and minerals, were important economic considerations, as was the eradication of Druidism – a cult deeply disliked by the Romans as a focus of tribal resistance. In AD 43 some 40,000 troops and auxiliaries were landed at Richborough under the leadership of Aulus Plautius. Named Rutupiae by the Romans, the site once overlooked a great natural harbour and provided an ideal bridgehead for the invading army. The Kentish coastline has gradually silted up over the centuries, and today the impressive remains of Richborough Fort are stranded about 3.2 km (2 miles) inland from the retreating sea.

The army moved rapidly north, engaging the Britons in a two-day battle by the River Medway in Kent. Further advances were swift as several tribes – especially those with trading connections – welcomed the Romans, and others surrendered without a fight. After successfully crossing the Thames, progress was halted to await the arrival of the emperor, who had been monitoring progress from Gaul. Claudius, accompanied by elephants, participated in a magnificent ceremony at Camulodunum (near Colchester), where the emperor received the formal submission of several British kings.

The new rulers of Britian were quick to consolidate their position, drawing upon their highly disciplined and effective legionaries to construct forts, bridges and roads. Supply lines delivering troops and equipment across the Channel were made more efficient by the development of Dover as an additional port. Ships were guided by twin lighthouses, built on high cliffs on either side of the harbour. One still survives and stands within the defences of Dover Castle. It is octagonal from the outside, although rooms within were rectangular, and it originally possessed eight stepped storeys, reaching over 24 m (80 ft) in height. A brazier on the top storey was kept constantly alight.

Britain remained far from stable in the wake of the invasion. Tribes such as the Durotriges of Dorset and

2

1 Wheeldale Roman road runs for a mile across an isolated stretch of the North York Moors and is one the few surviving examples of an original military road. Although the surface has disappeared, the larger stones of the base remain in place, as do the drainage channels dug out from each side of the road.

2 Hardknott Fort sits at the summit of one the Lake District's highest passes.

Built between AD 120 and 138, the fort was intended to control the road linking Ravenglass and Ambleside.

3 Few Roman legionaries stationed in Britannia were from Italy. Auxilliaries from other European provinces formed highly trained and well disciplined units.

2

Somerset mounted ferocious resistance from the immense hillfort of Maiden Castle, an apparently impregnable defensive position. However, even steeply rising concentric ramparts and ditches protecting a central core would have been overwhelmed by the tactical skill and weaponry of a Roman legion. A mass grave by the eastern gate of the castle offers possible evidence of a battle, although archaeologists interpret the discovery differently. Certainly the deaths were violent; one body still had a ballister-fired bolt embedded in its spine.

Seventeen years after the invasion, most regions had settled into the new regime as Celtic tribal structures were consciously drawn into the Roman administration. However, the death of Prasutagas, chief of the East Anglian Iceni tribe, proved a catalyst for a major native rebellion. In effect the leader of a 'client kingdom', Prasutagas sought to preserve this fragile autonomy in his will, dividing his assets equally between his family and the Emperor Nero. Local centurions interpreted this as submission and appropriated Iceni land. They flogged Prasutagas's widow, Boudicca, and raped her daughters.

The Iceni rose in revolt, joining forces with the Trinovantes to strike at key symbols of Roman occupation. Boudicca and her followers destroyed the province's capital, Colchester, including its vast stone temple of Claudius, and indiscriminately slaughtered the inhabitants. Encountering little opposition (the Legions, led by Suetonius Paulinus, were conducting a final assault upon the Druid stronghold in Anglesey), Boudicca's army moved upon London, destroying Chelmsford and Verulamium (near St Albans) en route. The 9th Legion sent to intercept them was annihilated in a forest ambush near Colchester, and London, a major source of Roman investment in the province, razed to the ground. The legacy of such devastation

recurs in excavations in the capital today, as layers of soot, ash, burned pottery and the possessions of those killed and tortured by the rebellious tribes.

It is estimated that around 70,000 people died in the uprising, including many Romanized Celts. Roman forces eventually killed tens of thousands of the rebels in a bloody pitched battle believed to have been at Mancetter near Nuneaton. Boudicca took poison, but reprisals on the Iceni territory of Norfolk were savage. A huge chain of forts was constructed across East Anglia, for example at Saham Toney and Warham, to prevent further uprisings.

Having quelled Boudicca's uprising, the harshness of Suetonius's revenge led to his recall to Rome. More conciliatory regimes followed, gradually allowing the colonized regions of Britannia (mainly the south and east) to recover and prosper, contributing valuable resources to the empire's economy. London was re-established as a thriving commercial centre, minerals were mined across the country, and agricultural production improved. But territorial expansion remained at the mercy of external events: Civil War in Rome during the late 60s AD, for example, temporarily removed many troops, delaying plans to subjugate the remote north and west. Renewed activity between AD 71 and 74 saw the submission of the northern Brigantes tribes, whose last stand occurred near Scotch Corner in North Yorkshire.

During those nationwide campaigns, efficient movement of men and materials over long distances was made possible by a rapidly expanding road network. The work was carried out by disciplined and versatile legionaries, supplemented by local conscripted labour. All roads were kept as straight as possible through meticulous surveying, a feat not always achievable on the inhospitable terrain in the wilder

3

1

2

3

1 Hardrian's Wall remains one of the greatest feats of civil engineering in Europe. Extending across England from Wallsened on the Tyne to the Solway Firth, the wall was built on the order of Emperor Hadrian around AD 123.

2 Jewellery and other artefacts of gold and semi-precious metals have been excavated from several sites along the wall.

3 Housesteads Fort on Hadrian's Wall had its own military hospital. These surgeon's instruments indicate that wounded legionaries received at least basic medical care.

4 Most Roman forts had bath complexes, although they were seldom as lavish as civilian ones. The elaborate King's Bath at Aquae Sulis (Bath), featured decorative arches and stonework.

parts of upland England. The legacy of the roads is still visible today (page 294), sometimes in boundaries or as trackways, but often in the shape of modern constructions that follow the Romans' well-chosen routes. The gravelled surface on a solid flag base ensured an efficient movement of troops and horses, reflecting the strategic military function for which they were designed.

The Roman army itself was an invaluable part of the imperial machine. Its soldiers were highly trained in combat and other skills, including building techniques, civil engineering and cookery, so each unit was self-sufficient in the field. Legionaries signed up for 25 years, but the subsequent rewards of a grant of land or equivalent financial gratuities enabled them to contribute successfully to civilian life. Many of the ill-fated inhabitants of Colchester at the time of Boudicca's rebellion were ex-legionaries and their families, helping to colonize the new territory.

Despite their professionalism, the Legions were unable to subdue the furthest reaches of Britannia. On his visit to the island in AD 122, Hadrian determined upon the construction of a permanent, fixed frontier linking Carlisle and Newcastle. The scale of the enterprise is apparent only at the physical site: 113 km (70 miles) in length and a remarkable feat of engineering, it is a monument not merely to Hadrian, but to the three Legions of Chester, Caerleon and York who built it.

Modifications were made to the wall as it progressed, including a substantial reduction in height to speed construction. Locally quarried stone was used wherever possible, although the last few kilometres of the western sector running to the Solway Firth was simply a turf wall surmounted by timber palisades. The wall was not one long unbroken barrier: soldiers were stationed at fortified gateposts, or milecastles, along the wall and manned lookout turrets were spaced at regular intervals in between. The gates allowed soldiers to pass through on raids to the north; they also acted as customs posts, exacting tolls from traders. Military units were garrisoned at large forts, generally set some distance back from the wall, as with the cavalry base of Chester. A

notable exception is Housesteads, which straddles the wall on one of its most exposed sections. After Hadrian's death in AD 138, the new emperor, Antonius Pius, ordered the frontier to be moved 160 km (100 miles) north. Built of turf, the Antonine Wall linked the Clyde and Forth estuaries, supported by an even greater number of forts. It was abandoned after a decade and

4

Hadrian's Wall again became the empire's northern front line. After the Legions' final departure, its ready-dressed stone was used for farms, churches and towns.

From Agricola's time, the Roman authorities sought to invest some of their power in regional municipalities. St Albans, Colchester, Lincoln, Gloucester and York were the five principal cities, providing a powerful focus of Roman culture and commerce. London achieved a level of prosperity that it would not equal for centuries. A vast basilica on Cornhill was 150 m (500 ft) long, its arcaded walls lined with marble 21 m (70 ft) high. Baths were established at the city gates and a Temple of Mithras by the Walbrook. Rich citizens lived north of the basilica, in porticoed villas with the accoutrements of Roman life – ink wells and styli, perfumes, blue and amber glass dishes and bowls, oil lamps and silver plates. A sophisticated trade network imported olive oil and wine from Italy, fabrics from Egypt, and ivory, silks and spices from the East. To those who had adopted Roman ways, life before the conquest have seemed alien indeed.

THE NORMAN CONQUEST

THE VICTORY OF WILLIAM DUKE OF NORMANDY IN 1066 STRUCK AT THE HEART OF SAXON POWER IN ENGLAND. A NEW RULING ELITE BROUGHT RADICAL CHANGES TO THE COUNTRY'S LANDSCAPE AND BUILDINGS, REINFORCING POLITICAL POWER WITH IMPOSING CASTLES AND CATHEDRALS. THE SAXON OWNERSHIP OF LAND WAS VIRTUALLY ERADICATED AND A MORE STRINGENT FEUDAL SYSTEM ESTABLISHED BY A BRUTAL MILITARY REGIME. MANY SAXON TREASURES WERE PLUNDERED AND ASPECTS OF ITS CULTURE SUPPRESSED, YET THE DOMESDAY BOOK CONTINUES TO PROVIDE A PARADOXICAL TESTAMENT TO ITS EFFICIENT AND SOPHISTICATED ADMINISTRATION.

THE LEGACY OF a pre-conquest England is still evident today, particularly in small villages such as Bosham in Sussex. Its shoreline cottages are dominated by a Saxon church with an impressive chancel arch containing stones from an earlier monastery that occupied the site. Harold Godwinson earl of Wessex celebrated mass there in 1064 before his ill-fated visit to France, at which time the interior would probably have been highly decorated. Saxon churches contained wall hangings and painted wall plaster, gilded statues and stained glass, while their monasteries were sources of magnificent illuminated manuscripts and considerable scholarship. Charlemagne used scholars from English universities and in the previous century Athelstan's court had harboured pilgrims, poets and churchmen from throughout Europe. Famous for goldwork, textiles and carvings, pre-conquest England was more culturally advanced than Normandy – Saxon social graces drew contempt from William's barons.

England's ruler at that time was the ageing, childless Edward the Confessor. He had a Norman mother and had lived in exile at the Norman court until 1042, estab-lishing a close association between the two countries. Significant Norman links and influence, both political and architectural, existed in England well before William's invasion. Norman clerks had been brought into Edward's administration; Robert abbot of Jumièges was made archbishop of Canterbury in 1051; and Westminster Abbey was built of Caen stone in a cruci-form Norman design. As the king's health declined, potential claimants to the throne emerged from a tangled web of dynastic links and allegiances extending from Normandy to Scandinavia. William duke of Normandy, despite being only a distant cousin, steadfastly maintained that the English monarch had promised him the throne during a visit to the French court in 1051. He was equally adamant that, during Harold's visit to Normandy in 1064, the English earl had sworn on sacred relics that he would support William's claim when Edward died.

Harold firmly denied the validity of his oath to William, saying that the holy relics had been deliberately obscured. As Edward's brother-in-law, he was present at the king's deathbed, and claimed the succession on the

1   The tiny village of Bosham in West Sussex, with its surviving Saxon church. Bosham was Harold's point of embarkation for his ill-fated encounter with William duke of Normandy in 1064.

2   The Bayeux Tapestry, sewn by Saxon women after the conquest, illustrates the events leading up to the battle of Hastings and its aftermath. The sections feature (from left to right)

Edward the Confessor's death and burial in his newly completed Westminster Abbey; Harold's subsequent coronation there; the new king's prophetic nightmare of a Norman fleet invading.

3   Pevensey Castle, originally a Roman fort of the Saxon Shore, was adopted by William as a fortified bridge-head following his landing.

basis of the Confessor's alleged final request that Harold should take care of his wife and his kingdom. Those last few whispered words were accepted by England's ruling council, the Witan, and Harold was crowned king the following day, 6 January 1066.

When informed of the coronation, William assembled an invasion army and fleet with which to cross the Channel and seize the English throne by force. Harold maintained coastal defences on high alert until September, when the escalating cost and prospect of stormy autumn weather, in which an invasion would become impossible, encouraged him to disband the levies (a local form of home guard). However, the winds that had delayed William were favourable for the Norwegian king, Harald Hardrada, also a contender for the English throne. Harald entered the Humber and anchored at Ricall, while Harold of England made a legendary forced march up existing Roman roads to East Yorkshire. The Norwegians were defeated at the battle of Stamford Bridge on 25 September, at which Harald Hardrada was slain. From a flotilla of 300 boats, the Scandinavians needed only 24 to ferry the survivors back home; the bones of their dead were still a landmark for travellers in the Yorkshire wolds in the 1130s. Meanwhile William had sailed on 27 September under a papal banner (papal support had been granted to William on the grounds of Harold's allegedly broken oath).

While Harold celebrated the victory at Stamford Bridge, William landed unopposed at Pevensey. He consolidated his position by strengthening the fortifications of the existing Saxon Shore fort and then moved eastwards towards Hastings. News of the Norman landings reached Harold on 2 October. He rallied his exhausted men and immediately headed south to make camp on Caldbec Hill, several kilometres north of the Norman positions near Hastings.

On the morning of 14 October, Harold had assembled his depleted forces – many are believed to have been still in transit – in battle formation on Senlac Ridge. Even today, it is clearly a superb defensive position which ensuredthat the Normans would have to fight uphill and over marshy terrain. The main body of the English consisted of the shire levy of Sussex, the

2

3

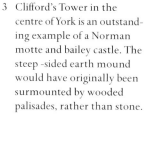

1 An artist's impression of the battle of Hastings in which Norman archers and cavalry eventually broke the fierce resistance of the Saxon thegnhood.

2 An aerial view of Old Sarum near Salisbury, Wiltshire. Originally a heavily fortified Iron Age fort, the strategic site was later occupied by Romans, Saxons and Normans. A castle, bishop's palace and great cathedral were built on the site, eventually abandoned owing to lack of water.

3 Clifford's Tower in the centre of York is an outstanding example of a Norman motte and bailey castle. The steep-sided earth mound would have originally been surmounted by wooded palisades, rather than stone.

Saxon aristocratic thegnhood, probably some Danish mercenaries, and Harold's elite force of housecarls. The main tactic of the housecarls was to form an almost impenetrable shield ring, repelling the enemy with deadly two-handed battle axes. William's troops, by contrast, were a fresh and highly effective military machine, dominated by a skilled body of knights in chainmail with lances and swords, supplemented by infantry and archers.

William ordered the archers to unleash a hail of arrows on the English ranks, a tactic that failed due to effective shield cover. The Norman infantry then attacked at close quarters, but Harold's housecarls did not break ranks. The cavalry were equally unsuccessful, but as they fell back down the slopes, an undisciplined charge after them by English foot soldiers, stationed behind the housecarls, caused these fyrdmen to become isolated. They were easily slaughtered, and later in the afternoon a similar incident occurred which reduced the English forces still further.

Desperate to achieve victory before dark, William ordered his archers to fire in a high arc. A determined group of Norman knights then fought their way through the ring of housecarls protecting Harold to cut down the man they called 'the oath breaker'. Harold may have received an arrow wound from the deadly shower, as recorded in the Bayeux Tapestry scene, but the English king of just nine months was hacked to death by Norman swords.

Seeing their leader slain, the English fyrdmen fled in terror; the housecarls tried to maintain formation but were eventually forced to retreat. After allowing his troops a few days rest, William marched east through Kent, burning much of Dover before passing through Canterbury and Maidstone en route for the capital.

Stiff resistance occurred at London Bridge, in response to which William razed Southwark. He then headed west to cross the Thames at Wallingford, leaving a trail of destruction in his wake. The circumnavigation of London proved successful: by the time he reached Hertfordshire, Saxon nobles had started to surrender and most paid homage to the monarch elect at Little Berkhampstead during December. He was crowned William I in Westminster Abbey on Christmas Day 1066.

William proceeded immediately to tighten his grip on a restive and rebellious kingdom. He retreated to Barking in Essex after the coronation and remained there while 'certain strongholds were made in the town against the fickleness of the vast and fierce populace' – a measure of his distrust of Londoners that continued throughout his reign. In the rest of the country, a chain of castles was rapidly established, strategically sited near river crossings and roads, or in the very heart of Saxon

2

1 Launceston Castle guarded one of the main routes into Cornwall. The sheer size and height of the motte, or mound, provides a vivid impression of how such fortresses must have dominated the local Saxon population.

2 Battle Abbey was founded by William I around 1070 upon the site where Harold was slain at the battle of Hastings. Most traces of the Norman monastery have disappeared, but the impressive medieval gatehouse survives.

3 The chapel of St John in the Tower of London, built by William in 1097, celebrates the simple austerity of Romanesque architecture.

1

towns and cities. Fortified dwellings were not new to England – the Roman fort at Portchester, for example, part of the Saxon Shore defences, contained a late Saxon building with a tower thought to have been a thegn's residence – but the quantity and scale of the Norman castles were new. They were designed to control and intimidate the local population, not to give communal defences from exterior threat as walled *burhs* had done.

Many of those initial structures, known as motte and bailey castles, were built of timber rather than stone. They consisted of a huge, flat-topped conical motte, or mound, usually about 24 m (80 ft) in height, the excava-tion of which formed a natural ditch around the site. Gangs of local men were pressed into the service of their new masters, and a motte could be thrown up in several days. On top of the motte, wooden buildings were erected to provide a secure garrison for the lord and his family. The bailey was an apron or courtyard, fortified by additional stake-filled ditches and a wooden palisade, accessed by wooden bridges. If an attack threatened, the bridges could be withdrawn to secure the site. Excavations of Hen Domen ('old mound' in Welsh), an early border castle near Montgomery, have revealed a partially self-sufficient structure, with a garrison, stores, smithy and bakery crammed into a claustrophobic bailey.

Where castles were deemed necessary in the very heart of Saxon towns, William's men had no qualms about simply demol-ishing whole areas of housing to make way for giant mounds. The Domesday Book records that 166 dwellings were lost in Lincoln and 98 in Norwich, while at Winchester in 1067 a castle mound was simply con-structed across a sizeable street. Clifford's Tower in York, soaring above the surrounding buildings, still shows the impact the structures would have had on local commu-nities. It would have been impossible, even in a city, to lose sight of the motte, an ever-present reminder of where political power lay.

The Normans perceived castle bases as a means of annexing territory, and in more rural areas, such as Launceston, the building of a castle frequently preceded the creation of a town. The castle at Launceston guarded

2

the main route into Cornwall and the borough grew up in the shadow of its mound. Older sites were also adapted to Norman needs, as there were few Anglo-Saxon structures to develop. The Iron Age hillfort of Old Sarum in Wiltshire, the precursor to Salisbury, had been a town (known as Sorviodonum) under the Romans. It was developed into one of the Conqueror's major regional centres, with vast ramparts encompassing a castle, a bishop's palace and a great cathedral. An initial earth motte was succeeded by stone buildings, including Bishop Osmund's cathedral, on which work began in 1087. Unfortunately, Old Sarum was poorly served by natural water, which proved to be impossible

3

to overcome. Combined with disputes between military and clergy, it caused the move in 1226 to more suitable land 3.2 km (2 miles) down the valley.

Rebellions continued to occur across England in the early years of Norman rule, and they were suppressed with almost unprecedented brutality. Herefordshire was the first area to rebel under Edric the Wild, and his guerrilla campaigns continued periodically throughout the Welsh Marches, Cheshire and Staffordshire. The revolt in the West Country ended with the submission of Exeter in 1068, but the most serious challenges were mounted in the north, supported by Scandinavian interests. The combined Danish and Saxon forces, including Edward the Confessor's great nephew Edgar, captured York before moving south into Lincolnshire. William had despatched his lieutenants to deal with the uprisings in the south and west but elected to deal with the northern problem in person. He laid waste to large areas around York, causing the Saxons to retreat further north towards Durham and Northumberland, and the Danes to seek the safety of their ships in the Humber estuary. The king proceeded to conduct a near-genocidal act of repression, known as the 'harrowing of the north', which shocked even the warriors of the time. In the winter of 1069, he marched as far as the river Tees, ordering his men literally to erase towns and villages from the map. All farm animals were killed and everything flammable was burned, including farming implements, food supplies and seed corn. So great was the devastation that when the compilers of the Domesday Book came to document certain northern areas 20 years later, they noted simply, 'waste'.

The Danish forces, who had formed a coalition with the rebel leader Hereward the Wake in East Anglia, established the Isle of Ely as their base. The swamps and hidden waterways of the Fens were convenient territory for guerrilla activity, and for a time they conducted a successful hit-and-run campaign. Eventually the rebels were trapped in a naval blockade and largely annihilated by troops using an overland causeway. Hereward himself escaped to continue his orchestrated resistance

1

before he was finally betrayed and killed.

A spate of castle building followed the various regional repressions and local landowners were dispossessed in favour of the new Norman lords. Initially this took the form of granting strong blocks of territory in the most sensitive areas to William's closest supporters, following the feudal structure well established in Normandy and other parts of Europe. This feudal system, alien to England, was essentially based upon the tenancy, rather than ownership, of land. The king was the owner and from him the aristocracy operated as tenants-in-chief, holding their estates in return for military service with a prescribed number of knights. The lords imposed similar conditions of service upon their vassals, who placed them in turn upon the villeins. The villeins paid the rent for their smallholdings by working for part of the year on the local estate land.

The redistribution of land that took place saw the virtual annihilation of the Saxon thegnhood. Of the thousands of English landowners existing before 1066, virtualy none remained by William's death in 1087. It is estimated that only eight per cent of the country was still in English hands, and most of the thegnhood were dead, impoverished or in exile overseas.

The church, too, had undergone significant upheaval after the conquest. Its upper echelons had been replaced by Norman bishops and abbots, and a radical rebuilding programme saw ancient cathedrals such as Winchester pulled down and replaced. Romanesque architecture, often associated with the Norman invasion, was in fact appearing in England before the invasion: Westminster Abbey bears a strong resemblance to Jumièges Abbey, completed in 1037, which Westminster Abbey's founder, Edward the Confessor, would have seen in exile. Caen stone was shipped to England for the new building, creating echoes of churches in Bayeux or Rouen, yet the post-conquest rejection of existing church design and Anglo-Saxon saints' tombs shows a political impetus behind the new architectural style. The magnificence of Norman cathedrals such as Durham and Ely is tribute

1 Following the 'harrowing of the North', Norman barons consolidated their hold over the Saxons by replacing their earlier wooden fortifications with stone castles. Conisbrough Castle in South Yorkshire, built during the 12th century from gleaming white magnesian limestone, possesses the oldest circular keep in England.

2 Rochester Castle defends a strategic crossing point on the River Medway The massive square keep faces the city's cathedral, both begun under the direction of Norman bishop Gundulf.

3 The Domesday Book is a record of the survey carried out by William I in 1086 to assess the taxable value of his newly acquired kingdom and monitor the power of his vassal barons.

2

not only to piety and organization, but also to the wealth inherited with the conquest of England. This also found its way to the owners of individual castles, who, as they became more established, replaced timber with stone from England or France.

The most prestigious buildings, of course, had always been constructed in stone. William drew upon parts of London's Roman wall to construct temporary fortifications following his coronation. The site was later developed into the capital's great fortress, palace and prison, known as the Tower of London. Its massive stone keep, or 'donjon', later known as the White Tower, was begun by Bishop Gundulf around 1078, using stone imported from Caen. Moving raw materials by water was considerably cheaper and easier than overland and the high quality French stone was more familiar to castle and church builders than any from English quarries.

The White Tower was completed in 1097 and originally consisted of three floors, a basement and two upper levels, each divided into three rooms. The upper storey contained the chapel of St John, one of the earliest Romanesque chapels to be built in England and a movingly beautiful place of worship. The Tower was subsequently embellished by other Norman kings to include armouries, a menagerie of exotic beasts, quarters to accommodate a garrison and the king's yeoman guard, rooms for sleeping, and council rooms. However, the main living palace of later Norman kings was the Palace of Westminster, of which only Westminster Hall (pages 234–35) survives today.

Despite the brooding presence of the Tower of London, much of the capital's land and trade remained in pre-conquest hands. Norman architecture had begun to appear in the city with Edward the Confessor and it continued to alter the city's physical aspect, but its markets, such as Billingsgate and Eastcheap, continued as in Saxon times and the tortuous street layout remained. Property boundaries and street layout have, in fact, been

3

1 The New Forest was the largest of the 80 royal hunting grounds established by the Norman kings, who protected their rights with the introduction of draconian forest laws. Vast tracts of ancient woodland and many Saxon villages were cleared in the creation of the forests.

2 A medieval manuscript taken from the *Historia Anglorum* by Matthew Paris, *c.*1250. It depicts the four Angevin kings as patrons of the church and reveals how closely dynastic power was linked with monumental construction. The kings are, left to right, top to bottom: Henry II, Richard I, John and Henry III.

1

unchanged in several cities for centuries: archaeological surveys in York and Durham have revealed a constant disposition of houses and streets from the 10th century onwards, apart from the occasional disruption of cathedral or castle. An awkward bend in the road around York Minster, for example, is due to the Norman cathedral's liturgical alignment, contrasting with underlying Roman roads followed elsewhere in the city.

Even outside the towns, much of the social and physical framework of Saxon England survived. Areas of land, estates and parishes continued to divide along roughly the same boundaries for centuries, and the agricultural population did not substantially change. The Domesday Book, commissioned by William in 1086, was in fact masterminded by a skilled Anglo-Saxon administration and provides a meticulous account of social and fiscal change. Every village was required to supply information on the identity of landowners, the extent and use to which the land was put, and the value of such land at the time of the conquest, when given to new owners by William, and at the present time (ie 1086). The truth of the responses was attested by juries comprising equal numbers of Englishmen and Normans, and no item was left unaccounted for. The *Anglo-Saxon Chronicle* highlighted the thoroughness with which the survey was conducted by observing, 'that not even one ox or one cow or one pig escaped notice' – a parsimony of which it felt the king should be ashamed.

When completed, the Domesday Book showed at a glance the power of every tenant, and equally important, how much could be extracted from him or her in taxes. Two volumes still exist today in the Public Record Office at Chancery Lane, London, and (as a related book) in the cathedral library at Exeter. They are invaluable records of both a dispossessed aristocracy and a labouring underclass for whom many aspects of life continued much the same.

One way in which the Normans did impact upon the villeins' lives was in their reshaping of the landscape for private hunting grounds. William ordered that much of the ancient woodland be cleared away and any inconveniently sited Saxon villages be simply removed. Land set aside for hunting was protected with draconian laws and regulations. To kill a deer meant the death penalty, and even inadvertently disturbing one could result in being blinded. Many of these original tracts have dwindled or been ploughed out, but the New Forest, one of the largest areas of former hunting land in the south of England, still covers *c.* 375 km² (145 sq miles).

Losing access to the forest was a serious blow to the local population, who relied heavily on its natural resources for firewood and game. Some commoners living within the forest were allowed to keep certain grazing rights, but even those were strictly controlled. Many of the laws peculiar to the New Forest and administered by the Verderers' Court have their origin in those set out by the Norman kings.

William the Conqueror died in 1087, to be succeeded by his third son, William Rufus. As the Norman dynasty eventually gave way to the Angevin, the buildings and landscape of England moved increasingly further from the older Saxon kingdoms. The legacy of the latter was concealed in foundations and land boundaries, common language and rural traditions, so that England never became an essentially Norman country. The loss of Normandy in 1204 severed the ties of its new aristocracy with old estates in France and encouraged them to adapt to an emerging English consciousness, in which both strains were intertwined.

enrie reformator ordinis ecce cenobuli et [...]
ter officinarum edificator. et amic special bufactor ecc[...]
albi munifie. regnauit ann. xxxu. dim. Huf fili e nu

te xii ai impotet bellior regnacoe fera fca magine prec[...]
Achon et rope potent fbegit. eccam de fco thoma mie ibide est ru[...]
Redict i alemania capt. pro e redepcoe calices anglie dabantur.

tande spiclo ba
liste apd chaluz
tiem ir anis er
dim regnauit
inceptus apud
fonte ebraudi
sepult qctur.

Rjcardus Rex
sertus ann
annann

Henricus III
Rex octau
annann

ine
cep
us

Iste Johannes fundauit abbatiam eiê ordis
et bellus locus apllatur. cuit quoqz tempe pa[...]
fa est anglia ruindin uldgia detinê ta mifa

Iste huricuf. iii. mlto tempe regnauit in pace anglia gu
uit. eccam fci petri westmon magnifice restaurauit.
amator fci adwardi special. feretru cr auro puriffim[...]

DYNASTIC STRONGHOLDS

FOLLOWING THE NORMAN CONQUEST, CASTLES BECAME THE RECOGNIZED POWER BASES OF BARONIAL FAMILIES FOR CENTURIES. THE FLUCTUATING FORTUNES OF THESE DYNASTIES ARE REFLECTED IN THE FABRIC OF THE BUILDINGS, AS IS THE IMPACT OF A VOLATILE POLITICAL CLIMATE. MANOR HOUSES WERE FORTIFIED AND CASTLES CHANGED TO COUNTRY HOUSES, REVEALING A COMPLEMENT OF ARCHITECTURAL STYLES AS INHABITANTS ADAPTED TO INSTABILITY OR PEACE. FOR DEFENSIVE REASONS, CASTLES ARE ALWAYS INDIVIDUAL STRUCTURES, UNIQUELY TAILORED TO THEIR OWN PARTICULAR SITE, YET THEY POSSESSED THE FLEXIBILITY TO EVOLVE IN RESPONSE TO CHANGING SOCIAL NEEDS.

THE CENTURIES after the battle of Hastings were dominated by instability in England. Between 1066 and the Black Death in 1348, only one period of domestic peace lasted for more than 30 years. The need for well-fortified castles was high, particularly during the anarchic government of Stephen (1135–54), when many castles were constructed without the requisite royal warrant. Henry II, reconstructing order and government in England, enforced the 'licence to crenellate' policy, whereby permission from the king was required before any fortifications were put in place. He destroyed many of the illicit, 'adulterine' castles and

was reluctant to grant new licences, encouraging the transition to sturdy manor houses, protected by a courtyard, stone gateway and moat. Manor houses became popular in southern and midland counties in the Plantagenet years, but tall stone structures remained on the border regions, where territory was under greater threat.

Both Alnwick and Warkworth are impressive Northumbrian border strongholds, and examples of Norman motte and bailey castles that were extended and elaborated over centuries. The former evolved into a palatial ducal residence which visiting Victorians referred to as the 'Windsor of the North', while the latter has become

1

1 Warkworth Castle was one
of two Northumberland
strongholds owned by the
powerful Percy family. The
cutaway illustration shows
the complex arrangement
of rooms and services
needed to maintain such a
self-contained unit. The
great hall forms the focal
point of castle life.

2 Alnwick has been the
principal seat of the Percy
family, earls and dukes of
Northumberland, since
1309. The keep of the
Norman castle later formed
the core of a classical palace.
The distinctive straight
tailed lion that is the family
crest features prominently
throughout the town and
estate.

an elegant, well-preserved ruin. Both became associated with the Percy family in an era when Northumberland was a virtual 'no man's land' between England and Scotland – a remote and alien region to many at the English court.

Alnwick, the earliest parts of which date from the end of the 11th century, became the seat of the Percy family when Henry Percy bought the barony from Anthony Bec, the bishop of Durham, in 1309. Warkworth was granted by the crown to the second Henry Percy in 1332 and the castles were linked with the family, albeit with intervals of confiscation, until 1670. This was an unusually long dynastic association: many landowning Norman families in the Domesday Book, for example, had disappeared completely by the end of the 12th century, a pattern repeated in subsequent generations. Those who survived did so in part through strategic marriages to consolidate the power of their estates – those not transmitted by hereditary means were forfeit to the crown under the rule of escheat.

Warkworth is a dramatically sited fortress, set on high ground overlooking a strategic loop in the River Coquet, and within sight of the sea. The river effectively creates a horseshoe peninsula, providing a natural moat to protect both castle and village. The castle's most striking feature is its massive keep, built around 1380 on the raised mound that formed the original heart of the castle. It soars above the narrow village street linking church and castle, underscoring the power wielded by great medieval dynasties over their territories. At a time when the feudal system in England was starting to collapse, and villeins conscious of the labour shortage were demanding mobility and wages, the dominance of Warkworth over its estate seemed absolute.

Castle keeps were intended to provide a strong defensive capability and to be self-sufficient in times of siege, but by the 14th and 15th centuries their owners were also seeking residential comfort. The majority of Warkworth keep's ground floor was given over to storage of food and wine cellars. Water, or rather lack of it, often determined how long a besieged stronghold could

endure, and the builders of Warkworth sought to combine additional light with a device for collecting rainwater. The lightwell is a rectangular open space extending up through the keep's full height and pierced with windows at regular intervals. Rainwater was funnelled down from the steeply pitched roof and collected in a tank at the lightwell's base. Normally used for flushing out the discharge shafts of the garderobes, or latrines, the supply could have been used for drinking in times of emergency. Hygiene, always a problem in an enclosed keep, was particularly important in siege conditions, when the atmosphere could quickly become unhealthy. Paradoxically, clothes were often stored in the vicinity of latrines as moths were deterred by the odour.

Alnwick's magnificent development in the 14th and

1 A reconstruction of Lady
   Anne Clifford arriving at
   Brougham castle in 1670.
   The size of her own travelling retinue highlights the
   problems faced by castle
   owners when dignitaries or
   royalty sought hospitality.
   Simply finding enough food
   or suitable accommodation
   could impoverish a region
   for months afterwards.

2 The portrait by Nicholas
   Hilliard of George Clifford
   3rd earl of Cumberland,
   depicts him in his role as
   elegant courtier. For a time
   he was Elizabeth I's jousting
   champion.

3 Although set amidst
   tranquil surroundings,
   Brougham nevertheless
   occupied a strategic position
   close to Penrith and the
   route to Scotland.

1

15th centuries, including a fine gatehouse and barbican
of 1440, is evidence of the more domestic architecture
that was turning fortresses into palaces in the more
secure south. The reconstruction at Alnwick coincided
with the Percys' most prominent period in medieval
politics, centring around their support for Henry
Bolinbroke, who overthrew Richard II in 1399. Having
successfully helped Bolinbroke to the throne, the family rapidly became disenchanted with his reign as Henry
IV. Less than three years later Henry Percy (who had
been created 1st earl of Northumberland at Richard's
coronation in 1377) and his son Hotspur, named for
his daring impetuosity on and off the battlefield,
plotted an unsuccessful rebellion to overthrow
their protégé. The plot was hatched within the
walls of Warkworth, a location prominent in
Shakespeare's *Henry IV Part II* and referred
to unflatteringly as 'this worm-eaten hold
of ragged stone'.

Hotspur was killed in battle at Shrewsbury in 1403. His father also died on the field, at
Bramham Moor in 1408, after joining an unsuccessful
alliance against the king with Owen Glendower and
Edmund de Mortimer. The Percy castles and estates

were forfeited by the king, but a Percy was reinstated by
Henry IV's successor and the line continued until 1670.
Elizabeth Percy, the heiress, married into the family
of the dukes of Somerset, and both Warkworth and
Alnwick fell into disrepair. Alnwick's fortunes were
revived in the 18th century by Hugh Smithson earl and
1st duke of Northumberland. In response to the period's
more domestic requirements, Robert Adam created
a new interior and 'Capability' Brown landscaped the
grounds.

Another great northern dynasty, the Cliffords,
inherited the strategically important castles of Brough
and Brougham through marriage in 1268. Both fortresses were built adjacent to earlier Roman garrisons
established to guard the trans-Pennine route now occupied by the main A66 trunk road. Brough is the more
isolated, set on a prominent ridge surrounded on three
sides by inhospitable fells.

The first medieval castle was erected there by
William II in about 1100 on the northern part of Verteris,
a Roman fort. It was largely destroyed in 1174 during
one of the frequent Scottish incursions into England's
northern counties. Brough was substantially rebuilt
towards the end of the 12th century by one
Theobold de Valoines, and altered again during
the latter part of the 13th century by Lord
Robert Clifford, who acquired the castle and
added the distinctive round tower. Warden
of the Marches and governor of Carlisle,
Clifford campaigned extensively in
Scotland, forming a close relationship with the English monarch
Edward II. He was killed at the
battle of Bannockburn in 1314.
Further improvements and
additions followed until the
castle was virtually gutted by
fire after Christmas celebrations in
1521. It was restored by the vigorous
Lady Anne Clifford, the last member of the
family to own the castle, in 1676.

2

Brougham enjoys a more tranquil rural setting than its near namesake but encompasses an even busier intersection. The Roman fort of Brocavum, on the same site, commanded four key routes: the River Eamont crossing on the outskirts of Penrith; the western route to and from Scotland; the Pennine route which linked up to Brough; and a Roman road which climbed over the Lakeland Fells via High Street. The castle itself, on the banks of the River Eamont, has a 13th-century keep. It also was restored by Lady Anne, who instigated repairs and rebuilding on all six family castles in 1643, as well as setting up trusts to provide foundations for the poor.

During the later medieval period nobles frequently possessed estates and castles in different parts of the country. Bolinbroke, for example, owned land at both Hereford and Lancaster, while the 'kingmaker' earl of Warwick held estates in Wiltshire and Yorkshire as well as Warwick. Such acquisitions were usually either through considered dynastic marriage, or gifts from a grateful sovereign for services rendered. In the latter instance, monarchs deliberately sought to break up territories to prevent too great a power base being established in any single area. Many titled landowners consequently spent the year moving from one residence to the next in a succession of regional progresses. Such flux may have contributed to the instability in which much of the barony remained, as well as to the claims of the villeins that their masters drained, rather than protected, manorial resources.

Middleham Castle was in the ownership of the Neville family from 1270. During the two decades from 1461, it became one of England's most important power bases. Following the execution of Richard Neville earl of Salisbury, captured at the battle of Wakefield, the castle passed to his elder son Richard earl of Warwick through his wife. He assumed the sobriquet 'kingmaker' as a result of vigorous support for Edward duke of York, during the Wars of the Roses. When Edward was crowned king following the battle of Towton in 1461, Warwick became the power and wealth behind the throne. He ruled in all but name during the first three years of Edward's reign.

The king's younger brother, Richard duke of Gloucester (later crowned as Richard III), spent several years around 1465 with Warwick at Middleham, learning military skills and court etiquette. In less than five years, Richard had married Warwick's younger daughter, Ann Neville, and received the lordship of Middleham from Edward, following Warwick's death at the battle of Barnet in 1471. Combining the wealth of his estates and the royal favour of his brother, the duke of Gloucester was the north's dominant figure in subsequent years. He managed the region for the crown and secured a large personal following both in Middleham and in the surrounding areas.

The exceptionally complete ruins of Middleham convey a strong impression of its importance during the 15th century. It was, in essence, a miniature court, providing a focus for patronage and influence, military authority and aristocratic social life. At the heart of the castle is the great 12th-century keep, built of harsh grey

1,2 The impressive medieval
fortress of Middleham
Castle was inhabited by the
young Richard duke of
Gloucester, firstly while in
the care of Richard Neville
earl of Warwick, and later
after the earl's death. The
castle was gradually
extended outwards from its
somewhat spartan 12th-
century keep to provide
more comfortable
accommodation.

stone. One of the country's largest castles in terms of
ground area, Middleham measures some 32 x 24 m² (344
x 260 sq ft). Rooms and facilities in the keep combined
security with grand living quarters. The hall, adjacent to
the main chamber on the first floor, was the site of lavish
entertaining, as well as the administrative centre for
local disputes or petitions, and the manorial court.

Other parts of the castle were improved and expanded
during Middleham's years of elevated status. Lavish
suites for important guests were created by additional
walls within the existing curtain. The west and south
ranges were connected to the keep by footbridges.

After Richard III's defeat at Bosworth, his estates and
castle were seized by Henry VII and remained in royal
ownership until the early 17th century.

FIELDS OF BLOOD

ENGLAND'S HISTORY FOR CENTURIES WAS DOMINATED BY BATTLES, BOTH INTERNAL AFFAIRS AGAINST ITS OWN PEOPLE AND OTHERS CONFRONTING A NATIONAL THREAT. THE WARS OF THE ROSES PROVIDED A SEEMINGLY INTERMINABLE SEQUENCE OF BRUTAL SKIRMISHES, TO WHICH MOST OF THE POPULATION REMAINED INDIFFERENT; THE CRISIS OF INVASION OR CIVIL WAR, HOWEVER, IMPACTED MORE STRONGLY UPON THE COUNTRY AT LARGE. AS WEAPONS BECAME MORE SOPHISTICATED, TECHNIQUES OF WARFARE CHANGED IN RESPONSE, WITH EFFECTIVE USE OF TERRAIN BEING AN INCREASINGLY IMPORTANT MILITARY SKILL.

THE BATTLE OF TOWTON was probably the bloodiest conflict ever fought on English soil. It took place on 29 March 1461, when weather conditions were terrible, with driving snow and strong winds impeding visibility and misdirecting arrows. Towton itself is close to Tadcaster and York, a significant site for a battle between the rival Houses of York and Lancaster. The terrain is relatively level, with a steep escarpment sloping away to Cock Beck, a tributary of the River Aire. Today the battlefield is agricultural land, and a simple memorial marks the site.

Although decisive in securing the English crown for Edward IV, Towton was just one of several battles fought over a 30-year period in the bitter factional feud known as the Wars of the Roses. The dynasties of York and Lancaster each claimed rights to the throne through complex lines of descent from Edward III's 12 children. In many ways a localized conflict, it was not a civil war of principle: most of the population sought merely to avoid the fighting, and changing of sides among the participants was not uncommon. The nobles and the knights supporting them suffered severely: those who survived the battles were often executed if those in the opposition were ascendant, and great estates were confiscated to enrich the crown further. Fighting was savage, unlike at Crécy or Agincourt: high standards of archery were maintained on either side, so both armies moved swiftly to close combat with swords and bills.

The forces of Henry VI and his queen, Margaret of Anjou, had defeated a Yorkist army at the second battle of St Albans in 1455, but subsequently retreated to their power base in the north. Edward duke of York had entered London in Henry's absence to be proclaimed king, and now sought a decisive military victory to consolidate his position. He therefore set off in pursuit of the Lancastrians, mustering forces as he headed north.

The weather was bitterly cold and the Yorkist army must have spent a miserable night in the open near the village of Saxton, exhausted from a long march and poorly fed. The Lancastrian forces were close by between Towton and Saxton, under the command of the duke of Somerset. The harsh, grey light of dawn revealed the close proximity of the two sides to each other, and although Edward was reluctant to engage until the delayed duke of Norfolk's force arrived, there was little choice under the circumstances.

Both armies drew up, in long battle lines because of the level ground. A strong wind drove snow straight into the faces of the Lancastrian forces. Realizing that the elements were in his favour, the Yorkist commander Lord Fauconberg ordered the massed ranks of archers to advance, fire one salvo and retreat. Accelerated by the wind, the arrows found their target with startling accuracy, and when the Lancastrians attempted to return fire, their own missiles were impeded by the gale and fell well short. Their opponents advanced once more, picking up the spent arrows and firing them.

Unable to withstand further barrages, the Lancastrian army moved forward to engage the Yorkists in savage hand-to-hand combat with swords, mallets, maces and daggers. Many of the archers were killed and both sets withdrew exhausted, to be replaced by infantry. The battle raged until well into the afternoon, 'with so great slaughter that the very deade carkcasses hindered them that fought'. As the day progressed, the Lancastrians appeared to be in the ascendancy but, just when Edward feared the battle was lost, the duke of Norfolk's army finally appeared with reinforcements who began to swing the tide back in the Yorkists' favour. Their demoralized opponents began to retreat, many ending in the swollen torrent of Cock Beck, weighed down by heavy armour. Those who did not drown in the icy waters

1 The great seal of Edward IV, who assumed the Yorkist claim to the throne following the death of his father in 1460.

2 A simple roadside cross between the villages of Towton and Saxton near Tadcaster is the only memorial to the thousands who were cut down during a battle fought in atrocious wintry conditions.

3 The site of the battle of Towton, which took place on 29 March 1461. The level terrain ensured neither side could gain strategic territorial advantage, so much of the battle consisted of savage, hand-to-hand combat.

2

1   The battle of Bosworth was
    fought on Redmoor plain
    near Market Bosworth in
    Leicestershire. Henry Tudor
    was victorious, thanks
    largely to the timely
    intervention of Sir William
    Stanley's force on the
    Lancastrian side.
2   The parish church of St
    James, Sutton Cheney, in
    Leicestershire, where
    Richard III took his last
    communion.

3   A boulder allegedly marks
    the spot where Richard was
    killed 'fighting manfully
    in the thickest part of his
    enemies' and the
    Plantagenet dynasty was
    extinguished.

were slaughtered on the banks by pursuing Yorkists, turning the waters red with blood. The estimates of casualties vary, depending on which side's herald compiled them, but several thousand men were killed that day. The toll included large numbers of the Lancastrian nobility, easily identified by heraldic devices.

In 1996, the accidental discovery of a mass burial pit on the edge of Towton village revealed to modern excavators the savagery of medieval warfare. Archaeologists from the University of Bradford confirmed that at least 38 corpses had been stripped and placed in the pit. Many of the skeletons exhibited signs of horrendous injuries from an assortment of weaponry. The scientists were

able to identify a total of 113 wounds on 27 skulls examined, the most severe damage having been inflicted by blunt weapons such as the mace.

Following Towton, Henry VI fled to exile in Scotland and Edward secured the throne. The new king ruled until his death in 1483, apart from a year-long interlude in 1470 when Henry was briefly restored to the throne. After Edward's death in 1483, the crown passed to his 12-year-old son, Prince Edward. Richard duke of Gloucester, the boy's uncle, was appointed Protector.

The throne did not remain indefinitely in Yorkist hands, however. Edward V and his younger brother both died in mysterious circumstances, having been

2

3

taken into the Tower of London on Richard's authority, ostensibly for their own protection. Many blamed Richard for their disappearance and death, and his subsequent acquisition of the crown was controversial amongst many of his followers. Having swept away all opposition, Richard was declared king on 8 July 1483, but he remained unpopular. New alliances failed to come to fruition, and his increasing isolation gave hope to Lancastrian supporters exiled in France. Their challenge materialized in Henry Tudor earl of Richmond, who landed at Milford Haven in Wales with 2,000 French mercenaries in early August 1485.

Bosworth, at which King Richard confronted Henry Tudor, was to prove the last conflict of the Wars of the Roses – although to contemporaries it may have seemed merely the next Lancastrian triumph in an apparently endless struggle. It occurred on 22 August 1485, over a relatively bare area of Leicestershire upland, south of Market Bosworth and close to the village of South Cheyney. Ambion Hill offered some strategic height, but the ground was boggy and awkward terrain for fighting. Today, a stone boulder set in sodden turf marks the site of Richard III's death; white roses are often left at its base.

The Tudor forces ultimately to defeat the king had moved into Leicestershire via Lichfield, gathering support as they went. A large Welsh contingent combined with the sheriff of Shrewsbury and 2,000 levies (the local militia). The earl of Oxford, later to lead the rebels at Bosworth, produced a force of about 8,000 men. A significant number of Henry Tudor's troops came from families hitherto loyal to the Yorkist cause. Others, including the powerful Stanleys of Lancashire, former allies of the king, declined to commit themselves, despite Stanley's son being held hostage by the king to secure his father's participation. Stanley held a secret meeting with Henry at Atherstone on 20 August, and it was his forces who would turn the tide of battle in the Lancastrian's favour.

Having gathered together an army of some 9,500 men, Richard elected to fight Henry before the Tudor army grew any larger or slipped past the king to head directly to London. The king's army consisted of archers, handgunners and artillerymen, pikemen armed with long spears, and cavalry. The vanguard, with 1,200 archers and 200 knights, was under the command of John Howard duke of Norfolk; the king controlled the main body himself and Henry Percy earl of Northumberland was in charge of the rearguard. The forces drew up on the heights of Ambion Hill, while the rebel force, similarly equipped and led by the earl of Oxford, manoeuvred across marshy ground at its foot. In so doing, they were in some disarray and a charge by Richard's vanguard might have sealed victory, but its commander, John Howard duke of Norfolk, maintained formation and waited for his opponents to scale the hill.

The battle began with rebel cannon fire, largely ineffective but demoralizing through its noise and smoke. Repeated salvoes from the archers of both sides were followed by the infantry engaging in close combat. In the ensuing bitter fighting, Norfolk was killed and his son, the earl of Surrey, captured – losses which seriously demoralized the king's men. The news was reported to Stanley, observing the battle's ebb and flow from a distance to see who gained the upper hand. He launched an attack on the king's right flank.

In the royal rearguard, the earl of Northumberland, Henry Percy, declined to send his troops to reinforce the king's ranks. Richard's cause appeared increasingly hopeless, mired in apathy and treachery. Surrounded by his personal bodyguard of some 80 mounted knights, Richard resolved to take matters into his own hands and eliminate Henry Tudor. He led a charge straight for his opponent, hacking his way through Welsh foot soldiers and killing at least two of Henry's knights before his own horse was cut from under him.

1 A memorial cross overlooking the rolling border farmland to the southeast of
Coldstream commemorates
the battle of Flodden,
fought on 9 September 1513.
James IV and many of the
Scottish nobility were
among the thousands slain
by an English army under
the command of Thomas
Howard earl of Surrey.

2 Arundel Castle is the seat of
the dukes of Norfolk, a title
restored to Surrey by Henry
VIII after his victory at
Flodden. The earl had
fought for Richard III against
the king's father, the future
Henry VII, at Bosworth, but
his prowess at Flodden had
established his loyalty to
Henry VIII.

More of Stanley's soldiers rushed in to aid the Lancastrians and King Richard III died under a savage rain of
blows from swords and battle axes. His crown, allegedly
recovered from a nearby thornbush, was presented to
England's new monarch, Henry VII. Elsewhere on the
battlefield, fighting gradually ceased as men from both
sides realized the issue had been, at least temporarily,
resolved. Partly because of this, and also because of the
reluctance of key participants to engage, casualties were
relatively light. The king's army lost about 1,000 men in
total, and the Lancastrian forces about one-quarter of
that. As Henry VII, the new king succeeded in keeping
the country at peace for much of his reign, but his ener-
getic son saw military conquest as an important element in his royal prestige.

An imposing stone memorial cross overlooking the
Northumbrian village of Branxton is the only visible
evidence of the savage battle fought at Flodden Field
between English and Scottish armies on 9 September 1513.
Although the Cheviot Hills form much of the border,
the countryside around Branxton consists of more gently rolling hills, while the battlefield itself is now agricultural land. The corpses from both sides were slung
into two large burial pits, one to the southwest of the
site and the other by the diminutive parish church, but
neither is marked and so the cross serves as their communal epitaph.

Earlier that summer, England's monarch, Henry
VIII, had led an invasion force to France. He feared such
action might cause a renewal of the 'Auld Alliance',
forged between Scotland and France in 1292, and cau-
tioned Surrey, his Lord Lieutenant of the North, 'to forget not the old prankes of the Scottes, which is ever to
invade England when the King is out'. Henry's intuition
proved well founded, and the army that Surrey faced
under the Scottish king James IV was the largest ever
assembled in Scotland, estimated at more than 25,000
men. Before Flodden, it had already captured the formidable English border castles of Wark, Norham and Etal.
Each castle was besieged and overwhelmed, partly due
to the Scots' heavy artillery. Surrey's hastily gathered
English force numbered at least 5,000 fewer than their
opponents as the weary English advanced to Wooler.

An attempt to lure James away from his impregnable
hilltop by offering battle on 9 September on nearby
Millfield Plain was unsuccessful: James accepted the
challenge, but rejected its logist-
ical terms. The suicidal consequences of a full frontal assault on
Flodden Hill are apparent today.
Surrey ordered his forces to
march away northwards, but the
Scottish army merely tracked
their opponents, relocating about
0.6 km (1/3 mile) further west on
the heights of Branxton Hill.

As battle could no longer
be delayed, the English army
wheeled round and headed south
to face the Scots. Each army split
into five groups, four of which
faced each other, with one unit
each held in reserve towards the
rear. This effectively turned the

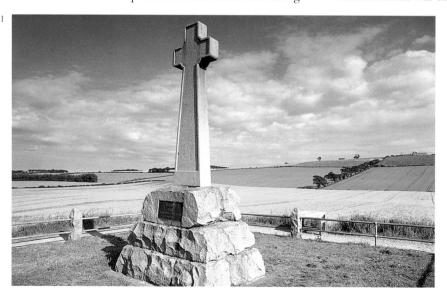

1

conflict into separate battles to be fought by the opposing phalanxes of about 5,000 men each.

Both sides opened fire with their respective artillery pieces, the Scots appearing to have an advantage in their heavier weapons. However, most of the Scottish fire overshot its mark, while lighter English guns proved far more accurate. Together with salvoes of arrows, they began to carve holes in the stationary Scottish ranks.

Despite the numbers involved, the actual fighting was over in a few hours. First to attack were Earl Home's borderers, careering headlong into Edmund Howard's men and causing mayhem, unhorsing the earl's son twice. Spurred on by Home's attack, the Scottish king and Earl Crawford led their respective forces into a brief but bloody mêlée. The Scots were seriously disadvantaged by their unfamiliar weapons – 5-m (16-ft) long, cumbersome pikes imported from France. By contrast, the English were armed with the shorter halberd, or bill, possessing a lethal combination of spike, hook and blade. When the battle developed into close combat, the long Scottish pike shafts were chopped to pieces by the English bills. Shorter Scottish swords proved equally ineffective in the confusion.

In the carnage of defeat, it took hours of searching to locate James IV's badly mutilated body. His bloody surcoat was torn from the body and despatched to Henry in France as proof of victory. It is estimated that over 10,000 Scots were slain that day alone – an astonishing number in the days of non-mechanized warfare. Almost an entire generation of the Scottish nobility was destroyed: the haunting tune 'The Flowers of the Forest', most frequently heard on occasions of remembrance, was originally composed to mourn the nation's grievous loss at Flodden.

When the Scottish king James VI became James I of England and Scotland, the two countries were united for the first time. However, the Stuart dynasty generated its own conflicts, most significantly the Civil War between Charles I and Parliament. After three years of conflict, the Civil War effectively ended at the battle of Naseby (14 June 1645). It took place to the northwest of Naseby in Northamptonshire, on an area of flat, open

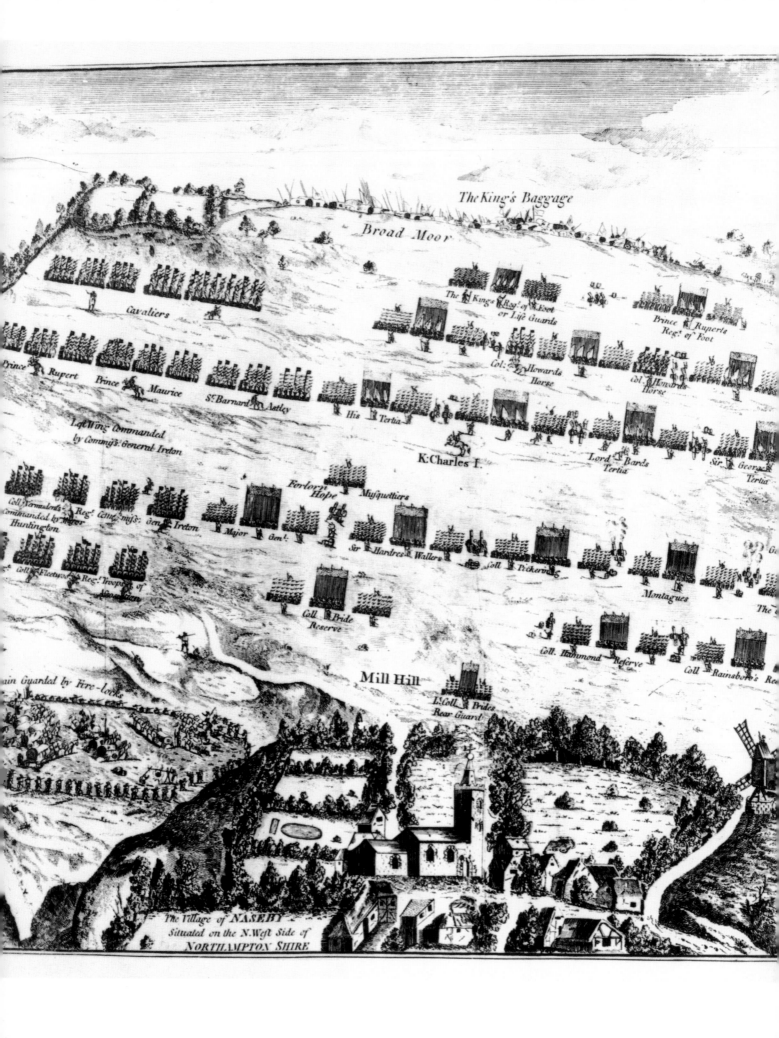

The King's Baggage

Broad Moor

Cavaliers

The King's Regt of Foot or Life Guards

Prince Ruperts Regt of Foot

Prince Rupert Prince Maurice

St Barnard Astley

Coll Howards Horse

Coll Howards Horse

His Tertia

Left Wing Commanded by Commiss: General Irton

K: Charles I.

Lord Bards Tertia

Sir George Tertia

Forlorn Hope

Coll Vermuden's Regt Commanded by Major Huntington

Commiss: Genl Ireton

Major Genl

Musquettiers

Coll Fleetwood Regt Troops of Association

Sir Hardres Wallers

Coll Pickering

Montagues

Coll Pride Reserve

Coll Hammond Reserve

Coll Rainsboro's Reg

Mill Hill

Lt Coll Prides Rear Guard

main Guarded by Fire-locks

The Village of NASEBY
Situated on the N. West Side of
NORTHAMPTON SHIRE

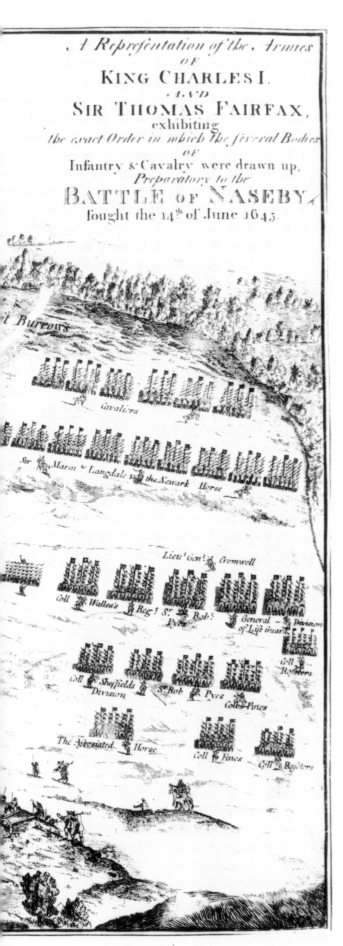

A contemporary engaving of the battle of Naseby, which took place on 14 June 1645. Royalist forces led by Charles I and Prince Rupert were engaged by the Parliamentarian 'New Model Army' under Sir Thomas Fairfax and Oliver Cromwell. The panoramic view shows the village of Naseby in the foreground with the Parliamentary forces ranged immediately above. The Royalists were significantly outnumbered.

ground with higher slopes on each side. The terrain favoured cavalry divisions and the excellence of the Parliamentary cavalry was decisive in Naseby's outcome.

The Civil War in the 17th century had a much greater effect on the country than the feuds of York and Lancaster. It was a conflict of constitutional principle, sustained on the Parliamentary side by taxation, excise duty and commercial loans. Naseby marked the debut of the Parliamentarian 'New Model Army', commanded by Sir Thomas Fairfax with Oliver Cromwell as second-in-command. It was the first time that anything resembling a standing national army had been assembled, characterized by organization, discipline, better trained officers and uniformed, properly remunerated men. Royalist troops had spoken of the new army in derogatory terms, but their contempt was ill-founded.

Both armies took up positions on the higher ground in the early morning, and battle commenced at about 10 am. Charles commanded the Royalist army, about 10,000 strong, with Prince Rupert as Lord General dictating manoeuvres from Charles's side. Parliamentary forces consisted of approximately 13,500 men.

The first engagement between the cavalry resulted in a victory for the Royalists, but Rupert's impetuous charge drew him away from his advisory role. An attack by the New Model Army cavalry, led by Cromwell, then overwhelmed the Royalist soldiers, both mounted and on foot. The king's hesitation to send in reserve forces confirmed the Royalist defeat, and both he and Prince Rupert fled to Leicester. The Parliamentarians captured over 4,500 Royalist prisoners, plus Charles's papers, which revealed secret dealings with the Irish and French. Royalist morale sank further as New Model Army artillery demolished their garrisons across the country – ending the era of castles as viable fortifications.

Both sides knew that a definitive battle such as Naseby had to happen eventually. Charles capitulated at Oxford a year after the battle, and was subsequently tried – by a court he steadfastly refused to acknowledge – on charges of waging war against his kingdom and Parliament. He was executed on 30 January 1649.

'THEY SHALL NOT PASS'

The need to protect England against invasion from the sea has dominated coastal areas for centuries. Early hillforts on strategic clifftop sites were replaced by castles, frequently adapted in turn as military technology and political circumstances changed. The fabric of these structures bears a complex historical legacy, revealing not least the financial impact of maintaining powerful fortifications. England's internal borders were also volatile regions, subject to local raids and larger incursions. Numerous castles were built to secure these defences, forming important focal points of baronial prestige.

1

DOVER'S TOWERING white chalk cliffs, a natural obstacle for potential invaders, have supported man-made fortifications since Iron Age times. The shape of Dover Castle follows the ramparts of an Iron Age fort around the natural contours of the hill; its defensive position overlooking the Straits of Dover has been exploited by English rulers up to recent times. Believed to have contained a Saxon *burh*, or fortified town, the potential of the site was perceived by the advancing Roman army in ad 78. They established the walled town of Dubris around the natural harbour and constructed the twin pharos, or lighthouses, to improve continental supply lines. One of the pair still stands within the present castle, its top rebuilt in the 15th century as a bell tower for the nearby church.

William of Normandy erected an earthwork fortress shortly after defeating Harold at the battle of Hastings. A motte and bailey structure characteristic of Norman castles was replaced in the late 12th century by Henry II's massive stone keep. This vast building was 25 m (83 ft) high and almost 30 m (98 ft) square, with walls up to 6 m (20 ft) thick. It needed major expenditure, even for Henry II, a prolific castle builder: more than £6,000 was spent on the keep between 1179 and 1188, far more than any other site. The keep still dominates the town today.

Before the Norman invasion, the Anglo-Saxon ports of Sandwich, Dover, Hythe, Romsey and Hastings had formed a mutually protect-

ive alliance to secure the Channel crossing. Known as the Cinque Ports, this federation was adapted by the Normans, who added the towns of Winchelsea and Rye. Special privileges, such as exemption from certain taxes and the right to hold their own courts, were extended to these towns, which in return were required to provide ships and men to defend the coast in times of need. Before the existence of a formalized navy, medieval monarchs were heavily dependent upon the Cinque Ports. Raids on Rye and Winchelsea in 1377 and 1380 resulted in the construction of Bodiam Castle in East Sussex. Drum towers were set at each corner of the moated fortress to enhance its defensive capability, but although the River Rother was navigable up to Bodiam, the castle was never subjected to attack.

The dual function of Bodiam, both private residence and military stronghold, had been anticipated in the earlier structure at Dover. Within the keep's solid walls were apartments designed to accommodate foreign royalty or dignitaries. Its main rooms were paradoxically relatively bare shells, as medieval monarchs and nobles tended to travel everywhere with their own possessions for comfort and security. A more convenient hall and chamber for the monarch were built along the eastern side of the inner bailey in 1240, but resulted in some deterioration in the keep. Significant modernization of the great hall and chamber also occurred, most notably in 1539 prior to a

1

visit by Henry VIII and Anne of Cleves, and further improvements took place before the arrival of Charles I's French bride, Henrietta Maria, in 1625. The keep's chapel, dedicated to Thomas Becket, is remarkable in its Romanesque decoration. Chapel, nave and chancel all feature deeply incised chevrons, dog-tooth carved vault ribs and pillars adorned with foliated capitals, but whether Henry II made the dedication to his martyred archbishop personally is not known.

Nevertheless, Dover's primary function was a military one. 'Who commands Dover, commands England' simplifies an often-quoted medieval phrase, but it had validity, confirmed by the castle's resistance to Prince Louis of France's prolonged and determined siege in 1216. The Crusades also exerted significant influence upon military structures and practices in England. This was reflected at Dover Castle, where concentric defensive walls with regularly spaced towers, the first example of their kind in western Europe, proved one of its great strategic strengths. The design technique originated in the Holy Land, where similarly constructed Moslem castles had persistently thwarted the Crusaders' attempts to storm them.

The labyrinth of tunnels beneath Dover Castle is an important example of a defensive feature modified through the centuries. They were developed under the direction of Hubert de Burgh, the chief justiciar of England to Henry III, as a direct result of the siege in 1216. The landward northern tip of the castle had proved the most vulnerable point when parts of the walls and barbican were undermined by French engineers. They succeeded in toppling one of the gate towers, allowing French troops to penetrate the castle before hand-to-hand combat drove them back.

The medieval tunnels were designed to provide a protected line of communication for defenders on the northern outer perimeter and to allow a besieged garrison to muster unseen before launching surprise counter-attacks. The northern entrance was abandoned in favour of a more strongly fortified western gate known as Constable's Gateway, whose six towers exuded an impression of impregnability.

A further system of tunnels was introduced during the Napoleonic Wars, when invasion became a very real threat. Flat-bottomed barges were ready to transport 150,000 French troops across the Channel, and only the

2

PRECEDING PAGES
1 An aerial plan of Dover
   Castle shows how its
   defences have followed the
   contours established by an
   Iron Age hillfort.
2 Dover Castle was the first
   fortification in western
   Europe to arrange its walls
   in concentric circles. This
   innovative defensive
   technique was imported
   from the Holy Land after
   the Crusades.

1 The chapel and sacristy are
   lavishly adorned with the
   carved dog-tooth ornamentation associated with
   Norman architecture.
2 Carronades, able to fire
   heavy shot over short distances, were ideal weapons
   for covering the moat.
3 An anti-aircraft operations
   room located within the
   secret World War II tunnels.

French defeat at Trafalgar, establishing English naval supremacy and removing viable naval protection for a French invasion, caused it to be aborted. Large numbers of reinforcements were drafted in to strengthen the garrison at Dover, in a castle already congested with soldiers, army stores, weapons and ammunition. A logistical solution was produced by Royal Engineers, who commissioned the excavation of seven parallel tunnels entering the castle from the cliff-face. The network, linked at its far end by a communication passage, was constructed approximately 15 m (50 ft) below the clifftop. These temporary barracks, able to hold up to 2,000 troops, were fitted out with fireplaces, sanitation and a well to supply fresh water, although they remained dark and unsuitable for lengthy habitation.

Dover's ability to modify its defences has extended into the more recent past. The Admiralty Look-out on the high cliff to the south of the castle site sheltered the Admiralty Port War Signal Station in World War I, monitoring all shipping entering and leaving the harbour. It was used again in World War II, in which Dover's underground tunnels were expanded and converted to bombproof control centres. A lower tier, known as 'Dumpy', was constructed to provide the naval headquarters for the Dover Command, the Coastal Artillery operations room and the Anti-Aircraft operations room, where the progress of enemy aircraft was charted on screens. In 1940 'Operation Dynamo', the evacuation by sea of over 250,000 British troops from Dunkirk, was masterminded from the tunnel centres by Vice-Admiral Bertram Ramsay and Winston Churchill. More recently still, the tunnels were adapted in 1962 to provide a Regional Seat of Government in the event of a nuclear attack.

In contrast to Dover's medieval tunnels, other Napoleonic War defences in the south are more contemporary in origin. The flat, almost treeless expanse of Romney March in Kent was fortified by the Royal Military Canal, a combination of trenches and channels from which British troops could mount a surprise attack. On the coast itself, the Martello Tower at Slaughden, near Aldeburgh in Suffolk, was based on a similar version at Mortella Point on the Mediterranean island of Corsica, attacked by British warships in 1794. The naval authorities were impressed by the tower's ability to withstand concerted attack from land and sea, and built a chain of 74 similar towers along the south coast between Folkestone in Kent and Seaford in Sussex. Others extended to the east, from Brightlingsea to Slaughden, all circular, built of brick and more than 9 m (30 ft) in height. Armed with a 24-pounder cannon and two equivalent weighted carronades, they were capable of directing an intense barrage of gunfire. Thick walls deaden external noise, but the Martello's domed ceilings produce high-quality acoustics.

3

1 Deal Castle was built by Henry VIII as an artillery fortress to counter the threat of invasion from Catholic nations following his break with Rome in the mid-16th century. Carrying 66 guns, its rounded bastions were designed to deflect incoming shot.

2 Portchester Castle near Portsmouth had an almost unbroken continuity of use, from one of the Roman Saxon Shore forts to prisoner of war camp and subsequently a hospital during the Revolutionary and Napoleonic Wars. Its Roman walls are the most complete in Europe.

Dover is not the only English fortress with a legacy of military modification. The Roman forts of the Saxon Shore formed England's first formally structured line of coastal defences, extending from the Wash in East Anglia to the Solent on the south coast. They varied in size, but 10 major forts, manned by a garrison of soldiers and a detachment of the Roman fleet, were established to guard the most important harbours.

Following the Roman withdrawal from Britain, several of the forts were maintained by Romano-British forces. Pevensey, one of the key fortifications of the period, was besieged by Aelle, the king of the South Saxons, who subsequently overran the fort and massacred its defenders. William the Conqueror made Pevensey his first secure base after landing nearby in 1066, and its strategic medieval importance led to a substantial stone construction, replacing earlier fortifications on the site.

The most westerly of the Saxon Shore forts was Portchester, a secure base for a fleet anchored in nearby Portsmouth harbour. The walls of Portchester, highly impressive in size and scale, are believed to be the most complete example of a Roman fortification wall in Europe. They are among England's greatest Roman ruins, once enclosing a total area of 3.4 ha (8.5 acres) and enhanced by 20 bastions and a double ditch. Unlike many Saxon Shore forts on the southern coast, the sea has not left Portchester marooned inland and contributes to the dramatic atmosphere of the site.

The fort's history of occupation during the Dark Ages is not known, but it almost certainly sheltered some form of civilian settlement after the Roman withdrawal and became a fortified *burh* during Wessex's 10th-century struggle against the Vikings. After the Norman Conquest Portchester was developed into a medieval royal castle. It proved a convenient and secure base from which to cross the Channel to Normandy, and was in regular use by both Henry I and Henry II. Portchester keep provided not only royal lodgings, but also a safe deposit for Treasury bullion.

In the early part of the 14th century, the beginning of the Hundred Years War aroused expectation of French attacks on the coast. Large sums were spent on increased security for the castle's three gates, and the buildings on the west of the inner bailey were improved to create a self-contained royal palace. Edward III stayed there while assembling his 15,000-strong army prior to departure for France and the victory at Crécy. Henry V also sailed from Portchester with his soldiers and legendary longbowmen to victory at Agincourt in 1415.

Developments in military technology are reflected in the design and use of strategic coastal forts. Until the 16th century, they had largely consisted of well-fortified garrisons with sufficient troops to repel raids or seaborne landings. The powerful artillery forts created by Henry VIII after his break with the Roman Catholic Church in 1531 revealed new techniques of attack and defence. Heavy guns could quickly reduce square keeps and rectilinear walls to rubble, and a basically circular, clover-

1

leafed design was developed instead. Projecting semi-circular bastions served to increase fields of fire and deflect incoming cannonballs.

Aware of possible attack from Catholic Europe, Henry built 20 powerful artillery forts along England's Channel coastline, stretching from Cornwall to Kent. The low-lying areas of ground around Deal and the flanks of Romney Marsh were considered particularly vulnerable and their defences were prioritized. Five castles – Sandown, Deal, Walmer, Sandgate near

Folkestone and Camber – were built to cover that region. Deal was the most powerful of the five and remains the best preserved.

Deal consists of a round, three-storey keep from which jut six two-storey bastions. These are in turn ringed by six single-storey bastions on which the castle's main armament of 66 cannon was mounted. The entire fortress is surrounded by a broad dry moat, carefully constructed to follow the exact contours of the walls. Embrasures are set into the walls at regular intervals,

2

1 The Martello tower near Aldeburgh was one of many similar coastal defences built to counter the threat of a Napoleonic invasion in the early 19th century. The brick towers were named after a similar structure that resisted a sustained English attack at Mortella Point on Corsica in 1794.

2, 3 Upnor was an Elizabethan artillery fortress built to guard a strategic point on the River Medway where it narrows before reaching the naval dockyards at Chatham. The fort failed in its designated role a century later in 1667 during the second Anglo-Dutch War when the Dutch fleet attacked Chatham, destroyed several ships and towed away the flagship *Royal Charles*.

which allowed small arms and musket fire to be directed at intruders in the moat. A near neighbour and almost identical fort, the structure at Walmer became the official residence of the Warden of the Cinque Ports in 1708. Successive Lords Warden have transformed the castle's martial appearance into a stately home of unusual dimensions. Past holders of the now largely ceremonial title include William Pitt the Younger and the duke of Wellington, who died at Walmer.

The Tudor artillery forts were considered particularly vital in restricting foreign warships' access to ports, harbours or river estuaries. A heavily armed vessel could inflict considerable damage on both vessels and port installations, and major royal dockyards had been established at Portsmouth, Chatham on the River Medway, and Deptford on the Thames (page 134). Important commercial ports such as Southampton were also vulnerable to attack, although the Isle of Wight offered limited protection with a natural blockade. Two of the most beautifully sited estuary forts are Pendennis and St Mawes in Cornwall, built to guard the narrow entrance to the vast natural harbour of Carrick Roads and Falmouth. They are offset to avoid damage from crossfire, as are the 15th-century castles on opposite sides of the Dart estuary. A heavy chain suspended between the two castles also sought to prevent enemy ships gaining entrance to the river mouth.

Hurst Castle, built on a projecting shingle spit to protect the western entrance to the Solent, is a Tudor artillery fort which underwent major reconstruction in later centuries. It was a relatively late Tudor fort, built between 1541 and 1544, of a complex and highly fortified design. The 12-sided tower at its core was surrounded by a curtain wall, including three substantial semi circular bastions and originally a moat, There was scope for 71 gun positions in six tiers from a combination of vaulted gun chambers and embrasures in the parapets and curtain wall. Extensive changes were made to Hurst Castle in the Napoleonic Wars, when the central tower was gutted and replaced with a solid brick vault to accommodate 24-pdr artillery guns on the roof and protect the

magazine. In the 1860s two vast wing structures were added to the east and west. They were designed to withstand explosive shells and accommodate up to 30 heavy guns, able to tackle the new, steam-driven warships.

At the same time a circle of fortresses was constructed around Portsmouth, facing inland to confront an enemy who had disembarked successfully elsewhere. One of the five forts, known as the Gosport Advanced Line, was Fort Brockhurst. It represented a new style of fort, polygonal in shape to allow a flexible response to the building's location and gun positioning requirements. As ordnance became increasingly powerful during the 19th century, forts such as Brockhurst could become more versatile in military terms, adopting an offensive as well as defensive role.

3

1

CHAPTER

4

England, as an island nation, has always been vulnerable
to seaborn invasion whether from Viking longships, the massed
fleet of the Spanish Armada or French barges assembled during the
Napoleonic Wars. The need for defence, and the need to trade, prompted
the growth, by the end of the 19th century, of the largest naval and
merchant fleet in the world. The infrastructure required to service this
vast enterprise encompassed harbours and dry docks, shipyards and
warehouses, rope walks, sail lofts and forts. Whole towns were largely
devoted to building, fitting-out and victualling ships and their crews,
and the growth and prosperity of cities like Bristol were very much
dependent on the wealth accrued from the many voyages of
exploration, or plunder, financed by the various
companies of merchant adventurers.

A MARITIME NATION

RULING THE WAVES

ENGLAND'S SECURITY AT HOME AND PROSPERITY OVERSEAS DEPENDED ON NAVAL SUPREMACY FOR CENTURIES. A ROMAN FLEET WAS CREATED TO COUNTER SAXON ATTACKS IN THE 3RD CENTURY AD, AND THE ENGLISH KING ALFRED ALSO INVESTED HEAVILY IN MARITIME DEFENCE. THE DEVELOPMENT OF A STANDING NAVY IN TUDOR TIMES ESTABLISHED CLOSE LINKS WITH COMMERCIAL INTERESTS, AS MARITIME POWER HELPED TO SECURE TRADE ROUTES AROUND THE WORLD. YET THE 'SENIOR SERVICE' ALSO MAINTAINED A DEFENSIVE ROLE ON ENGLAND'S SHORES, WITH LARGE DOCKYARDS AND SHIPBUILDING BASES DOMINATING AREAS OF THE COAST. DESPITE OFTEN DEPLORABLE CONDITIONS ON BOARD, THE NAVY'S SAILORS, SHIPS AND BATTLES BECAME THE FOCUS OF AN EVOLVING NATIONAL IDENTITY.

THE IMPORTANCE of a regular, sea-going force was recognized by the Romans during their tenure of Britain. Medieval monarchs, however, for whom most warfare consisted of major land battles, sustained coastal defences through the *ad hoc* resources of the Cinque Ports (page 122). Only with the literal and metaphoric expansion of horizons in the 15th and 16th centuries did England begin to invest in the commercial potential of maritime adventure. Henry VII gave financial support to John Cabot's voyage to the New World and strengthened the mercantile marine fleet. A permanent royal dockyard was constructed at Portsmouth of Portland Roach stone, and in 1496 it received a purpose-built dry dock, enabling warships to be drawn out of the water to have their hulls cleaned and repaired. Several new vessels were commissioned, including two four-masted carracks – ships significantly bigger than the normal merchant vessels of that period.

When Henry VIII inherited the throne in 1509, he acquired five new royal warships built at Portsmouth. The new king sought the construction of a permanent fighting fleet, well adapted to ocean sailing and manoeuvrable in combat, and to this end he increased the number of ships, dockyards and coastal defences. The *Mary Rose*, flagship of the Tudor fleet, was one of the new style of vessels built at Portsmouth between 1509 and 1511. She was designed to be an efficient and heavily armed fighting platform, as advances in shipbuilding technology allowed gun ports to be safely cut in the lower parts of the hull. This in turn permitted more guns to be carried without upsetting the ship's stability and enabled the famously devastating 'broadsides' to be fired.

The *Mary Rose* saw plenty of action during the French wars of 1512–13 and 1522–23. Her armaments included 15 cast bronze muzzle-loading guns, and 24 heavy and 30 lighter wrought-iron guns. The heaviest were located on a specially constructed and reinforced gun deck. Henry VIII encouraged a national gun-founding industry, and the bronze cannon were some of its first examples. Wrought-iron guns were among the most sought-after products of the Wealden iron industry, but basic construction limited their accuracy.

The *Mary Rose* sank close to Portsmouth in 1545, during combat with the French. Eyewitness accounts vary, but it appears that the lower gun ports were open and the ship simply keeled over too far, sinking in minutes with the loss of nearly all hands. The recovery of the wreck and its cargo from the seabed in 1982 provided invaluable information about life on a Tudor warship.

As conscripted merchant ships no longer provided adequate defences, the navy continued to grow. It was established as a standing force in the king's pay, maintained by the Navy Board with policy being made by the Board of Admiralty. Portsmouth expanded as a naval base and harbours such as Dover were fortified with gun emplacements. One problem attached to building ships on the Channel coast, however, was that a journey had to be made after launching to fit the ships out with ordnance from the national arsenal at the Tower.

In 1512, Henry elected to build a new royal dockyard on the River Thames at Woolwich, followed a year later by one at Deptford. Both were conveniently located near the royal palace at Greenwich. The first commission for Woolwich was to build the *Henri Grâce à Dieu* (or the *Great Harry*), which was to be the largest ship afloat. Deptford, the bigger of the yards, expanded to over 12 ha (30 acres), encompassing two wet docks, three slips, workshops, rope manufacturers and officers' quarters. Ancillary

2

PRECEDING PAGES

Main picture: *Embarkation of Henry VIII on board the* Henri Grace a Dieu *in 1520* by Friedrich Bouterwek, after an original painting by Vincent Volpi.

Detail: The statue of Captain James Cook at the Queen's House, Greenwich.

1 One of the few original gates to Portsmouth's historic dockyards to survive the bombing raids of World War II.

2 The salvaged hull of Henry VIII's battleship *Mary Rose* is now housed in the Number 3 dry dock at the Portsmouth dockyards, after being raised from the sea bed in 1982.

3 A painting by Joseph Farrington (1747–1821) of the dockyards at Deptford on the River Thames. The dockyards were established by Henry VIII around 1513.

3

1

industries sprang up around the dockyards, including cooperage works to make the barrels in which all ships' stores were supplied, and roperies to provide the miles of rigging needed for each vessel. Each dockyard became a virtually self-contained community, especially Deptford, base of the East India Company. During the first 20 years following its incorporation by royal charter on 31 December 1600, the company built over 10,000 tons of shipping in the Deptford yards.

When Elizabeth inherited the throne in 1558, the navy had become run down and corrupt. The new queen recognized the commercial and political benefits of maritime power, and in 1570 a new major royal dock-yard was created at Chatham on the River Medway, at the head of a vast sheltered anchorage. It became the most important naval dockyard for much of her reign. Approximately 50 ships could be moored on the Medway, making it an ideal base for winter repair work.

A major overhaul of the English fleet took place following the appointment of John Hawkins, one of

Elizabeth's favourite seafarers, as treasurer of the navy in 1577. Each vessel was streamlined by increasing its length and the huge platforms at the bow and stern were lowered for greater speed and manoeuvrability.

The possibility of invasion from England's hostile Catholic neighbours had existed since Henry VIII's break with the pope in 1533. Elizabeth encouraged Francis Drake and other privateers to plunder Spanish bullion ships in the Caribbean, reinforcing the links between commerce, exploration and naval strategy. The constant drain on the revenues of Philip II of Spain, plus Elizabeth's execution of Mary Queen of Scots, the main Catholic contender for the throne, finally led to an attempted Spanish invasion in 1588.

Spain was the leading maritime power in Europe and the weaponry of the *Felicissima* ('Invincible') Armada arguably superior; their fleet of over 100 ships carried heavily armed soldiers and was, in effect, an army on the move. The English response, commanded by Lord Howard of Effingham, drew upon the navy's professional

1 The 'Armada Portrait' of Elizabeth I, attributed to George Gower (1540–96). The painting is thought to have been undertaken in 1588, almost immediately following the English victory. The outcome had been a personal triumph for Elizabeth, whose speech to her land forces at Tilbury had sought to present a woman as a convincing war leader.

2 The famous statue of Sir Francis Drake on Plymouth Hoe, the site of his allegedly leisurely game of bowls as the Armada approached. Drake's leadership was an important factor in defeating the Spanish galleons.

3 A contemporary engraving of a chart showing the tortuous route around the British Isles followed by the fleeing Armada.

warships and the armed mercantile marine. Their sailors were expert in seamanship and the handling of their own gunnery, but they confronted a formidable force. Significantly, the Armada seems to have engendered unity in England against external threat, regardless of religious divide.

The Armada reached Cornwall during the latter part of July 1588, its first sighting signalled by the lighting of beacons along the Channel coast. Isolated skirmishes took place as the Spanish fleet made its way up the Channel, but no major encounters ensued. This was largely due to the speed and handling of the English ships, able to attack the lumbering galleons and quickly retreat. Engagements off Portland Bill and the Isle of Wight on 6 August also resulted in few casualties. The Spanish fleet anchored undeterred off Calais, preparing to embark the duke of Parma's army, based in Flanders, on to landing craft for a final assault.

During the night of 7 August a small flotilla of English fireships, packed with explosives and burning straw, were steered towards the Armada. Many Spanish ships cut their anchor cables and were swept away by the fierce tides and currents of the Channel, losing the tight defensive formations on which they relied for security. On the morning after the fireship attack, English squadrons led by Howard, Drake, Hawkins and Frobisher engaged the smaller galleon groups midway between Calais and Dunkirk, near the coastal town of Gravelines. Spanish galleons, accustomed to grapple an enemy ship and fight at close quarters with muskets, light guns and archers, were frustrated by the rapier-like thrusts and longer-range guns of lighter English vessels.

Despite the intensity of the battle, few Spanish ships were actually lost, but the fleet suffered 600 dead and over 800 wounded, with many officers held for ransom.

In the stormy night, the beleaguered Spanish fleet found itself driven towards the Zeeland Banks, treacherous sand banks off the Belgian coast. A sudden shift in wind direction carried them into the North Sea's deeper waters, and subsequently northwards towards Scotland. Negotiating the coast of Ireland proved perilous, and less than half the Armada eventually returned home.

When the English sailors started to dock, they discovered little remuneration awaiting them on shore, although they had lacked pay for weeks at sea. Lord Howard of Effingham was moved to complain to the secretary of state, Francis Walsingham: 'It were pitiful to have men starve after such service and if men should not be cared for better than to let them die and strive miserable, we should very hardly get men to serve.'

England's victory over the Armada had consequences in both the political and the economic sphere. It illustrated the shift of maritime power to the north of

135

A Maritime Nation

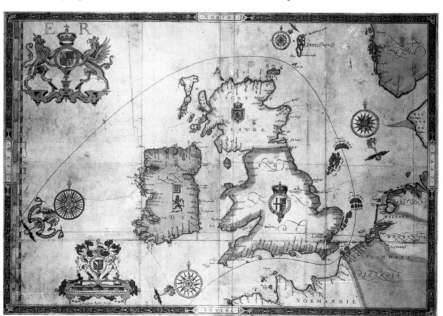

Europe from the Mediterranean, and anticipated the new trading impetus that was to accompany it. English adventurers were released to trade and plunder, establishing a commercial rivalry with the Dutch that provoked the Anglo-Dutch Wars of the 17th century. In 1614 the East India Company developed a new dockland site at Blackwall, east of the Isle of Dogs, as London grew into one of the leading trading emporia of Europe.

Maritime supremacy was not maintained, however. Neither James I nor Charles I was able – or willing – to invest, and naval power declined under their respective regimes. The Dutch East India Company exploited its greater naval backing to extend their influence in the Malayan Archipelago, controlling the lucrative Spice

Islands, the Moluccas. Closer to England's shores, pirates from north Africa conducted raids in the Channel and the navy entered the Civil War on the parliamentary side. With the forming of the Commonwealth, Oliver Cromwell recognized the seriousness of the naval situation and appointed the brilliant Admiral Blake as commander. He achieved notable English victories over the forces of Charles I's nephew, Prince Rupert, and in battles at Portland and Beachy Head in 1653, during the first Anglo-Dutch War. Charles II inherited a stronger navy after the Restoration, but lack of money and an outbreak of the plague coincided with further Anglo-Dutch hostilities in the Thames Estuary. In 1666 the English sustained nearly 4,000 casualties in an engagement of the second Anglo-Dutch War. The following year the Dutch commander, de Ruyter, inflicted serious damage on the Chatham dockyards. Three ships of the line were burnt at their moorings, and the 90-gun *Royal Charles* was towed back to Holland as a prize. However, the war did encourage further naval reforms in an effort to create a reliable national force. The royal dockyards at Woolwich and Deptford entered another prolific era of shipbuilding, producing better designed and more efficient vessels on which it was easier to distribute armaments and supplies. Such was the status of English shipbuilding that Peter the Great of Russia lived for four months at John Evelyn's house in 1698, studying shipbuilding at Deptford dockyard. He proved to be an unruly tenant.

Another diarist, Samuel Pepys, played a major role in transforming the Stuart navy as secretary to the Navy Board. Charles II took a keen interest in the Royal Navy (as the service became known during his reign) and Pepys approved of the king's involvement, commenting that he 'best understands the business of the sea of any

1

prince in the world'. As part of his attempts at modernization, Pepys introduced in 1677 examinations for aspiring lieutenants in mathematics and navigation. He was concerned that naval commanders should possess greater theoretical and practical knowledge of the sea, in contrast to a traditional preference for military leaders. The Royal Mathematical School at Christ's Hospital had been established four years earlier to train boys in 'the Art of Arithmatique and Navigacion' for use at sea.

Pepys also sought to address the welfare of sailors. Their diet was notoriously poor and after the third Anglo-Dutch war of 1672–74 it was alleged that rations included mouldy bread and diseased meat. Pepys, aware that 'Englishmen and more especially seamen, love their bellies above anything else', established minimum standards for crews' rations, although the absence of fresh fruit and vegetables meant that scurvy continued to ravage ships' companies.

Remuneration was another problem confronted by Pepys. At the Restoration, government funds were so low that some sailors were owed approximately three years' back-pay. Citing Cromwell's New Model Army as an example, Pepys forced the Navy Board to acknowledge that a professional fighting force required adequate and regular pay. Navy discipline remained harsh for several centuries, however, with brutal floggings considered almost commonplace.

One of the greatest memorials to Stuart naval reform is the Greenwich Hospital, created at the behest of James II's daughter Mary during her joint rule with William of Orange. Appalled by the injuries of English sailors sustained in conflicts with the French (culminating in the battle of La Hogue in 1692), she wished to establish a hospital for disabled sailors similar to the Royal Military Hospital in Chelsea. Queen Mary's choice of site maintained the association between Greenwich and the navy that began with the Tudor monarchs. Inigo Jones had designed the perfectly proportioned Queen's House for Anne of Denmark in 1616 – the first royal commission in the Palladian style – but the palace degenerated during the Commonwealth. Charles II had held ambitious plans for a new 'King's House' nearby,

2

1 *Portsmouth Harbour* by
John Cleveley the Younger
(1747–1786), shows the
activity surrounding the
naval dockyard. Portsmouth
became the principal base of
the Royal Navy during the
18th century, when France
replaced Holland as the
main threat to England's
sovereignty.

2 A painting by Joseph
Farrington of the royal
dockyards complex at
Chatham, executed around
1792. The vast scale of the
site is exaggerated by the
surrounding countryside.
The complexity of ship-
building in the age of sail,
requiring long rope-making
sheds and other ancillary
buildings on site, is evident.

3 A 19th-century depiction of
the 'triangle and congreve
rockets' at Chatham. Naval
and military punishments
were harsh during the
Georgian era, with brutal
floggings routine for relatively minor offences.

but lack of funds brought work to a halt after the completion of one wing.

Mary died before work could begin, but William determined to honour what she described as 'the darling project of my life'. Christopher Wren had been appointed to design the hospital, although his initial proposal to demolish everything on the site, including Inigo Jones's creation and the Tudor buildings, was fortunately rejected by the queen in 1694. The diarist John Evelyn was appointed treasurer, and he and Wren jointly laid the foundation stone on 30 June 1696. Over the next 50 years Hawksmoor and Vanbrugh were among the celebrated architects who continued the project. The final hospital building consisted of two equal segments, symmetrical masterpieces with the Queen's House as their axis. Although the Queen's House is architecturally inconsistent in scale, the view from it, and the historical legacy of the site, remain intact. The Royal Naval College moved there in 1873 and remained until the late 20th century, while the Queen's House is the present home of the National Maritime Museum.

One of the hospital's triumphs is the Painted Hall, planned by Wren as the dining hall. It is remarkable for the glorious decoration by James Thornhill, which he began in 1707 and completed 19 years later. The room became too small to accommodate the increasing numbers of pensioners and was unused until January 1806 when the ceiling painting

3

1, 2 H.M.S *Victory* was the flagship of Admiral Horatio Nelson at the battle of Trafalgar in 1805, one of the greatest of all British naval victories. *Victory* was one of the first of a new breed of Ships-of-the-Line. The ship weighed over 2,000 tonnes, and carried 104 guns and 850 men. The *Victory*'s keel was laid in dry dock at Chatham dockyards on 23rd July 1759.

3 Buckler's Hard near Beaulieu in Hampshire was one of England's leading shipyards during the 18th century. Being on the edge of the New Forest ensured plentiful supplies of oak.

4 A painting of one of the most famous military signals in English naval history by Walter William May. Nelson had wanted to use the word 'confides' but was informed that 'expects' existed in the flag vocabulary and would thus be quicker to execute.

1, 2

(depicting Peace and Liberty triumphing over Tyranny) provided an appropriate canopy for the body of Admiral Lord Nelson. Having been brought from Trafalgar, it lay in state there until it was taken up the river for burial at St Paul's Cathedral.

The Georgian navy in which Nelson served kept up Pepys's standards of recruitment; unlike their counterparts in the army, who could buy their commissions, naval officers had to survive a rigorous apprenticeship and pass examinations. But influential connections or patronage were essential to gaining a place on board a naval vessel to begin training. As a result, most officers were drawn from the professional middle classes, minor landed gentry and sons of existing naval officers.

Recruiting seamen was a perennial problem for both Royal Navy and merchant ships. Three methods were used – volunteers, the impress service and, from 1795, the Quota Acts. A volunteer was paid 'conduct money' from which he was expected to purchase appropriate clothes and a hammock; he also avoided any threat of debtor's prison (the navy protected a sailor from his creditors if the debt was less than £20). The impress service allegedly targeted only existing sailors, and each major port had a captain in charge of 'recruitment'. In reality, in England's coastal towns and harbours, the press gangs employed notorious tactics, seizing men from ale houses, streets or even the church door. The term for such forcible recruitment derived from the

Old French *prest*, meaning a loan. A 'prest' man's fate was sealed as soon as, voluntarily or otherwise, he accepted the 'King's shilling' to enlist.

The Quota Acts, which were introduced by Pitt the Younger, required each county to provide a quota of seamen, based on its population and number of sea ports. Bounties provided an inducement, but as few free men showed enthusiasm for a life at sea, petty criminals were given a choice of the navy or prison. During an era of harsh jail terms for quite trivial offences, the option of going to sea provided quite an attractive alternative.

In the latter part of the 18th century, naval action abroad served to consolidate England's maritime authority. Naval support was a decisive factor in the capture of Quebec province by General Wolfe in 1759, as well as the island of Guadeloupe in the Caribbean, considered by many to be the greater prize. As the conflicts of the 18th century continued, the navy demanded increasing resources to expand. Nelson's flagship *Victory* was a product of the naval shipyards at Chatham, eventually to decline as larger vessels struggled to negotiate the Medway. A new shipyard at Bucklers Hard, set on the fringes of the New Forest, came into prominence in the 18th century. Bucklers Hard launched ships into the River Beaulieu, which flowed into the Solent. Oak from the forest was plentiful and there was an ironworks nearby with a water-powered forge hammer. As many as 56 naval vessels were built there between 1745 and 1808, including the 64-gun *Agamemnon*.

Napoleon knew that he had to defeat the Royal Navy before invading England. Cape Trafalgar, off the Spanish coast between Cadiz and the Straits of Gibraltar, was the setting for the conflict that ended his plans. Nelson's triumph was a combination of brilliant tactics and superior gunnery from the British fleet. He instructed his ships to

3

form two columns and sail at the centre and rear of the enemy fleet, thus enabling them to attack over half the French and Spanish vessels before the vanguard could turn and rejoin the action. In addition to firing cannon balls directly into a ship's hull, naval captains raked the enemy decks and rigging with shot. The carnage caused by a single, well-directed burst from a ship's short-range carronades could be devastating; in conjunction with a long-range broadside, an opponent could be crippled within minutes. Such was the damage inflicted on the French admiral's flagship by Nelson's first attack in the

Victory, effectively removing the Frenchman from the battle; the same pattern was repeated down the line.

Nelson's plan worked well. The combined enemy fleet was split into three, with each part forced to conduct a separate battle. Every one of the 27 British ships survived the battle, but of the 33 enemy vessels, 18 were taken as prizes. Nelson himself was fatally wounded by a sniper, but Trafalgar broke France as a maritime power. British naval supremacy would not be challenged again for a century, by which time steamships had transformed the fleet and the conduct of war at sea.

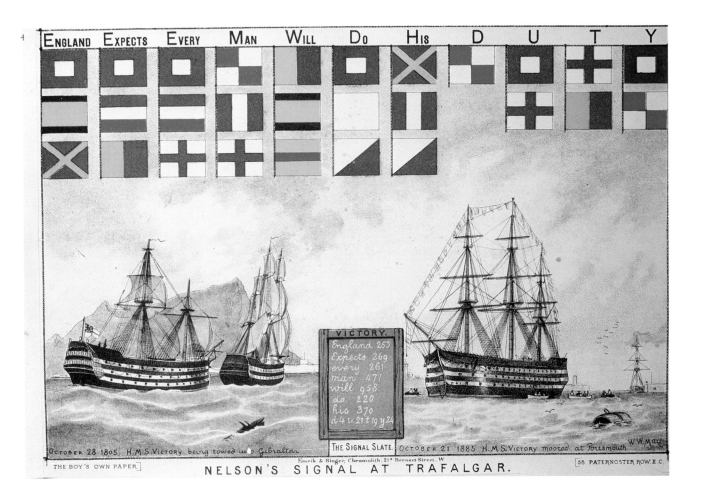

NELSON'S SIGNAL AT TRAFALGAR.

EXPLORATION & TRADE

FROM THE TUDOR PERIOD ONWARDS, MARITIME EXPLORATION BECAME A MAJOR FOCUS OF ENGLAND'S COMMERCIAL ENDEAVOUR. NEW TRADING RELATIONSHIPS WERE ESTABLISHED IN THE CARIBBEAN AND THE AMERICAN MAINLAND TO THE WEST AND INDIA AND CHINA TO THE EAST, HERALDING A FLOOD OF EXOTIC IMPORTS SUCH AS FOODSTUFFS, TEXTILES AND CERAMICS. THE ECONOMIC IMPERATIVE TO CONTROL OVERSEAS TRADE ROUTES AND MARKETS WAS THE ENGINE BEHIND COLONIAL EXPANSION, AND RAW MATERIALS BECAME INCREASINGLY IMPORTANT.

THE INVESTMENT of Henry VII and Bristol merchants in John Cabot's voyage to the New World in 1497 emphasized the commercial incentives behind contemporary exploration. The greatest maritime empire of the 15th century belonged to the Portuguese, excellent sailors trained by the school of navigation founded at Sagres in 1418. The Portuguese established a presence in India and the Malayan archipelago early in the 16th century, monopolizing the lucrative spice trade until the Dutch seized control in 1609. The tiny, nutmeg-producing island of Pulroon, an English acquisition of great pride to James I, was also lost in 1620, followed by the Amboyna massacre in 1623.

From the mid-16th century, English sailors sought direct access to the Orient through routes to the east and west. Martin Frobisher made three voyages to the northern Canadian waters in search of the elusive North-West Passage, but without success. Cabot's son, Sebastian, founded a company of Merchant Venturers in an attempt to secure an alternative North-East Passage to Asia. Two separate expeditions led by Sir Hugh Willoughby and Richard Chancellor were mounted in 1553, Chancellor reaching Moscow to establish a trading link with Russia.

Other English trading organizations, such as the Levant Company (1581) and the East India Company (1600) followed suit, seeking to dominate European trade in a particular region. Traditional tactics of plunder and piracy continued to be employed in the Spanish Caribbean, encouraged by Elizabeth I and Walsingham as

a demonstration of English maritime power. Francis Drake's remarkable voyage of circumnavigation in 1577–80, in which he sailed westwards to the East Indies and back to England via the Cape of Good Hope, was a remarkable feat in an era of limited navigational technology. He received a knighthood in 1580 from the queen on the deck of the *Golden Hind* – still laden with Spanish bullion looted on the voyage's outward leg.

By the mid-17th century, England's commercial interests abroad had begun to expand. In the Caribbean, the islands of St Kitts, Barbados, Nevis, Antigua and Montserrat were acquired between 1623 and 1632, followed by Jamaica in 1655. Many of these territories developed prosperous sugar plantations whose owners began to wield political influence in England. The East India Company, established at Surat in Gujarat, began to develop new factories, or trading stations, at Madras, Hooghly in Bengal, and Bombay. Quality Indian calicoes were exported to England in significant quantities, rising from 220,000 pieces in of cloth in 1625 to approximately one million in the early 1680s. As reliable sea travel became an economic necessity, scientific instruments, such as a new quadrant, were developed to improve navigation. Much of the scientific study, including accurate mapping, took place at the Royal Observatory at Greenwich whose first home, Flamsteed House, was built by Wren in 1675. Its distinctive façade, surmounted by the famous Time Ball, dominates the Greenwich Park skyline, and overlooks the Old Royal Naval College and the Thames.

1 The Time Ball was set up on the roof of the Royal Observatory at Flamsteed House in Greenwich in 1833 to serve as a visual time signal for mariners on the Thames by which to calibrate their chronometers. The ball was dropped at 1pm rather than noon as the astronomers were engaged in their own duties of measuring the sun as it passed the local meridian at mid-day.

2 Captain James Cook was renowned for his exploration of the South Pacific during the 1770s and was largely responsible for Britain's initial acquisition of colonies in Australasia.
3 Dartmouth in Devon has been an important harbour since Roman times and many historic naval expeditions have sailed from its sheltered anchorage.

2

John Flamsteed was appointed the first astronomer royal by Charles II, who commissioned the observatory building in the hope that the compilation of accurate astronomical charts and lunar tables might help to reduce the uncertainties of navigation. Among commercial requirements was an accurate calculation of longitude, essential in plotting a position at sea. 'Dead reckoning', the traditional method, required considerable skill to be effective, based as it was on simple calculations of distance and speed. More sophisticated navigation techniques, able to accommodate the effect of currents, involved latitude and longitude, both measured as segments of a 360-degree circle. Latitude is relatively straightforward to calculate from astronomical observation, but even minor miscalculations of longitude, where one degree equals 60 nautical miles (111 km), could be disastrous. Following the passing of the Longitude Act by Parliament in 1714, a competition was launched to discover a method of determining longitude to an accuracy of half a degree. Much to the chagrin of leading scientists and astronomers, the winner of the £20,000 reward was a clockmaker, John Harrison. He devised a pendulum-free chronometer (page 136), impervious to extremes of temperature and the pitch and roll of a vessel at sea. However, the new device did not become widely available to sailors until the late 18th century. Captain Cook's second voyage (1772–75), during which he sailed round Antarctica, confirmed the instrument's accuracy and reliability. It followed his remarkable 1768–71 expedition, when he produced detailed maps of the Pacific, Australia and New Zealand, claiming the eastern part of Australia itself for the

3

crown. The landing site was named 'Botany Bay' after the quantity of new species encountered there.

Exotic foreign crops and produce such as coffee, tea, chocolate, Indian calicoes and silks were introduced into England during the 17th century, and previously luxury items such as sugar became more affordable as supplies increased. The country's volatile domestic climate – Civil

War, execution of Charles I, plague and external conflict – were counterpointed by burgeoning overseas trade as the balance of economic power in Europe began to shift. The Italian wool trade, for example, declined as overland travel to the east became uncompetitive compared with English and Dutch Cape routes. Southampton, the main port used by Italian merchants, suffered in turn, but London increased in prosperity, conducting foreign trade through the Thames Estuary in predominantly English ships. The Pool of London below London Bridge compared only with Amsterdam in the volume of shipping it contained, including barge traffic with domestic produce from local inland ports, such as Gloucester, or from coastal regions. London's trade far outstripped that of other English ports; Custom House administration at the Port of London cost £20,000 a year in 1680, compared with £2,000 at Bristol and £900 at Newcastle.

Outside the capital, ports had begun to specialize in particular produce. Newcastle exported large quantities of coal, primarily to London, from where it was shipped by river across the country; Hull focused upon whaling

and fishing; and Plymouth fostered transatlantic trading links as well as its connections with the Royal Navy. Declining Scandinavian trade impacted upon England's eastern ports, although shipbuilding maintained a presence at Whitby and Yarmouth, and the silting up of the Dee estuary gradually curtailed Chester's trade. Bristol, described by Pepys in the 1660s as 'in every respect another London', was the dominant coastal port of the southwest, and controlled river traffic far up the Severn. It maintained close associations with sugar and tobacco, forming the base of the cigarette and cigar manufacturers W.D. and H.O. Wills, later Imperial Tobacco. The crop had proved the salvation of the struggling English colony at Jamestown, Virginia – virtually extinguished through starvation in 1609. A tobacco variety brought from Spanish plantations in the West Indies, *Nicotiana tabacum*, changed the colony's fortunes, and exports from the area soared, rising from 20,000 lbs (9,000 kg) in 1617 to 28 million lbs (12.7 million kg) by the mid-1680s.

Tobacco plantations were increasingly worked by slave labour, employed even more intensively in the

1 Gloucester is an important inland port on the River Severn. It is linked by a canal, completed in 1827, to docks at Sharpness on the Bristol Channel c.26 km (16 miles) away. This valuable connection enabled ships of up to 1,000 tonnes to navigate the waterway and discharge their cargoes for distribution across England through the network of inland waterways.

2 The lighthouse on the island of Lundy in the Bristol Channel. Its construction was funded by Bristol merchants, anxious to safeguard their investments. Although navigational aids had improved maritime safety by the turn of the 19th century, England's inshore waters still represented a considerable hazard.

Caribbean sugar industry. Its exports of sugar to England more than doubled between 1660 and 1700, Barbados becoming the greatest producer in the trade by the 1670s. The sugar arrived unrefined, in a crystallized, muscovado form, which gave rise to refineries around the ports themselves, in cities such as Bristol and Whitehaven, Kingston upon Hull and Newcastle. As England's colonial population grew wealthier, it created a welcome export market for European furniture and other goods, encouraging England's manufacturing, shipbuilding and mercantile marine. The Long Parliament's Navigation Act of 1651 sought to strengthen English commercial interests further, declaring that the colonies must trade with, and import manufactured goods from, England alone. Such legislation aroused bitter resentment in the colonies themselves.

The scale of slave labour required for the sugar plantations gave rise to the highly profitable 'triangular' trade, with ports such as London, Bristol and Liverpool providing the English nexus. Ships carried iron goods, finished cotton fabrics and guns to the trading stations on the west coast of Africa. The produce was exchanged with local traders for slaves, who were then transported to America under appalling conditions; an average of 10 per cent died on any one crossing – more if the ships became marooned in the Doldrums. Having discharged their surviving human cargo, the ships would load up with raw cotton, sugar and dried tobacco leaves for the return voyage to England, before starting the round trip once more. Between 1680 and 1783, some two million West African slaves were carried across the Atlantic Ocean in European ships, and profits were substantial. In 1771, over 180 ships engaged in the trade sailed from the docks of London, Bristol and Liverpool (almost two-thirds of which were dispatched from the last, primarily loaded with cotton).

Lancashire's high concentration of cotton mills made Liverpool the principal entrepôt for cotton in the 18th and 19th centuries. As early as 1800 it had overtaken Bristol as England's second port, a status reflected in the elegant town hall, designed by John Wood (who created much of Bath) in 1754, and embellished later in the century. As cotton manufacture became fully

1

mechanized, the industry required huge supplies of raw material. Indian cotton, too coarse for English machines, was replaced by finer American thread, strengthening the industry's western focus. From 1813 to 1833 Liverpool's raw cotton imports grew eightfold, and the impressive Albert Docks were constructed in 1841–45 in response to the rising demand. The warehouses' simple, imposing Doric columns are built of iron, revealing the complex influences behind the new industrial age.

Commercial pressures and new engineering skills transformed England's coastal ports in the early 19th century. Lighthouses were established by the naval authority of Trinity House and new docks constructed across the country. In the capital, the West India Dock, the London Docks and the East India Dock all opened between 1800 and 1805, as the city captured virtually all the East India traffic, together with much of the European, African and American trade. The vast infrastructure was sustained by large numbers of unskilled

dockers and casual labourers who lived – often in awful conditions – in the hinterland of markets and ports.

Much of the East India traffic related to the tea trade, one of the company's most lucrative commodities in the 18th and 19th centuries. China tea was an expensive luxury when it first arrived in England and was often kept in a locked caddy in private homes. Imports rose from 50 to 15,000 tonnes over the 18th century, creating huge profits for the company, who held a monopoly. Demand for tea soared, encouraging the establishment of plantations in India, with plants and seeds literally smuggled out of China in 1851 on the company's behalf. China tea was still prized, however, and after the company's monopoly had ended in 1834 sleek clipper ships raced one another to London with the new season's tea. For the crews, the race was a three-month marathon of endurance, but the prestige of victory was high.

Britain maintained maritime dominance well into the steamship era, its rapidly expanding empire making long-distance sea travel both a political and an economic necessity. In 1885 one-third of the world's seafaring ships were registered British, and 80 per cent of its steamships. Ocean transport had become both cheaper and faster by the end of the 19th century than had been conceivable at its start. Technology transformed geographic distance and commercial possibility, just as navigation aids and exploration had done in the 16th century. England was at the forefront of both developments, and sea power the medium through which this was expressed.

2

1 In 1706, Thomas Twining bought Tom's Coffee House in the Strand, a meeting place for some of London's most eminent businessmen. A major business developed from the initial investment, centred around the increasingly popular commodity of tea.

2 The tea clipper races of the mid-19th century that brought the new season's harvest from China created considerable excitement in England, and fortunes were staked on the outcome. Of all the ships that took part in that trade, the best known is the *Cutty Sark*, now moored at dry dock in Greenwich.

3 The achievements of the clippers – and the wider expansion of England's maritime trade – were essentially dependent upon reliable navigation techniques. The Royal Observatory in Greenwich remained at the forefront of astronomical investigations, adding new rooms or observatories every time a new or better positioned telescope was required. The Altazimuth Pavilion shown here was built towards the end of the 19th century to measure the moon's orbit..

3

CHAPTER

5

Parish churches, with their individual towers, spires and steeples,
form an integral part of the English landscape, while the medieval cores
of many cities are still dominated by majestic cathedrals. Little remains of
the first timber buildings, but many Saxon stone churches have survived to the
present. Sturdy, unbuttressed towers reveal a distinctive surface decoration, the
simple beauty of which belies their age. The Normans introduced Romanesque
architecture to England, typified by heavy, imposing stone-work carved with
vigorous patterns and primitive animal forms. The Early English, Decorated
and Perpendicular phases of Gothic architecture, which succeeded one
another between the 13th and 16th centuries, provided some of the
country's greatest church and cathedral buildings. Walls and
windows were filled with graphic depictions of the joys
of heaven and the dire consequences of damnation.

IN FEAR
& PRAISE

SHAPING THE FAITH

For centuries Christianity has been the established religion of England, underpinning much of the country's artistic and cultural heritage. It was popular in the latter years of the Roman occupation, before being virtually extinguished by the Anglo-Saxons. Christian communities of monks on the Celtic fringes of Britain, such as Iona and Lindisfarne, kept Christianity alive. When Roman missionaries under Augustine arrived in Kent, divergences between the two strands — Celtic and Roman, monastic and episcopal — led to ecclesiastical disputes that would take years to resolve.

CHRISTIANITY FIRST REACHED Britain from Gaul in the 3rd century AD, and before long claimed its first martyr, St Alban. In 313 the Roman emperor Constantine proclaimed Christianity one of the tolerated cults and towards the end of the same century Theodosius declared it the sole religion of the empire. Almost simultaneously, pagan barbarians overran Britain.

By the 5th century six or seven groups of these pagan invaders had settled there. It took a further 200 years of concerted efforts by both Roman and Celtic missionaries for Christianity to become the nation's accepted faith. Pope Gregory I evidently regarded Britannia (or at least the souls of its inhabitants) as part of Rome, even though the legions and administrators had long since departed the island province, and at the close of the 6th century he elected to send Augustine, prior to the monastery of St Andrew in Rome, and some 40 missionaries to England in an attempt to re-establish the Christian faith. Augustine was reluctant to undertake the task, but nevertheless landed on the Isle of Thanet, off the coast of Kent, in AD 597 to begin his ministry. Directing Augustine initially to Kent was a deliberate ploy by the pope, as he was aware that Aethelbert king of Kent was married to Bertha, a Christian Frankish princess, and therefore unlikely to be entirely unsympathetic to the cause.

Aethelbert gave a cautious welcome to Augustine's group, granting them the freedom to preach locally. Some months later he agreed to be baptized himself, and in due course he sanctioned the building of a church. The remains of St Augustine's Abbey, located

just outside Canterbury's city walls, bear traces of that first Saxon foundation and also contain the graves of some of the first archbishops of Canterbury. In the 1,500-plus years since, Canterbury has remained the Mother Church of Anglicanism.

The abbey was in addition to other churches that already existed, for the Venerable Bede mentions 'a church built in ancient times while the Romans were still in Britain, next to the city of Canterbury on its eastern side'. This church is thought to be St Martin's in Canterbury, where Bertha is said to have worshipped, making it the oldest church in continuous use in England. The abbey and the church are both representative of a pattern to be repeated across the land down the centuries — one in which buildings were built over, altered or expanded upon according to the tastes of the day by later generations of Christians.

With much of the countryside then heavily forested, the earliest Saxon church builders exploited the available natural resource and erected wooden churches, of which St Andrew's at Greensted in Essex still offers Europe's oldest wooden nave. It was not until the later Saxon period that stone churches were built in any number, but even so relatively few complete ones have survived. However, the parts of them that have been incorporated into later buildings stand out as powerful statements of the strength of the faith that had developed throughout England in the pre-Norman Conquest period. Saxon architecture and detail is so distinctive that the merest remaining fragment is instantly recognizable. Saxon church towers can be identified by their small rounded windows and curious arched door-

PRECEDING PAGES

Main picture: Canterbury
Cathedral, looking west
down the nave.
Detail: 'Apocalypse of St John',
detail of wall painting at
Westminster Abbey chapter
house.

1   The statue of St Aidan in
the churchyard of St Mary
the Virgin, Lindisfarne, faces
directly towards the monastery he established in 635.

2   The Carpet page from the
Lindisfarne Gospels, c.700,
reveals the artistry
and technical capabilities
achieved by the monks.
Ascribed mainly to Eadfrith
bishop of Lindisfarne, the
opening page of each Gospel
is remarkable for its depth
of colour and spectacular
elaboration woven around
the Latin text.

1 Engravings on one of the
two rare 9th-century Anglo-
Saxon crosses in the small
market square at Sandbach,
Cheshire. The crosses,
which tower above the
cobblestones, are thought to
have been erected to mark
the Saxon kingdom of
Mercia's conversion to
Christianity. They portray
biblical scenes, animals and
dragons, some of which
reflect a pagan past.

2 The gaunt ruins which
occupy the cliff top at
Whitby today are the rem-
nants of a medieval abbey
built on the site of a monastery established by St Hilda
in 567. It was there that the
Synod of Whitby was
convened in 664 by King
Oswy of Northumbria to
resolve the differences
between the Roman and
Celtic churches.

ways that are set high above ground level, as well as the
ornate pilaster stripwork that adorns the smooth plastered exteriors of churches such as St Peter's in Barton-
on-Humber, Lincolnshire, and All Saints in Earl's
Barton, Northamptonshire. Both these churches also
feature impressive examples of 'long-and-short work'
on the quoins, the alternation of upright stones with
flat slabs that project beyond the angles to clutch the
walls. The towers and raised doorways of the Saxon
churches may well have been defensive measures,
enabling the community to seek refuge from attackers
by withdrawing into the more secure upper chamber
of the tower.

As St Augustine sought to establish his mission, ten-
sions arose between the British-evolved form of Celtic
Christianity and that which had arrived with Augustine
from continental Europe. Following consultations with
Rome in AD 603 on how the church should be organized,
Augustine attempted to implement the papal plan for
the creation of archbishoprics and the division of the
country into dioceses. Augustine sought a meeting with
those bishops who had kept Christianity alive during
the post-Roman invasions, but contemporary accounts
indicate that the gathering failed to achieve any consen-
sus. It would be another six decades before the Roman
and Celtic factions of the English church met again to
attempt some form of reconciliation.

During the first quarter of the 7th century, the papal
mission suffered numerous reversals of fortune, partly
due to the deaths of converted tribal kings, including
Aethelbert, whose successors had rejected the new religion. Mellitus bishop of London, who had built a church
called St Paul's, was expelled from the city by a pagan
mob. Pope Gregory in his letters to Augustine had
counselled that pagan practices should be adapted to
Christian usage, but in some cases both continued to
be observed simultaneously: Raedwald king of the East
Angles, having been baptized, erected a Christian altar
immediately next to the sacrificial table in his temple,
where he worshipped alternately at both. In the north,
however, Aethelbert of Kent's daughter married Edwin,
king of Northumbria, and converted him to Christianity.
Paulinus, a member of Augustine's mission, was dispatched to minister to the pagan Northumbrians. But
in 633 Edwin was killed and the exiled son of a previously overthrown ruler of what is now Yorkshire returned
to seize control of Northumbria as King Oswald. This
was to present an opportunity to breathe new life into
the indigenous Celtic Christian church. Oswald had
been converted to Christianity by an Irish monk, Aidan,
during a period spent exiled on the island of Iona off the
west coast of Scotland. A Celtic monastery had been
established there by Columba in about 563. In 635, at
Oswald's behest, Aidan and a group of monks travelled

to Northumberland where, near Oswald's fortress at Bamburgh, they founded a community on Lindisfarne, later known as Holy Island. The ruins of the 12th-century priory can still be visited today.

The way of life adopted by the Celtic Irish monks was significantly different to that led by those who worked within the Roman church. The Celtic monks had little interest in creating parishes through which to organize group worship, and, in effect, govern territory; instead they divided their year into segments of fasting and penitence spent in small individual cells and combined with long periods of touring throughout the north, preaching and baptizing.

The spur to reconciling the differences between these two forms of Christianity was provided by Oswald's brother and successor, Oswy. He sought a synod to resolve the fundamental issue of the date of Easter that had to be resolved, among other doctrinal concerns. In 664 representatives of Celtic and Roman Christianity were brought together at the Synod of Whitby. The

synod was presided over by Hilda, a descendant of the Northumbrian royal line and abbess of the religious house she had founded at Whitby in 657 for men and women, a 'double foundation' that numbered among its followers Caedmon, the first English religious poet.

The case on behalf of Rome was outlined by Wilfrid, a Northumbrian monk, and the Celtic arguments were put forward by Colman, an Irish monk from Mayo and Aidan's successor as abbot of Lindisfarne. Intellectually, the aggressive Wilfrid dominated proceedings; his determination to 'extirpate the rank weed sown by the Irish' faction won the day and Roman practices were largely adopted thereafter. King Oswy pronounced that 'the rule of St Peter, to whom Jesus gave the keys of heaven' should be obeyed henceforth.

Having lost the doctrinal argument, some Celtic monks elected to return to Ireland, while others continued their ministry in England. One of the latter founded Malmesbury Abbey in Wessex, now Wiltshire. In the 10th century its celebrated patron Athelstan, the

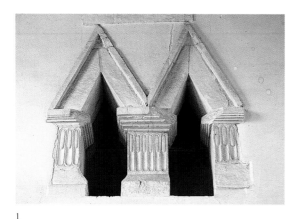

1

Saxon king, was buried there. The town was also home to the 12th-century chronicler William of Malmesbury, the best known English historian since Bede. A third group returned to Lindisfarne, including a young prior named Cuthbert, one of the disciples of St Aidan. Large periods of Cuthbert's time there were spent as a hermit on an uninhabited island adjacent to Lindisfarne and he impressed many with his willingness to endure the physical and mental demands of the ascetic life – so much so that in 685 he was invited to become bishop of part of Northumbria. Two years later he died and his body was buried by the altar of the church on Lindisfarne. With his memory increasingly venerated, 11 years later the monks dug up the remains in order to enshrine the bones in a casket. They found Cuthbert's body in the same perfect condition as the day it had been interred. A wooden coffin containing the untainted corpse became a sacred relic of northern Christianity and helped to establish Lindisfarne as a major place of pilgrimage (page 176).

During the formative years of the English church, between 650 and 850, kings and bishops built hundreds of monasteries, although these early establishments were far from uniform and bore little resemblance to the houses pioneered by the Benedictines. Most were more like settlements, small communities founded by a nobleman on his estate, ruled by his relatives and staffed by his dependents, but still observing most of the functions of a parish church. Women of noble lineage such as Hilda could not become priests, so an appointment as abbess represented an alternative to dynastic marriage.

One of the oldest surviving examples of a Saxon monastic foundation is incorporated into the parish church at Brixworth in Northamptonshire. The church dates from the mid-7th century, when the Saxon kingdom of Mercia was in its Christian infancy, and still evokes Roman colonial traditions both in style and fabric. Thin red bricks recycled from abandoned Roman villas feature prominently around the arches and doorways, and the plan itself reflects the basilican one (that of a public hall), linking it to Augustine's group of

Roman-inspired churches in Kent. The rectangular plan, with transepts and an eastern sanctuary ending in an apse, was well established by the time the English kingdoms became converted to Christianity.

Considerable wealth accrued in the early monastic communities as a result of pilgrimages by the faithful. It was suggested by some theologians that when the first Viking raid on English shores took place in 793, the fact that Lindisfarne was chosen was God's judgement on the monks' luxurious lifestyle. A letter that year from the English scholar Alcuin to King Aethelred of Northumbria stated, 'It is nearly 350 years that we and our fathers have inhabited this most lovely land, and never before has such terror appeared in Britain from a pagan race, nor was it thought that such an attack from the sea could be made.'

After further raids Lindisfarne was abandoned. The monks dismantled the wooden church and took it and Cuthbert's remains on a 200-year quest to find a secure place in which to erect a permanent shrine to the saint. In 998 the monks finally found the ideal location – a rocky hill almost completely encircled by water, where a simple chapel was built over Cuthbert's body. Within two centuries that humble shrine had been replaced by one of the most impressive examples of Romanesque architecture in Europe – Durham Cathedral (page 158).

In addition to Cuthbert's relics, Durham was once home to the remarkable 7th–8th-century illuminated manuscript known today as the Lindisfarne Gospels, now in the British Museum. The scribe was Eadfrith, bishop of Lindisfarne from 698 – the same year that Cuthbert's body was exhumed. A great deal of painstaking work went into the gospels, and each one begins with a magnificently

2

1 Twin triangular-headed windows fashioned from pale oolitic limestone illustrate the Saxon origins of St Mary's Church at Deerhurst, Gloucestershire.

2 Romsey Abbey in Hampshire possesses what might be the oldest low relief carving of the crucifixion in England. The unique Saxon carving was originally gilded, with jewels in the eye sockets and it may well be the crucifix recorded as being given to the abbey by King Edgar *c*.960.

3 Apart from the insertion of windows and the addition of a porch, the tiny Saxon church in the former pit village of Escomb has remained virtually unchanged since it was built, possibly as early as the 7th century.

decorated page featuring intricate lettering and illustrations, all rendered in colours of indescribable intensity. The parchment on which they were inscribed was produced from calf-hide. Each skin yielded two pages, the whole book requiring the hides of well over 100 calves. Similar in execution to Ireland's Book of Kells, the Lindisfarne Gospels exhibit an amazingly accomplished synthesis of Anglo-Saxon, Celtic and Mediterranean influences, and illustrate how the skilled craftsmanship evident in pagan jewellery and metalwork could be adapted into new Christianized art forms.

In the wake of the Whitby synod, the church in England began the process of rationalization originally envisaged by Pope Gregory I – effectively re-creating the governing structures of the Roman empire but on behalf of the church. This was done under the guidance of Theodore of Tarsus, archbishop of Canterbury from 668, who in 672 summoned a council of the whole English church at Hertford, at which he established Canterbury's authority and laid the foundations of the parochial system. His reforms left the church in a far more self-confident and well-organized state, presaging the political union of England itself. The two seats for archbishops established at Canterbury and York reflected the secular power of Kent and Northumbria respectively. (The rise of Mercia in the late 8th century

1 St Mary's at Stow-in-Lindsey, Lincolnshire, is one of the most monumental and impressive churches of the pre-conquest period. It retains its true cruciform plan, with central tower and crossing arches of equal proportions.
2 Earl's Barton, in Northamptonshire, is justifiably famous for the Saxon tower of All Saints Church. It provides an outstanding example of surface decoration, with pilaster strips laid over the plastered surface to form geometric patterns.
3 St Andrew's Church at Greenstead-juxta-Ongar in Essex is reputed to be the oldest surviving wooden church in the world. The nave walls are made from massive oak logs, tongue and grooved for draught-proofing, fixed with wooden pins. They have been scientifically dated to 845.

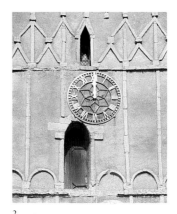

2

led to another archbishopric, at Lichfield.) By 750, much of the original scheme for dioceses had been realized, the boundaries that were established being based on the secular ones already extant in Anglo-Saxon society. Remarkably, despite centuries of change and upheaval, the majority of those territorial delineations survive today, more than a millennium after the distribution of parishes and their associated churches had begun to appear in the English landscape.

The concept of the communal parish church as it is accepted today did not exist during these early years. Churches were owned and built by the local lord, who had sole control over them and could turn the buildings over to other uses if he so wished. The lord also appointed the parish priest, a right that continued throughout the Middle Ages. The proximity of many rural churches to a manor house bears witness to this close social relationship.

In many communities, the Saxon churches have endured in various ways. The Saxons preferred to change old buildings rather than start afresh. One of the finest examples of a Saxon church surviving in its entirety is the starkly simple two-cell building of St John's at Escomb in County Durham. Escomb is also remarkable for the size and smoothly sculpted finish of the blocks used to construct its walls, a legacy of a Roman fort located 3 km (2 miles) from the village. The site on which the church stands may have been connected in some way with an earlier form of religion, a clue to which is provided by the ancient sundial on the south wall. Still fixed in its original position, the device is thought to be the oldest in England and has a remarkable carved serpent entwined above its dial. There are distinct similarities between this beast and representations of the Teutonic creator god who was a feature of the pagan religion of the Angles, tribes of whom settled in parts of north-eastern England.

There is further evidence for the merging of the old religions with the new one. Christian baptism spoons were among the mainly pagan treasures unearthed from the site of the lavish ship burial discovered at Sutton Hoo in Suffolk. Carved stone crosses such as the ones from Middleton, Yorkshire, and Gosforth, Cumberland, bear testament to a fusion of faiths by incorporating Christian iconography with representations of armed Viking warriors or pagan mythological elements. Even some Scandinavian runic stones include references to the Christian crucifixion, notably the Gotland picture stones.

As the first millennium drew to a close, pagan influences were largely eradicated and considerable purpose and direction prevailed within the English church. Within a generation, however, its architectural legacy was to be reduced to incidental details and foundations as most Anglo-Saxon cathedrals, abbeys and churches in England were rebuilt in the new Romanesque style.

POWER & PATRONAGE

The Norman Conquest of 1066 brought England politically and ecclesiastically closer to Europe. William I erected great stone cathedrals and churches across the land, not only 'to the greater glory of God' but also to symbolize the permanence of the new regime. The administrative structure of the church also changed, with Norman bishops and abbots becoming powerful political figures. The growing prosperity of the Benedictines prompted the foundation of a number of ascetic monastic orders, such as the Cistercians, while friars and canons preferred to do God's work in the secular world. They attended the sick and needy, preached and served as teachers and scholars.

Durham Cathedral is arguably the finest surviving Romanesque church in Europe, but it also constitutes, by its sheer size and overwhelming atmosphere, a statement of intent. It is no coincidence that this most enduring of legacies from the Norman Conquest was built in a region that had been so reluctant to submit to the invaders. Durham's thick stone walls and massive stone piers exude an air of power and permanence, meant to leave northern Saxons in no doubt that the new regime was there to stay. A great castle was built alongside the cathedral, on the same elevated peninsula. These two edifices, twin symbols of medieval authority towering high above the town, represent a perfect illustration of what the arrival of the Normans must have meant – the imposition of a new and alien ruling class.

The church containing St Cuthbert's body formed part of a Saxon monastery that had occupied the site since AD 998. Walcher of Lorraine, the first Norman bishop to be appointed to Durham, deemed the community too lax and ordered it to be refounded with 23 Benedictine monks from Monkwearmouth. The monastery was replaced by the current cathedral complex, on which work started in 1093. Excluding the towers, which were a later addition, construction was accomplished in around 40 years. Durham's bishop during the first phase of building was William of St Calais, who had just returned from three years' exile in Normandy having been accused of plotting against William II. The time spent in his native province would have provided the bishop with opportunity to absorb the styles and techniques employed during a time of prolific church building in Normandy.

In Durham Cathedral one's eyes are drawn to the great piers that support the nave vault. These alternate between clusters and massive single columns, each approximately 2 m (7 ft) in diameter and deeply incised with a different geometric pattern. Although many Norman churches and cathedrals bear typical zigzag, beak-head or nail-head ornamentation, nowhere outside Durham uses it to such effect. In common with other Romanesque churches Durham has a paucity of windows and is dimly lit, but there is more than enough light from the clerestory to illuminate the nave's rib vaulting. The cathedral was the first church in Europe to be rib vaulted throughout. Durham's chancel was completed by 1104, some 40 years before St Denis in Paris where it is generally agreed the style originated.

Another new cathedral was built at Ely, an island in the Cambridgeshire Fens, heartland of Saxon resistance to the Norman invaders led by Hereward. Among other forms of protest, he had led raids on abbeys and other church buildings where Normans had replaced Saxons, and he had resisted all William's attempts to seize the island. Finally, the Benedictine monks at Ely betrayed him in return for protection of their lands from the new crown. In 1081 the first Norman abbot of Ely, Simeon, was appointed and the foundations of the cathedral were laid. Built in pale Barnack limestone, it has been little altered in the 10 centuries that have followed.

Although the foundation stone of Durham Cathedral was not laid until six years after William I's death in 1087, his strict reform of the English church had begun almost immediately after the Norman Conquest with the removal of Stigand, the Saxon archbishop of

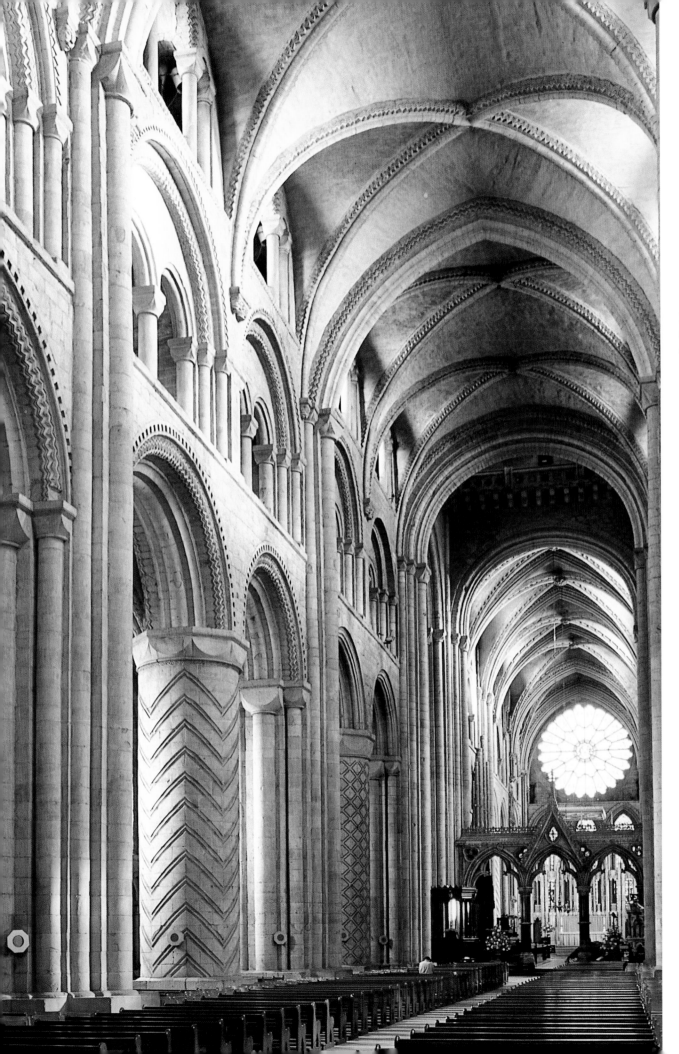

1

Canterbury, in favour of Lanfranc. Long accustomed to selecting his own abbots and bishops in Normandy, William, in conjunction with his new archbishop, continued that role within his new territorial acquisition. Normans and Frenchmen replaced nearly all the native bishops. Some were deposed immediately on Lanfranc's orders, others were replaced when they died or retired. Within 20 years of the conquest, virtually all the religious houses in England were ruled by French-speaking superiors, who initially had little more than a passing interest in the language, history or traditions of the Anglo-Saxon monks they governed.

Winchester, the ancient capital of the West Saxons (and Alfred the Great), was largely destroyed by William. During the 10th century it had become a vigorous

2

centre of religion and learning, exemplified by the building of a new minster there containing the tomb of St Swithun and the creation of illuminated manuscripts such as the Benedictional of St Aethelwold. William's replacement of the relatively small minster by a huge Norman cathedral signified his intention to dominate the English church.

It had been the power of patronage through Aethelbert that had enabled Augustine to re-establish Roman Christianity in England some 500 years earlier. Under Norman control this power was used to replace or modify Saxon institutions, both religious and secular. The Norman bishops who took up new posts were often wealthy landowners, and although they were appointed to the church, they were subject to the feudal system imposed on those Norman barons who had acquired land and estates at the expense of their previous Saxon owners. Bishops were still obliged to render payment to the king in the form of armed knights. William had therefore not only begun the process of forcing the church to conform with his strictly held views, but by inserting a favoured few into key positions, he was using this reform as an instrument of imperial rule.

This tightening of the links between church and state was advanced even further in Durham, where the king appointed William of St Calais prince-bishop in 1081, giving him the power to administer the city as a county palatine. The royal powers vested in the bishop allowed for the provision of his own private army and as both a religious and a military leader he was expected to rule on William I's behalf.

Prior to the Norman Conquest, Anglo-Saxon sees had been based largely on political divisions, but Archbishop Lanfranc and his successor, Anselm, reorganized some in accordance with the Norman practice of situating the see at the heart of large centres of population. Once established within towns and cities, bishops could more readily fulfil their dual role of being both spiritual leader and national administrator, the latter reinforced if necessary by the use of military power, normally at the command of the local earl.

PRECEDING PAGES

1 A detail from one of the
deeply incised pillars in the
nave of Durham Cathedral.
2 The view eastwards down
the nave at Durham
Cathedral. The effect of
heavy stonework is offset by
elaborate decoration to
pillars and arches.

1 The deep chancel arch at
Tickencote in Rutland is
a fine example of Norman
carving. There is a wide
variety of decoration

throughout the six
different orders.
2 The richly carved 12th-
century font at St Michael
and All Angels, Castle
Frome, Herefordshire,
exhibits detail that verges
on the barbaric.
3 One of the most richly
ornamented Romanesque
parish churches is St Mary
and St David, Kilpeck,
Herefordshire. Due to
the durability of the local
sandstone, the 12th-century
carvings still remain sharp.

Benedictine monasticism – adherence to the 6th-century rules of St Benedict – had already become established in England before 1066, largely due to the inspired leadership of King Edgar and St Dunstan the abbot of Glastonbury, who was consecrated as the arch-bishop of Canterbury in AD 959. Dunstan had revitalized the monastic movement after the depredations of the Vikings and the destruction of many of the monasteries. A few cathedrals had been monastic before the Norman Conquest, but afterwards there were many more. Canterbury, Winchester, Westminster, Worcester, Ely, Peterborough, Durham and Norwich were some of the more important Benedictine houses. Once they were established in their new sees, the Norman bishops undertook a wholesale campaign to reconstruct the kingdom's religious buildings in Norman form.

The established Benedictine monasteries enjoyed royal patronage and prospered under Norman rule. Rebuilt and increasingly rich, the foundations were surrounded by an expanding number of satellite cells and parish churches, many of which had earlier been simple Saxon wooden structures but which, too, were now rebuilt, paid for in part by the new-found wealth accruing from various forms of income and endow-ments. Even some of the smallest rural churches had the attentions of master craftsmen lavished upon them during their construction, resulting in standards of decorative stonework that would not have seemed out of place on abbey churches or cathedrals.

But with wealth there came a laxity in the monastic standards laid down by St Benedict, and some monks sought a return to an austere, simple life. These new movements, such as the Cistercians (from Burgundy's Cîteaux forest), gradually filtered through to England as they became more firmly established. The first Cistercian house in England was established in 1128 at Waverley in Surrey. The second abbot of Cîteaux, who served from 1109 to 1133, was in fact an English monk named Stephen Harding and he played an important role in developing the order's fundamental principles. Together with the son of a French knight, Bernard of

3

1

1 Michelham Priory in East Sussex, founded for Augustinian canons in 1229, resembles a fortified manor. It is encircled by a moat and guarded by an austere stone bridge and gatehouse.

2 Leigh Court Barn, Worcestershire, is a magnificent 14th-century tithe barn built for the monks of Pershore Abbey. It is the largest of its kind in England.

3 Gloucester was the first cathedral in England to introduce claustral fan vaulting. It was extended to cover the monks' washing place outside the refectory.

2

wool, under a black scapular, or apron – chose to establish new monasteries shocked even those patrons who chose to support them. Remote locations in wild countryside, often far up small river valleys, were thought ideal, and although the ruins of one of their greatest houses in England, Fountains Abbey in North Yorkshire, now stands amid landscaped gardens, it was not always so.

Cistercian monasteries were intended to be architecturally austere buildings. Furnishings were basic, a vegetarian diet was mandatory and although meals were taken communally, the strict observance of silence was allowed to be broken only by the voice of the refectory scripture reader. Their rules forbade the Cistercians from accepting any material donations. They could accept only land from prospective patrons. That stipulation, coupled with an ethos of hard manual labour, resulted ultimately in the irony of the Cistercians becoming prosperous agriculturists.

The Norman era's system of patronage – the making of large donations of money or land to monasteries, priories and abbeys – continued the relationship that had existed earlier between Saxon aristocrats and the early church and prolonged it for centuries. It was a mutually beneficial system: the church obtained the funds it required to function, while the aristocracy could continue their wealthy lay lifestyle. By the act of patronage, nobles and barons believed that they were acquiring the possibility of salvation without having to endure the rigours of monastic life themselves – in effect, they were paying others to suffer on their behalf. The system helped to institutionalize the relationship between church, state and landed gentry.

Fontaine, he won Europe-wide support from the pope, royalty and the nobility. From humble beginnings, the movement flourished and by the beginning of the 13th century there were some 500 Cistercian monasteries in Europe. The estimated numbers of monks in England at the time of the Norman Conquest is about 1,000, but by the early 13th century there were 13,000 or more.

In every Cistercian monastery the same standards of dress, liturgy and conduct were strictly observed. New abbeys were colonized by monks from existing monasteries, perpetuating the sense of family within the movement. The harshness of the environments in which the 'white monks' – they wore habits of undyed sheep's

However, it also sowed the seeds of conflict. Rich rural monasteries and their occupants were despised by many, including poor parishioners whose own priests and churches often struggled. The material trappings of a monastery made it a target requiring some element of fortification, which only served to alienate it further from the peasantry. Also, the power and influence of the church made it a rival to the secular authorities, creating the conditions for a volatile relationship and one that could on occasion erupt into violence – such as happened with the murder of Archbishop Thomas Becket in 1170 – and resulted finally in King Henry VIII's dissolution of the monasteries in the 16th century, when they were officially described as places of 'manifest sin, vicious, carnal and abominable living'.

The ruins of the abbeys at Fountains and Rievaulx, among hundreds of others, bear witness to this history, although up to the dissolution both were particularly highly regarded. Such institutions were prevailed upon by would-be patrons to establish satellite or 'daughter' houses, drawing settlers from the main houses and into new areas of the countryside. Soon a network extended from the Wash to the Scottish borders. As the monasteries expanded, the brothers found themselves having to spend much of their day working the land, at the expense of prayer and devotion. That situation was rectified by the arrival of lay brothers, whose involvement within the Cistercian movement, although they worshipped in the abbey church twice a day, centred only around the manual labour required for building, horticulture and the tending of the increasingly large flocks of sheep on which the order grew richer than could have ever been contemplated.

Although many benefactors were perfectly content to donate the seemingly untenable land on which the Cistercian movement thrived, others gave those parts of their estates that were already established with farms and villages. Unwilling to reject a generous offer, the monks resorted to transforming the land back into barrenness by evicting tenants and even, on occasion, demolishing entire villages – practices that effectively

turned the Cistercians into enclosing landlords. The order grew wealthy on the sheep production that was so suited to the hill country of Yorkshire and Lincolnshire, where many of their estates were located. During the medieval period, when the English wool trade was flourishing, Cistercians were one of the major contributors to the export market.

As time passed, lay brothers became more difficult to recruit. Towards the end of the 14th century this reduction in the labour force was exacerbated by the effects of the Black Death. Deprived of so many farm workers, the Cistercians were forced to become landlords and to derive ongoing income from tithes and rents, which meant they were travelling back towards the materialistic ways they had once sought to abandon.

Another monastic order prominent in the religious fabric of medieval England was that of the Augustinian or Austin canons (followers of the 5th-century writings and instruction offered by St Augustine bishop of Hippo), also called the 'black canons' due to the colour of their habits. The Augustinians was the church's first religious order of men to combine clerical status with a full common life. During the era of Saxon Christianity, canons had been bodies of clerks who had served those cathedrals and larger churches known as minsters, from where they fanned out into the surrounding countryside to spread the word of God and promote the cause of early church building. A movement in Europe to bring such chapters of canons under a stricter form of monastic rule gathered momentum and in 1059 culminated in the Lateran Council. This led many canons to choose to live together according to monastic ideals under the guidance and leadership of a prior.

Augustinian canons came to England around 1100, replacing the existing clergy at St Botulph's priory in Colchester. Henry I and his queen, Matilda, were enthusiastic and generous supporters, settling them in foundations throughout England. One of the larger priories established for them by Matilda was at Holy Trinity in London's Aldgate, a foundation that rapidly created five subsidiary houses in Oxford, Dunstable, St Osyth,

Plympton and Launceston – a geographical spread that encompassed the Midlands and Cornwall. Not to be outdone by his wife's munificence, Henry I established canons at Carlisle in 1122, where their house became the cathedral of a new diocese a decade later, and in Cirencester, where they built both an abbey church and a parish church located at the abbey gates.

Lay society readily embraced the movement because of its accessibility and the charitable work it undertook within large centres of population. The Augustinians also gained respect because they were modest. The canons performed a particularly valuable function in caring for the sick, elderly and infirm through their establishment of hospitals and almshouses – the latter confusingly also referred to as hospitals in medieval times, after their founders, the Knights of the Hospital of Jerusalem. The oldest church in London was once the choir of an Augustinian priory – St Bartholomew the Great in Smithfield – and its associated hospital forms part of the ancient foundation of Bart's Hospital.

Also supporting such relief works were the four great medieval mendicant orders (whose members took a vow of poverty and supported themselves by work and charitable contributions), which rose to prominence from the 13th century. These were the Augustinian hermits, or Austin friars (not to be confused with the canons); the Dominicans, or 'black friars'; the Franciscans; and the Carmelites. The orders were significant in London and other major towns where their preaching drew vast crowds, often to the ire of parish churchmen. A friary was like a monastery, but the friars (from the Latin *fratres*, brothers) made excursions and were exempt from the jurisdiction of the bishop. Many place names in London refer to the one-time presence of friars, for example the district of Blackfriars.

The almshouse tradition was continued through the actions of wealthy private benefactors who sought an alternative to making a financial contribution to an actual monastery. Architecturally, English almshouses provide a rich legacy, ranging from the diminutive cloistered seclusion of Ewelme in Oxfordshire to the

1. Beamsley Hospital near Skipton, North Yorkshire, was founded as an almshouse by the Countess of Cumberland in 1593. The circular building alludes to the churches of the Templars and contains its own central chapel.
2. The 13th-century gatehouse of Kirkham Priory, North Yorkshire. The Augustinian foundation was one of three established monasteries by Walter L'Espec, the lord of Helmsley.
3. Thornton Abbey gatehouse, Lincolnshire, is a remarkable brick structure dating back to the 14th century. The stone fortifications might be attributed to the fact that it was built around the time of the Peasant's Revolt and an isolated location rendered it vulnerable.

impressive tall-chimneyed houses that flank the large quadrangle of St Cross in Winchester. Ewelme was built by William de la Pole duke of Suffolk in 1437 after he had been granted a licence for its foundation by Henry VI. The statutes provided for a corporation of two chaplains and 13 poor men 'having a common seal'. Land from as far afield as Buckinghamshire, Wiltshire and Hampshire was given as the endowment and men from those places still have priority when appointments to the houses are made today. Almshouses were also established to care for elderly or disabled soldiers, one such being the delightfully half-timbered Lord Leycester Hospital in Warwick, which was founded by Robert Dudley earl of Leicester in 1571 to house his old soldiers. On a somewhat grander and more public scale, the Royal Chelsea Hospital was founded by Charles II in 1682 for veteran and invalid soldiers. Designed by Sir Christopher Wren, the buildings were one of his most successful secular architectural achievements, and are still in use today.

3

THE GOLDEN AGE of GOTHIC

THE PERIOD FROM THE END OF THE 12TH CENTURY TO THE END OF THE 15TH CENTURY WITNESSED THE CONSTRUCTION OF AN UNPRECEDENTED NUMBER OF GREAT CATHEDRALS AND CHURCHES. LIKE THEIR COUNTERPARTS ON THE CONTINENT, THESE GOTHIC STRUCTURES WERE LIGHT AND AIRY, BUT THEY CAN BE DISTINGUISHED BY THEIR EMPHASIS ON LENGTH RATHER THAN HEIGHT. THE EARLY ENGLISH STYLE OF THE 13TH CENTURY GAVE WAY TO THE MORE ORNATE DECORATED ARCHITECTURE IN THE 14TH CENTURY, AND THIS IN TURN WAS REPLACED BY THE VERTICAL LINES OF THE PERPENDICULAR PERIOD. MOST LARGE GOTHIC CHURCHES FEATURE A MIXTURE OF THE STYLES, AS FASHIONS CHANGED DURING THE USUALLY LENGTHY CONSTRUCTION PROCESS.

LINCOLN CATHEDRAL – begun in 1192, with its long, low nave – and Wells in Somerset – started *c.*1180, at the same time as rebuilding commenced at Canterbury – are good examples of the re-interpretation of French ideas to accommodate English taste. Each serves to reveal a distinctly home-grown version of Gothic architecture known as Early English, which concentrated on creating vistas of linear richness. The Early English religious building is typified by pointed or 'Gothic' arches; elongated lancets grouped together into three- or five-light windows; multiple ribbed vaults; and the use of soaring columns of dark, Purbeck marble, clustered around pillars for a delightful, polychromatic effect.

The finest surviving example of Early English, however, is found at Salisbury, where the cathedral (begun in 1220) was built as a single entity on a virgin site. Consequently, the building was neither influenced nor restricted by earlier architecture, nor was it significantly added to during the later Gothic periods known as the Decorated and the Perpendicular.

Although rib vaulting was pioneered in Durham, the structural role of such vaulting in distributing weight was first exploited systematically in France, where the Gothic style originated. This style was introduced into England by the master mason William of Sens when he was commissioned by the monks of Canterbury to rebuild the choir after it had been destroyed by fire in 1174. In Normandy, William had witnessed a new cathedral being erected utilizing techniques first explored in the rebuilding of the abbey of St Denis near Paris and he sought to put this revolutionary approach into practice at Canterbury. The chronicler of the cathedral, Gervase, recorded the work as it progressed and the fact that

William fell 15 m (50 ft) to the ground from scaffolding in the fifth year, to be replaced by an Englishman.

The French pioneers of the Gothic style sought to flood churches with light and banish the dark and often gloomy atmosphere of many Romanesque churches and cathedrals. Interiors were transformed by elegant pillars and windows of stained glass that glittered and shone like precious stones. Buildings could now provide an experience of light, colour and beauty that was sufficiently awe-inspiring to move the worshipper emotionally and spiritually.

The basic technical innovations on which the new architecture was founded centred around the realization that there was an alternative to the wide, load-carrying walls characteristic of the Romanesque style. If the pillars were sufficiently strong to carry the arches of the vaulting, then the massive walls between those pillars became redundant. The walls could be thinned and used to hold large windows. In effect, the French architects strove to erect a kind of stone scaffolding with which to hold the entire building together. This task was complicated by the introduction of the pointed arch in place of the semicircular one. If the gap between two pillars is bridged by a semi circle, the height of the vault above will remain constant, but by fitting two segments together to create a pointed arch, the height can be varied at will by making it either flatter or more pointed.

Significant additional height, however, could not be accommodated without some means of countering the greater outward thrust generated by both the roof and the heavy stone vaulting – a challenge for medieval architects and masons with so few technological resources at their disposal. The problem was overcome

1 One of the most beautiful stone staircases in any church is that which leads to the chapter house in Wells Cathedral. The first entirely Gothic cathedral in England, with pointed arches used throughout, Wells is renowned for the remarkable medieval sculpture gallery that comprises the west front.

2 Few cathedrals can match the majestic setting of Lincoln, set high upon a 61 m (200 ft) limestone plateau that was once occupied by a Celtic hillfort. Bishop Hugh of Avalon began the present cathedral at the end of the 12th century after an earthquake badly damaged its predecessor. His work produced one of the purest expressions of the Early English style.

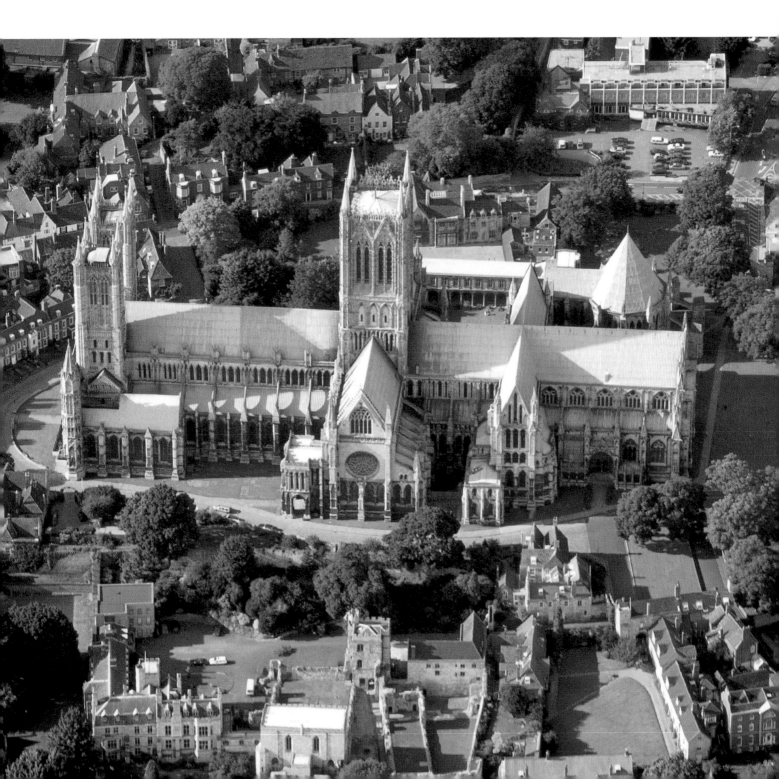

1 The decorative carving within Southwell Minster's chapter house is a remarkable mass of intertwined foliage. Hidden amongst the leaves and branches are several 'green men', figures more pagan than Christian, but which are often found in churches.

2 Exeter Cathedral's early 14th-century stone pulpitum, adorned by 17th century paintings, looks out over a nave that is perhaps the most beautiful expression of Decorated Gothic in any cathedral.

3 The 14th-century nave of Beverley Minster features delightful carvings of men, women and angels playing musical instruments above every pillar.

1

by introducing flying buttresses to the high naves as an essential contribution to the even distribution of weight. These flying buttresses were supported by tower buttresses, crowned with pinnacles that provided both decoration and powerful stabilizing downward pressure. Early English Gothic architecture, though, often favoured length, and placed far less emphasis on height than did the architecture of the great French cathedrals such as Notre Dame, Sens, Amiens and Beauvais. There was consequently less need for buttresses. Lincoln Cathedral is regularly presented to visitors as it would have appeared centuries ago, without any seating in the main body of the nave. To stand by the west door, looking down the entire length of the nave to the choir beyond, is a truly humbling experience.

Predicting how the framework of such edifices would cope with the additional burdens placed upon them was not easy and there were many reversals in fortune. In 1239 Lincoln's central tower collapsed, a disaster that resulted in the bishop having to petition Henry III to dismantle sections of the city's Roman wall in order to use the masonry. In 1338 a similar fate almost befell the tower at Wells Cathedral, but the crisis was averted by the genius of master mason William Joy. Having spotted significant cracks in the masonry, he conceived the idea of introducing the scissor arch braces that are such a unique feature of the cathedral. These giant whalebone-like devices provided additional support for the tower and helped in the distribution of its weight down into the foundations.

In addition to the slender lancet, other types of Early English windows and triforium arcading can be readily identified by their tracery designs. The first Gothic period featured both plate and geometric tracery; the former represented by decoratively shaped openings cut through the solid stone infilling at the head of a window, the latter consisting of either circles or foiled circles.

Cathedrals were, of course, immense building projects for their day that took many years to complete. Few of those who initiated such projects lived to see them finished. The drawn-out construction also meant that many cathedrals reflected in their structure and decoration centuries of changing taste and technical innovation. Because a cathedral was invariably built extending westwards from the chancel to the nave, the prevailing architectural style may have changed significantly by the time the building reached its conclusion at the west front. Those cathedrals that have Early English west fronts display the gracious elegance sometimes lacking from the more exuberant decorative styles that followed – the dignified simplicity of Ripon's series of lancets, Peterborough's great recessed triple entrance

2

2

arch adorned with symmetrical blind arcading and, of course, the medieval west front sculpture galleries of Wells and Salisbury, two of the finest in the country.

As the 13th century drew to a close, a more ornamental phase known as High Gothic can be identified. In England this is referred to as the Decorated period, and can be seen in much of the carved work at Westminster Abbey and Gloucester. England's most impressive ecclesiastical building of the Decorated period is the cathedral church of St Peter in Exeter. When Bishop Walter Bronescombe returned there after attending the dedication of Salisbury Cathedral in 1258, he resolved to transform the city's Romanesque cathedral into a building that would match the beauty of Richard Poore's creation. Work on bringing Bronescombe's wish to fruition began in 1270 and continued for a century, funded initially by his generosity and tithes from the then thriving Cornish tin mines that provided the bishopric with a substantial annual income. St Peter's twin towers occupied an unusual position over the transepts but that architectural idiosyncrasy did at least ensure that there was no central crossing to take into account when creating the vault. The consequence was that the vaulting runs over nave and choir for nearly 91 m (300 ft), representing the longest uninterrupted stretch of vaulting in the world. The effect created by Exeter Cathedral's elaborate vaulting is one of being in the midst of a stone forest, with the vaults fanning out like branches before descending to merge with the thirty Purbeck marble columns.

Other cathedral builders, no longer content with the clear majestic outline of the earlier buildings, sought to show off their improved technical skills and greater artistic awareness by the use of sculptural decoration and complex tracery, which became the hallmark of that period. As technical skills improved, cathedral masons gave full vent to artistic improvisation: arcades became wider, columns taller and more slender, and vaults were given an increased number of ribs – some of which still performed a structural function, while others were purely ornamental with carved and painted bosses at their intersections. Walls became thinner and were more freely decorated both internally and externally with blind tracery, while many towers and spires were embellished with parapets, pinnacles and crockets. Window tracery acquired a new freedom of expression through the addition of flowing curves and floral patterns, some of which were so complex in their composition that the patience of even the most skilled glaziers must have been sorely tried.

Bishop Bronescombe's creation in Exeter was continued by his successors, with the final phase completed during the 42-year bishopric of John Grandisson (1327–69). The building culminates in the glorious swirling tracery of the great west window, beneath which the exterior façade is lined with row after row of stone statues. Bishop Grandisson was sufficiently proud of what had been accomplished to draft a letter to Pope John XXII, informing him that 'the cathedral at Exeter, now finished up to the nave, is marvellous in beauty and when completed will surpass every church in England'.

The contribution of sculptors and carvers to the Decorated period cannot be understated. Their artistry is shown to particularly good effect in the chapter house of Southwell Minster: a narrow passageway links the Romanesque church and the Decorated chapter

1

house, where there is a profusion of naturalistic carving that envelops every capital and twines around columns like petrified green shoots. The fascinating detail evident in these legacies of craftsmanship would have confirmed the view of Abbot Suger of St Denis, who had argued, 'Through the beauty and splendour of the church the dull mind would be awakened to the majesty of God.'

By the late 14th century the era of Late Gothic architecture was emerging. This phase was exclusive to England, where it manifested as the Perpendicular (the French continued with their flamboyant High Gothic style until the Renaissance). Perpendicular was typified by light, airy proportions; straight, lattice-like tracery over the windows and wall surfaces; shallow mouldings; and perhaps the greatest feature of that period, the fan vault. The effect of Perpendicular was to create shallow, cliff-face styles of walls and windows, but craftsmen were given free rein in their execution of the detail. Of all the buildings from that period, King's College Chapel in Cambridge (built 1446–1515) perfectly illustrates the potential of the genre. Because there are no side aisles, and therefore no pillars or arches, the dramatic effect created by the delicate vaulting is increased considerably. The fans radiate from supporting vaults in a filigree network of stone that covers the entire ceiling.

The new style of architecture had not, however, originated in King Henry VI's glorious college chapel. This honour goes to Gloucester Cathedral, where Master William Ramsey remodelled the choir in the Perpendicular style. Ramsey managed to achieve walls rising to a height of 28 m (92 ft), which he covered with a magnificent lierne rib vault. Gloucester's vast east window vies with York for the most impressive area of glass in the country.

Within the context of cathedral building, the Perpendicular style was exemplified by architects such as Henry Yevele, who worked on both Westminster Abbey and Canterbury Cathedral. His nave in the latter cathedral is quite outstanding for its daring emphasis on massed vertical lines, which branch upwards into the sprays of rib vaulting joined in a long central row of gilt bosses. That phase of Canterbury's rebuilding was completed around 1405, a few decades after Perpendicular was introduced, and it can be contrasted with the more florid fan vaulting accomplished more than a century later within the underside of the Bell Harry tower.

The Perpendicular age was deemed to have ended sometime around the middle of the 16th century, by which time all the great medieval churches had been completed. Architecture was soon embracing the Renaissance period, when the emphasis was on public and domestic buildings and ecclesiastical work slowed until the end of the 17th century and the age of Wren during the decades following the Great Fire of London.

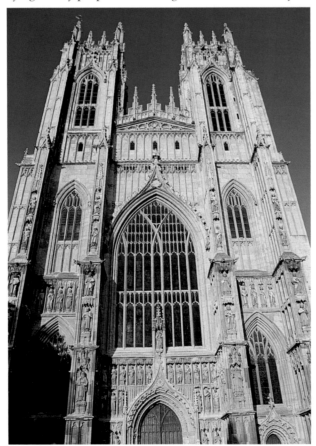

2

MEDIEVAL PILGRIMAGES

DURING THE MIDDLE AGES PILGRIMS WOULD VISIT SHRINES OR HOLY PLACES FOR A VARIETY OF REASONS — SOME WERE DEEPLY PIOUS, SOME WERE INSTRUCTED TO DO PENANCE BY THEIR PRIESTS AND OTHERS CAME IN HOPE OF A CURE. THE VERY RICH MADE PILGRIMAGES TO ROME, JERUSALEM OR ONE OF THE OTHER GREAT CHRISTIAN CENTRES, BUT THERE WERE PLENTY OF NATIONAL, REGIONAL AND LOCAL SHRINES FOR THOSE WITH LESS MONEY AND TIME. THE CATHEDRALS, MONASTERIES AND TOWNS ATTACHED TO SHRINES BENEFITED GREATLY FROM THE PILGRIMAGE INDUSTRY — VISITORS NEEDED FOOD AND SHELTER, AND WOULD OFTEN LEAVE AN OFFERING AT THE HOLY SITE AS PART OF THEIR PENANCE OR IN HOPE OF REWARD IN THIS LIFE OR THE NEXT.

THE STEPS ASCENDING TO THE TRINITY CHAPEL in Canterbury Cathedral have been worn smooth by the feet of countless pilgrims over the centuries. They have made their way there to honour Thomas Becket – in Geoffrey Chaucer's words, 'the holy blisful martir for to seke' – the murdered archbishop who was canonized in 1173, little more than two years after he was killed. Becket had resisted Henry II's encroachments upon ecclesiastical privileges and an angry outburst by the king had led four of his knights to rid him of his 'turbulent priest'. In 1174, in an act of public repentance at Becket's shrine, Henry was scourged by all 70 of the monks there.

Canterbury Cathedral's eventual splendour was paid for by the wealth accrued from centuries of pilgrimage. Had Becket not been martyred there and given the cathedral one of the most visited shrines in Europe, Canterbury would not have been able to fund the rebuilding necessary after two disastrous fires, in 1067 and 1174. At the time of the second fire, Becket's tomb was lodged in the magnificent crypt built by Lanfranc, first of the great Norman bishops appointed by William I. The saint's resting place remained untouched, thus preserving the steady source of revenue with which to create a cathedral worthy of the fame that had come to Canterbury.

From the 11th century, the church had actively encouraged the faithful to express their repentance and gain remission for their sins by making a pilgrimage. The established cult of collecting and visiting relics gained new momentum. The act of canonization made the physical remains of a saint, or of objects associated with a saint, sacred things believed to possess the power to intercede and cause God to heal the body and absolve the soul. But while relics represented a source of hope to the faithful, they also constituted a source of wealth to their owners. Some clergy whose churches or monasteries did not possess relics of their own, were not averse to creating them. Not every church was fortunate enough to have the body of a venerated person, such as Durham did with St Cuthbert. Even so, at their height there were probably 70 main pilgrimage shrines sited throughout England.

Many English churches attempted to profit from pilgrims through the introduction of obscure saints and unsubstantiated relics found their hopes dashed when the Normans denied recognition to a number of Celtic and Saxon saints – an act that tells us much about the

Norman method of wielding power and about the strong demand for English objects of reverence among the subject population. From the 12th century onwards, canonization required papal approval and this was only granted after investigations into the miracles attributed to a particular saint. Attempts were even made on behalf of more 'political' candidates. For example, the tomb of Edward II at Gloucester Cathedral was a favoured destination for many, and the contributions made there paid for a massive building programme in the 14th century. But it remained an unofficial cult, albeit a popular one, and canonization for the king murdered at Berkeley Castle was not forthcoming.

1   Steps leading up towards
    the Trinity Chapel and pre-
    Reformation site of Thomas
    Becket's shrine in
    Canterbury Cathedral. The
    flights of steps through both
    nave and choir were
    designed to create a
    sensation of triumphant
    ascension towards the high
    altar and the glittering
    shrine beyond, encrusted
    with jewels.

2   St Lucy's Chapel in Christ
    Church Cathedral, Oxford
    commemorates the
    martyrdom of Thomas
    Becket in glass. It is thought
    that the insertion of a small
    fragment of plain glass to
    obscure his face and secure
    anonymity may have
    preserved the window from
    destruction in the
    iconoclastic fervour of
    the Reformation.

2

1

In the case of Thomas Becket, however, the shocking nature of his death led to rapid canonization, and in order to cope with increased demand from the visiting public his relics were transferred in 1220 to the newly completed Trinity Chapel. Experiencing Canterbury as a 21st-century tourist is perhaps not too dissimilar from its medieval heyday when bands of travellers – such as those depicted in Chaucer's *Canterbury Tales* – would arrive after completing the prescribed pilgrim routes, or ways, which still exist and are still used for their original purpose. The narrow medieval streets leading up to the

2

cathedral remain awash with visitors, although the medieval pilgrim's visit would have been painstakingly organized by monks rather than tour guides. Pilgrims would have been escorted through the cathedral, pausing at the murder spot and the high altar where Becket's body was laid out. Finally, they would be allowed to savour those few blessed moments of prayer, thanksgiving or supplication before the shrine. It really was an awe-inspiring sight according to the description given by one medieval visitor, 'The shrine surpasses all belief, covered over with plates of pure gold, but the gold is hardly visible for the variety of precious stones with which it is studded.'

As shown by Henry II's own example, pilgrims came from every social station. Indeed, security considerations alone made it likely that different groups of people would band together on their journeys. Whatever the destination, the rigours of medieval travel restricted most pilgrimages to summertime, when days were longer and the climate more benign, enabling those who could not find accommodation in a hospice or monastery to sleep under hedges or in barns.

1 Gloucester Cathedral flourished on the proceeds of pilgrimages to the tomb of Edward II, interred there following his murder at Berkeley Castle in 1327.
2 St Cuthbert's coffin was carried around the north of England by the monks of Lindisfarne for two centuries before settling at the site on which Durham Cathedral was founded.
3 The Shrine of Our Lady of Walsingham is a legacy of pilgrimages that have taken place to the Norfolk village. They began in the 11th century, when the lady of the manor had a vision commanding her to build a replica of the Nazarene House of the Annunciation.

The departure of a pilgrim from his home village might be attended by great ritual, including a special mass being said and the consecration of the staff, cloak and bag taken on the journey. Bearing a letter from the parish priest confirming his genuine status, the pilgrim would be escorted to the parish boundary and given a further blessing to help him on his way. Once the security of home was left behind and the pilgrimage embarked upon, the journey was intended to be both physical and spiritual – a life-transforming experience. Returning home to his community, the pilgrim might bear holy water and wear emblems associated with the site. Although many cults lost devotees after a generation or two, the more profound underlying reasons for making a pilgrimage serves to explain their continued significance for many today.

Not all pilgrimages were made to prominent shrines, and examples still survive all across England of some of the lesser, more local, ones. The church of St Candida and the Holy Cross at Whitchurch Canonicorum in Dorset is probably unique in that it actually retains the relics of its patroness in a 13th-century shrine. Holy wells featured prominently as places of pilgrimage and some waters were associated with pagan worship long before the Christian practice of baptism was adopted in England – a continuity of bond between people and landscape. In one of the more remote areas of Northumberland, near the village of Holystone, a silent pool is overlooked by a lone Celtic cross. It recalls the time when the missionary Paulinus baptized more than 3,000 people there in AD 627. Although currently named Lady's Well, the spring has also been known as St Ninian's Well, after the Scottish evangelist who predates Paulinus. Although it is linked primarily to the Middle Ages, pilgrimage seems to speak of a timeless inner human need and it has never actually died out – in some areas it is in fact undergoing something of a renaissance. Canterbury apart, two of the more enduring pilgrimage destinations in England are Glastonbury, associated with Joseph of Arimathea, and the Marian shrine to Our Lady of Walsingham in East Anglia. Long popular with women pilgrims as a place of solace, Walsingham is said to mark the site where, in 1061, the Virgin Mary appeared to Richeldis de Faverches, the lady of the manor – the only such visitation in England. The subsequent shrine and adjacent Augustinian priory were victims of the Reformation, but interest in Walsingham revived during the late 19th century. A new statue of Our Lady was carved and now the shrine and Slipper Chapel are visited by Roman Catholics and Anglo-Catholics in the Church of England.

3

PARISH CHURCHES

At the centre of their communities, parish churches were for centuries the settings for the most important events in a person's life — baptism, confirmation, marriage and burial. Over the years the ideal manner of worship changed many times, in response to which parish churches were altered or rebuilt in a new style. From the 13th to the 19th century a priest was supported by his parishioners, either through a landed endowment, a local tax or semi-voluntary donations. Although usually associated with the country, some of England's finest parish churches were built in London by Sir Christopher Wren after the Great Fire of 1666. They include St Paul's Cathedral, one of the great architectural triumphs of the age.

Nowhere in England are the contrasts between different forms of Christian worship more clearly highlighted than in the Gloucestershire market town of Tewkesbury. Located almost within touching distance of one another, the Old Baptist Chapel and the abbey church of St Mary the Virgin were equally revered by the different denominations that created them. Built c.1620, the chapel is the oldest Baptist house in England, following the movement's introduction into the country just eight years earlier. Because the Baptist doctrine required adult baptism only, fonts were replaced by large water tanks — but in Tewkesbury's case, the adjacent River Severn served instead. The chapel has today been restored to its original condition and features a distinctive three-sided wood-panelled gallery with hard bench seating and a pulpit in close proximity to the worshippers. A chapel was the equivalent of a parish church to the nonconformists who worshipped there, and the deliberate absence of elaborate decoration was not seen by them as a barrier to the effectiveness of prayer.

At the other end of the scale, Tewkesbury Abbey is one of the finest post-dissolution churches in England. A cathedral in all but name, its collection of medieval monuments is second only to that of Westminster Abbey. Through the quality of its architecture and fittings, one can glimpse something of the grandeur that would have been a part of most Benedictine churches at the height of the monastic movement. That the abbey managed to survive the Dissolution almost intact is due to the fact that the townsfolk bought it from Henry VIII before his commissioners arrived. The

most dominant feature of the church is its Norman tower, which at 45 m (148 ft) high, is the tallest structure from that period in the country. The interior successfully blends Norman work with later modifications, most notably the 14th-century vaulting to both nave and transepts, whereas the majority of monastic churches retained for parish worship have been significantly truncated. One of the most commonly adopted conversions was to form a church from the chancel, transepts and tower, dispensing with the original nave. In other instances, the nave or one aisle alone has been saved, but in the case of Malmesbury and Croyland abbeys and Binham Priory (Wiltshire, Lincolnshire and Norfolk respectively) the fragments of wall, arches and windows that stand forlorn alongside the surviving segment bear witness to the acts of destruction that took place. Elsewhere, in North Yorkshire for example, there was wholesale removal of the contents and vandalism of the structures of many religious buildings.

As testified by the generosity of the citizens of Tewkesbury, a church was a reflection of its parish. The parochial system as the local unit of church organization in England has existed from pre-conquest days, and arose to replace the minster system in which a larger church served a wider area. It was also connected to the growth of secular clergy, living among those they served, as distinct from regular clergy, who were the educated class of monks subject to religious orders.

Some of the earliest parish churches were founded during the Saxon period in the 10th and 11th centuries, and were often built to replace minsters. Surviving

2

PRECEDING PAGES

1 The ornate chancel of Tewkesbury Abbey, Gloucestershire.
2 An atmosphere of composed simplicity defines the interior of the Old Baptist Chapel, Tewkesbury.

1 Needham Market in Suffolk is endowed with a remarkable example of the skill of medieval carpenters. The nave roof of St John the Baptist is a magnificent achievement, with angels on every beam.
2 Some of the finest bench ends in Cornwall are housed within the secluded church of St Andrew, Launcells. The church boasts almost a complete set of around 60 benches, mostly dating back to the 16th century.
3 The parish church of the delightfully named Norfolk village of Little Snoring has one of the only two detached round bell towers in the country.

Saxon churches or remains also, of course, reveal that they favoured building by accretion, so their roots often go back further still. At this time parish churches were still built by a lord for his immediate family and their tenants, but when the population expanded rapidly during the 11th century, churches had to be enlarged to provide adequate accommodation. That programme was brought to an abrupt halt by the Black Death in the 14th century, when the devastation visited upon whole communities left enlarged churches almost empty. By this time, the major programme of cathedral rebuilding had been completed, freeing skilled labour for the expansion of parish church building if required.

The level of patronage and a church's location clearly affected the quality of finish and the raw material from which it was fashioned. Many of the finest churches are located over, or near to, the limestone belt that curves from Yorkshire to Dorset. The counties that benefit most from having access to limestone quarries are Leicestershire, Gloucestershire, Wiltshire and Somerset – the latter in particular exploiting the stone's fine texture, shown to good effect by a stunning series of finely traceried towers in the Taunton area. The overall prosperity of an area was important too; in some parts of the country very few churches were altered much, yet in wealthy East Anglia almost all churches were rebuilt in the 15th century.

Whether constructed from limestone, flint or timber, no two churches in England are the same, and for more than a thousand years these buildings have lain at the heart of community life. The construction and decoration of a church was the expression of a community's religious faith and a declaration

to those outside the community – that is, the parish – of how they wished the world to see them. These places of social and religious ritual serve as repositories of centuries of communal memories: generations of local people have used them to mark the important stages of life's events through to death itself, and they reflect the wealth or monetary sacrifices of a community, its taste in materials and design, and the very culture of those people for whom it was built to be used.

Prior to the industrial revolution and improvements in transportation, the choice of building materials usually reflected what was available locally. The plentiful supply of timber into the late medieval period enabled there to be a degree of continuity with Saxon times, but whereas many Saxon churches had been built entirely of wood, the vast majority of churches now had at least an exterior fabric of stone. Where wood was used extensively was in the formation of the interior. Some of the best examples of the genre are in East Anglia, at St Wendreda's at March in Cambridgeshire and St John the Baptist's at Needham Market in Suffolk. Both churches

3

are remarkable for the hosts of carved wooden angels that seem to have settled like butterflies on every available beam end or strut from which the elaborate roof structures are formed. St John's mundane exterior belies the astounding feats of carpentry located within. Its nave roof is an excellent example of how medieval carpenters dealt with the problems posed by bridging wide spans without creating too much outward thrust. Wide hammer beams carry tall posts strengthened by lateral struts and also support cambered tie beams.

In addition to making extensive use of timber, East Anglia is also noted for having large numbers of round flint towers, many of them dating back to the late Saxon or Norman periods. Much of the region is devoid of good building stone, but it does have an abundance of flint. The small, irregular-shaped stones were readily gathered from fields, but to make effective use of them for building required large quantities of mortar to act as a binding agent. As it was impossible to create sound and secure corners using flint, the round towers were adopted as the obvious practical solution. In a region

that once bore the brunt of raids from Scandinavia and northern Europe, some of those built near the North Sea coast appear to have been constructed with defence in mind and have been provided with narrow arrow slits.

Other church builders in East Anglia discovered that knapped flints were excellent for exterior decoration when used in conjunction with limestone, the resulting technique being referred to as flushwork. The dark exposed faces of the fractured flints were used to create geometrical patterns on lighter-coloured church walls, an effect that can look quite dramatic if employed with discretion, but rather confusing if overdone. Flushwork is prominent on some of the more lavish Suffolk churches – built as a result of the region's prosperity through the medieval wool trade – and Holy Trinity Church at Long Melford, with its cathedral-like proportions, is finished with flint.

Most of East Anglia's 'wool' churches are remarkable for the height and strength of their towers, features accentuated by the region's relatively flat countryside. The tower and nave were the responsibility of the laity, and it was the tower that soared above the fields as the symbol of a wealthy town or village. For those communities that had grown rich through the demand for English wool, the church was much more than a place of worship – it became the focal point of their ambitions and aspirations and an expression of the solidarity they felt. That communal pride was often manifested through the fabric of the church, which became a means of honouring themselves as well as God, and although they might not confess to it openly, it provided the opportunity for an extravagant gesture to neighbouring villages. The builders, however, were also pious, as is suggested by the noticeable lack of ornamentation inside the great 'wool' churches. Certainly they were well built and used craftsmen of the highest calibre, but the temptation to continue the flamboyance of the tower was firmly resisted when it came to the nave.

But all these are country churches and while their variety of form has played an important role in making the English countryside distinct, over the centuries England has become an increasingly urbanized country. It is in the towns and cities that church building is most likely to reflect the congregation rather than the patron and where one can most readily compare the rich architectural legacy left by generations of architects, builders and craftsmen. Nowhere is this more true than in London. The capital was largely left unaltered by the Normans in the 11th century. During the church building of the 12th century the foundations used were Saxon ones and in terms of parish churches alone, it is believed there were well over 100. As the city prospered, stone came into greater use; then the friars gave fresh impetus and the number of churches continued to grow.

And so the dynamic has continued across the centuries. In recent years the City of London's historical skyline has been transformed by soaring structures of concrete, steel and glass, but for more than 300 years before such development it was steeples, spires and the immense dome of St Paul's Cathedral that dominated views of the capital – the consequence of an inspired period of reconstruction following the Great Fire of London in 1666. In particular, the buildings of Sir Christopher Wren and his younger colleague Nicholas Hawksmoor have come to symbolize the artistic resilience of an age emerging from the dual disasters of plague and fire. Despite war damage, Hawksmoor's six churches and 16 of Wren's original 50 survive today, primarily in the City and the East End, but keen vision and a degree of patience may be needed to track all of them down. The scale and grandeur of these urban parish churches continues to impress today, but their original

1

impact – in a city where the surrounding buildings were much lower – must have been even more remarkable. The innovative vision of both men aroused mixed reactions in their contemporaries and each had to overcome resistance and setbacks in realizing their radical designs.

London was devastated by the fire of 1666, in which over 100 churches and 13,000 medieval wooden houses were lost. 'It made me weep to see it,' wrote the diarist Samuel Pepys. 'The churches, houses and all on fire and flaming all at once.' Reconstruction commenced, and in 1669 Wren was appointed king's surveyor of works and plunged into a major programme of church design and construction. He was to create over 50 new churches, including the handsomely fronted St Martin's, Ludgate, the small and simple St Benet's in Upper Thames Street, and the elegantly furnished St Margaret's, Lothbury, but it took time – more than half of those he designed were not started until 10 years after the fire. A relatively early example of Wren's originality appears in the form of St Clement Danes, built in 1680–82 and set just beyond the City's boundaries. It combines the design of a traditional Gothic church with a centralized plan characteristic of the Renaissance, while also reflecting influences of a classically inspired basilica. Despite his position, Wren did not always have *carte blanche* when designing new churches, a point well illustrated by St Mary Aldermary. A wealthy local parishioner had donated £ 5,000 for the church's reconstruction, but with the stipulation that it should replicate the Perpendicular Gothic style of the original. Wren adhered to his patron's request in shape and form, but nevertheless introduced his own contribution subtly through the magnificent vaulting. He used plaster instead of stone and created delightful little saucer domes between the fans.

The physical environment also exerted an influence upon Wren's designs. Even in 17th-century London restricted urban space encouraged architects to build upwards, directing much of Wren's creative expression towards towers and steeples. The most monumental steeple is arguably that of St Mary-le-Bow in Cheapside, in which the traditional structure is adorned with classical details such as colonnades, balustrades and volutes. None of Wren's towers or steeples are identical, and all reveal individual influences in their design. The five-tiered spire of St Bride's, Fleet Street, has been an important landmark for centuries – and has provided inspiration for thousands of wedding cakes. However, Wren's genius also manifested itself through his treatment of interior space. St James's, Piccadilly – believed by Wren to be his best design for a parish church –

2

marries a plain exterior with a beautifully light, airy interior, complemented by the exuberant wood carvings of the Dutch-born sculptor Grinling Gibbons.

Wren's knowledge of geometry, which is revealed in the Sheldonian Theatre's system of timber roof trusses, enabled him to create sensations of depth, space and light that one might have thought impossible from a basic rectangle. St Stephen's, Walbrook, is an outstanding example of his skill in dealing with a restricted ground area. The interior is a perfect rectangle, divided into bays, aisles and sanctuary by the introduction of 16 Corinthian columns. The central space is covered by a large, lantern-illuminated dome, creating an effect more associated with the Byzantine tradition than that of western Europe. The design, planning and erection of St Stephen's dome were all used by Wren as a rehearsal for the ultimate challenge of St Paul's, where the result is so perfectly placed that the acoustics of the church are considered by many to be the finest in London.

In addition to supervising the ongoing church rebuilding programme, Wren was continuously working on designs for the new cathedral. A solution was represented by his First Model of 1672; it was approved by the king, who sanctioned demolition of the burnt-out ruins and the commencement of work. Despite having the royal seal of approval, Wren's scheme was widely criticized as being too modest, obliging the king to request a more elaborate design. This was duly presented in the form of an intricate wooden model in 1673, referred to as the Great Model (both versions are now displayed in St Paul's). However, the new design was rejected by the clergy for being excessively flamboyant in the manner of European Catholic cathedrals — a resemblance thought inappropriate for a staunchly Protestant England, anxious to preserve the legacy of the Reformation under its newly restored monarchy.

Wren redrafted the plans and eventually came up with an acceptable compromise. This was an adequate blend of Gothic and classical styles, but a design that in his eyes lacked the vital inspiration that sets great buildings apart. A royal warrant for the work was issued in May 1675, the king including a vital clause permitting variation on the approved design that might be 'rather ornamental than essential'.

Because Wren determined to build the cathedral as a whole and not in traditional sections, it would have been difficult to assess the building's form during those early stages, particularly when it was screened by so

2

1 The choir of St Paul's Cathedral is probably the nearest that Protestant England came to the baroque. Its ornate gilded mosaics and saucer domes are extravagant features, not normally associated with a rather restrained Anglican Church.

2 One of Wren's architectural drawings for St Paul's Cathedral. Construction eventually began in 1675, following the architect's presentation of several schemes to King Charles II and church leaders. The version finally constructed was not necessarily the design officially approved.

3 The Dome of St Paul's is still one of the great features of London's skyline, despite modern glass and steel monoliths. It is an outstanding technical and aesthetic achievement.

much scaffolding. The structure that gradually rose from the foundations bore an uncanny resemblance to Wren's own favoured design, the rejected 'Great Model' version, including hundreds of modifications to enhance the monumental nature of the building. Much of the work was carried out using 50,000 tonnes of gleaming white Portland stone. Great blocks of it had to be hauled up from the River Thames and then pulled with great difficulty through the narrow streets. In addition, 25,000 tonnes of other stone, 560 tonnes of chalk and 11,000 tonnes of ragstone were required – the cathedral accounts detail many compensation payments to those whose buildings were damaged by the cumbersome materials.

Progress became so painfully slow that eventually Wren's salary was halved in an attempt to spur the work on at greater speed. By the time his son placed the last stone on the lantern in 1710, Wren was 79 years old. In the meantime throughout the city the phrase 'a St Paul's workman' had become a synonym for slowness. Nevertheless, conceived, planned and built under one man's direction, St Paul's is unprecedented among English cathedrals. It is also an architectural triumph, an articulation of the confidence of an age.

Wren's magnificent creation distilled key elements from the palaces, churches and châteaux of France. This is most notable in the two tiers of paired Corinthian columns that grace the façade, reminiscent of the Louvre Palace, which Wren saw on a visit to Paris before the Great Fire of London. Wren's other sources included the Italian baroque architect Borromini, whose work inspired the twin towers flanking St Paul's west front, and he overcame the technical complexities of supporting the vast dome by studying Ely Cathedral's 'gravity defying' octagonal lantern tower, dating from the 14th century. In St Paul's, a huge outer drum is constructed above an inner, lower dome. This contains a tall cone of bricks, reinforced by iron chains, upon which rests the lightweight timber dome covered in lead sheeting. Light falls onto the crossing below through eight triple openings in the dome.

Working with Wren on St Paul's and other projects was Nicholas Hawksmoor, who became deputy surveyor of works on Chelsea and Greenwich hospitals, two of Wren's most celebrated secular buildings, and was clerk of works at Whitehall, Kensington Palace and Westminster Abbey – where he was later responsible for the west towers. As Hawksmoor moved from the status of protégé to exceptional colleague, his influence can be sensed in the verve and vitality of Wren's later work. Hawksmoor realized his own distinctive fusion of classical authority and Gothic fancy in his six great London churches: St George's in the East; Christ Church, Spitalfields; St Anne's Limehouse; St Alphège's in Greenwich (site of the murder of Alphège archbishop of Canterbury, by the Danes in 1012); St Mary Woolnoth, east of Mansion House in the City; and St George's, Bloomsbury – a relatively late creation and one of the grandest. St George's remarkable stepped steeple is based on Pliny's description of the tomb of Mausolos at Halicarnassus, and an implausibly canonized George I appears as St George on an obelisk.

The architecture of both Wren and Hawksmoor survived to bring a timeless elegance to the capital today. Perhaps the most appropriate epitaph is Sir Christopher Wren's own, a simple Latin inscription inside St Paul's: 'Reader, if it is a monument you seek, look around you.'

MESSAGES OF HOPE & DOOM

THE EXTERIORS OF MANY OF ENGLAND'S CHURCHES HAVE NOT CHANGED A GREAT DEAL SINCE THE 16TH CENTURY, WHEN ATTENTION TURNED TO SECULAR BUILDINGS, BUT THEIR INTERIORS WOULD BE UNRECOGNIZABLE TO RENAISSANCE EYES. DURING THE REFORMATION AND ITS AFTERMATH, ALTARS TO THE SAINTS WERE REMOVED OR DESTROYED, AS WERE STATUES IN WOOD OR STONE. STAINED GLASS, TOO, WAS DEEMED IDOLATROUS, AND SO WERE PAINTINGS THAT ADORNED CHURCH WALLS. FURTHER CHANGES WERE MADE IN THE 19TH CENTURY, WHEN REFORMERS ADVOCATED THAT CHURCH INTERIORS WERE REMODELLED TO INCREASE THE AMOUNT OF PROCESSIONAL SPACE AND GIVE A GREATER EMPHASIS TO THE ALTAR.

WE HAVE BECOME so accustomed to the bare church interiors of today, with their bland, neutral colours of stone and plaster, that it is easy to forget that even the most humble village church was once a riot of colour. Almost every available space was taken up by painted decoration or by representations of the Christian mysteries and the drama of salvation, a biblical story, or the martyrdom of a saint: images that would help ram home to a largely illiterate congregation the essential precepts by which they should live their lives.

Architectural styles and internal layouts of churches vary widely, but the earliest conformed to the basilican plan with a dominant axis leading from the western main door to the chancel, the eastern end of the church facing the rising sun, where the focal point of worship,

the altar, is situated and where the eucharist is celebrated. In the medieval period a cruciform layout evolved with side transepts leading off the main axis, or nave. After 1215, when the doctrine of Transubstantiation was enunciated, it was necessary to separate the nave from the chancel: the nave was reserved for the congregation, while the chancel was the priest's domain where God was present through the sacrament as the bread and wine changed into the substance of the body and blood of Christ. Over time, the physical barrier represented by the chancel screen became increasingly elaborate.

The north side of a church was painted with representations of the Old Testament and the south side with the New Testament. The Last Judgement, Paradise on Earth and an Afterlife for the Righteous were all popular subjects. The ecclesiastical imagery – expressed in

2

1 The restored wall paintings in the nave of St Peter and St Paul, Pickering, give an impression of what medieval churches might have looked like before the Reformation's whitewash obliterated them. The martyrdom of saints was a commonly employed theme and Pickering has a particularly graphic version.

2, 3 St Mary's Church at Kempley, Gloucestershire, is a rare example of a completely painted chancel dating from the mid-12th century. Attempts to uncover them by a 19th-century vicar caused damage, but what remains is remarkable. Almost the entire chancel is given over to an Apocalypse. Rows of apostles line the walls, gazing up at a Christ in Majesty on the low barrel vault.

sculptures (both stone and wood, with highly decorated baptismal fonts first used in Saxon times), mosaics, paintings, and coloured glass as well as wall frescoes — included God, Christ, Mary, the saints, the apostles, heaven and hell, and events from the scriptures and Christian history. During the Puritan era of the post-Reformation in the 16th and 17th centuries, when the worship of images was regarded as idolatrous, many churches had their decoration removed, their stained glass replaced, and their frescoed walls whitewashed.

The role of the paintings located within the nave in sight of the congregation was to teach through the commonly portrayed themes of the Life of Christ and the Saints, the Seven Deadly Sins and the Seven Works of Mercy. Specific topics particularly pertinent to every-day life might include the consequences of swearing (Christ's body being torn apart by those who swear by it) or the warning to gossips (two chattering women seen with a horned devil hovering between them). Last Judgement, or 'Doom', paintings were customarily located above and around the chancel arch, with most of them drawing upon the apocalyptic passages contained within the Gospel of St Matthew. Although artists did usually give equal wall space to the fates of both the blessed and the damned, the latter offered far greater scope for creative interpretation and the horrors of hell were quite graphically portrayed to provide the necessary incentive for sinners to repent in time.

Which saints and apostles were included within the confines of the nave might well have been determined by the individual patron's preferences as he, and not the priest, would have been responsible for the commissioning of and payment for such work. Stained glass windows very often gave as much prominence to biblical stories as to the coats of arms of the church's local patrons. One saint universally represented was St Christopher, patron saint of travellers, who was allocated space by the door so that parishioners would be ensured his blessing for their journey home. Local saints, too, would be important, as was the saint to whom the church was dedicated.

191

*In Fear
& Praise*

3

As congregations grew naves were often rebuilt and aisles added, providing more space for paintings. Quite a large number of parish churches, especially in Devon and Cornwall (such as Holy Cross, Crediton, and St Mary's, Launceston, respectively), were planned with aisled chancels and so the function normally fulfilled by the arch dividing it from the nave was performed by a rood screen, which in some cases was continued across the church's full width. Although that structure was not able to accommodate the 'Doom' paintings found on many arches, they were often highly decorated with figures that, having been painted on wood, have often survived the passage of time. Those that have faded have been easier to restore than their mural counterparts, and some excellent examples survive in churches such as All Saints at Kenton in Devon.

With one or two exceptions, the wall paintings currently visible on parish church walls have been rescued from centuries of obscurity under layers of whitewash. During the Reformation, the Order in Council issued in 1547 decreed 'the obliteration and destruction of popish and superstitious images, so that the memory of them shall not remain in the churches'. The uncovering of old wall paintings has therefore been something of an accidental process, much of which occurred during the 19th century, with varying degrees of success.

Medieval artists applied paint using one of two methods: fresco or secco. In the former technique pigments are painted onto freshly applied plaster, so that the

1

paint becomes bonded to the surface by a process of carbonization. In England, secco was the most commonly used of the two and involved simply painting onto a prepared, dry surface, the paint encouraged to adhere to the plaster by the use of a medium such as oil, egg or animal glue. Paint that has been simply coated onto a plaster surface was obviously more vulnerable than a true fresco, which had greater pigment depth.

Although no parish church has paintings to match the quality of those at Canterbury and Winchester cathedrals or Westminster Abbey, the tiny Norman church of St Mary's at Kempley in Gloucestershire possesses the most complete set of wall paintings anywhere in the country. The chancel is filled with the colour and figures of the 12th-century Romanesque murals, the most powerful of which is an Apocalypse scene painted on the barrel vault. At its heart is Christ in Majesty, surrounded by evangelists, angels and solar bodies, the walls on either side containing apostles, bishops and pilgrims with eyes firmly focused on the events above.

The Kempley murals were originally thought to be true frescoes, but later research suggests that although the paint was applied to wet plaster, the work was finished later using the secco technique. Joins detected in the plaster reveal the extent of each day's work as scaffolding was moved up to reach the next level, but each individual segment was actually too large to have been painted in one session while the plaster was wet.

Church wall paintings largely used natural pigments, the earth colours of red and yellow ochre, lime white and black. Where budget permitted, this was enhanced by the introduction of more exotic pigments, such as blue from lapis lazuli. Lapis lazuli was used to particularly stunning effect in two of Canterbury Cathedral's finest murals, the *Taming of the Viper by St Paul* in St Anselm's Chapel and the *Naming of St John* in St Gabriel's Chapel, both executed during the mid-12th century. In fact, English wall painters were so admired that their skills were in demand across the Continent.

While the loss of so many wall paintings is unfortunate, the wholesale destruction of medieval stained

glass by the 16th century iconoclasts was a major disaster. More than half of England's cathedrals and an even greater percentage of parish churches possess little or no old glass. The sheer brilliance and artistry exhibited in those windows that have survived intact make the loss seem even greater.

The appeal of stained glass to the Christian church was both aesthetic and spiritual in origin. 'Let there be light' are the first words spoken by God in the Book of Genesis and Christ described himself as being 'the light of the world', promising that those who believed in him would become the children of light. Archaeological and documentary evidence shows that coloured glass was used in England during the 7th century: in his *History of the Abbots of Monkwearmouth and Jarrow* Bede reveals that in

675 Abbot Benedict Biscop sent to Gaul for craftsmen to glaze the windows of his monastery at Monkwearmouth.

Stained glass really began to flourish as an art form in Gothic Europe around the mid-12th century, thriving in an architectural climate that sought to eliminate the solid masonry of the Romanesque and replace it with ever larger and more decorative windows, but little in England survives from this era – York Minster's nave clerestory windows contain some panels from a one-time series of narrative windows, one of which depicted the life of St Benedict. The favoured rectangular format of English churches perfectly lent itself to the inclusion of huge expanses of glass, most notably in the east windows of larger churches and cathedrals. Such great windows made spectacular backdrops to the high altar,

1,2 In St Mary's, Fairford, Gloucestershire, every window is used in a chronological journey through Old and New Testaments. Eve and the serpent begin a biblical story that culminates in the Last Judgement on the great west window. The mood changes in the lower right hand panels where purgatory is not a pleasant prospect.

3 St Neot's in Cornwall is another parish church with a remarkable legacy of glass, most of which dates from the 16th century. Its star window is the Creation in which God is seen with mathematical instruments planning the earth and the final panel shows Noah, doffing his cap to God, having received his instructions for the ark.

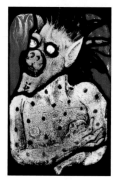

1

the focal point of worship. The great east window in York Minster represents a superb example of work by masons and glaziers, resulting in a window 23.5 x 9.75 m (77 x 32 ft), one of the largest areas of stained glass in the world. Assembled at the beginning of the 15th century, the window took just three years to complete.

The subjects portrayed on windows followed the same themes as wall paintings. The York window depicts God holding a book inscribed 'I am Alpha and Omega', the theme of the beginning and the end continuing from the Creation in Genesis to a monumental Apocalypse cycle based on the Book of Revelation.

When looking at medieval stained glass, it is tempting to linger on the merits of the individuals responsible

2

for the design at the expense of the skills of the glass makers. Colour was a vital consideration and the glass received its tint at the manufacturing stage through the addition of various metallic oxides while the material was in its molten state. Because oxides were introduced into the molten glass in clay pots, medieval glasses are referred to as pot-metals and are particularly noted for the depth and intensity of their colour. One exception to that process concerned the creation of red or ruby glass, which if produced in the normal way would have possessed a colour of such intensity that it would have appeared as almost black. That was overcome by producing what was termed a 'flash-ruby', whereby a thin, even layer of red was blown onto the surface of white glass. By the 15th century, other colours such as green and blue were being produced in the same way to give the glazier greater scope for controlling the use of light and shade within a particular panel. By grinding the surface of a 'flashed' glass, the glazier could expose the white glass beneath to create two colours with one piece.

The parish church of St Mary's, Fairford, Gloucestershire, is the only church in England to have retained a complete set of pre-Reformation stained glass. It was made between 1500 and 1517 under the direction of the king's glazier, Barnard Flower, in his Westminster workshops, and painted by Dutch artists. There are 28 windows in all, following a narrative sequence. The crucifixion dominates the east window and a dramatic interpretation of Christ in Majesty, the Last Judgement and heaven and hell appears on the great west window. One of the window's most impressive features is the management of the two lower panels. Apart from two or three figures in either blue or white, it is composed almost entirely of shades of red.

The glasswork of later periods can, of course, be as beautiful and as instructive. There are many examples throughout the country, including work overseen by the Victorian architects G.F. Bodley at St Helen's, Brant Broughton in Lincolnshire, and St Michael's, Brighton, Sussex, and William Burges at St Mary's, Studley Royal, North Yorkshire.

CHAPTER

6

From the arrival of St Augustine in the 6th century, there
has been an unbroken tradition of learning in England's ancient
cities. Initially monastic, these early foundations continued under royal
patronage after the dissolution. With no other form of education available,
it was left to wealthy laymen to found their own charity schools, many
to later blossom into the great public schools of Victorian England. The
'grammar' schools which offered free education to local boys were a
feature of Tudor England and maintained their role throughout the
following centuries. The ancient universities grew out of religious
institutions attached to monastic foundations, but it was the
19th century which saw a great expansion in education
with the founding of new schools and universities and
the belated provision of education for women.

PILLARS OF
WISDOM

ANCIENT FOUNDATIONS

EDUCATION AND LEARNING WERE THE PROVINCE OF THE CHURCH IN ENGLAND FOR CENTURIES. CELTIC MONASTERIES PRODUCED MAGNIFICENT ILLUMINATED MANUSCRIPTS THROUGH THE LARGELY ILLITERATE DARK AGES AND CULTURED SAXON KINGS SUCH AS AETHELRED AND ALFRED MAINTAINED A TRADITION OF SCHOLARSHIP THAT WAS RESPECTED ACROSS EUROPE. THE FIRST SECULAR FOUNDATIONS OF THE 14TH AND 15TH CENTURIES REFLECTED THE RELIGIOUS LEGACY IN THEIR MONASTIC STYLE OF ARCHITECTURE, ENCLOSED COURTYARDS CONTRIBUTING TO THE CLAUSTRAL ATMOSPHERE. THOSE RECEIVING INSTRUCTION WERE STILL THE PRIVILEGED FEW. EVEN THE RADICAL DEVELOPMENT OF PRINTING, BROUGHT TO ENGLAND IN 1476, COULD BE APPRECIATED BY ONLY A SMALL MINORITY.

THE UNBROKEN TRADITION of learning in England, both in schools and universities, is a remarkable historical achievement. Physical continuity is an important aspect; a few of England's public schools have occupied the same site for a thousand years, often with ruins to match, and several are on World Heritage Sites. One such is the King's School, Canterbury, which claims to be the oldest school in the country. Its list of headmasters only goes back to 1259, but the tradition of learning in the shadow of the cathedral dates back to the arrival of St Augustine in 597. His brief was to convert the English to Christianity, and education played a large part in the process. It was not

long before the novice monks of Canterbury's monastery were busy learning Latin in order to help disseminate the Gospel. They sat at carrels in the cloisters, a system that in Canterbury's case continued up to about 1395, when the cloisters were remodelled and a proper schoolroom was built instead. The claustral system operated in many other religious centres as well, and the schools that emerged from it in Ely and Rochester still exist today.

Most of the early pupils were young boys preparing for the religious life. But the rich sometimes sent their sons to be educated at a monastery, and at Romsey Abbey in Hampshire, regarded as a secure centre of

1

learning in uncertain times, the Saxon nobility sent
their daughters as well. A substantial number of monasteries were sacked in the Viking raids of the 9th century,
but most survived into Norman times. The curriculum
slowly broadened, and sport later began to feature – a
13th-century window in Canterbury Cathedral shows a
boy with a ball and hockey stick, all set for a game. The
schools were still monastic in character, but they were
beginning to reach out also to the wider populace and
become centres of learning serving the whole community, not solely the church.

And they were being copied, notably by William of
Wykeham, who in 1382 founded a new school in
Winchester, catering for 70 poor scholars and 10 'commoners' – sons of the gentry and nobility. Intended as a
feeder school for New College (Wykeham's other foundation at Oxford), Winchester was unique in being the
first school established as a sovereign and independent
corporation, existing 'by and for itself, self-centred and
self-controlled'. It was built close to the cathedral, but
in grounds of its own, its architecture echoing the contemplative nature of the monastic schools - an attractive mix of quadrangles and mellow cloisters designed
to inspire godliness and good learning in its young
charges. Although not the oldest school in England,
Winchester has the oldest school buildings designed for
the purpose and still in continuous use. College Hall is
still occupied by Wykehamists, the scholars still wear
the original quasi-religious black gown, and they still go
on to New College in appreciable numbers.

The language of instruction was also changing as the
14th century advanced. A chronicler, John of Trevisa,
noted in 1385 how 'John Cornwaile, a maister of grammar chaunged the lore in gramar scole and construc-
cion of Frensche into Englische; and Richard Pencriche
lerned that manere teaching of hym... in alle the
gramere scoles of Engelond children leveth Frensche
and construeth and lerneth in Englische.' Significant as
this change was, it still affected only the privileged few.
For most people in the Middle Ages there was no education at all. Apart from a few aristocrats, the only ones

1

able to read or write were the clergy, although the emerging profession of law required literacy as well. The remainder simply grew up illiterate, full of ignorance and superstition. Every village church in England used to have Bible scenes painted on the walls - many still do - to bring God's word to a population unable to study the Good Book for themselves. And every cathedral had a chapter house, where monks gathered daily to have a chapter of the Bible read to them. Other than that, there was virtually no popular education.

Gradually, however, the situation began to improve, usually at the behest of benevolent individuals rather than any central initiative. At Ewelme in Oxfordshire, for example, the earl of Suffolk and his wife (Geoffrey

Chaucer's granddaughter) built a village school in 1437 that continues today, still in the same building, still educating local children 'freely without exaccion of any Schole hire'. Ewelme has not developed into a public school, as most did in similar circumstances, but remains part of the state system, continuing to teach local children free of charge, just as it has always done.

If they could not afford to finance a school by themselves, like-minded individuals sometimes clubbed together instead. Such was the case of medieval guilds (page 76), who extended the principle of a good practical training enjoyed by their own apprentices to others as well. The Mercers' Company was incorporated in 1444, its charter stipulating that it was to found a grammar school in return, better known today as the Mercers' School. The Mercers later took over St Paul's as well, while the Grocers maintained Oundle and the Skinners took care of Tonbridge. The Haberdashers and Merchant Taylors founded their own schools which have endured to the present day, and other guilds did the same. The educational establishments they established were tiny at first, but developed into thriving institutions that have prospered far beyond anything the founding fathers could have imagined.

The greatest founding father of all was Henry VI, an undistinguished king but an inspired educationalist. Impressed by the success of Winchester and New College, he established a similar feeder school at Eton, just across the river from Windsor Castle, to supply undergraduates for his newly founded college at Cambridge. After several false starts, the number of poor scholars to be educated at Eton was fixed at 70, and in 1443 a former headmaster of Winchester was appointed to teach them. Henry took a close personal interest in the school, often visiting the scholars and taking note of their progress. He was angry when they visited in return, telling them 'not to do so again, lest his young lambs should come to relish the corrupt deeds and habits of his courtiers.' Eton still educates 70 scholars on the foundation, but the number of commoners on the roll has risen from the original 13 to almost 1,200.

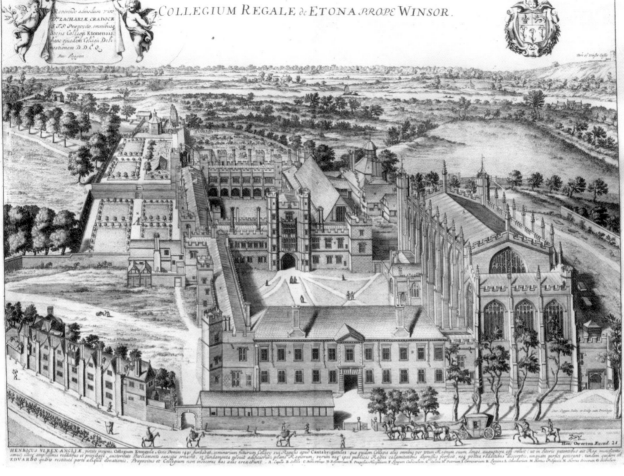

2

3

Chief among Eton's old buildings is the Chapel, begun in 1441 and completed over the next 50 years. It was intended to be much larger, but Henry was murdered during the Wars of the Roses, so only the choir was actually built. The building is a smaller version of King's College Chapel, Henry's other foundation at Cambridge. King's was begun at the same time as Eton, its statutes providing among other things for 16 choristers, 'poor and needy boys, of sound condition and honest conversation, being ascertainably under the age of 12 years'. The college still maintains 16 choristers today, educating them at King's College School. This foundation is perhaps the most famous of several English choir schools, its roots in the ancient statutes of an era when education was beyond the reach of all but the very rich.

Nowadays such schools serve a more privileged clientele. Eton College today is second only to Christ's Hospital as the most lavishly endowed school in the country, boasting a huge selection of investments and a library full of treasures. These include several Caxton volumes, the earliest printed works in the English language. William Caxton did not invent printing, but he did introduce it to England. Educated in Kent – perhaps at Canterbury, which had a Caxton on the monastic roll at the relevant time – he lived abroad for years before returning to Westminster in 1476 with the country's first printing press. 'It is not wreton with penne and ynke as other bokes ben,' he explained, of his first publication, 'to thende that every man may have them attones, ffor all the bookes of this storye empryntid as ye here see were begonne in oon day, and also fynysshid in oon day'.

The first book was a sensation, as were those that followed, including Geoffrey Chaucer's famous tales. Caxton grew rich and other printers joined in. The scene was set for a major expansion of learning, making education available to anyone with access to a book.

EXTENDING EDUCATION

The expansion of learning in the Renaissance, complemented by the European humanist tradition, had a natural impact on English scholarship. Academics such as John Colet instigated the development of grammar schools, an initiative continued by Henry VIII whose secular foundations replaced the cathedral schools of the dissolved monasteries. Many of England's famous institutions began as Tudor grammar schools, and they fostered some of England's greatest literary talents. The availability of education remained limited and only in the 19th century were free elementary schools established for all. Secondary education remained a remote prospect for many until recent times.

A major influence behind England's educational reforms was the scholar John Colet, a friend of Erasmus and Thomas More who was to become Dean of St Paul's. He also founded St Paul's School in 1509 to encourage classical learning in the burgeoning middle class "for boys of all nacions and countres to be taught free in the same in good literature both Laten and Greke'. It was a success from the start and rapidly became a model for other grammar schools around the country. Harrow, Rugby and Uppingham, or example, all began as grammar schools in Tudor England, offering free education to local boys. So did Berkhamstead, Felsted and many others. Some later developed into fee-paying public schools, but others have retained their original purpose, quietly serving the local community for hundreds of years. Dixie Grammar School at Market Bosworth, a couple of miles across the fields from the spot where Richard III charged to his death, was founded in Tudor times on the site of a much older school that had fallen into disuse. The school was rebuilt again in 1828, leaving only a plaque to record its previous 800-year old history on the site.

One of the most interesting of the Tudor foundations was Christ's Hospital. Today it is the richest school in the country, but it was founded by Edward VI as a charitable establishment for the education of London's poor. Only a few years after its foundation, Christ's had 400 children on its books, all wearing the distinctive uniform of black breeches and yellow stockings under a full-length blue coat that continues to this day. The school years were named in recognition of classical heritage and humanist scholarship, progressing through Little Erasmus, Great Erasmus, Deputy Grecians and finally Grecians in the most senior part of the school.

Initially the school occupied the former Greyfriars monastery in Newgate Street, near St Paul's. It lost half its buildings in the Great Fire of 1666, but employed Wren and Hawksmoor, among others, to design the reconstruction. A few years later, Samuel Pepys persuaded Charles II to grant the school a second charter founding a royal mathematical school within the same walls. Boys learned maths and techniques of navigation as a preparation for a life at sea, and Christ's Hospital became the first school in England to study science as a regular part of the curriculum – a possible consequence of having Sir Isaac Newton on the board of Governors.

Christ's Hospital was also a religious institution, as its name implies. The church had enjoyed a monopoly of literacy for centuries and expected to continue playing a major role in education at every level. But times were changing at the beginning of the 16th century and the church was not changing with them. Despite the modernising zeal of John Wycliffe, it remained a backward-looking institution, jealously guarding its privileges and reluctant to address reform. Paying a visit to St Thomas' shrine in Canterbury Cathedral, Colet and Erasmus had been appalled to see the monks selling fake phials of the martyr's blood to gullible pilgrims, or inviting them on payment of a fee to touch a skull that plainly was not Becket's. The murdered saint was a lucrative business to the monks, but to an increasing number of influential thinkers such behaviour was idolatry of the worst kind. In their view, the church needed to reform itself from top to bottom, or else suffer the consequences.

The church failed to reform and monastic power was broken with the dissolution of its establishments by Henry VIII. In seizing the assets of more than 600 monastic houses, many extremely rich, Henry also deprived the cathedral schools of their sources of funding, removing the governing body that took care of them. In 1541 Henry reconstituted them as reformed grammar schools, renaming the cathedral schools of

1 A late Tudor foundation, Dixie Grammar School was founded in 1601 on the site of an earlier establishment that had fallen out of use. It was restored again in 1828, when the plaque was produced to celebrate its historic origins.

2 An engraving of Christ's Hospital, London, dating from 1776. Founded by Edward VI in 1553, the school was located in the former Grey Friars building in Newgate Street. Christ's became known as the 'Blue Coat School' in recognition of its distinctive uniform — long blue coats and yellow stockings.

2

1 Edward the Confessor was
a pupil at Ely's cathedral
school in 1010. After the
dissolution of the monas-
teries, King's, Ely took over
the monastic buildings,
including this gatehouse. It
still occupies them today.

2 The Norman Staircase at
King's, Canterbury was built
20 years before Thomas
Becket's murder in 1170. It
led to a great hall where in
later years pilgrims to his
tomb were accommodated.
Christopher Marlowe won a
scholarship to the newly
renamed school in 1578.

Canterbury, Rochester, Ely, Chester, Worcester and elsewhere as the King's Schools, after himself. They remained in the same buildings as before, with the same headmaster and the same pupils, but with a different set of governing statutes and a new name. In all essential respects, their educational curriculum and links with the past remained unbroken.

Some consequences of this modernisation can be perceived in the next generation, when some outstanding playwrights and poets were active in the country. Shakespeare, Marlowe, Jonson, Beaumont and Fletcher, Kyd, Sidney, Spenser and Nashe served to celebrate the beauty of the contemporary English language. All had well furnished minds and most had attended one of the new grammar schools instead of learning at home. Quite a few were from humble backgrounds and in previous generations might have remained illiterate.

The family of William Shakespeare were unable to read, and he probably acquired his learning at Stratford grammar school. Christopher Marlowe, a cobbler's son, won a scholarship to King's, Canterbury in 1578 – no longer a monastic foundation, although it still used the same buildings in the cathedral precincts. The school's reconstituted statutes of 1541 were typical of the period:

'The boys shall be taught to know the Latin syntax readily, and shall be practised in poetic tales, the familiar letters of learned men, and other literature of that sort. In the Fifth Form they shall commit to memory the figures of Latin oratory and the rules for making verses... Then they shall be versed in translating the most chaste Poets and the best Historians. Lastly in the Sixth Form they shall be instructed in the formulae of *De Verborum Copia ac Rerum* written by Erasmus, and learn to vary speech in every mood, so that they may acquire the faculty of speaking Latin so far as is possible in boys. Meanwhile they shall taste Horace, Cicero and other authors of that class.'

Marlowe proved to be a quick learner. As a scholarship boy, he wore a white surplice on Sundays, joining the procession of King's Scholars which assembled at the school's Norman Staircase and proceeded to the cathedral by way of a gloomy and forbidding passageway known then and now as the Dark Entry. It surfaced later in Marlowe's play *The Jew of Malta*, a memory of his schooldays cheerfully adapted for a scene in which a servant delivers poisoned broth to a nunnery:

'There's a dark entry where they take it in,
Where they must neither see the messenger,
Nor make inquiry who hath sent it them.'

Henry's heir, Edward VI, continued the Tudor commitment to education, establishing many grammar schools in his short reign. Educational opportunities were largely restricted to boys, however, unless girls happened to be aristocratic and supplied with learned tutors and governesses. Elizabeth herself was formidably well educated, capable of conversing in Italian to Italians, and in Latin and Greek to the dons of Oxbridge. She also endowed numerous grammar schools, although these again were designed for boys. Her cousin Lady Jane Grey was considered

CANTERBURY. 15
NORMAN STAIRS.

equally talented, a 16-year-old familiar with Latin, Greek, Hebrew, Italian and French. But for ordinary girls, without access to governesses or tutors, the chances of acquiring even a limited education were not high. Schools for girls did exist – Christ's Hospital took 'poor maiden-children' in a separate establishment – but they were few and far between.

It was many years before the situation improved to any appreciable degree. The Red Maids' School was founded at Bristol in 1634 to educate 40 'poor women-children', and there were any number of short-lived ladies' seminaries in the 18th century, but the absence of any famous girls' schools before the late 19th century speaks for itself. Boys received the lion's share of whatever education was available; girls were left behind.

For the working classes, the situation was even worse. The only education most could hope to receive in the 18th century was a spasmodic attendance at the village school, often housed in a cottage and run by an incompetent, ill-educated teacher purporting to teach the alphabet and not much else. The majority of children were in any case too busy working in the fields – and later the factories – to attend school very often. Plenty of village school buildings survive from the period, but they are almost always small and cramped, with

children of all ages studying together in the same room. As seats of learning, they left a great deal to be desired.

The most significant breakthrough for working-class education came in 1870, when the Government introduced compuslory schooling for the first time. In part this was a consequence of the extension of male suffrage, achieved in the Reform Act of 1867. The prospect of ill-educated masses with influence proved so alarming that the politicans were forced to reconcile the conflicting religious views of educational bodies. Previously schools had been voluntary, funded overwhelmingly by the Church of England. Now, in areas where there were no voluntary schools, local authorities were required to set up and maintain free, non-denominational schools for all children of primary school age. In practice, this meant that most schools at village level continued to be run by the Church of England – a long standing grievance among Dissenters. Although non-denominational, the new board schools were mostly urban, limited to little more than the three R's. However, the radical legislation achieved results: school attendance rose from 1.25 million in 1870 to 4.5 million in 1890, and the money spent on each child doubled. By the end of the century the vast majority of the population could at least read and write.

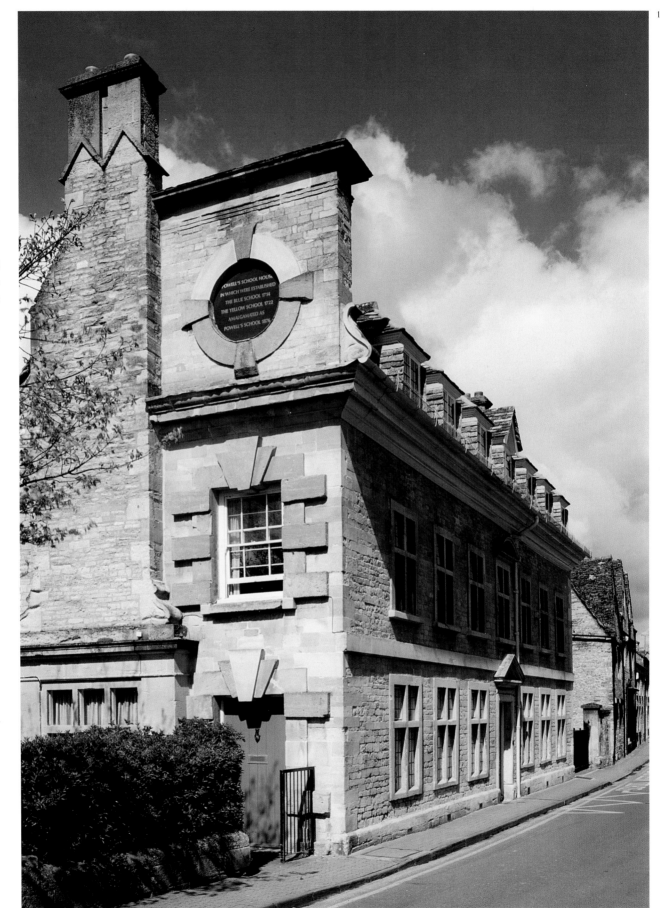

2

1 Powell's School forms an impressive building in Gloucester Street, Cirencester. It dates from 1714 when it contained the Blue School; the Yellow School was added in 1722. The two establishments amalgamated in 1876.

2 William Wordsworth's home in Cockermouth, Cumbria. Together with other Romantic poets, including Coleridge, Shelley and Keats, he became increasingly popular with the rise in literacy in the 19th century.

3 Greens Norton school in Northamptonshire is typical of the local elementary schools of Victorian times. The three Rs were taught, in a utilitarian environment, with little provision for secondary education.

The schools themselves, however, were rather grim. In getting the act through Parliament, the government had committed itself to 'the least possible expenditure of public money' and the new buildings were functional rather than aesthetic. Most were utilitarian in design and looked more like workhouses than temples of learning. And still only a rudimentary schooling was provided – the provision of secondary education was not resolved until 1902.

For much of the 19th century, public schools were the aspirational ideal; many grammar schools had suffered through lack of investment, and the Academies that had

3

served Dissenters well in the previous century had also declined. Dr Thomas Arnold, Rugby's headmaster in the 1830s, sought to reform the public schools through religious services, discipline, monitors and a strong sporting emphasis. Others followed his example, making Victorian public schools a popular social melting pot for the middle and upper classes. The curriculum was somewhat limited for a new industrial economy, and, despite the historic buildings, English secondary education was seldom an intellectual challenge. Matthew Arnold, son of Thomas, condemned it – with some exaggeration – as 'the worst in Europe', producing ruling 'barbarians' and middle class 'Philistines'.

Nevertheless, it did provide opportunities for those able to participate. Girls received little formal secondary education for much of the 19th century and the newly literate working class had largely to fill the gap for themselves. The trade unions ran self-improvement classes, as did an increasing number of working mens' educational associations. And in 1880 the Corporation of London and the livery companies launched a bold new venture, the City & Guilds of London Institute,

with a brief to promote technical education and research. At one level, the Institute set the examination standards for technical apprenticeships; at another. it made a major contribution to Imperial College and other technological institutions. (London University's Queen Mary College in the East End began as a People's Palace of Delight with a technical school attached.) For many seeking university education, such as Jude Fawley in Thomas Hardy's novel, the barrier was physical and absolute: 'Only a wall divided him from those happy young contemporaries of his with whom he shared a common mental life; only a wall – but what a wall.'

Increased literacy brought new enthusiasm for poets such as William Wordsworth – himself educated at Hawkshead grammar school in Cumbria. His championing of nature and the common man against the horrors of industrialization struck a common chord. Hawkshead today has Wordsworth's comment on the pleasure of books painted in large letters on the walls: 'Round these with tendrils strong as flesh and blood our pastime and our happiness will grow' – a reminder of the importance of England's educational achievements.

DREAMING SPIRES

Oxford and Cambridge are not only England's oldest universities; they are amongst the most famous educational institutions in the world. The medieval architecture of many Oxbridge colleges — courts, quadrangles and rooms resembling monastic cells — is evidence of their original religious connections. Diverse architectural styles celebrate the colleges' secular power and prestige. Colleges such as Christ Church and Trinity, founded by Wolsey and Henry VIII respectively, were set in opposition from the outset, and the Civil War also saw divided allegiances in the universities. Competition from other universities in the 19th century forced Oxbridge to adopt a more liberal curriculum and improve academic standards.

LIKE THE CATHEDRAL SCHOOLS, both Oxford and Cambridge Universities began as religious institutions attached to adjacent monasteries. It had been the practice for English scholars, always clerks in holy orders, to complete their education at the University of Paris, where they studied canon law at the behest of Henry II. But Henry quarrelled with the king of France in 1167 and ordered the scholars home. They settled at Oxford, where the monks of Osney Abbey and St Frideswide's Priory gave lectures on Roman law and theology. From these slender origins developed one of the most famous universities in the world.

The early students lived in halls of residence, of which only Beam Hall in Merton Street now survives. Later they became attached to colleges, religious foundations centred around a chapel and the cloistered calm of a quadrangle, with monastic-style cells for sleeping quarters — a pattern that continues today. The colleges were originally developed to provide food, maintenance and an element of protection to the young and impoverished scholars, some of whom were only 14 or 15 years old. The oldest college is probably Merton, with a chapel dating from 1290 and a quad from the 14th century; Balliol was established at much the same time.

Cambridge developed in a similarly arbitrary way, the consequence of a 'town versus gown' quarrel at Oxford. A prostitute was killed in 1209, the town hanged two students in revenge, and the situation became so unpleasant that a number of scholars took refuge in the Fens, where there were abbeys and monasteries to sustain them. The oldest college

building in Cambridge is the chapel at Jesus, formerly the church of St Radegund's nunnery. The college moved into the nunnery and found the buildings ready-made, including a dining hall that now has been in continuous use for more than 800 years. Additional accommodation was later built on the same monastic pattern, notably the 17th century range where Samuel Taylor Coleridge had ground floor rooms. A friend remembered him there in 1791, tossing Aeschylus and Plato aside in order to discuss Edmund Burke's latest pamphlet over supper.

But if Oxbridge colleges began as religious institutions, their subsequent development owed much to the traditions of the grand country house — those wonderfully palatial establishments that noblemen designed for themselves from the Middle Ages onwards (page 256). Knole, Audley End, Hampton Court and many others were all built as a series of quadrangles, one leading on to the next to impress visitors and emphasize the owner's standing in the world. Quite often these owners endowed an Oxbridge college as well, so it was only natural that they should employ the same architect to do the same thing again in a university setting.

A good example is St John's College, Cambridge, founded in 1511 by the will of Henry VII's mother, Lady Margaret Beaufort. The splendid gateway was built to withstand a siege — and indeed took a battering from Parliamentary forces during the Civil War, when the original statue of St John was removed and lost. Restored after the king's return, the gateway boasts the Tudor rose, the Beaufort portcullis, the

1

effect. The whole place is presided over by a magnificent Master's Lodge in which Lady Margaret's portrait takes pride of place. The Master of St John's might not be a medieval baron, but he is certainly housed like one.

It is a similar story in other colleges, albeit some more than others. Oxford's grandest college, Christ Church, owes its origins to the vanity of Cardinal Wolsey, Henry VIII's chief minister. Not content with building Hampton Court, he wanted to build something comparable at Oxford, to be called Cardinal College, but fell from grace before the work was completed. Henry VIII took it over, but it was another century before Christ Church was finished, by which time the college was grand enough for Charles I to use it as his headquarters during the Civil War.

It is no coincidence that Henry was responsible for Cambridge's grandest college, Trinity. Irritated by Wolsey's pretensions, he was not to be outdone when it came to lavish endowments. Trinity and Christ Church both have an enormous main court (or quad) with a fountain in the middle; Trinity's is slightly larger. Nevile's Court at Trinity was built after Henry's death, although its cloisters are traditionally medieval, with doorways leading off to the undergraduates' rooms. The flagstones have such a resonant echo that Sir Isaac Newton used them 300 years ago to calculate the speed of sound, stamping his foot and measuring the time it took before the echo return to him.

royal coat of arms and a recurring pattern of marguerite daisies (to symbolize Lady Margaret). All the trimmings signified an important establishment within, backed by a rich and powerful patron. St John's three courts (Cambridge never calls them quadrangles) then unfold one after the other, adding considerably to the

Much of the money for the college buildings was acquired from the dissolution of the monasteries, the

2

endowments being transferred from the church to the colleges. There was a certain logic to this, since the most scholarly monasteries had enjoyed quasi-university status in medieval times. The academically minded monks simply moved to the universities after the dissolution, bringing their books with them. Archbishop Parker happily pillaged Canterbury's monastery to furnish the library of Corpus Christi at Cambridge. The books included King Alfred's copy of *The Anglo-Saxon Chronicle*, Thomas Becket's Psalter, and a 6th-century Gospel probably belonging to St Augustine. Today the collection is worth over one billion pounds and Canterbury Cathedral would dearly like it back.

The intellectual excitement of the Reformation was followed in due course by the more prosaic upheavals of the Civil War, which affected both universities badly. Most colleges were for the king, some melting down their plate to pay for his troops. Most of the townspeople were for Parliament, investing the traditional town versus gown hostilities with a sharper edge. It was not until long after the Restoration that either university was in any shape to consolidate its position and start planning again for the future. A burst of architectural activity followed, transforming Oxford in particular from a sleepy collection of medieval cloisters to something altogether more distinguished. Sir Christopher Wren built Tom Tower and the Sheldonian Theatre, Nicholas Hawksmoor the Clarendon Building and James Gibbs the Radcliffe Camera, the world's first library in the round. The buildings were extraordinarily bold and adventurous for their time, but unfortunately both universities went into a steep decline during the 18th century. This was largely because the individual colleges enjoyed far more power than the

university, yet remained resolutely monastic in outlook. Among other things, they persisted in reserving academic posts almost exclusively for celibate clergymen – a outdated medieval concept. The situation became so grave that in 1750 only 190 freshmen entered Oxford and 127 Cambridge, about half the figure of early Stuart times. Few were poor scholars hoping to enter the church; most were young gentlemen idling time away before a Grand Tour. Aristocrats did not even have to sit exams, and serious scholars were better off at Edinburgh Univesity or Trinity College, Dublin.

Improvements occurred in the 19th century, largely due to competition from new universities. In 1871 religious entrance restrictions were finally abolished, allowing Noncomformists to study for degrees as at London and Durham (both founded in the 1830s). The curriculum widened to include the natural sciences and other new subjects, and women's colleges were founded, such as Girton (1869), Newnham (1875), Lady Margaret Hall (for Church of England students) and Somerville (for others) in 1878. Despite the fake medieval crenellations of the Gothic revival, Oxbridge at the end of the 19th century was moving closer to modern times.

3

CHAPTER

7

Cromlechs, barrows, funerary brasses, tombs and churchyard monuments were all created to honour the dead, and to mark
their status in life. England is particularly rich in such visual reminders
of past lives. Current advances in archaeology allow a much greater
understanding of such burials. The great variety of funerary monuments
in England's parish churches is unparalleled anywhere in the world.
Tombs of recumbent knights and their ladies get ever more decorative
as the centuries pass until they reach their zenith in the great
architectural confections of the 17th century, tiered like wedding
cakes and ablaze with marble and gilt. The Victorian
era marked an explosion in sentiment as rows of
temples, obelisks and weeping angels
were erected to the memory of
countless loved ones.

DEATH & REMEMBRANCE

EARLY TOMBS

ANCIENT BURIAL PLACES ARE AMONG THE MOST IMPORTANT ELEMENTS OF ENGLAND'S EARLY ARCHAEOLOGICAL RECORD. THEY PROVIDE A WIDE RANGE OF ANTHROPOLOGICAL AND HISTORICAL INFORMATION, PARTICULARLY WHERE GRAVE GOODS ARE PRESENT TO HELP ESTABLISH RELIGIONS AND CULTURAL PROVENANCE. FROM THE EARLIEST SURVIVING PREHISTORIC BARROWS TO THE SUTTON HOO SHIP BURIAL, THEY CAN INDICATE TRADING LINKS, BELIEF SYSTEMS, MEDICAL DETAILS AND THE CHANGING RELATIONSHIP OF PEOPLES AND CUSTOMS. NEVERTHELESS, SUCH EVIDENCE IS OF NECESSITY PARTIAL AND THE COMPLEXITY OF MUCH EARLY ENGLISH HISTORY REQUIRES IT TO BE INTERPRETED WITH CAUTION.

Many of England's prehistoric burial sites are found in the Wiltshire countryside. The hump-backed mounds of boulders and chalk that dominate the landscape date from before 4000 BC and extend through the Neolithic and Bronze ages. The henges at Avebury and Stonehenge are surrounded by clusters of both round and long barrows, structures in which piles of earth have been heaped over wooden or stone burial chambers. In contrast to our modern view of graves, such barrows provided collective burial sites to which new bones were added over time and the diverse chambers of which may have reflected the houses of the living.

West Kennet Long Barrow is one the largest and best preserved Neolithic burial chambers in England. It is thought to have been in use from approximately 3500 to 2000 BC, when it was finally sealed by the so-called Beaker people. Although it exceeds 91 m (300 ft) in length, the actual stone-lined burial chamber, divided into five inner rooms, extends inwards for only about 12 m (40 ft). The hump-backed mound was excavated from parallel ditches on either side, while the separate inner chambers were constructed from sarsens of local origin, and roofed with flat capstones. The huge stones now guarding the tomb entrance were used to close it, following the backfilling of the chambers and passage with chalk, earth and rubble. While the tomb was still in use, a curved forecourt provided space for funerary rituals. At Crichley Hill near Gloucester, the site of several prehistoric monuments from the Neolithic era to the Iron Age, a shallow mound placed in a ditch is complemented by a circular platform edged with stones. Some archaeologists believe that such platforms may have once accompanied most barrows and

been lost through ploughing. Ceremonies outside the tomb may have held greater significance than the bones within, regularly disturbed to accommodate fresh burials. At West Kennet, fewer than 50 individuals were buried in the ancestral barrow and only one was a complete skeleton; piles of vertebrae and long bones had been tidied into heaps, and skulls placed along one wall. Analysis of the bones revealed that the four side chambers and the larger end cavity were divided by age and sex, and several of the bones had been interred long after any flesh had rotted away.

Wayland's Smithy in Oxfordshire, named centuries later for Wayland the Smith of Saxon myth, is another Neolithic communal tomb. It was built in two stages, one slightly before West Kennet and the other slightly later, and contained parts of more than 40 bodies. The original mortuary chamber of wood had been strengthened by surrounding sarsens and covered by a mound of chalk, secured by stones; large slabs designate the barrow's end.

The chambers of the long barrows have yielded large quantities of pottery fragments from different periods and other small grave goods such as beads, flint tools and animal bones. More comprehensive finds have been associated with the later round barrows, which came into use towards the end of the Neolithic era and continued well into the Bronze Age. Significantly, round barrows usually represented the graves of individuals, normally males, rather than groups of ancestral bones, and cremation became increasingly common. Ashes were interred in an earthenware urn and accompanied by early grave goods, including the hallmark bell-shaped beakers (for which the Beaker people were named), delicate stone arrowheads and metal tools and weapons.

2

3

1

Relatively few burial sites have been discovered
from Iron Age Britain, excepting the 'Arras culture' of
localized settlements at Wetwang Slack in Yorkshire.
Excavations have revealed elaborate burials involving
chariots and carts, presumed to be the province of tribal
chiefs and their families. An unusually plentiful array of
grave goods accompanied the person whose ashes were
buried around 10 BC at the site of present-day Welwyn
Garden City. These included five amphorae containing
the equivalent of 350 bottles of wine, a silver drinking
cup, a bronze plate and knife, food stored in numerous
pots, a gaming board and pieces and several items of
jewellery. Ordinary people were probably cremated,
given water burial or interred in simple style.

Roman burials, even before the impact of
Christianity, were relatively sparse, with minimal grave
goods. Burials took place in cemeteries outside the city
walls, with bodies interred in stone sarcophagi for the
affluent, wooden coffins for middle-ranking citizens and
simple shrouds for the poorest. Their tombstones
showed some of the first portraits of individuals or
family groups rather than abstract symbols or gods.
Many such carvings in the cemetery at Colchester were
desecrated during the Iceni uprising of AD 60, memorials to distinguished legionaries proving a particular
target for Boudicca's rebellious tribal forces.

Grave goods are recurrent features of Saxon burials,
reflecting practices that were common in much of
northern Europe. After the departure of the Romans
and the complex population movements of the 5th
century AD (page 20), variations in the burial patterns of
southeast England do indicate some degree of cultural
change. A rich vein of Saxon burial sites has been
unearthed in this region, often containing sophisticated
metalwork – shields and weapons, elaborate brooches
and jewellery, although their distribution is not rigidly
determined by gender. The presence of Roman
objects, such as the prized
Samian ware ceramics,
or items of British
origin adopted as
Saxon heir-
looms, com-
plicate the
analysis fur-
ther. Nor,
in the early
decades of
Christian
resurgence in
England, do

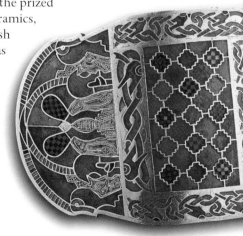

3

grave goods always provide clear demarcation between Christian and pagan beliefs. St Cuthbert, for example, was buried at Lindisfarne in 687 adorned with robes and jewels, and provided with a cross, a portable altar and a copy of St Jerome's Gospel.

As Christianity became established in England, however, grave goods were gradually abandoned in favour of simple, unaccompanied burials. Among the final flourishes of neo-pagan culture was the celebrated Sutton Hoo ship burial, which was excavated from an escarpment overlooking the Deben estuary in Suffolk in 1939. The site was known to be a barrow cemetery and archaeologists

2

discovered in the largest mound the skeletal framework of a ship. Its timbers, and indeed the body it contained, had long since disintegrated in the acid sand, but iron fittings indicated the position of a central coffin, around which magnificent grave goods were deposited. These included the famous helmet, a sword decorated with gold and garnets, elaborate jewellery and an ivory chess set, arousing speculation that this was a royal burial site. It is now believed that the grave was that of Raedwald, king of the East Anglians, who died around AD 625 — a date contemporary with gold coins found in an exquisitely decorated purse. The possessions were appropriate to a warrior king of the 7th century; silver 'baptismal' spoons indicate a possible Christian influence, although this is at variance with traditional ship burials.

Even with the actual skeleton, graves are a complex legacy to interpret. A Viking axe in a grave at St Wystan's Church at Repton in Derbyshire reveals an intriguing combination of pagan and Christian beliefs. Despite such inconsistencies a general pattern emerges in which cremation and grave goods were replaced by relatively modest burials. The modification reflects the growing power of English Christianity, and the absorption of diverse cultures into an evolving national fabric.

MONUMENTS OF DEATH

Memorials to the deceased, whether idiosyncratic or conventional, often say more about the society that constructs them than the individuals they commemorate. Grief may be universal but it is expressed in a social and cultural context, particularly through funerary architecture designed to impress future generations. England's churches and grave-yards contain a rich diversity of memorials, from simple crosses and discreet brasses to the elaborate Victorian tombs that revel in conscious sentiment. They reflect the country's religious changes, secular fashions and artistic styles and show how individuals of the past adjusted to the inevitability of bereavement.

For the majority of people from Saxon times up to the later Middle Ages, anonymity in death was as certain as the act of dying itself. Intermural burial (burial inside a church) was not sanctioned until the Council of Nantes in 658, and for some time afterwards outside burial remained the normal practice. Some use was made of both head-stones and footstones in medieval town and village churchyards, but they never exceeded 0.9 m (3 ft) in height and carried no inscriptions. Their use declined gradually, and had ceased by the end of the 14th century. A person of importance, such as a local lord and

his family, would probably have secured a place inside the church, perhaps in a dedicated family chapel (page 223), but for the majority of the population the large churchyard cross, signifying holy ground, served as a communal epitaph.

Some of the earlier memorials used in churches and cathedrals were coffin lids made in the late 11th century from slabs of imported Tournai marble or Caen stone, but they lacked significant decoration. Later versions from the 12th century carried more elaborately engraved imagery, such as one in Ely Cathedral that commemorates Bishop Nigellus, whose soul is shown

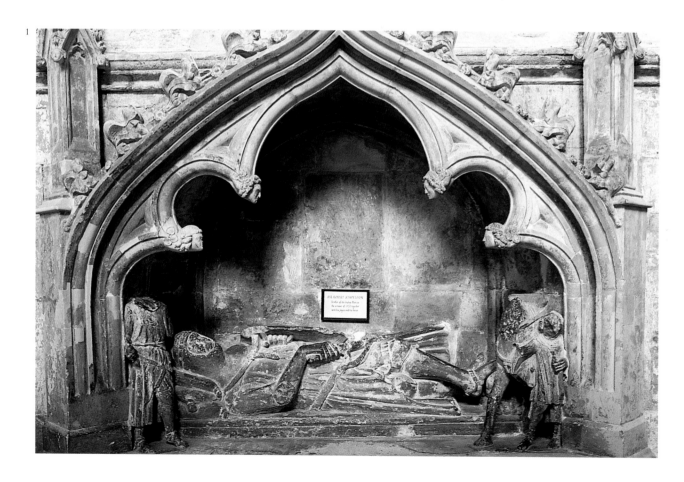

1 The tomb of Sir Richard Stapledon, who died *c.*1320, in the north choir aisle of Exeter Cathedral exhibits many of the features associated with knight effigies of the early medieval period. An ornate canopy emphasizes his status as a member of one of north Devon's leading families.

2 The brass of Sir Robert de Septvans in St Mary's Church, Chartham, Kent, is one of the earliest military brasses in the country, dating from the early 14th century. This life-size monument is remarkable for the minute details in the armour, most notably the extraordinary wing-like epaulettes on the shoulders, known as *ailettes*.

being transported to heaven in the hands of a severe-looking angel. It was also during the 12th century that effigies began to appear, usually as memorials to past bishops. They were executed in low relief and carved out of the stone surround.

Bishops were also those most commonly featured on carved tombs in the early decades of the 13th cen-tury. They were gradually joined by knight effigies, medieval warriors portrayed in helmets and full armour: many bear a shield on one arm and appear to be either draw-ing or sheathing their swords. One of the most celebrat-ed of English knight effigies appears on an unknown tomb in Dorchester Abbey, Oxfordshire, dating from 1280. The carving has been interpreted as a knight about to engage in his final duel with Death, and features a recumbent figure charged with a remarkable latent ferocity. The swirling drapery of his surcoat brings a touch of naturalistic energy to the cool stone.

Similarly powerful, monumental sculptures from the 13th century occur on the magnificent tombs of the Knights Templar in the Temple Church in London. Their prone, crossed-leg posture was a sepulchral fashion that lasted well into the 14th century. It was succeeded in aristocratic echelons by a more static, devotional posture with hands joined in contemplative prayer. Whether this manifested an expression of real faith or merely conventional piety depended upon the skill of the artist concerned.

A public expression of very private grief occurs in the Eleanor Crosses, commissioned by Edward I in 1290 after the death of his queen, Eleanor of Castile. His mourning lament 'my harp is turned to mourning, in life I loved her dearly, nor can I cease to love her in death' took physical form in the construction of 12 similar crosses, to be placed at the 12 resting points of the cortège on its journey from Lincoln to Westminster Abbey. Three of the Eleanor Crosses survive, at Geddington in Northamptonshire, Hardingstone in Bedfordshire and Waltham Abbey in Hertfordshire, and their legacy also lives on in the name of Charing Cross, the final halt on the queen's last journey to Westminster.

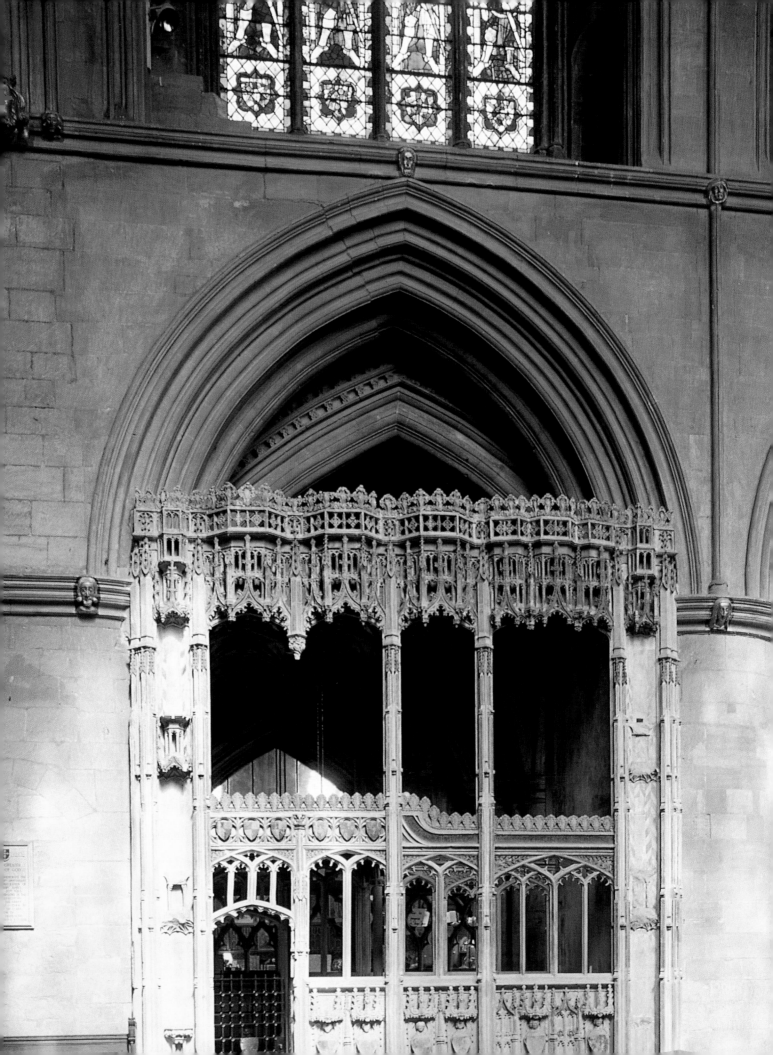

2

1 Tewkesbury Abbey in Gloucestershire is endowed with some of the finest chantry chapels. The Beauchamp Chapel is a fine expression of the Perpendicular; its repeated canopy and gable motifs give the chantry an unusually vivacious style.

2 Alice duchess of Suffolk is portrayed in exquisite detail on her 15th-century alabaster tomb in St Mary's, Ewelme, Oxfordshire.

3 The Eleanor Cross at Geddington is one of 12 memorial crosses erected by Edward I. They served to mark each of the places where the cortège bearing the body of his queen, Eleanor of Castile, rested on its journey from Harby near Lincoln to London.

For the majority of Edward's subjects, even a free-standing effigy in stone or marble proved to be prohibitively expensive. An alternative memorial developed in the form of an engraved brass, a style that escalated rapidly in popularity. The earliest depictions of knights were of full length and there exist some noteworthy examples: Sir Robert de Bures' brass at All Saints, Acton, Suffolk, dates from 1320; Sir Robert de Septvans' at St Mary's, Chartham, Kent, four years later; and one each of Sir John D'Abernon and his son at St Mary's, Stoke D'Abernon, Surrey, date from the 1320s. All exhibit meticulous reproductions of the knight's armour, and where there is chainmail every link has been etched accurately in the metal.

Cheaper than stone, brasses were actually made from latten, an alloy similar to brass but made from copper and zinc, which was then hammered into thin sheets. Because they could be virtually mass-produced, the quality of the brasses varied substantially, from a very high standard to poorly designed efforts showing limited technical competence. Some wealthier clients in the east of England took their custom abroad to Flemish metalworkers, whose methods of production were considered superior, not least in the way the brass was composed. The Flemish engraved rectangular sheets of brass with figures, background and appropriate heraldic ornamentation, whereas the English favoured cutting out the different elements individually. When affixed to the matrix stone, the latter method frequently resulted in unsightly gaps being visible, which detracted from the finished work.

As production techniques improved and brasses became readily available, so they became increasingly more affordable to lay society, and were consequently an illustration of a more flexible social structure. During the 14th and 15th centuries, brasses of newly affluent merchants began to appear alongside those of knights, lords and ladies. In the parish church of All Saints at Stamford in Lincolnshire, the 15th-century brass of John Browne and his wife reflect the contemporary concerns of those with recently acquired wealth and social status. He wears a purse at his waist and two woolsacks lie at his feet, symbols of the foundation of his fortune. His wife flaunts the latest high fashion, including an elaborate and popular headdress of incongruously horned design.

Portraiture as a means of identification did not exist at that time and few attempts were made by artists to achieve any form of likeness. Sculptors and patrons seldom encountered one another, and although the requirements of a memorial might be laid down in quite specific detail, individual features were not expected to be accurately reproduced. Artists occasionally

3

1 The Sackville Chapel within
   the parish church of St
   Michael and All Angels at
   Withyham, East Sussex
   contains a wonderful array
   of family memorials. One of
   the most arresting is the
   white and grey marble
   monument to Thomas
   Sackville, who died in 1667
   at the age of 13.

2 Hidden away in the Wind-
   rush Valley in Oxfordshire,
   the tiny village of Swin-
   brook houses one of the
   more endearing family
   tombs. Six members of the
   Fettiplace dynasty are
   immortalized in matching
   trios of effigies. Although
   separated by only 70 years,
   they seem centuries apart
   in style.

took account of a person's reputation in life, endowing the subject with facial expressions appropriate to their deeds, but an appearance commensurate with social rank or occupation was the norm. Fashions, both civilian and military, were portrayed with minute attention to details of style, colour and content. Funerary sculpture is consequently often an invaluable aid to historians of medieval dress.

In conscious rejection of such worldly decadence, a trend for portraying the body's physical dissolution on tombs emerged from France in the early 15th century. Such tombs emphasized the role of the body as an expendable vehicle for the soul, the degeneration of one leading to the liberation of the other. The style was first

adopted in England by leading members of the clergy, Bishop Fleming of Lincoln providing the earliest known example. His tomb features a traditional sculpted effigy on the top, counterpointed by a skeletal cadaver directly beneath. Abbot Wakeman of Tewkesbury Abbey took the theme even further by abandoning all his vestments and appearing as a skeletal corpse, over which a variety of unappealing creatures crawl and slither.

Some of the more sumptuous tombs of the 15th and early 16th centuries were encased within their own miniature chapels known as chantries. The term derived from the chantry, an intercessionary mass recited for the wellbeing of a founder during his lifetime and for the continued repose of his soul after death – a practice significantly reduced after the Reformation. The presence of chantries is usually restricted to larger collegiate or abbey churches and cathedrals, because the endowment of a chantry was very much the preserve of a wealthy individual. Such an endowment was usually in the form of rent from lands, which would pay for the services of one or more priests to undertake a daily ritual entirely separate from the formal conduct of services within that church.

The establishment of chantries resulted in many priests, whose stipends came directly from the endowments, performing no other religious or pastoral duties other than the recital of masses for the deceased several times a day. Chantries allowed rich men and their families the psychological comfort of knowing that the future welfare of their souls could be influenced by continuing actions in this life; it also created a bridge between the living and the dead.

The importance attached to the endowment of a chantry is well illustrated by the history of the Cantilupe Chantry within Lincoln Cathedral. Founded in 1345 during the lifetime of Nicholas and Joan Cantilupe, the endowment initially provided for two chaplains to say occasional masses on their behalf. Thirteen years later, and following the death of Nicholas Cantilupe, his widow's anxiety became more acute, and the endowment was increased to five chap-

HEARE LIETH THE BODY OF WILLIAM / FETIPLACEE SQVIER SONNE AND HEYR
OF ALEXANDER FETIPLACEE SQVIER HEES / POWSE ELIZABE HASHFIELDDAVGHTERANO
HEYROF SEOMVNDASHFIELD KNIGHT HEHADI / VETSONNS HE DECEASOTEI DAYOFMAYI 602

HEARELVETHFIE BODY OF ALEXANDER / FETIPLACESONNEA HEVREOFANTHO
NVEFFTIPL ACEESQVIER HEWASFIRSTSPO / WSEOTOANN OAVCHTERANOHROFWILLIAM
ESQVIERFENTOCOORITY ASHLLOHEHAOISVE550 / NNSANO7OAVGFEESILON CESEOTEI OFSEPEYIO.0M

lains reciting masses on a daily basis. Even that was later deemed insufficient and more assets were realized; after her death the chantry establishment included a warden and seven chaplains, a substantial house and an elaborate tomb in the cathedral for the founders.

One particularly telling comment about the supposed benefits of chantries to their benefactors is inscribed on a tomb inside Tewkesbury Abbey. The abbey is renowned for having several splendid memorials, including the famous Despenser Chapel, which features a knight on its roof who, kneeling, faces the high altar in prayer. All the most prestigious chantries are clustered near the altar, but the tomb, as its inscription observes, occupies a less exalted position:

Here I lie at the Chancel door
Here I lie because I'm poor:
The further in, the more you pay
Here I lie, as warm as they.

Not all chantry endowments served self-interests, however. Several have been responsible for the foundation of ancient educational establishments, from Winchester and Eton to many of the small village schools that developed during the 15th century to enable rural children to receive some perfunctory schooling. Parish churches have also benefited from such legacies, and in some cases patrons made provision for substantial rebuilding works to take place – one such was St Augustine, Stoke by Clare in Suffolk, which received a new nave in 1535 following the establishment of a foundation by Matthew Parker (later to be archbishop of Canterbury under Queen Elizabeth I).

One of the most impressive architectural and monumental chapels of that era is the Beauchamp Chapel within the Collegiate church of St Mary in Warwick. Commissioned in his will by Richard Beauchamp earl of Warwick, who died in 1439, the family chapel was begun in 1442 and took 21 years to complete at a cost of nearly £2,500. Delightful as the surroundings are, it is the tombs and monuments – as well as the marvellous anachronisms – that draw the eye. Beauchamp's gilded tomb stands in the centre of the chapel: he is clad in a style of armour that originated in Milan a decade after his death. His hands are raised in supplication but held slightly apart, so that his gaze might constantly rest on a roof boss of the Virgin Mary. The effigy is encircled by an unusual cage-like construction known as a 'hearse' –

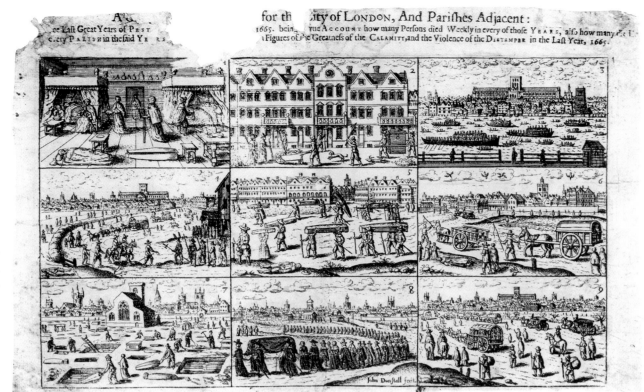

A[...] for th[...] ity of LONDON, And Parishes Adjacent:
[...]e Laft Great Years of Pest 1665. bein[...] rue Account how many Persons died Weekly in every of thofe Years, alfo how many [...]
[...]ery Parish in the faid Years [...] Figures of [...]e Greatnefs of the Calamity, and the Violence of the Diftamper in the Laft Year, 1665.

John Dunftall fecit

one of only three in the country, the others being over the tomb of William I's son, Robert, in Gloucester Cathedral and the Marmion tomb at West Tanfield in North Yorkshire. It is thought that the hearse was used to support some form of fabric covering, which would be withdrawn from the effigy during the mass recital. The Beauchamps' illustrious neighbours are members of the Dudley family; their brightly coloured tombs include those of Robert Dudley (Queen Elizabeth's favourite courtier) and his wife, their infant son and Dudley's brother Ambrose.

The contrast between the late medieval simplicity of the Beauchamp tomb and the garish decoration of the late 16th century reflects the changes in attitude towards death that took place in Elizabethan England as a consequence of the Reformation and its aftermath. The Protestant doctrine of the afterlife, in which the living could no longer assist departed souls by prayer, made the deathbed an irrevocable turning-point. Life became essentially a preparation for death, a concept powerfully expressed by the 17th-century dean of St Paul's, John Donne (author of the celebrated *Songs and Sonnets*), in an extraordinary sermon, 'Death's Duel', preached shortly before his own death in 1631. In his memorial sculpture Donne wears a shroud, a concept for which he posed alive to indicate to the sculptor, Nicholas Stone, how the fabric might hang from his standing form. The modified emphasis of funerary ritual was reflected in the fashions of tombs. Hands were

still closed in prayer, but the monuments now represented a final summation of the earthly achievements that would determine the occupant's fate. Social status was important in these memorials and tombs were decorated accordingly.

One item of centuries-old church furnishing was expressly spared from the ravages of the Reformation: family memorials and tombs. These were held in high esteem, and the craftsmanship that might otherwise have gone into the creation of rood screens was instead lavished on these pieces. In St Mary's at Great Brington, Northamptonshire, 20 generations of the Spencer family lie in tombs in the church's north chapel. These sculptures, the final resting-places of centuries of locally important figures, remain today both as a testament to artistic skills and as a symbol of the imperishable connection between a family, the community, the parish church and the hereafter.

The insecure nature of historic existence was compounded by epidemics of plague. The Great Plague of 1665 was the last, and not even the most severe, of several recurrent outbreaks. The Black Death in the 14th century, for example, decimated populations across Europe, reducing them from an estimated 6 million to 4 million, its victims mostly anonymous in their demise and disposal. Plague lingered in England for centuries, and its social effects included a great upheaval in rural society, agriculture, and the economy. Thousands of villages were abandoned or reduced to ruins: the inhabi-

1 The graphic depiction of life and death in London during the Great Plague of 1665. Although some mass burial sites were established outside the City's walls, other victims were interred in the normal manner. As a result, churchyards were overwhelmed, and corpses buried dangerously near the surface perpetuated the risk of disease.

2 The collection of infant tombs known as 'Pip's Graves' is located on the bleak Hoo peninsula between the Thames and the Medway estuaries. It is an appropriately sombre location, thought to have inspired the opening passages in Charles Dickens' *Great Expectations*.

tants of Eyam in Derbyshire imposed an heroic quarantine on themselves in 1665 in an attempt to save the region from infection. Most of its inhabitants died. As the situation in congested 17th-century cities became even more acute, traditional forms of burial were abandoned and infected bodies were cast into plague pits. The sites of these mass graves are still encountered in construction projects; others are preserved as open spaces and gardens, such as Vincent Square in London.

Although cathedrals and larger urban churches house excellent examples of sepulchral sculpture, small rural village and estate churches contain some of the greatest treasures. Some churches feature monuments to entire dynasties spanning several centuries, such as Exton, near Oakham in Rutland, where nine important monuments encompass a period of more than four centuries, beginning in 1390. A black and white marble memorial to Lady Bruce of Kinloss, who died during childbirth at the age of 22 in 1627, is executed with great sensitivity, while that erected in 1686 to the 3rd Viscount Campden, depicted in Roman dress and sculpted in marble by Grinling Gibbons, is slightly bizarre. In addition to the complex fusion of classical and contemporary fashions, figures were often shown physically rising from their coffins, an attractively literal representation of the Christian resurrection theme.

Mausolea are common in those churches associated with large landowners. The de Grey family, who owned Wrest Park in Bedfordshire, for example, established a mausoleum that was entered by means of a door set in the chancel. The monuments extend from the 16th to the 19th

centuries and feature the full range of styles, fashion and materials that were used for funerary sculpture, including alabaster and marble. Other churches seem physically overwhelmed by the proliferation of monuments and, in some instances, the family themselves seem to have made little provision for the display of later memorials. At St Mary's, Bottesford, Leicestershire, the chancel was rebuilt in the 17th century to accommodate an ever-expanding collection of memorials for the de Roos and Manners families (earls and dukes of Rutland), which eventually became so numerous that they blocked views of the altar from the nave.

In previous centuries, mortality rates were much higher, especially for women, who frequently died in childbirth, and for infants. Among the more affluent

2

1 Kensal Green in northwest London was the first privately run cemetery to be licensed. It was established under an Act of Parliament in 1832, in an attempt to alleviate London's crisis of burial space. Monuments vary from elegant simplicity to Egyptian extravagance, illustrated in the mausoleum of circus impresario Andrew Ducrow.

2,3 Not all Victorian cemeteries were filled with elaborate memorials, but prevailing neoclassical tastes resulted in a disproportionate number of draped urns and versions of Cleopatra's Needle. Bradford's Undercliffe cemetery is a typical example, where monuments to industrialists and civic dignitaries are arrayed in regimental precision.

1

social classes, children were sometimes remembered on their parents' tomb by being featured as small sculpted 'weepers', placed around the base or at each corner. Children who had pre-deceased their parents were shown holding a skull in the slightly macabre version of heraldry that was commonly applied to monuments of death. Skulls and crossbones appear on a number of surviving gravestones, sometimes accompanied by an hourglass to symbolize the inexorably flowing sands of time.

It is impossible to know how parents coped with the loss of so many children. Some historians argue that their emotional investment in each must have been more limited, but sepulchral sculptures often indicate a very real grief. The memorial to Penelope Boothby at St Oswald's, Ashbourne, Derbyshire, who died aged five in 1791, is a very moving marble portrait of the sleeping child. So disconcertingly lifelike are its features that when it was exhibited at Somerset House by the sculptor, Thomas Banks, King George III's wife Queen Charlotte was moved to tears. The epitaph perfectly echoes the mood created by the sculpture: 'The unfor-

tunate parents ventured their all on this frail Bark, and the Wreck was total.'

The deaths of most adults and children, however, would not have been marked by any form of memorial, just a simple shroud and an unmarked grave. Some churchyards dating back to the 18th and 19th centuries in industrial town centres still contain 'guinea graves', such as Beckett Street Cemetery in Leeds. These were essentially common graves in which those who could scrape together a guinea had their names collectively inscribed on the stones. Many of the stones were completely covered on both sides.

The Victorian fascination with death translated into a diverse and elaborate range of tombs and memorials. Cemeteries of the 19th century contain a strange blend of neoclassical, Egyptian and High Gothic mausolea, interspersed with angels, draped urns and scaled-down versions of Cleopatra's Needle. Most of England's industrial towns and cities have their own distinctive Victorian cemeteries, such as Jesmond Old Cemetery in Newcastle. Some of the memorials in cemeteries established around London during the 1830s are of sufficient architectural merit to have received Listed Building status.

By the beginning of the 19th century, some of London's parish burial grounds and churchyards were full. Some churches purchased land outside the city boundaries to create additional space, but continuing high mortality rates coupled with outbreaks of disease, such as cholera, led to the establishment of privately run cemeteries after a bill was passed in Parliament in 1832. Kensal Green, the first to be consecrated, had initial difficulty attracting clients until Augustus Frederick duke of Sussex and Princess Sophia, both children of

2

3

1

2

King George III, were interred in front of the Anglican chapel. Kensal Green promptly became a fashionable burial place and competition for the best sites became intense. The topography of the cemetery became a microcosm of society, with royalty and nobility at the centre in the most architecturally exotic tombs, the affluent middle classes radiating outwards, and the poorer graves, marked by simple crosses, near the edge.

Highgate Cemetery was consecrated in 1839, later than Kensal Green. Both have their share of celebrity graves from the worlds of art, literature and politics, but Highgate became the more prestigious of the two. It is particularly renowned for its layout of serpentine paths crowned by the Circle of Lebanon, a sunken ring of Egyptian-style catacombs erected around an existing cedar of Lebanon tree, Another famous feature is the Egyptian Avenue, entered through an impressive gateway flanked by paired lotus-topped columns. The tombs feature an intriguing array of architectural styles: Gothic, Greek, Egyptian and Byzantine confront one another in glorious memorials to the dead.

The Albert Memorial in London's Hyde Park, designed by Sir George Gilbert Scott, sought to convey a memorial of 'monumental and national character'. Scott's winning design was selected by Victoria herself; it was completed in 1882, after 12 years of construction. The memorial, recently restored by English Heritage, proved to be a masterpiece of Gothic Revival architecture, intricately crafted from white Italian marble, bronze, agate, wrought iron and granite. A combination of brilliant paintwork, bronzes and glittering mosaics reflects Albert's wide range of cultural and economic interests. Culture features prominently on the Parnassus Frieze, in glittering representations of

Pottery, Painting and Sculpture. Symbolic statues of Geometry, Astronomy, Chemistry and Medicine bear witness to Albert's scientific concerns, while allegorical figures of Engineering, Manufactures, Agriculture and Commerce reveal the prince's enthusiasm for business and economics. The Great Exhibition of 1851, one of Albert's greatest achievements, is commemorated by the catalogue in his statue's hand. He is in fact buried with Victoria at the Royal Mausoleum at Frogmore, close to Windsor, but the memorial remains an essential symbol of mid-Victorian England – its aspirations, achievements and enviable self-confidence.

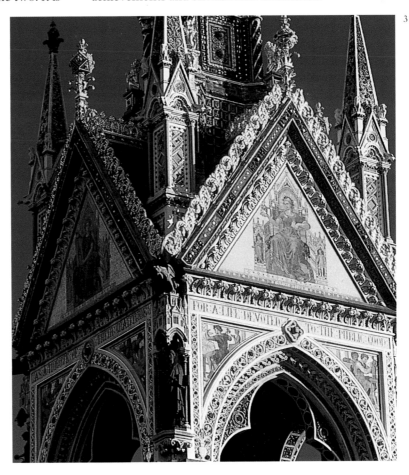

3

CHAPTER

8

The full majesty of the law, a ringing phrase, was
meant to strike those who heard it with a reasonable sense of
dread. As did the rest of the panoply of the law: the full-bottomed
wig and gown which obscured the humanity of the judge, the raised
dais on which he sat, the dock which contained the accused, and the
cathedral-like court where legal proceedings took place. Once convicted,
this deliberate attempt to coerce was carried through to the design of
prisons themselves, gatehouses like barbizans of old with portcullises
and heavy doors to shut out the last vestiges of freedom. And
the punishments meted out could be savage: from the
early horrors of hanging, drawing and quartering,
to the 19th century monotony of the treadmill
or the stone-breakers yard.

LAW, CRIME &
PUNISHMENT

ESTABLISHING THE LAW

Magna Carta, signed at Runnymede by the reluctant King John, is often thought to be the source of legal rights in England. In fact common law, from which much of the country's legal system still derives, had been established a generation earlier by Henry II. Henry drew upon a complex legal inheritance, including Norman, Roman, Saxon and Viking traditions, to establish a codified system. Later centuries had to wrestle with the complexity of religious conscience and jurisdiction of the law, epitomized by the trial and execution of Sir Thomas More. Despite such challenges, buildings such as Westminster Hall endorsed through their magnificence both the power and longevity of the English legal system.

On a grassy knoll overlooking the River Thames near Windsor stands a simple stone memorial, erected in the 1960s by the American Bar Association. It marks the spot at Runnymede where in 1215 King John was presented by his barons with the list of demands known as Magna Carta. The list was not the charter of civil liberties that later generations have imagined, but it did establish the principle of the rule of law in England – a law to which the king was subject, as well as everyone else. From this simple notion developed all the other ideas about freedom of speech and trial by jury that have since become enshrined in the legal systems not only of England, but of English-speaking countries all over the world. Hence the American lawyers' enthusiasm for Runnymede.

Legal systems had been established in England before, of course. Lawmaking was an important element of Saxon kingship in the 9th and 10th centuries, acknowledged in the coronation promise of Alfred's grandson and successor, Athelstan, 'to keep his people in peace, to forbid robbery and wrong-doing by all men, no matter how high in society, and to promote justice and mercy through the rule of law.' Athelstan proceeded to refine the fierce, retributive legislation he inherited, based on an eye-for-an-eye concept of justice, into more sophisticated codes that strengthened royal control. He held large assemblies, or councils, to discuss policies and laws appropriate for a complex kingdom of seveal different tribal groups. Penalties were still harsh, including banishment and severe physical injuries, but Athelstan appears to have been a humane as well as a politic wielder of authority. Sometimes the king seems to have been well ahead of

his time; he objected, for example, to the execution of anyone under the age of 15, a common practice in England as late as the 19th century.

However, it was not until the reign of John's father, Henry II, that an attempt was made to centralize the various elements of Roman law, the Viking courts of the Shire and Hundred, Saxon ordeal by fire, and the ecclesiastical and local courts. Norman additions included the concept of trial by combat, where litigants with wooden weapons slugged it out until one of them admitted defeat. But all of it varied from place to place, according to local custom. Henry's great and lasting achievement was to codify the legal processes and place it on a common, comprehensible footing.

He began by sending people abroad to study the civil law of the old Roman empire and the canon law of the church. Such emissaries bore fruit in later centuries with the establishment of home-grown centres of civil and canon law at the Universities of Oxford and Cambridge. The college of Trinity Hall, for example, was founded at Cambridge specifically to produce lawyers following a shortage after the Black Death; it still has some of the original books in the old library, chained to desks so they cannot be stolen. The college still specializes in producing lawyers, over 650 years after its foundation.

More importantly, however, Henry II also appointed a central panel of judges – professionally trained lawyers whose job was to travel all over the country bringing his newly standardized laws with them and applying them uniformly to local courts. It was a daunting task, but gradually these travelling judges brought order out of chaos, setting up a system of common law across the

PRECEDING PAGES

Main Picture: Walsingham's House of Correction, built in 1787.

Detail: The famous statue of Justice holding a set of scales on top of London's Central Criminal Court.

1 Above the Thames at Runnymede, a memorial overlooks the spot where King John was forced by his barons to sign Magna Carta in 1215.

2 John's father Henry II, shown in a 18th-century painting, was the first to codify England's chaotic legal practices into a single system of common law.

3 The 17th-century lock-up at Bradford-on-Avon is a converted chapel, perched on the 14th-century bridge.

2

233

Law, Crime & Punishment

3

1 In the 18th century it was common to leave executed criminals hanging for months as a warning to others. Winter's Gibbet at Steng Cross in Northumberland was functioning in 1791, when one William Winter was hanged on it for murder.

2 Diagrams showing the internal and extenal structure of the prison tower at Dover Castle.
3 The elegantly designed gateway to the House of Correction at Folkingham in Lincolnshire.

1

land that was the same for everyone. The system was established initially in French and Latin, but was always wholly English in character, a judicial process that drew on European legal experience but developed quite differently in England. Most significant of all, it was independent of the king, although conducted in his name. Henry died, and monarchs after him came and went, but the common law was still the common law and continued regardless. The institution of common law was Henry's outstanding legacy to his successors – even if, like John, they did not always appreciate it.

Henry's system of itinerant judges worked very well in his own time and was continued after his death. It still operates today, with circuit judges presiding over a number of county courts. The judges travelled in some degree of pomp, attended by flunkies. They stayed with local grandees to begin with, whose duty it was to accommodate them, but were later housed in judges' lodgings specially provided for the purpose. Court

rooms were built where proceedings could be heard in proper legal surroundings, with a suitably professional atmosphere. And because the king's judges were properly trained, there was less emphasis on trial by combat and other absurdities, and more on reasoned argument. Lawyers were retained by the various parties, appealing to a jury composed initially of local people who knew something about the case, but developing gradually into a system of 12 good men and true, listening impartially to a variety of evidence before delivering their verdict. It was the beginning of the system as we know it today.

An appearance in court often presaged a spell in prison, and prison buildings have survived from very early days. Felons were often incarcerated in church buildings or the dungeons of the nearest castle, as a reminder of the local lord's feudal powers. In consequence, most of England's old castles still have a dungeon or two somewhere in their walls. Dover Castle ran to a proper prison, and Berkeley Castle retains part of the cell where Edward II was brutally murdered in 1327. Most illuminating of all, Warwick Castle still has an oubliette (from the French *oublier*, to forget), a terrifying hole in the ground little bigger than a man into which the prisoner was shoved and literally forgotten.

However, it is Westminster Hall more than anywhere that illustrates the might of the law from its earliest days. The hall was built in 1097 as part of William II's London palace, but owes

3

its present appearance to the remodelling of the 1390s. It is a vast structure, measuring 73 m (240 ft) long and 28 m (92 ft) high at the apex, with a soaring hammer-beam roof of finest oak: when built, it was almost the biggest of its kind in Europe. The king's great council met there from Norman times onwards, and it was from that council that both Parliament (from the French *parler*, to speak) and the Royal Courts of Justice evolved.

Westminster Hall is, in fact, the very seat of British justice, as it is where the highest courts in the land sat from the time of Magna Carta right up until 1882, when they moved elsewhere. There were four different courts, each specializing in various branches of the law. The Court of the King's Bench occupied the southeast corner of the hall and was initially presided over by the king himself. A wonderful medieval painting shows the court in session, the judges on the bench in scarlet robes, the clerks at a green baize table scribbling busily on long rolls of parchment, and a row of sad-looking prisoners in shackles awaiting their turn in the dock, while the court officials stand over them with their staves of office.

At the same time as the King's Bench was in session, the Court of Chancery was busy in the southwest corner of the hall. The Court of Common Pleas sat near the middle of the west wall, and the Court of the Exchequer sat just outside the hall, in a building on the other side of the west wall. The exchequer was responsible for

raising taxes and sat at a huge chequered table divided into squares, which in pre-computer days facilitated the calculation of tax returns. From it descends the office of the present chancellor of the exchequer.

These courts at Westminster Hall formed the bedrock of the legal system, building up a body of carefully reasoned case law that has served the country superbly over the centuries – and also other countries around the globe, including Ireland, Australia and India, whose legal institutions descend from the British. When you remember that Westminster Hall was also the scene of many famous trials – the Scots patriot William Wallace, Sir Thomas More, Guy Fawkes, Charles I – it is no wonder that American lawyers regard it as a shrine.

Sir Thomas More was a celebrated former lord chancellor and a distinguished lawyer in his own right. His fall from grace came in 1535 when he was found guilty of high treason for refusing to acknowledge Henry VIII's supremacy over the pope. Such a challenge to the king's authority meant that issues of religion in England became subject to the jurisdiction of the law, and individuals were forced to choose between two loyalties. The walls of Westminster Hall once rang with the words of his sentence, traditional for traitors to the crown: 'You are to be hanged till you be half dead, after that cut down yet alive, your bowels to be taken out of your body and burned before you, your privy parts cut off, your head cut off, your body to be divided in four parts,

1

diately hailed as Protestant martyrs, and the place where they died is marked today by an elaborate memorial in Broad Street, outside the college of Balliol.

Mary's successor, Elizabeth I, persecuted Catholics in their turn, although she declined to burn them at the stake. Elizabeth had sympathy with the view that the law should not concern itself with religion, as it had not been designed to 'look into men's souls'. But that view was radical at a time when English Catholics were suspected of being agents of the Spanish, so Catholics continued to be pursued for treason.

The Jesuits, closely associated by the authorities with Spain, were pursued more vigorously than any. Their most famous martyr was Edmund Campion, executed at Tyburn in 1581. A government spy caught him holding mass at a country house in Berkshire. The spy fetched a Justice of the Peace with powers of arrest and the house was surrounded. Campion and his associates promptly disappeared into a priest hole and could not be found. The house was searched from top to bottom, but it took 50 men almost 24 hours to locate them. 'David Jenkins, by God's great goodness, espied a certain secret place, which he quickly found to be hollow; and with a pin of iron ... he forthwith did break a hole into the said place: where then presently he perceived the said Priests lying all close together upon a bed.'

Such priest holes and secret places for saying mass were common in Catholic houses at the time. A good example survives at Sawston Hall in Cambridgeshire, complete with a lavatory for the occupants. The persecution reached its peak in 1597, when so many Jesuits were being interrogated under duress that, at least according to Catholic sources, 'the rack never stood idle at the Tower'. Among the recusants imprisoned that year was one Sir Thomas Tresham. He relied on his faith to bring him through, and after his release built a triangular lodge on his Rushton estate in celebration of the Holy Trinity. It still stands today, providing a bizarre reminder of a time when freedom under the law meant one thing for followers of the established church, and something quite different for everyone else.

and your head and body to be set at such places as the King shall assign.' In fact, More's sentence was commuted to beheading, as was usual for the upper classes, but it was still a savage end. He was executed on Tower Hill – the scaffold's site is marked by a stone in the pavement by Trinity Square Gardens – and his head exhibited on London Bridge until his daughter managed to retrieve it and give it a decent burial.

Many in the 16th century suffered under law for religious beliefs. The bloodiest repression came in the 1550s, when Queen Mary had hundreds of Protestants burned at the stake for heresy. Most notoriously of all, Bishops Latimer and Ridley were burned together at Oxford in 1555, Latimer dying very quickly, Ridley suffering horribly as the flames took their time. The two were imme-

2

1 A portrait of Sir Thomas More, one of the period's greatest lawyers, by Hans Holbein. The former lord chancellor fell from Henry VIII's favour by setting the pope's authority above that of the monarch.

2 The martyrs' memorial outside Balliol College, Oxford, commemorates Bishops Latimer and Ridley. Both were burned at the stake in 1555, bearing their ordeal with great courage. 'We shall this day light such a candle, by God's grace, in England, as I trust shall never be put out.'

3 After his release from the Tower of London, the recusant Sir Thomas Tresham built a triangular lodge at Rushton in celebration of the Holy Trinity that had sustained him in his ordeal.

3

3

BEHIND CLOSED DOORS

THE CONDITIONS IN ENGLAND'S PRISONS WERE NOTORIOUS FOR CENTURIES, ALTHOUGH PRISONERS' ACTUAL EXPERIENCES DEPENDED ON THEIR ABILITY TO PAY FOR PRIVILEGES. THE TOWER OF LONDON, WHERE HIGH-PROFILE POLITICAL PRISONERS WERE HELD — FREQUENTLY BEFORE THEIR EXECUTION ON TOWER GREEN — WAS ESPECIALLY FEARED. THE TOWER'S ASSOCIATION WITH TORTURE, IN PARTICULAR THE RACK, WAS ENCOURAGED BY THE AUTHORITIES AS A DETERRENT. MORE RELEVANT TO ORDINARY CRIMINALS, HOWEVER, WERE THE CONGESTED, DISEASE-RIDDEN GAOLS IN WHICH THEY AWAITED EXECUTION OR TRANSPORTATION, OFTEN FOR RELATIVELY MINOR OFFENCES. REFORMERS CAMPAIGNED FOR CHANGES IN PRISON CONDITIONS, BUT EFFECTIVE IMPROVEMENTS PROVED HARD TO ACHIEVE.

THERE WERE SEVERAL different kinds of prison in England in the 16th century. Some were designed for debtors, some for church offenders, others for common criminals. The Tower was the state prison, for important political detainees, and many of the Catholics imprisoned in Queen Elizabeth's time were to end up there. The four-turreted White Tower in the centre was built by William the Conqueror in 1078, primarily as a fortress capable of withstanding a siege. Subsequent monarchs added two rows of curtain walls and a moat, and the Tower served both as fortress and prison from the earliest days right up until World War II. Some prisoners were held captive for a few weeks, others for the rest of their lives. A few, including Henry VI, the duke of Clarence and the two little princes, were murdered out of hand. More than 100 were executed, usually by beheading on Tower Hill. Most were released sooner or later, however, unless there was a good reason for keeping them locked up for ever.

In medieval times the majority of prisoners arrived by water, stepping reluctantly ashore at the Watergate by the riverside. So many arrived this way that it has been known as Traitors' Gate ever since. The gate still looks much as it did when Sir Thomas More and John Fisher passed through it in 1534, on their way to martyrdom and Catholic sainthood. Once inside the Tower, prisoners were accommodated according to their rank — royalty in the royal apartments, the rest in the small outlying towers linking the curtain walls. As with prisons elsewhere, occupants were allowed creature comforts if they could pay for them. Sir Walter Raleigh enjoyed conjugal visits from his wife; Sir Thomas More and Bishop Fisher

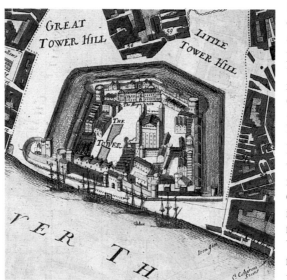

swapped food, exchanging oranges for a dish of custard, although Fisher ended up so emaciated that he had to be carried to his execution on a chair. Inmates were usually free to roam the inner keep as well. It was only lower-class prisoners who were thrown into dungeons and kept in strict confinement. And it was only lower-class prisoners who were subjected to torture and other discomforts: people of gentle birth were usually spared the worst in deference to their rank.

The Tower has always had a terrible reputation for torture, but actually much of it was exaggerated by contemporary propagandists for their own purposes. Torture was not even legal: it required a warrant, signed either by the monarch or a privy councillor under the royal prerogative, and such warrants were only signed in exceptional circumstances. It appears to have been used chiefly against Catholics during Elizabeth's reign, although the torturers were at pains to point out that it was treason they were investigating, not religion. Edmund Campion was certainly subjected to the rack in 1581: 'He used to fall down at the racke-howse dore upon both knees to commend himself to God's mercie.' His fellow Jesuit John Gerard left a graphic account in 1597 of hanging by his arms from a dungeon wall in the White Tower until he fainted from the pain. But Gerard's torturers were reluctant and spared him the rack when they saw he would not talk. The Tower's governor resigned in disgust afterwards, after only a few months in the job. He shared the view of the public that torture was not acceptable and declined to have any part in it.

His successor proved less particular in 1605, when Guy Fawkes was brought to the Tower after the failure

1 This hand coloured engraving of 1754 provides an early map of the Tower of London. The moat and two rows of curtain walls made it a most forbidding prison, from which few inmates escaped.

2 The central White Tower of the Tower of London was first constructed by William I in 1078. In the centuries that followed, so many prisoners entered the Tower by the Watergate that by the 16th century it had become known as Traitors' Gate. Sir Thomas More entered in this way, as did Princess Elizabeth, accused of conspiring against her half-sister Queen Mary.

of the Gunpowder Plot against James I and Parliament. Fawkes refused to name his fellow conspirators, so the king signed a warrant for his forcible interrogation, stipulating only that 'the gentler tortours are to be first usid unto him'. Fawkes was thrown into the so-called Dungeon of Little Ease, a hole so cramped that he could neither stand nor lie, but had to crouch in pitch darkness until his tormentors released him. When that failed to work, they tied him to the rack – the Tower had the only one in England – and stretched him until his bones began to crack. Not surprisingly, Fawkes broke down

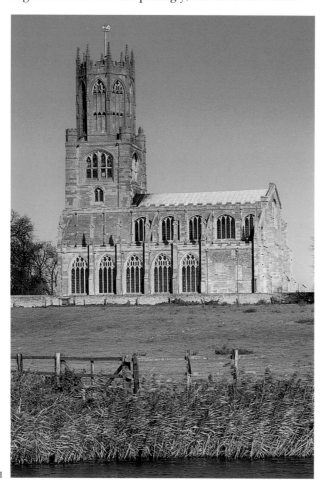

1

on his second day in the Tower and confessed to everything. He was one of the last people to be tortured in England, however. Even by royal warrant, the practice was phased out soon afterwards as part of a general move towards curbing the absolute powers of the king.

It was a difficult time for the monarchy. Like his predecessors, James believed firmly in the divine right of kings, the idea that monarchs had been specially selected by God to occupy the throne and should therefore be regarded as all-powerful. King John may have signed Magna Carta, but he repudiated it immediately afterwards, claiming duress, and the issue of the monarch's exact position in relation to the law has remained unresolved. The question surfaced again during the last years of Elizabeth I's reign, when her increasingly erratic rule served to alienate many of her subjects. The earl of Essex led a rebellion in protest, only to be executed in 1601. The earl's protest nevertheless struck a chord with the general public. He was beheaded on Tower Green, within the privacy of the prison walls, an action explained at the time as a special privilege for an old courtier. The real reason, however, was that many people shared Essex's view that it was time for the public to have a wider say in government. There would have been a riot if he had been executed on Tower Hill in front of a sympathetic crowd.

Essex's old enemy Sir Walter Raleigh was another high-profile figure in the growing unrest about royal powers. Partly in response to the Gunpowder Plot, James I kept him prisoner in the Tower for 12 years, and later, most unjustly, had him executed outside Westminster Hall. His death did not provoke a riot, but the revulsion at the king's high-handedness was universal. Among the outraged witnesses to the execution were John Hampden and John Pym, who subsequently threw themselves into the struggle for Parliament against the arbitrary powers of the king. In the best traditions of Magna Carta, they questioned the divine right of James to do as he pleased, asserting instead the right of Parliament to assist in the making of laws and be consulted on matters of national importance.

1 Following James I's accession in 1603, it was claimed that he had Fotheringay Castle destoyed in revenge for the execution of his mother (Mary, Queen of Scots) there in 1587. In fact, the stones were taken for other building purposes. All that now remains of it is Fotheringay Collegiate Church nearby.
2 Charles I portrayed by Edward Bower at his trial for his life in Westminster Hall. No precedent existed for a Parliamentary court and Charles refused to recognize it. His execution was an unpopular act, seen by most people as a form of judicial murder.
3 Carisbrooke Castle on the Isle of Wight, where Charles I was held prisoner during his conflict with Parliament.

2

3

The crisis came to a head during the reign of James's son, Charles I. He, too, believed in the divine right of kings, to the extent of trying to arrest five members of Parliament, including John Pym, who had opposed him. However, an outraged Parliament would have none of it. The five remained free and in the ensuing Civil War, it was Charles who was defeated. After being taken prisoner at Carisbrooke Castle, he was brought to London and put on trial at Westminster Hall in January 1649, on a charge of waging war against his own people.

It was an astonishing turn of events. From being the embodiment of the state, before whom all subjects knelt in homage, the king was now on trial himself, an event unparalleled in British history. And he was on trial at Westminster Hall, the very seat of royal justice! There were no legal precedents for anything of the sort,

1

so Charles was in some sense justified in refusing to recognize the Parliamentary court that proposed to examine him. 'I would know by what power I am called hither,' he demanded. His accusers had no answer, but they found him guilty anyway. Charles was beheaded outside the Banqueting House on 30 January 1649, to widespread disquiet and a feeling that Parliament had taken a step too far. Charles had been very careful to quote the law in his own defence, and most people agreed with him. The official axeman flatly refused to execute his sovereign, as did many others. A significant number of Parliamentary leaders found an excuse to be out of town for the king's trial, and therefore unable to sign their names to his death warrant.

The legal status of the Parliamentary Commonwealth was problematic from the start. Nominally operating without the sanction of law, the constitutional government required a legal head of state if it was not to degenerate into a military dictatorship. It was not long before Parliament's leaders considered offering the 'vacant' throne to Oliver Cromwell in order to fill the vacuum. He declined, taking the title of Lord Protector instead. The monarchy was restored in 1660, two years after Cromwell's death, and the former Protector's exhumed head was displayed on Westminster Hall. From 1688 the monarch ruled constitutionally, occupying the throne by the will of the people, rather than by divine right. Magna Carta had come of age at last.

Of course, all of this meant little to ordinary people, whose lives were far removed from events at Westminster. Whether the law was administered by the king's officials or a junta of major-generals, the result tended to be the same for the people on the receiving end. It was the rich who made the laws, the poor who swung from the end of a rope. Punishments had been draconian throughout the Middle Ages – branding, mutilation, boiling alive and pressing to death were commonplace – and they remained so as the 17th century gave way to the 18th, the so-called Age of Enlightenment. Women were still burned as witches in the reign of George III, death was mandatory for stealing a sheep or a horse, and young children could be hanged for the theft of a handkerchief or a piece of beef. Transportation was introduced as a substitute for the death penalty, but it owed more to the need for labour in the colonies than any concept of mercy. A little shop lifting, or a theft of small change from an employer, and people could find themselves bound for the shores of America, or later the penal colonies of Australia, never to see their families again. The sheer numbers exported in this way seem incredible today – 80 years after the first convict ships reached Australia in 1788, more than 150,000 prisoners had been transported there.

Many convicts died en route, because conditions on board ship were appalling. The same was true of prisons at home. Every kind of vice and disease flourished in

2

1 Metropolitan policemen, with their distinctive top hats, photographed around 1890. Law and order was greatly improved in the 19th century by the introduction of a uniformed police force, the initiative of Sir Robert Peel.
2 The old courthouse at King's Lynn is decorated with a set of manacles, a visible deterrent to would-be malefactors.
3 By contrast, the gate of Wormwood Scrubs prison is decorated with plaques commemorating John Fry and Elizabeth Howard. Both important prison reformers, they devoted their lives to improving conditions for inmates.

English prisons and Hogarth's caricatures were no exaggeration. Unhappiest of all were those prisoners who had been acquitted at their trial but lacked the money for their release expenses and so were left to rot. They found a champion in John Howard, the sheriff of Bedfordshire, who made a tour of provincial prisons in 1773 and was horrified at what he found: smallpox, gaol fever and prisoners of both sexes locked up together. Howard promptly made it his life's work to reform the prison system, lending his name to the Howard League for Penal Reform that continues to this day.

As a result of his efforts, the appalling conditions were slowly eradicated and a building programme started to provide every prisoner with a cell to themselves. Howard's work was continued in the 19th century by Elizabeth Fry, who devoted her life to improving the conditions for female prisoners. In 1817, she described her attempts to comfort a woman condemned to death for theft: 'I have just returned from a most melancholy visit to Newgate, where I have been at the request of Elizabeth Fricker, previous to her execution tomorrow morning at eight o'clock. I found her much hurried, distressed and tormented in mind … Is it for man thus to take the prerogative of the Almighty into his own hands …? Besides this poor young woman, there are also six men to be hanged, one of whom has a wife near her confinement, and seven young children.'

Mrs Fry's words fell largely on deaf ears, although Robert Peel's reforms to the criminal law in the 1820s abolished the death penalty for over 100 crimes. Public hangings continued until the 1860s, however, and it took another 100 years before the death penalty was abolished. Other punishments remained draconian – both the treadmill and cat-o'-nine-tails were legal until well into the 20th century.

There were innovations, however. A civilian police force was another of Robert Peel's achievements at the Home Office. Armed only with batons and less politically controversial than soldiers, the 'Peelers' were established in London in 1829. Such was their success that by 1856 every county and borough was required to employ a force, subject to national training and discipline.

At the dawn of the 21st century, prison conditions still leave room for improvement. John Howard's goal of a cell for every prisoner still seems as far away as ever, and Britain continues to imprison a greater percentage of its population than almost anywhere in Europe. It is not a distinguished record.

3

KEEPING THE PEACE

THE FAMOUS INDEPENDENCE OF ENGLAND'S JUDICIARY FROM THE MONARCH WAS ESTABLISHED BY HENRY II. THE LAWS IT APPLIES ARE DETERMINED BY PARLIAMENT, LINKING TWO GREAT NATIONAL INSTITUTIONS THAT HAVE SHAPED ENGLAND'S CHARACTER FOR CENTURIES. AN ELABORATE GOTHIC DESIGN EMPHASIZED THE POWER AND AUTHORITY OF THE NEW HOUSES OF PARLIAMENT. IN THE GREAT DEBATING CHAMBERS, CONFRONTATIONAL ROWS OF OPPOSING SEATS REFLECT THE ADVERSARIAL NATURE OF POLITICAL THEATRE, STILL CLOSELY LINKED TO THE LEGAL PROFESSION TODAY. IN CONTRAST, THE ROYAL COURTS OF JUSTICE ON THE STRAND, WITH THEIR DELIBERATE ECHOES OF A GOTHIC CATHEDRAL, INVEST THE COUNTRY'S JUDICIAL PROCESS WITH A SENSE OF VIRTUAL REVERENCE.

1

IN THE DAYS BEFORE Britain joined the European Union, the law in England was derived from two main sources. One was case law — the judgement handed down in a particular case, thus setting a precedent. The other was statute law — a bill drawn up by legal experts to meet a particular need, then examined in detail by both Houses of Parliament before going to the monarch for the royal assent. Either way, the function of the legal system in England were interlinked with an outstanding collection of Parliamentary buildings clustered around Westminster Abbey, now officially recognized by the United Nations as a World Heritage Site.

Everybody is familiar with Westminster Abbey, of course, but a surprising number of people have never noticed the Chapter House to the side. It is a splendid building, a 13th-century rotunda, still with the original tiled floor. According to one account, it is where the forerunner of the House of Commons convened for the first time, a gathering of elected representatives of ordinary people, summoned most reluctantly by Henry III under pressure from Simon de Montfort earl of Leicester.

The official proclamation promised much: 'In this year on the octave of St Hilary [20 January 1265] there came to London, by summons of the Lord King, all the bishops, abbots, priors, earls, barons of the whole kingdom, and of the Cinque Ports, of each city and borough 4 men, to be present at the Parliament. In which Parliament, on St Valentine's Day, it was made public in the Chapter House at Westminster that the Lord King had bound himself, on oath, by his charter that neither he nor the Lord Edward in time to come would do

injury to, nor cause to be injured, the earls of Leicester and Gloucester, nor the citizens of London or any of those who adhered to them, on account of anything done in the former time of disorder in the kingdom; and he ordered expressly that the charters of liberties [Magna Carta] and of the forest which were made in the ninth year of his reign, should be kept inviolate.'

The king broke his word, of course: his followers caught up with de Montfort later that year and dismembered him. And the gathering in the Chapter House was not the first meeting of the House of Commons so much as an assembly of the national council that happened to include local people for the first time. However, it was certainly the beginning of the idea. When the House of Commons did emerge, it had no meeting place of its own and used the Chapter House for its deliberations right up until 1547. The building is one of the cradles of the English legal system.

Otherwise, the only other Parliamentary building to survive from the earliest days is Westminster Hall. Everything else burned down in the disastrous fire of 1834, when the ancient Palace of Westminster was razed to the ground. However, the hall survived, and from the ashes of the Palace beside it rose the new Houses of Parliament, grandiloquently designed by Sir Charles Barry to dignify the seat of the legislature and its place at the centre of events. The new Houses were built in the Gothic style favoured by the Victorians and the effect was certainly striking. At the time of its completion, the tower housing Big Ben was the tallest structure in the world.

Most imposing of all are the two debating chambers, one created for the Lords, the other for the Commons.

2

PRECEDING PAGES
1   The Houses of Parliament, rebuilt in Tudor Gothic style after the fire of 1834, are the country's supreme law-making body. Laws have been made on this site for more than 800 years.
2   *The House of Commons*, 1888. The elaborate interior was deliberately designed without sufficient seats to add to the atmosphere on important occasions.

1   Until its removal in 1878, Temple Bar in the Strand marked the western gate to the City of London.
2   Based near the ancient Templar church, the lawyers of the Middle Temple use the Templars' Agnus Dei as their emblem.
3   The Royal Courts of Justice were designed to resemble a cathedral, inspiring awe and reverence for the law.

as a venue for concerts and cultural events, with the crown court and civil court accommodated almost as an afterthought – and incongruously – at either end of the Great Hall. Police cells were in the basement.

The new Parliamentary buildings, also an imposing structure, were completed in 1850. For the next 30 years they existed side by side with the law courts in Westminster Hall, an increasingly chaotic arrangement that had long outgrown its usefulness. In 1882, the lawyers moved out of the hall altogether, after almost seven centuries, and transferred to the newly built Royal Courts of Justice on the Strand. The Royal Courts were another Gothic extravaganza, resembling a cathedral inside and out: their intent was to inspire awe in the 'congregation' and a reverence for the law. The statue of King Alfred on the east gable served as a reminder that the administration of justice was nothing new in England, and the whole building expressed the spirit of Queen Victoria's England at its most ebullient.

The Queen, herself a descendant of King Alfred, opened the building on 4 December that year. Her speech emphasized the unique place of the legal system in the country's history and identity: 'I have all confidence that the independence and learning of the judges, supported by the integrity and ability of the other members of the profession of the law, will prove in the future, as they have in times past, a chief security for the rights of my Crown and the liberties of my people.'

The courts stand at the heart of lawyers' London, midway between Lincoln's Inn and the Temple. The Temple takes its name from the ancient church of the Knights Templar, still extant. The Middle Temple also takes its emblem from here, the Agnus Dei, known to publicans as the Lamb and Flag. Temple Bar, the official gateway to the City, stood outside the Royal Courts of Justice; it was removed during construction to provide a better view of the site. Designed by Sir Christopher Wren, the Bar still had Jacobite heads on it in 1773, impaled after the 1745 rebellion. Daniel Defoe once spent time in the pillory by the gatehouse for his satirical pamphlet 'The Shortest Way with the Dissenters'.

3

1

Much of lawyers' London still looks as it did in Defoe's day, a labyrinth of narrow passageways and barristers' chambers, with small old courtyards from Shakespearean times and formal dining halls on the Oxbridge pattern. The lawyers look the same, too, the barristers in wigs and gowns, the judges in knee breeches and buckled shoes. There have been moves to modernize their dress, but many of them are adamant that it should be retained, arguing that the law would lose its majesty if they went to work in an ordinary suit. Lawyers are firmly traditional by nature – hardly surprising in a profession that thinks nothing of quoting a legal precedent from 300 or 400 years ago.

Tradition actually plays an important part in their professional ethos. One of the more curious customs at the Central Criminal Court, better known as the Old Bailey, is the strewing of herbs across the prisoner's dock on the first two days of each session during the summer months. The judges carry a posy of sweet-smelling flowers as well, a reminder of the time in 1750 when 55 people caught typhus from a Newgate prisoner and died. The prison stood next door until 1902, when it was demolished and the stones reused to build the modern Old Bailey on the same site.

Newgate, constructed between 1767 and 1780, was the result of the decision by City of London authorities to rebuild a prison sited in the medieval gatehouse. John Howard criticized the 'manifest errors' of the new building – ventilation and natural light were very limited, as the outside of the building had no openings, and the inside plan allowed only cursory separation of prisoners by age and sex. The prison became an even greater focus of dread in 1783, when public executions were relocated there from their original site at Tyburn.

The main entrance to the Old Bailey stands on the same spot as the old debtor's door of Newgate. It was here that countless people were publicly executed in the first half of the 19th century. One of the most notorious hangings was attended by perhaps 40,000 people in 1840, among them two ambitious young journalists who arrived very early in the morning to make sure of a place. W.M. Thackeray could not bring himself to watch the actual moment of death, but Charles Dickens surveyed the entire spectacle, including the crowd:

2

'From the moment of my arrival – down to the time when I saw the body with its dangling head, being carried on a wooden bier into the gaol – I did not see one token in all the immense crowd; at the windows, in the streets, on the house-tops, anywhere; of any one emotion suitable to the occasion. No sorrow, no salutary terror, no abhorrence, no seriousness; nothing but ribaldry, levity, drunkenness, and flaunting vice in fifty other shapes.'

Dickens was always a fierce critic of the legal system. Childhood memories of his father's imprisonment for debt never left him and were revisited in several of his novels. In *Oliver Twist* he left a graphic account of Fagin's last hours at Newgate, sitting in the condemned cell waiting for dawn to come: 'Those dreadful walls of Newgate, which have hidden so much misery and such unspeakable anguish.' Dickens shared Elizabeth Fry's feelings about the unnecessary brutality of the law, the casual taking of life for what, by modern standards, were only footling crimes. He would have been delighted to see her statue adorning the Old Bailey's Great Hall.

The theme was taken up again by Oscar Wilde at the end of the century. Convicted in 1895 for something that was not even a crime across the Channel, the most talented writer of his generation was sentenced to two years' imprisonment with hard labour, the maximum the law allowed. Wilde was lucky to avoid being sent to Dartmoor, that bleakest of prisons in the West Country, where stones were broken, and men, too. He went to Reading Gaol instead, observing with deep sympathy a trooper of the Royal Horse Guards taking his last exercise in the courtyard before his execution:

I never saw a man who looked
With such a wistful eye
Upon that little tent of blue
Which prisoners call the sky.

A century later, some significant reforms have been achieved. Homosexuality is no longer a crime, hard labour no longer a punishment, and the death penalty has been abolished, except in time of war. Nevertheless, prisons are still a source of concern. Cells remain badly overcrowded, conditions insanitary, and drug abuse rife. Further improvements are essential to create a prison service that can look to the future as well as to the past.

CHAPTER

9

The history of the English country house is as much a
social history as a record of brick and stone, of turrets and porticos.
From the Lord in his hall, sitting at a high table underneath a dais,
the trappings of power and prestige have been faithfully reflected,
enriched and embroidered with each passing generation. The flight from
the hall to the solar was followed by the institution of the great chamber,
with its attendant arrangement of subsidiary rooms until finally the
formal strictures of the 17th century dictated that supplicants would
have to overcome a series of social obstacles represented by an entire
enfilade of rooms – the ante-chamber, the withdrawing room,
the bedchamber, the closet. Architectural styles, too,
came and went, reflecting the fashions and
ideals of each individual age.

A PLACE IN
THE COUNTRY

THE FIRST ESTATES

RECENT RE-CREATIONS OF IRON AGE FARMSTEADS, INHABITED BY VOLUNTEERS AS THEIR FOREBEARS MIGHT HAVE DONE, HAVE GIVEN SCIENTISTS AND ARCHAEOLOGISTS INVALUABLE INSIGHTS INTO HOW LIFE WAS LIVED THOUSANDS OF YEARS AGO. SURVEYS ARE DISCLOSING SUCH SITES IN LARGE NUMBERS, INDICATING THAT ENGLAND JUST PRIOR TO THE ROMAN INVASIONS WAS AN ORDERED AND SETTLED SOCIETY. THE ROMANS THEMSELVES STAMPED THEIR OWN STRUCTURAL IDENTITY ON THE NATION WITH THE VILLAS, ROADS, TEMPLES, THEATRES, FORTS AND BATH HOUSES THAT CHARACTERIZED THEIR EMPIRE. IN DUE COURSE THE BRITISH BUILT SIMILAR CONSTRUCTIONS, INCLUDING VILLA COMPLEXES WITH BEAUTIFUL MOSAIC FLOORS AND WALL FRESCOS.

SET AMIDST THE ROLLING chalk hills of Bascomb Down in Hampshire, the Iron Age roundhouses of Butser Ancient Farm, roofed in great conical funnels of thatch, replicate the type of settlement that would have been commonplace when the Romans first set foot on English soil. Their assumption that Britannia was a land of savage barbarians was misplaced, and when Julius Caesar led the first of his two exploratory expeditions, he discovered a more civilized and ordered society than he expected. Caesar noted in his written observations that 'the population is exceedingly large, the ground thickly studded with homesteads and the cattle very numerous'.

Butser is no Iron Age theme park, but was founded to explore archaeologists' theories and ideas through experimental practice. Because the majority of lowland Iron Age dwellings were timber based and left little tangible evidence, archaeologists have employed educated

1

2

PRECEDING PAGES
Main picture: Chatsworth
House, Derbyshire.
Inset: The Rotondo, Stowe,
Buckinghamshire.

1   An aerial view of Butser
Ancient Farm in
Hampshire. The farm is an
empirical project which
explores archaeologists'
interpretations of evidence
excavated on Iron Age sites.

2   A beautifully crafted gold
earring, discovered at
Lullingstone villa, near
Eynsford in Kent. Many of
the artefacts found at the
site indicate the prosperity
of the villa's owners.
3   The remains of Lullingstone
villa, which was excavated
in 1939. An unusually
complete floor plan has
been constructed from
the structural remains.

guesswork in areas where even the most painstaking fieldwork has provided insufficient data. Many of the questions about how Iron Age communities lived and worked are being answered by the research being conducted at Butser, through a combination of trial and error and meticulous scientific analysis.

3

The farm recreates the type of setttlement probably common around 300 BC. It is enclosed by banks, ditches and wickerwork fences, and its most arresting feature is the great roundhouse at the centre. Based on an analysis of postholes at other Iron Age sites, the roundhouse is a building of great sophistication, both in concept and execution. It is 15 m (50 ft) in diameter, with a total floor area of some 176 m² (1894 sq ft). The outer walls are of wattle and daub, and the framework is strong enough to bear the weight of an estimated 15 tonnes of thatch. Crucial to the design is the pitch of the roof. Too steep and it would be heavy and unstable; too shallow and the rain would not drain away, rotting the thatch. The roundhouse at Butser needed timber from 200 trees – a mix of seven-year-old coppiced hazel rods and 40-year-old oak. The roof itself needed the straw yield from at least 15 Celtic-sized fields. Each field would have required a day to plough, and the straw would have taken a skilled man about six weeks to lay.

Most Iron Age sites are surrounded by a series of pits, initially thought to be primitive houses, but now considered to be grain silos. Experiments at Butser have shown that between 1 and 5 tonnes of wheat and barley could have been stored underground, provided the pits were dry and airtight. Under these conditions grain cannot germinate – and decomposing bacteria cannot thrive, since they quickly exhaust the oxygen and water they need to live, leaving sterile carbon dioxide. Once a pit had been opened, however, all the grain had to be used at once to prevent it from going bad – which serves to indicate the number of people that each pit was intended to feed.

Storage was important because cereals were the mainstay of farming in the Iron Age, particularly the wheat species Emmer and Spelt. It had long been assumed that crop yields must have been significantly lower in prehistoric times, but the Butser experience suggests that they were not all that different, although the Iron Age was much more labour-intensive.

Cereal was the mainstay, but most farmers kept livestock as well. The Celtic Shorthorn cattle of the Iron Age are now extinct, but the small-horned Dexter cattle at Butser are thought to be their closest living relation. Some of them have been trained to pull replica ards (prehistoric ploughs). Yoked around the horns, they can plough half an acre a day in normal conditions. The ancient farmers kept sheep as well, a half-wild variety sometimes mistaken for a goat. Analysis of bones and

1

1 Remains of the baths at
Lullingstone villa. Even the
more modest villas featured
communal bath complexes,
and the highly decorated
one at Lullingstone was
extended by later owners.

2, 3 Roman villas are renowned
for the quality and colour
of their mosaic floors. Those
at Lullingstone feature
complex geometric designs,
framing pictorial scenes
from classical legends.

4 A bronze flagon recovered
from Lullingstone. Evidence
shows that the inhabitants
of the province's country
villas enjoyed plentiful
supplies of wine and olive
oil, imported from the
countries of the Roman
empire, as well as fruit and
vegetables grown on the
estates themselves.

hair found at Iron Age sites suggests remarkable similarities with today's Soay sheep, and other breeds now associated with the Hebrides and the Shetland Islands.

After the Roman invasion, new varieties of fruit and vegetable were introduced, along with ideas on crop rotation and intensive animal breeding. The Romans also built towns, creating an urban population that needed to be fed. Small farmers now had a market for their surplus produce, which they could dispose of at

2

the nearest town. However, the most significant change introduced by the Romans was the manner in which people lived. A communal way of life, all sleeping together in a single roundhouse, was gradually replaced by single family houses, rectangular in shape and much more Roman in appearance. Julius Caesar had remarked caustically that British women were held in common, their children brought up in a commune as no-one knew who the father was. Under Roman influence, they began to live as family units, each with a private house and area of land.

As society expanded still further, farming became an attractive business investment, drawing a more prosperous class away from the towns. Farms expanded into estates, with the wealthiest structured around increasingly large villas. Lullingstone villa in Kent is an example of an estate house that evolved over a period of time. Dating from AD 100, it was modified, refined and expanded during the period of Roman occupation.

Villas, like town houses, were lavishly decorated with marble or mosaic floors and plaster walls adorned with frescoes. Principal rooms would have been heated by a complex hypercaust system, which also formed an essential part of the bathhouse complex. Public baths were an integral part of urban life, but each villa also had its own private complex – an area clearly extended at Lullingstone during the life of the villa. The ritual aspect of communal bathing was important to the Romans, and the grandeur of the bath-house and its environs was a clear indication of wealth. Changing-rooms were elegantly tiled and heated, and the more affluent households possessed an elaborate sequence of hot and cold rooms similar to those in public urban bathhouses.

Lullingstone's expansion included a dining room with mosaic-panelled walls,

INVIDAS[...]DISSEI[...]NOT[...]AV[...]
[...]STIVSAHOLIASISSHADVSOVEDOMOS

depicting scenes from classical legend. The villa also contains evidence of changes in religious practice. Grave goods suggest that pagan beliefs prevailed during the earlier period, and a shrine in the cellar bears traces of frescoes of water nymphs. However, a Christian chapel was later created in the cellar. One of few such private places of worship to have been discovered among the 2,000 or so villas found in England, it clearly indicates that Lullingstone's owners were people of importance.

The concept of gardening for pleasure became part of villa life and a variety of herbs, vines and flowers were introduced from Mediterranean countries. As the rural villas expanded, structural modifications were made. Projecting wings originally used to encompass a veranda might have been extended and remodelled to create a

courtyard in which the more fragile and decorative plants would be grown.

Villas have been discovered in greatest concentration in the fertile lowland areas of the south, where arable and mixed farming were profitable. The cultured prosperity of their buildings and estates proved finite, however. After the departure of the Roman legions in the 5th century AD, isolated villas with few defences became easy prey, and most were abandoned.

4

FROM MOATS TO MANSIONS

As the conquerors of 1066 established their rights to land and property and lawlessness declined, the Englishman's home moved from castle to hall, house to Palladian villa. The progression mirrored the nation's developing political and aesthetic sense. Regional variations gave rise to spectacular black and white half-timbering in the midlands and northeast and the sculptural quality of free-hand pargetting in parts of the southeast. The desire to express social power and prestige gave birth to the great country houses, from Haddon Hall and the 'prodigy houses' to Blenheim Palace and Chatsworth, that continue to dominate the English countryside.

AFTER THE CONQUEST William I transferred virtually the entire estate of the English land-holding classes to his Norman followers. Castles, built of wood by this new generation of landowners, were erected with speed, not only to consolidate territorial gains but also to terrorize and demoralize the local population. Some 30 castles, mainly of the motte and bailey type, were erected in the five years after the conquest and this had advanced to between 80 and 90 at the time of William's death in 1087. It has been estimated that the number of motte and bailey castles may eventually have reached almost 1,000.

A balance had to be struck between the need to subjugate the populace through a network of powerful strongholds built and maintained by tenants-in-chief and the need to keep their territorial ambitions in check. Accordingly, the crown was careful not to control the development of fortifications and resist

excessive construction of stone castles. A further check to baronial autonomy was the consolidation of several thousand small estates extant before 1066 into less than 200 major lordships held by tenants-in-chief. This distribution of land provided for the maintenance of a castle, and the land so designated was known as a castellari.

It was easier to keep an eye on a smaller number of powerful barons who were well rewarded by the king than on thousands of fractious chieftains. The right had been established that the king could occupy any castle at will; no castles of stone could be built without his express approval, and only under stringent conditions. But after the death of Henry I in 1135 and the struggle for power between Matilda and Stephen I, the barons began to build their consolidate their local power bases in 'adulterine', castles of stone. An entry in the *Anglo-Saxon Chronicle* records 'and they filled the whole land with these castles. They sorely burdened the unhappy people of the country with forced labour on the castles.' By 1150 there were more than 1,000 unlicensed strongholds. The depredations on their livelihoods caused by constant internecine warfare took its toll on the major landowners who began to make private peace treaties amongst themselves. The treaty of Winchester in 1153 resolved the differences between Stephen and Matilda's son, the future Henry II.

The larger feudal landlords built great halls at the heart of their establishments to accommodate their retinues and to serve as the focus for entertainment and the formal ritual of eating, which was performed with great ceremony and a punctilious regard for rank and status. Many landowners consolidated their position and prestige by attaching to their household families of differing social grades by ties of service. For those of noble birth, a period in the lord's service acted as a form of education, imparting social polish, an understanding of administrative matters and experience in the martial arts and sporting prowess. The most important servants of the largest landowners would themselves be of noble birth, with their own houses and estates. In this way the gradations of power and prestige were demonstrated, and the theatre in which this was given visual emphasis, both by the archi-

1 The undercroft of Burton Agnes Old Manor House in East Yorkshire is one of few surviving traces of Norman domestic architecture. Built around 1170 by Roger de Stutville, the manor remained home to the local lords for some 500 years. An Elizabethan mansion was erected next to the manor house, the exterior of which was faced in brick to match the new house.

2 Aydon Castle near Corbridge in Northumberland is a fortified manor dating back to the 13th century. Built on the edge of the steep-sided Cor Burn valley, Aydon was originally built as an undefended house. It was later subjected to attacks from both Scottish and English raiders and required additional protection.

2

1 Stogursey Castle, Somerset, has a varied history. It originally formed part of the estate of one William de Courci, a Norman knight and steward to Henry I, but after the Wars of the Roses it was owned by the Percys. The castle was abandoned and fell into decay, but its gatehouse, a 17th-century addition, has been restored by the Landmark Trust.

2 Oxburgh Hall, Norfolk, is the home of the Bedingfield family, who built it in 1482.

3 Leeds Castle, Kent. The site was first fortified in wood by a Saxon noble during the 9th century. Rebuilt in stone, the structure was substantially enlarged by Edward I and transformed by Henry VIII. Leeds became a favourite country retreat of those seeking to escape the intrigues of court life.

1

tectural arrangements and the forms of ceremony observed, was the great hall. The lord and his family sat at the high table, raised on a dais underneath a canopy. Others disposed themselves strictly according to rank, those of more humble birth 'below the salt'.

A hall with a magnificent canopy from *c.*1500 still exists at Rufford Old Hall in Lancashire. The internal arrangements of the medieval hall (a word also applied to quite small spaces) varied little. The hall was open to the roof timbers, and in richer and more advanced households was heated by a large open fireplace and chimney. A central hearth on the floor and an opening in the roof covered by a louvre through which the smoke escaped, as at Penshurst, was a more usual arrangement and necessitated the typically high-roofed structure to aid smoke dispersal. At the lower end of the hall, opposite the dais, three service doors from the partition known as the screens gave entry to the hall from the buttery and the pantry, as well as access to the kitchen, usually a separate building, via a passage. Windows would have been closed to the elements by wooden shutters, expensive glass being used for the top sections only, and very often stone seats were formed in the window embrasures with footrests raised above the

2

3

dirty floor. The earthen floor, constantly trampled by many feet, was regularly strewn with rushes to reduce dust. Furniture would have been minimal, and removable, to accommodate large gatherings. Trestle tables, benches, a chair for the lord placed centrally at the high table under the dais, and a scattering of stools would have sufficed. Walls would have been plastered or wainscoted, then painted with formal decoration or pictorial subjects. By the end of the 14th century tapestry wall hangings were common in all larger halls.

In the more peaceful regions of the kingdom the house evolved from the castle hall, still raised above a vaulted undercroft for security, and further defended by a gatehouse and moat. The largest of the late medieval houses contained a whole feudal community, not just the members of one noble family, and by the mid-1400s a household of 150–200 was not unexceptional for the larger landowners. Communal living in the hall for the lord and his immediate retinue had been replaced by a more private arrangement of solars and closets that led off the hall. This trend accelerated with separate private apartments built for family and servants, and sometimes a garrison block, but the whole arrangement was still dominated by the hall, the public space built and furnished to impress, where all events of any importance took place. With the gradual imposition of law and order the primary concern for defence gave way to more domestic concerns in the appearance of the house, coupled with an ostentatious desire to impress. For several centuries even quite humble farmhouses were built within a moat as a very visible symbol of status.

The internal organization of the early castle observed a similar pattern. One of the best preserved examples of a late medieval courtyard castle, built in the 1380s, is Bodiam in Sussex. Sir Edward Dalyngrigge, one of Edward III's generals, was given licence to fortify his manor house: 'He may strengthen with a wall of stone and lime, and crenellate and may construct into a castle his manor house of Bodyham, near the sea, in the co of Sussex, for the defence of the adjacent county, and the resistance of our enemies …' As a rich man, Sir Edward ensured that his castle was not just a bastion against the French, but also supremely comfortable. His living quarters are now in ruins, having been razed during the Civil War, but the plan is still easily discernible: the door opposite the gatehouse leads into the screens passages of the great hall, with the family's apartments beyond to one side and the servants' quarters and garrison beyond the kitchen on the other. Large arched windows would have allowed light to flood into these rooms.

Oxburgh Hall in Norfolk, first mentioned in the Domesday Book as 'Oxeburgh', meaning the fortified place where oxen are kept, was rebuilt from a smaller house almost exactly a century after Bodiam. In 1482 Edward IV granted permission 'to enclose that manor with walls and towers of this kind; also embattle, crenellate, and machicolate those walls and towers.' Apart from a similar ground plan and a surrounding moat, intended more to reflect the mellow red brick of its beautifully executed walls than as a serious deterrent to attackers, there are few similarities between the two buildings: one was built to perform a serious defensive role, albeit with high standards of interior comfort; the other was constructed in such a manner that the defensive architecture of earlier castles had become mere decoration. The machicolations of the gatehouse at Oxburgh have no gaps through which to pour boiling

1 The black and white timber-framed house of Little Moreton Hall, begun by William Moreton during the 16th century, is a highly decorative example of the genre. A central cobbled courtyard is enclosed on three sides; the fourth gives access to a garden. The whole site is surrounded by the narrow moat.

2 William Moreton's grandson was responsible for the

addition of the long gallery, a popular feature in Elizabethan houses. It provided an elegant room in which to entertain formally and to display paintings.
3 Great Dixter in the Weald was one of many great houses built by wealthy ironmasters. The house was built in 1480 and boasts one of the largest timber-framed halls in the country.

2

oil on intruders below. The Hall is built of soft brick, easily demolished by artillery, and in place of the smooth ashlar of Bodiam the brick walls are highly decorated, the standards of the bricklayers, cutters and moulders impressively high. Complicated shapes and compound curves abound, particularly in the magnificent circular newel staircase that rises through the right-hand tower to the roof. On the first floor of the gatehouse is the King's Room, so-called because in 1487 King Henry VII lodged there on one of his progresses.

The royal progress served several functions: it permitted the monarch to be seen by as many of his subjects as possible, to hear petitions, collect revenues and dispense justice; and by lodging with his more powerful barons for variable amounts of time at huge cost to the hapless host, to impose a financial penalty on those seen to be overstepping the mark. The inventories compiled by his courtiers after the death of Henry VIII describe the specially made trunks that housed the king's effects on his continual journeys around his kingdom. The royal progress, however, had a marked influence on the development of the country house. It was in the reign of Henry's daughter Elizabeth that the great 'prodigy houses' were built. Until the reign of Elizabeth, country houses were generally built according to regional characteristics. The first books on architecture appeared in the mid-1500s and coincided with the rise of the master mason, who became the designer and overseer of major building works, the 'architect' of the house.

A rash of new buildings began to appear on an undreamt-of scale as a result of the wealth released by the suppression of the monasteries and by the increased enclosure of land. The three years that followed the dissolution of the monasteries

begun in 1536 by Henry VIII saw the biggest transference of land since the conquest. An estimated one-third of England was reputed to have changed hands. Between 1540 and the end of his reign, Henry VIII had either given away, sold or exchanged two-thirds of all monastic land and property, distributing this vast wealth amongst no more than about a thousand families.

The 'prodigy houses' were enormous, and built to impress. The queen was unmarried, and her favours alighted on several courtiers in turn. Those who hoped for advancement by entertaining the queen and her retinue required establishments large enough to house such numbers in new suites of rooms away from the hall that was now the preserve of the servants. Contemporary houses had resembled collegiate foundations with a gatehouse and buildings grouped around courtyards within. These inward-looking houses, their design still echoing the defensive needs of earlier times, were gradually replaced with outward-looking houses where the equivalent of one range of a courtyard was omitted. As the focus shifted from the ground floor hall

3

1

2

to the upper storeys where the family's own apartments lay, the fenestration became grander and more elaborate and the rooms within began to evolve different functions. The principal additions were the great chamber and the long gallery on the first floor, or sometimes at the top of the house.

The large houses that were now built elaborated on these new developments, principally Kenilworth, Burghley, Theobalds, Holdenby, Kirby and Longleat, and were in effect proxy palaces built to impress and divert the queen. Kenilworth Castle was given to Robert Dudley, created earl of Leicester by the queen in 1563. By 1570 he had transformed the old castle into a palace in the revived Gothic style, ready to receive the queen. In 1572 she visited briefly whilst staying at nearby Warwick, where she was entertained by the obligatory mock battles, assaults on canvas castles, flying dragons ablaze with spewing fireballs and squibs, and other

costly entertainments. She returned to Kenilworth in 1575 for 19 days and was entertained at enormous expense. At one point in the continuous round of plays, masques, routs and fireworks she was summoned by a trumpet blast to the edge of the lake where Arion was riding on the back of a 7-m (23-ft) dolphin with six musicians concealed in its belly. But the costly building works and lavish entertainment paid dividends. William Cecil, the elder statesman of the age, was the confidant and chief supporter of the queen from her accession to his death in 1598. He would entertain her for weeks at a time at phenomenal cost – but with an equivalent gain in influence and patronage.

Smaller houses for the lesser gentry were also built to reflect the new developments in internal arrangements, but still adhered to marked regional styles. In the northwest of England, where stone was difficult to come by, the art of building in wood flourished and

3

master craftsmen produced a number of ingeniously framed buildings of great structural complexity. The exposed timbers were treated with black pitch and the panels between the frames were plastered and whitewashed. The resulting geometric patterns, as at Little Moreton Hall in Cheshire, were echoed in contemporary knot gardens and embroidery. Little Moreton Hall was substantially added to in 1559 and again before 1580, when the famous Long Gallery spanning the whole of the top floor was added, with its long row of continuous mullioned windows. Long galleries were principally created to enable the household to take exercise in bad weather. Initially built above covered walks or arcades, the first-floor gallery at The Vyne, built by Lord Sandys between 1515 and 1528, is probably the first to be incorporated within the house. It is decorated with the arms, crests and armorial

1 Tudor and Elizabethan houses were built into the west front of Bury St Edmund's abbey church after the dissolution of the monasteries.

2 The small Tudor building with its distinctive chimney is the sole surviving fragment of a brick mansion built on the site of Warden Abbey, a 12th-century Cistercian monastery.

3 Bayham Abbey, East Sussex, was a Premonstratensian house located in the valley of the River Teise on the Kent/Sussex border. After the abbey's dissolution, the site was acquired by the Camden family who commissioned Humphry Repton to landscape the ruins into the garden design.

4 The prosperous Fountains Abbey was one of the first monasteries to be sold by Henry VIII after the dissolution. Fountains Hall was built by its second owner, Sir Stephen Proctor, early in the 17th century. Stone from the abbey's infirmary and surrounding buildings was employed in building the elegant mansion.

4

devices of all the Sandys relations and political allies. In later centuries it was customary to hang serried ranks of family portraits along the walls. A walk in the Long Gallery was therefore to be treated to a show of the connections, influence and prestige of the owner.

The medieval solar, where the lord and his retinue had by the opening of the Tudor period retired from the hurly-burly of the hall, became in the Elizabethan house the great chamber. In many ways it took over the functions of the old hall, chief venue for great gatherings and ceremonial occasions, and as such was decorated with some grandeur. The decoration of the Great Chamber at Gilling Castle in Yorkshire was an exercise in the worship of ancestry in pursuit of the consolida-

tion of family prestige. It was created in the upper floors of a 14th-century tower by Sir William Fairfax in 1575, and the colourful frieze he commissioned to decorate the walls contains the coats of arms of 433 Yorkshire families. The High Great Chamber at Hardwick Hall was by comparison built on a huge scale. Hardwick was built between 1590 and 1597 by the redoubtable Bess of Hardwick, the dowager countess of Salisbury, who had amassed a considerable fortune over four marriages.

The architectural pattern books that became so influential in introducing Renaissance ideas to England were not published in English until the 17th century. The most well known, Sebastiano Serlio's *Five Books*, detailing the classical orders, was published between

1 The Great Court at Athelhampton House near
Dorchester, Dorset, exhibits
fine examples of topiary. It
was a popular decoration in
formal gardens. The yews at
Athelhampton have been
sculpted into pyramids, 9 m
(30 ft) in height.
2 *The Tichborne Dole*, 1670,
depicts the annual Lady Day
ceremony (25 March) at
which the lord of the
manor, Sir Henry Tichborne,
distributes bread to the local
poor. It is a unique portrait
of rural society in the reign
of Charles II, framed in the
context of the great house
which dominates the estate.
3 Elizabeth countess of
Shrewbury, 'Bess of Hard-
wick', built Hardwick Hall in
Derbyshire to a design by
Robert Smythson in the late
16th century. The house is
remarkable for its extensive
and elaborate use of glass.

1537 and 1547 on the continent but not until 1611 in
England. Nonetheless, Sir John Thynne's Longleat, the
first of the 'prodigy houses', begun in 1567, was based on
Serlio's pattern books. The great Elizabethan architect
Robert Smythson first worked at Longleat and was in
turn responsible for two of the era's greatest houses,
Wollaton Hall outside Nottingham, built for Sir Francis
Willoughby in the 1580s, and Hardwick Hall in
Derbyshire. Hardwick was revolutionary: it was not a
courtyard house but symmetrical, with a high proportion of window to wall space. Its windows increased progressively in size from the ground up to reflect the status of the rooms within, the High Great Chamber being
on the second floor. Six towers containing rooms or
'banqueting halls' were reached from the roof.

It was the architect Inigo Jones who is credited with
establishing the fashion for the classical language of
architecture in England, following his first-hand experience of Italy in 1603–14, travelling with Lord Arundel,
one of the earliest 'Grand Tourists'. The greatest Italian
architect of the previous century had been Andrea
Palladio, who had in turn been influenced by Sebastiano
Serlio and his reinterpretations of classical theory. For
Palladio, perfection in architecture was achieved only
through the use of a governing set of proportions that
derived from the measurements of the human body.
He built a large number of celebrated villas in the mid-
16th century and summed up his theories, illustrated by
his own works, in the *Four Books of Architecture*, published
in 1570. A pupil of Palladio's, Vincenzo Scamozzi, carried
the Palladian tradition into the 17th century, and in the
second year of his Grand Tour Inigo Jones made a pilgrimage to meet this disciple of the master.

In 1615, a year after his return to England, Jones was
made surveyor general of the King's Works and by 1620
was established as the principal court architect. Jones's
public buildings for the circle of the court of James I had
a lasting impact. These include his Queen's House at
Greenwich of 1616, the Banqueting House at Whitehall
Palace begun in 1622, and the first classical church to be
built in England, St Paul's, Covent Garden. In 1734 the
architectural critic James Ralph decreed the latter 'one
of the most profound pieces of architecture that the art
of man can produce'. One of his few domestic works
was his collaboration on the refronting of Wilton House
near Salisbury – a favourite house of Charles I – for the
earl of Pembroke in 1636.

The Civil War brought the downfall of Jones – 'few
courtiers sought his services, and
no-one from the trading or
banking classes' – and wrought
havoc with the architectural
development of the nation and
the fortunes of its most powerful families. Those who had
begun to experiment with the
new classical style and all things
al Italiano were no longer in the
ascendant, whereas the lesser
gentry who had acquired new
power through Parliament and a
constitutional monarchy were
the main country house builders
after the Restoration in 1660.
Many of them had spent the

1 One of a set of architectural drawings produced by Placido Columbani *c*.1786, recording the completed decorative schemes in the Little Drawing Room at Audley End.

2 A palace in all but name, Audley End was built by Thomas Howard 1st earl of Suffolk between 1603 and 1614, the year that Suffolk was elevated to the position of lord high treasurer of England. The great mansion was designed to promote Howard's personal power and to accommodate the king and his entourage.

3 The Great Drawing Room is one of a suite of rooms designed by Robert Adam during remodelling of the house around 1760.

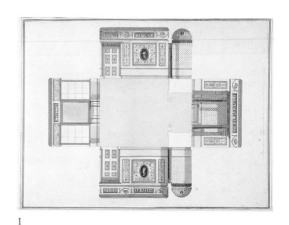

1

Commonwealth in exile in Holland and France and houses like Belton in Lancashire of the 1680s and Uppark in Sussex of the 1690s show a marked Dutch influence.

The first stirrings of the baroque style were seen in the work of Sir Christopher Wren, who took centre stage for more than half a century after the death of Inigo Jones in 1652. It was his pupils, the great baroque architects Vanburgh and Hawksmoor, who were in the ascendant at the turn of the century with theatrical houses, based on French and Italian ideas, of enormous

length. Examples are Castle Howard, built in Yorkshire for the earl of Carlisle in 1699, and Blenheim Palace in Oxfordshire, presented to the 1st duke of Marlborough by a grateful nation following his decisive victories over the French in 1704. Both houses were conceived on a gigantic scale and were festooned with decorative flourishes in the manner of Bernini and Borromini.

At Blenheim, Vanburgh saluted the military hero with a number of symbolic references: lions savaging French cockerels; ducal coronets on reversed fleurs de lis; and the 32-tonne bust of Louis XIV, captured at Tournai, hoisted above the central portico of the south front. The formal social conventions of the 17th century

dictated that rank was acknowledgement by the depth of penetration into the private apartments, those of lesser status being barred from going further than the ante-chamber or withdrawing room, while intimates and those of higher rank might progress through to bedchamber and closet. This *enfilade* of apartments decreasing in size from a central hall was employed by Vanburgh at Blenheim and by Talman in his remodelling of Chatsworth.

The death knell for baroque was the growing xenophobia of the English. Foreigners were increasingly depicted as victims of political or religious tyranny, or as sympathizers of the Jacobite cause, and consequently enemies of the Protestant succession. The interiors of Castle Howard are dominated by the work of Venetian artists and plasterers, and this foreign connotation led, in the political climate of the day, to the fall of the baroque style from favour.

It was Richard Boyle, 3rd earl of Burlington, who was responsible for a revolution in English architectural taste. He had set out on his Grand Tour in 1704, 100 years after Inigo Jones, and based on his studies of the classical theorist Vitruvius and the villas of Palladio, he built his villa at Chiswick, now in southwest London, which can still be visited today. By the 1730s Burlington was widely regarded as the supreme arbiter of architectural taste. Both his buildings and his theories had a profound influence on his contemporaries and were to become the models for hundreds of 18th-century country houses built by his disciples. One of the greatest of these was the Scottish architect Colen Campbell, who published between 1715 and 1725 the three volumes of *Vitruvius Britannicus*, a collection of plates of contemporary houses, and a clever work of propaganda for the Palladian cause.

HOUSES, PARKS & GARDENS

THE BEGINNING OF THE 18TH CENTURY HERALDED THE AGE OF CLASSICISM IN COUNTRY HOUSES, WITH THEIR NEWLY FASHIONABLE PARKS. LANDOWNERS, IMBUED ON THEIR GRAND TOURS WITH LOVE OF ALL THINGS GREEK AND ROMAN, CAME HOME TO BUILD MEDITERRANEAN VILLAS WITH DEEP, SHADY, COLUMNED PORTICOES. THOUSANDS OF VARIATIONS ON THE VILLAS OF PALLADIO'S NATIVE VENETO SPRANG UP IN RURAL SETTINGS, OFFSET BY SCULPTED LANDSCAPES STUDDED WITH FOLLIES, GROTTOES AND CASCADES. THE NEWLY RICH 19TH-CENTURY INDUSTRIALISTS SWEPT AWAY THE OLD ORDER IN FAVOUR OF GOTHIC BATTLEMENTS AND A RETURN TO MEDIEVAL ENGLAND UNTIL OVERTAKEN BY THE LESS BELLIGERENT DOMESTIC-VERNACULAR ARCHITECTURE OF THE ARTS AND CRAFTS MOVEMENT.

HOUGHTON HALL IN NORFOLK was commissioned in 1722 by Sir Robert Walpole, the king's chief minister (an office henceforth to be known as the 'prime minister') from the architect Colen Campbell, a disciple of Lord Burlington. Accordingly it was built in the new 'Palladian' style, severely symmetrical and based on Palladio's rules of harmonic proportion. Walpole was first lord of the Treasury for some 20 years during the reign of George I, and having raised his family from minor Norfolk gentry to be amongst the most powerful in the land, in time-honoured fashion he set about buying land and building a suitable power base to consolidate this success. Colen Campbell was one of the most fashionable architects of the day and William Kent, who was responsible for the

interiors, the most celebrated designer. Their work, together with the lavish furnishings and the finest picture collection in the country, made the incontrovertible statement that Sir Robert Walpole was a man of power, prestige, influence and taste.

Houses were commonly built or expanded to signify a change in status of the owner. In the decades before

the building of Houghton, the Cavendish family rebuilt Chatsworth in Derbyshire to celebrate the elevation of the 4th earl to a dukedom, awarded by King William III in recognition of his support during the 'Glorious Revolution' of 1688. The duke chose William Talman, an exponent of the baroque, shortly to be superseded by the more restrained classicism of Lord Burlington and his circle. The family had first settled at Chatsworth in the 16th century and by 1707 Talman had virtually rebuilt the house around the old Elizabethan core. The Duke ensured that the new exterior of the house was more than matched by the interiors, and he employed the best European artists and craftsmen of the period.

The baroque was a style of strong emphasis: columns were doubled or twisted, decoration and sculpture were monumental, and formal proportion was distorted by the use of curves instead of straight lines. Baroque houses were strung out in receding blocks, encompassing large courtyards, and were lavishly adorned with domes and turrets. All these features are found in abundance at Blenheim Palace, a gift from Queen Anne to the duke of Marlborough in recognition of his great victory at the battle of Blenheim in 1704. It was to be more of a monument than a home. The building was the work of Nicholas Hawksmoor and John Vanbrugh, who also worked at Castle Howard. In both cases, however, Hawksmoor's technical expertise played a considerable part in enabling Vanbrugh's artistic vision to be realized.

A particularly distinctive element of the English country house was its relationship to its site. In previous eras the house had been more of a working institution, a manorial farmhouse, but by the 18th century the house was regarded as one element in the triumvirate of

2

1 *View of Burghley House*, painted in the 19th century. This magnificent country seat near Stamford was built during the latter part of the 16th century by Sir William Cecil, later Lord Burghley, principal adviser to Elizabeth I. The painting shows the 32-acre lake created to enhance the landscape by Lancelot 'Capability' Brown.

2 The wild environment of Alnwick Castle presented Brown with one of his more arduous commissions. It involved levelling and banking the area directly in front of the castle.

3 Blenheim Palace was built between 1705 and 1722 for John Churchill Ist duke of Marlborough. It is held to be the finest work of the baroque architect Sir John Vanbrugh.

house, park and gardens. The fashion for emparkment gained ground rapidly and many an old but inconveniently sited village was swept away in the name of aesthetics. Generally conservative in taste, the English aristocracy regarded with favour those houses that blended harmoniously into the landscape in terms of scale, execution and materials, as opposed to dominating it, as the earlier fashion for terraces, walkways, allées and canals had done. Gardens from the Tudors to the early 18th century had attempted to constrain nature. The new fashion was to manipulate nature by subtly and gently transforming the countryside into carefully sculpted parkland, and bringing the 'wilderness' of trees, grass and deer up to the house. An illusion of Arcadia was thereby presented, hiding the fact that it was a carefully managed effect. Formal gardens were swept away; once straight canals were made to meander and balloon into lakes and cascades; trees were cut down and new groves of semi-mature trees were planted; hills and valleys were repositioned.

One of the new devices used with enthusiasm, which enabled a revolution in the natural approach to landscape design, was the 'ha-ha'. The horticultural equivalent to a defensive ditch, with a 1.5–1.8-m (5–6-ft) deep culvert cut into the ground surface, and a vertical wall built from the bottom of the ditch to ground level on

3

1   The south façade of Harewood House in Yorkshire looks out over an ordered landscape of carefully placed plantations and gently undulating parkland. The setting was created from fields and pasture land by 'Capability' Brown for the owner, Edwin Lascelles.

2   In 1767, Thomas Chippendale was awarded a commission to furnish Harewood throughout. The library writing desk dates from 1770.

3   Harewood's gallery is one of the most magnificent rooms in a quite extraordinary house, all of which was the work of Robert Adam. The ceiling was created to a design drawn by Adam in 1769. Much of the painted decoration was the work of Biagio Rebecca, an artist of Italian descent who had also worked at Windsor Castle, Audley End and Somerset House.

one side and a gentle grass slope on the other, it was invisible to anyone looking from the wall side. The result was an effective means of stock control, enabling animals to get much closer to the house without a high wall blocking the line of sight. Establishing a visual relationship between the country house and its carefully orchestrated landscape became of paramount importance, and for that to succeed there could be no barriers to impede the vistas to and from the house. At Stowe, Charles Bridgeman employed the ha-ha to unite previously unconnected areas into one, effectively 'ring-fencing' the park's boundary.

The house and its garden were now seen as a unit and the site for building a new house was often chosen for aesthetic rather than practical reasons, perhaps on rising ground 'to command the prospect', although the

prospect itself was often then modified to represent what was considered aesthetically ideal, as well as to set off the house itself. Over the decades the creation of these new Arcadian landcapes was dominated by three men: William Kent, Lancelot 'Capability' Brown and Humphry Repton.

One of the delights of Blenheim is the setting of the palace within its park, an effect significantly enhanced by the twin lakes created during a later phase of landscaping by Brown. Sir John Vanbrugh's great bridge had previously crossed no more than a marshy area through which trickled the River Glyme. Vanbrugh's retention of the ruins of Woodstock Manor in the Blenheim grounds as a romantic 'eye-catcher' make him the father of the later English picturesque tradition. By damming and redirecting the flow of water, Brown endowed the scene with a natural splendour that perfectly complemented the architect's work. The harnessing and manipulation of streams and rivers to create lakes and cascades was one of the attributes that set Brown apart from his contemporaries. His innate talent for knowing precisely where and when to use such features contributed greatly to the aesthetic appeal of many country houses and he was constantly in demand.

At Stowe in Buckinghamshire a seminal garden was created as part of a remodelling and restructuring process of both house and grounds undertaken between 1713 and 1776. The work was under the direction of three successive members of the Temple family, and several of the greatest innovative architects and landscape designers of the early and mid-18th century worked on it, merging together 160 ha (400 acres) of garden and park to transform Stowe into the finest example of the new form of landscape garden. Charles Bridgeman was the first gardener to be engaged and the layout and planting scheme he used at Stowe reflected his formal training. It was not until 1730 that the gardens assumed their true picturesque quality following the arrival of William Kent, considered the father of English landscape gardening. Until then, Sir John Vanbrugh had also been working at Stowe, both on the house and designing garden structures – he had placed a rotondo on a knoll to the southeast of the house, which provided views out over the park to the countryside beyond.

However, at around the same time as Kent arrived, architect James Gibbs replaced Vanbrugh. It was this new team of Kent and Gibbs that merged landscape and architecture and turned Stowe into a great landscape garden. Bridgeman's formal, straight lines – so typical of continental work – were softened and made irregular, and strategically sited Arcadian ornamental buildings, such as the Palladian bridge, were erected where they could be observed in a panoramic sweep from the rotondo, or appreciated individually on foot as each led on to a fresh and surprising change of composition.

One of the garden's most attractive features is the Elysian Fields, named after the paradise of classical mythology and created along what was once a public road to Stowe. A stream replicated the River Styx, whose banks were appropriately planted to create a Stygian gloom, its darkness gradually lightening as the valley progressed, and it was adorned with Doric arches, temples and other buildings.

It was in 1740, towards the completion of the Elysian Fields, that a young gardener named Lancelot Brown was recruited to the staff at Stowe. He must have been influenced by Kent's work, but once he was established his style became far less intimate than Kent's, working with broad sweeping vistas and concentrating more on creating desired effects by landscaping, judicious tree placement and water features than by dotting his creations with artificial eye-catchers. Brown thought nothing of altering contours as necessary by excavating tonnes of earth in order to create his beloved lakes and water features. Because his schemes relied heavily on the use of trees to achieve the sought-after effect, he developed a machine for digging up mature trees that enabled species over 6 m (20 ft) high to be successfully replanted. At Chatsworth, which underwent a fashionable landscaping, Daniel Defoe was astounded to see the changes that had occurred between his visits: 'The duke has removed a great mountain that stood in the way,' he wrote. 'I was perfectly confounded for I had lost the hill and found a new country in view.' Defoe's observation perfectly encapsulates the objectives of the great landscape designers such as 'Capability' Brown and Humphry Repton.

The inclusion in the landscapes of references to classical mythology was a reflection of the strong influence they wielded in England among those who commissioned the houses and gardens. Classical education and an exposure to Greek and Roman history instilled in young gentlemen a fascination with the ancient world, resulting in their culturally enlightening Grand

1

Tours to study Italian antique and Renaissance art and architecture. The focus for many was fixed firmly on the period of Imperial Rome, creating a desire to express the ideals they had read about and to experience them at first hand through their lifestyle and properties.

The picturesque movement sought to meet these desires, and it was Vanbrugh at Castle Howard who made one of the first attempts at transforming a proposed formal layout into a vast Elysian field with temples and obelisks erected on high ground so that the entire scheme formed some kind of cohesive link between monument and nature. Each vantage point opened up a fresh vista, the focal point of which was another temple or similar structure. At the many sites that were created during the ensuing decades of experimentation and refinement, the ultimate aim was to present viewers with a succession of different 'canvases' as they progressed on foot or by carriage. The same rules of composition and perspective used by artists were employed by the gardeners: hills, trees, water, fake ruins and statuary were fashioned in the natural equivalent of a landscape painting.

From 1715 onwards the classical revival was under way, led by Colen Campbell and Lord Burlington. It was to remain highly influential in England until the 19th century. One of their triumphs was the growing fashion for the Palladian style, which was regarded as 'natural', as opposed to the baroque, which was 'artificial'. A significant development was the penchant for Palladian-style country villas rather than traditional grand houses – although the villas were by no means small.

In 1720 Campbell began work on the square house of Stourhead in Wiltshire for a banker, Henry Hoare. As splendid as the relatively modest Palladian house was, the architecture that was added to the garden was sumptuous, for Stourhead is laid out with a series of walks punctuated by views containing the obelisk, the Pantheon, the Palladian Bridge, the Temple of Flora, the Temple of Apollo, St Peter's Church, the Bristol High Cross and a Grotto with statuary.

2

3

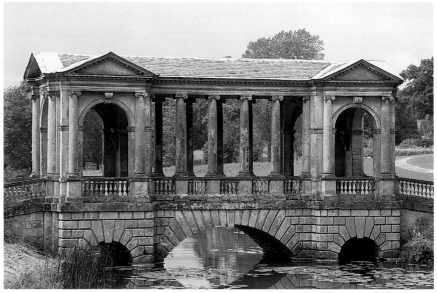

1, 2 Wrest Park in Bedfordshire was built during the
1830s by the de Grey family.
Its style is modelled on that
of an 18th-century French
chateau, and the garden
designs encompass more
than 150 years of changing
tastes and fashions. The
intricate formality of the
French garden gives way to
a extending landscape of
woods, canals, fountains
and follies.

3 Chatsworth's core dates
back to the Elizabethan
mansion built by 'Bess of
Hardwick', but the present
house dates from the end of
the 17th century. The 1st
duke of Devonshire added
the south front in 1687.
Other façades followed in
succession to create a house
of rich classical style.

Works such as Stowe or Stourhead established the desirability of enhancing a park with buildings, but tastes varied from patron to patron and although classical overtones were the most popular, by the 19th century Gothic ruins were in vogue. Ready-made designs could be ordered to suit all tastes, seasons and locations, but some landowners adapted the ruins of earlier buildings already on site. 'Capability' Brown was summoned to Sandbeck Park in Yorkshire, the newly built residence of the 4th earl of Scarborough, and asked to reorganize the landscape, which contained the Cistercian monastery of Roche Abbey, with a 'poet's feeling and painter's eye'. Alongside Brown's customary terracing, discreet water-

1

2

falls and artificial lake, substantial parts of the monastic buildings were 'remodelled'. The losses in pursuit of an artistic composition caused quite an uproar, but despite that the pattern was soon repeated throughout the countryside wherever old abbeys and priories could be found. Some landowners were more circumspect than others and the ruins of Fountains Abbey, for example, have been preserved for their intrinsic elegance and grace, rather than as an atmospheric ruin in the park.

In 1734 the painter and landscape gardener William Kent emerged as a fully fledged architect through his collaboration with Burlington at Holkham Hall, Norfolk. Little was known about classical interiors, so the Palladians had free rein, and in the entrance hall at Holkham their astonishingly original creation in marble encapsulated the nature of the classical revival. The Palladian interior is typically planned so that the important rooms are on the first floor and the entranceway has a staircase to access that floor.

Harewood House represents a fine example of how a wealthy landowner sought out the best designers and architects of the period to ensure that his house and grounds were at least the equals of those owned by house guests or visitors. In 1738 Edwin Lascelles, whose fortune derived from the sugar plantations of Barbados, had gone on the Grand Tour and returned with ideas and ambitions to re-create the classical styles he had seen. He commissioned Robert Carr of York as architect and in 1758 Lascelles showed his plans for the house to Robert Adam, who was at that time seeking to establish himself in London following a period of intensive study in Italy. The Harewood commission provided a perfect showcase for Adam's classical designs and his highly individual style, going beyond the Palladians and attempting the classical itself, subsequently called neo-classicism, featured in every room, from ceilings down to carpets – an attempt at artistic unity, all perfectly augmented by the furniture of the renowned craftsman Thomas Chippendale. Although Adam supplied drawings to other cabinetmakers, his collaborations with Chippendale were based on mutual trust and under-

standing of one another's artistic interpretations of a particular scheme. Chippendale, a Yorkshireman, favoured mahogany, newly introduced to England from South America. Although generally regarded as working within the rococo style, he avoided the excess that is sometimes exemplified by that style and was later much influenced in his designs and decoration by the work of Adam.

The scale of most country houses made them difficult places in which to live in warmth and comfort. Internally, a hall and the system of informal parlours and a suite of formal apartments had been consolidated in the Elizabethan era. In the 18th century, however, the influence of European models was felt and interior layouts underwent great change. The dining room or saloon remained with the hall at the centre of the house, but in baroque houses apartments were arranged in linear fashion so as to create a Versailles-like vista radiating from the saloon, whereby a visiting monarch might be made welcome. Such a layout resulted in extended façades – Stowe or Wentworth Woodhouse – as the wings extended off the centre. Over time these rooms became superfluous to the needs of the family, who required the comfort afforded by the smaller rooms elsewhere in the house. Such family rooms were

tucked away in a more private wing, often on the ground floor.

By the mid-18th century, display was evident not just in the building itself, but in its contents: a library was now considered a necessity, and the family's paintings and sculptures – often evidence of the grand tour – were displayed in surroundings to match, accompanied by Chippendale furniture or Wedgwood pottery. In the Palladian houses, a grand entrance would be accompanied by a variety of entertaining rooms – the library, music room and so on – which led off the saloon to provide a route for guests to follow. This plan is found in both Houghton Hall in Norfolk and Harewood House.

In older English houses access to individual bedrooms could only be effected by passing through other rooms. The newer house interiors introduced the corridor and the apartment system became the accepted format for guest accommodation, although one that was governed by strict rules of etiquette and rank. Family members and guests would each have their own 'apartment', varying from one room up to six or more for the most lavishly appointed state apartments.

By the late 18th century, state apartment interiors were commonly furnished with mirrored glass in preference to paintings. At Harewood, Chippendale had

1

the glass cut in special workshops to fit within bespoke frames and girandoles. Many examples can be found throughout Harewood, where they perfectly complement some of Adam's more elaborate ceiling designs – none more so than in the Gallery, which extends for more than 23 m (76 ft) along the entire west end of the house. One of Chippendale's more unusual contributions was to make pelmets to hang above each window, carved from wood in perfect simulation of a heavy fabric bedecked with gold tassels. To complement the interior work of these two master craftsmen, in 1772 Lascelles commissioned Brown – who had derived his nickname of 'Capability' through his practice of informing patrons that their properties almost certainly possessed capabilities for improvement – to 'improve' the fields and pasture surrounding Harewood House.

The early 19th century saw a revival of interest in Greek architecture and decoration, but it was the Gothic revival during the Victorian era that influenced a new genre of country houses. In the second half of the 18th century, Horace Walpole's villa at Strawberry Hill had presaged this development, but it was an exception

rather than the rule. In the 80 years to 1914 the country house changed far more in terms of its architecture and social assumptions than in the whole of the previous 120 years. From being the preserve of the hereditary landed classes, country house society became open to anyone rich enough to buy their way in. The later 19th century was the heyday of the Gothic country house, built mainly for the 'new aristocracy' of wealthy industrialists: Anthony Slavin's rebuilding of Scotney Castle in Kent (1835–43); Scarisbrick Hall in Lancashire by Augustus Pugin; Elvetham Hall in Hampshire by Samuel Teulon; Knightshayes Court in Devon by William Burges; Highclere Castle in Berkshire by Charles Barry.

The fashion for houses in the Gothic style was given a new direction with the Arts and Crafts movement, which offered a more domestic vernacular architecture in which great attention was paid to detail and to layout, and its great evangelists were Pugin, Ruskin and Morris. In praise of the new style William Morris wrote: 'In these walls you may cut windows wherever you please … you have no longer to make a lesson in logic in order not to sit in pitch darkness in your own home, as in the sham Roman style …' Examples include Standen in Kent; Wightwick Manor near Wolverhampton, which harks back to the Tudor-Elizabethan manor house; and Cragside in Northumberland. All had more comfortable, less formal, interiors and the garden was more a domesticated and floral refuge than a carefully landscaped monument for effect or contemplation.

By the turn of the 20th century, country houses were no longer expected to express the prestige, authority and power of their owners, which had been the guiding principle for a thousand years.

2

1 The spectacular Great Conservatory at Syon House was designed by Charles Fowler in the 1820s. It provides a focus for the 12 ha (30 acres) of garden enclosed within the 81 ha (200 acres) of parkland, cleverly landscaped by 'Capability' Brown.

2 Keddleston Hall in Derbyshire, built between 1758 and 1765 by Robert Adam, James Paine and Matthew Brettingham. The influence of the young Robert Adam is significant. Fresh from the Grand Tour, his references to the antique – in this case the Arch of Constantine – are evident.

3 Rievaulx Terrace and Temples illustrate the harmonious blend of man-made elements with natural surroundings typical of 18th-century landscape design. A long grass-covered walk links Tuscan and Ionic temples with avenues cut through the banks of trees to provide occasional glimpses of the abbey ruins below.

3

LONDON'S 'COUNTRY' HOUSES

ROYAL PALACES, SUCH AS ELTHAM OR HAMPTON COURT BESIDE THE RIVER THAMES, HAD EXISTED AROUND LONDON FOR CENTURIES. IN THE 17TH CENTURY, HAM HOUSE NEAR RICHMOND BECAME THE HUB OF COURT LIFE, CENTRED AROUND A CABAL OF PROMINENT ARISTOCRATS. HOWEVER, THE VOGUE FOR THE 'COUNTRY VILLA' WITHIN STRIKING DISTANCE OF TOWN WAS THE INSPIRATION OF THE 3RD EARL OF BURLINGTON. HE BUILT HIS HOUSE NEAR CHISWICK IN THE 1720S, DOMED AND PORTICOED IN EMULATION OF ANDREA PALLADIO'S VILLA ROTONDA. A RASH OF BUILDING FOLLOWED, INCLUDING THE EXQUISITE, MINIATURE PALLADIAN MANSION, MARBLE HILL HOUSE NEAR HAM HOUSE AND THE ADAM HOUSES OF SYON, OSTERLEY AND KENWOOD.

LONDON IN THE 18TH CENTURY was the world's economic powerhouse. A period of peace and prosperity following the defeat of the French, and the Unions with Scotland and Ireland made London more than a centre of political and imperial power. It became the focus of Britain's courtly, social and cultural life, especially before 'the season' ended in June each year. The governing élite, many of them graduates of the Grand Tour, increasingly regarded themselves as inheritors of a classical tradition established by Augustan Rome.

For the established, or those aspiring to be, it was

imperative to have a townhouse in London to complement a country seat. By the mid-18th century many people had created villas, executed in the latest taste, within the countryside adjacent to the capital. They echoed the traditions of Rome as well as the English court, which had long maintained palaces along the river from Westminster at Greenwich, Kew, Windsor and elsewhere. It was not unusual, therefore, for the élite and wealthy mercantile classes to establish country houses and villas in favoured locations within a 32-km

(20-mile) radius of the capital. Two such London country houses were created in the second half of the 18th century by Robert Adam. At Syon House (1762–69) in Twickenham, commissioned by the duke of Northumberland (who maintained a townhouse in central London, supplied with food from Syon's farm), a residence was planned that among other things enabled the women to retire well away from the men. The houses were used interchangeably to entertain political figures, although the summer was generally spent at Syon, before travelling to spend time at the family's principal country seat at Alnwick in Northumberland.

Meanwhile, Osterley Park at Isleworth in Middlesex (1761–80) gave physical embodiement to economic and social progress. The crumbling, late 16th-century Elizabethan mansion was acquired by the banker Robert Child (whose family owned Colen Campbell's creation of Wanstead House outside London until it was demolished in 1824). Child commissioned Robert Adam to transform Osterley into an elegant neoclassical villa for the entertainment of friends and business associates. The result is a most spectacular and complete example of Adam's work, featuring a magnificent open portico and long interior gallery.

Yet another example of Robert Adam's work was the neoclassical house of Kenwood, set high up on Hampstead Heath and surrounded by trees, ponds and green fields. Robert, together with his brother James, modified the already extant dwelling there, having been commissioned by the Lord Chief Justice, William Murray earl of Mansfield, to submit plans for the work in 1764. In their *Works of Architecture,* published in 1774, the brothers extol the virtues of the view over London from Kenwood, describing a panorama that encompassed the City, Greenwich Hospital and river traffic on the Thames. A painting dating from 1775 is the earliest known view of

2

Kenwood *in situ*; it shows the distinctive white building standing isolated in a landscape of rolling green wooded hills and pastures.

Robert Adam revelled in the creative freedom accorded him by Lord Mansfield. An open brief allowed his obsessive continuity of design to be realized fully in both interior and exterior, epitomized by the two principal façades. The north front portico is modelled on classical public architecture, specifically the Erechtheion on the Athenian Acropolis, but Adam devised his own columns and combined features from both the Ionic and Corinthian orders. Kenwood's interior and south front contrast strongly with the entrance's formality; the south façade in particular derived more from his experiments with interior decoration than from classical and Palladian precedents.

Adam created the symmetry now present in the south front of Kenwood by building the library wing to balance with the earlier orangery. The entire façade was then refaced in a newly patented oil-based cement, an economical way to reproduce architectural decoration. The gleaming white south façade is a complex essay in low-relief, similar to work found in the library and characteristic of Adam's growing tendency towards detail and refinement. In creating the white stucco façade, the brothers were architecturally ahead of a fashion more readily identified with Nash and the Regency period. Many people travelled from London to view the innovative designs, but not everyone was impressed. One critic proclaimed: 'While he [Robert Adam] aimed at elegance within, he covered the outside of his buildings with frippery.'

The Great Room or Library, together with its ante chamber, was the only room in Kenwood solely erected by Adam. In its basic form, the room is a double cube with an apse at either end and a curved ceiling, patterns from which are echoed in the carpet beneath. The pairs of Corinthian columns create a sense of constraint that effectively exaggerates the scale of the room beyond. Mirrored recesses contribute to the visual manipulation, directing one's gaze back out towards the grounds in what Adam acknowledged to be 'a most singular and beautiful effect'.

3

He sought to emulate the glory of ancient Rome by creating the kind of house and garden that might have been found in the suburbs there, and he built it adjacent to his older, Elizabethan house that was subsequently demolished in 1788. Lord Burlington drew his inspiration from several sources, including Palladio's own domed Villa Rotonda. The columns of Chiswick's portico were based on the Roman temple of Jupiter Stator, the shallow dome on Rome's Pantheon and the semi-circular windows directly below it on the ancient Roman baths of Diocletian. Burlington's creative debt to Inigo Jones and Palladio is acknowledged in their statues, which flank the main entrance. As with Northumberland, the house was for recreation and entertainment: Burlington also had a townhouse in Piccadilly, which, in a substantially altered building, now houses the Royal Academy. The garden at Chiswick pioneered naturalistic landscaping.

The principal rooms at Chiswick are located on the first floor. An octagonal hall at its heart is sparsely but grandly furnished, with room for functions or entertainment. However, the austere elegance of Chiswick House had no disruptive kitchen (a link had been built from the villa to his adjacent mansion, in which meals were prepared and eaten). Radiating from the central octagon, the colourful and opulently decorated rooms were more intimate – venues for affable encounters between like-minded connoisseurs and specifically designed to house some of Lord Burlington's art collec-

Kenwood's grounds and gardens underwent three distinct phases: a formal layout in the mid-18th century, followed by a more picturesque scheme, and finally a remodelling of the landscape by Humphry Repton in 1793 which remains largely intact.

It was, however, Lord Burlington, an enthusiast for the 16th-century Italian architect Andrea Palladio, who was responsible for the archetypal London country house – his startling innovation at Chiswick (page 282), built during the 1720s with an interior by William Kent.

1 Marble Hill House is an elegant Palladian villa occupying a secluded riverside setting on the Thames near Richmond. It was built during the 1730s, and although still in the same classical style as Chiswick, exhibits little of the flamboyance associated with Lord Burlington's villa.

2 A narrow stone staircase provides access to all three upper floors. Visitors would have been unaware of its presence, as the first floor state rooms were reached by more formal stairs which ended on the first floor.

3 Marble Hill exhibits the Palladian mannerism of introducing four pillars into a hall. The concept was derived from Palladio's original interpretation of the central court of a Roman house.

2

tion. Each room was also adorned with finely detailed allegorical ceiling paintings, some attributed to Kent. He also extended the garden's lawned area, bringing the house and river beyond into a unified visual relationship. The majority of Chiswick's gardens retain an Italianate appearance, with formal and informal walks and avenues leading to a succession of architectural features including statues, temples, urns and obelisks.

The year in which Chiswick House was finished also saw the completion of an equally beautiful Palladian villa overlooking the Thames near Richmond. Built for Henrietta Howard, mistress of King George II, Marble Hill House derives its impact from perfect proportions inspired by Palladio. The villa, in a highly fashionable location, features prominently in one of Turner's finest versions of Richmond Terrace, painted in 1836.

Marble Hill House's construction drew upon the proceeds of a settlement given to Henrietta by the king. In her quest to make provision for a life outside Court, she was assisted by Archibald Campbell earl of Ilay, who secured the land, and Henry Herbert, later 9th earl of Pembroke, her architectural advisor. Original designs were probably drawn by Colen Campbell, originator of the Palladio-Jones revival, then amended and taken to completion by Herbert. As heir to the owner of Wilton House in Wiltshire, Herbert grew up in rooms created by Inigo Jones, including the famous 'Single Cube' on which Marble Hill's Great Room was based.

As was customary in houses of that period, the most important room occupied the first floor and Marble Hill's Great Room is flanked by three bedrooms and a dressing-room. Below the deeply coved ceiling, which penetrates up into the third storey, the room is contained within a 7-m (24-ft) cube, and although each wall is different the symmetry is maintained by the inclusion of two false doors. Wilton appears to have influenced Herbert's treatment of the hall, which was accorded a white and gold colour scheme. It contained copies of Van Dyck paintings in frames almost identical to those in the original 'cube'.

Marble Hill's Gallery was the second finest room within the villa, owing more to Elizabethan and Jacobean architectural traditions than Palladio. Located on the floor above the hall, the Gallery extends along the full length of the house. Although the villa was designed for living in, it also became a well-known meeting place for leading literary and artistic figures.

The grounds surrounding Marble Hill House reflect the elegant simplicity of its design, mainly comprising areas of grass interspersed with judicious tree planting.

3

ESTATE LIFE

The status of the servant changed radically from medieval times to the 19th century. Willing accomplices in the complicated ceremonial that marked the grandeur of their feudal lords, the 'upper servants' had vanished to other career ladders by the end of the Elizabethan era. The 19th century was the apogee of the servant. Architects advised their clients to design their houses according to the number of staff available to run them. An army under the direction of the butler, cook and housekeeper ensured smooth running indoors; the head gardener and the gamekeeper did the same for the grounds. The whole hierarchy was to be swept away in the trenches of World War I, leaving sculleries, pantries and boot rooms to the encroaching ivy.

THE EARLY MEDIEVAL HOUSEHOLD accommodated master and servants together, the 'upper' servants generally being of the same class as their employer. In the late medieval period, the lord and his family moved from the communal hall to private apartments and left the hall exclusively to the servants and retainers, the hall being used by the lord only on the equivalent of state occasions. Servants were not to be ejected from the main house until the middle of the 17th century, when they were banished to a servants' hall with an accompanying set of rooms in the basement. By the 18th century, the saloon had replaced the great chamber and the hall began to reduce in size to the continental model of the vestibule inside the front door – though

well into the century many country houses still kept old-style large halls as ancillary rooms for entertainment. Simultaneously the back stairs were invented to keep the servants hidden. This became a national obsession, with stairs, tunnels and even railways being employed to keep the activities 'below stairs' hidden from the household. A 19th-century writer stated 'under no circumstances of course should the servants overlook the private life of the family … none of their windows should command the lawn or private garden'.

The last vestiges of the pomp and ceremony that accompanied the formal serving of food, every course preceded by an usher, and followed by a retinue of servants each with their own specialist function, died out in the early 18th century. No longer were servants required to sleep in truckle beds outside their master's door, or lady's maids near their mistresses, as had happened in earlier centuries. Specialist service wings were built, which reached their apogee in the 19th century

with rooms and servants for every conceivable task – the ultimate in specialization being a room kept exclusively for ironing the newspapers. The only visible servants were the butler and, in grand establishments, liveried footmen who waited at table and received visitors. Their function was largely ornamental and they were often hired as matching pairs according to height and width of calf. A liveried servant symbolized the household's wealth and prestige.

The indoor servants divided into three departments ruled by the butler (or steward), the housekeeper and the cook. Each took their orders daily from the mistress of the house and were in turn responsible for their staff. The butler was in charge of the footmen and ruled the pantry where the plate and the silver was cleaned. The walk-in safe with its heavy iron doors often led off his bedroom. He ensured the smooth running of the dining room and the transfer and serving of food. The housekeeper ran the house and was responsible for the laundry maids, who cleaned, mended, set fires, trimmed lamps and did the laundry. The cook's domain was the kitchen and its ancillary preparation rooms, and she was in charge of the kitchen and scullery maids. The organization of below-stairs life in the mid-19th century, when servants and the different rooms they inhabited were at their most numerous, was complex, vastly more so than in the equivalent houses of France or Germany. Never fewer than 15 and sometimes up to 40 servants (Mentmore had 34) catered for the needs of the household. They were constantly on call, summoned by a system of wires and bells from each room. They drew hot water for baths, trimmed, filled and distributed up to 70 oil lamps every evening, cleaned fireplaces and set fires in rooms all over the

1 A portrait of maids in service at Biddlesden Park House, Buckinghamshire at the end of the 19th century.
   Life for servants in Victorian households was one of hard work and equally strict discipline. Positions in country houses were held to be the most attractive.
2 Sir Robert Walpole, Britain's first prime minister, built Houghton Hall, his Norfolk mansion, on the site of two earlier houses. Work began in 1721, but the existing village proved an eyesore to Walpole and so was demolished. Servants and estate workers were relocated to a 'model' village located outside the park, which appropriately enough was named New Houghton.

house, and polished everything until it shone. For a lower servant, life was hard, yet in the 20 years between 1851 and 1871 female domestic servants increased twice as fast as the population as a whole. In comparison with other work, jobs in the large country houses were the best paid and most sought after.

The upper servants were given considerable trust and responsibility by their employers and their accommodation was comparatively spacious. They ruled the under servants with a rod of iron and in some households copied the rules imposed on them – that they should not speak unless they were spoken to. But there was also room for levity: some houses held weekly dances in the servants' hall to which the outside staff were invited, and an annual ball at which the master of the house danced with the housekeeper and his wife with the butler. These were legitimate occasions for servants of both sexes to meet in a period of strict segregation. With the decline in the number of servants employed, and their eventual devastation on the battlefields of World War I, the rooms and offices dedicated to various specialist tasks were the first to be abandoned.

287

A Place in the Country

2

1 The magnificent entrance to Clumber Park in Nottinghamshire. Beyond the gates is the longest planted avenue in England, a double row of over 1,200 lime trees. The mansion belonging to the dukes of Newcastle was demolished in 1938, but their 1618 ha (4,000 acre) landscaped park survives.

2 Hunting, shooting and fishing have always played a major role in country life, especially in past centuries when self-sufficiency was essential. Social functions such as shooting parties drew upon hired labour from across the estate.

3 A group of gardeners and estate workers from Biddlesden Park House, Buckinghamshire. Large country parks and gardens required an army of retainers to keep grounds and game supplies in order.

1

2

The outside servants also had a range of specialist tasks. The coachman and grooms looked after the stables and horses, and in due course the motor house and motor cars. They lived above the stables. The kennelman looked after the hounds if there was a hunt attached to the house; if not, the job was taken over by the gamekeeper. Dogs were bred for different purposes: terriers for hunting rabbits and ejecting foxes from their dens; labradors and spaniels for retrieving fallen birds. The gamekeeper lived in his own cottage and kept the estate clear of vermin, shooting and trapping animals that were regarded as pests. He also reared pheasants for the shoot, buying eggs and keeping them under broody hens until they hatched and then releasing them into the coverts where he fed them until ready for the beginning of the shooting season. He liaised with the master about which coverts to shoot in what order, and organized the beaters accordingly. The blacksmith worked in the smithy, shoeing horses and attending to the ironwork of the estate, the best craftsmen making ornamental gates and other decorative items. The joiners and sawyers worked with the timber from the estate, sawing the logs into planks in the sawpits, stacking them to season and dry, and then making and mending as required.

The head gardener was as redoubtable a figure amongst the outdoor servants as the butler was indoors. He lived in the gardener's cottage and ruled a staff of under-gardeners and apprentices who lived in bothies built into the walls of the gardens. His domain covered the formal gardens and their planting, the stretches of lawn and the gravel walks, as well as the walled kitchen garden where produce for the house was grown. The kitchen garden was a world of its own, enclosed in high

walls with a variety of glasshouses for fruits and exotics, specialist 'pits' for new imports like pineapples, and walls heated by flues to keep the first frosts from the emerging fruit. In the 19th century, during the London season, hampers of food were packed in vine leaves and despatched by train to feed the London household.

Most large estates let the land to tenants who, generated the income required to keep up the owner's lifestyle, with the exception of the home farm, which kept cattle, sheep and pigs for the needs of the household. The farm was usually sited some distance from the house, because the Victorians in particular had problems

3

with smells — kitchens also were as far away as possible and incorporated side draughts to dissipate smells.

With the huge increase in country-house visiting and a corresponding interest in the life of the estate, many houses open to the public have restored not just the state and family rooms, but also the servants' wing, stable and farmyard, kitchen garden, blacksmith's shop, and the sawyer's pit and joinery shop, to help visitors experience a now vanished way of life.

CHAPTER

10

The network of roads and railways which drive through
the topography of the English countryside were created to meet
the needs of trade and warfare – to take goods to market, or to move
troops between forts in times of war or civil unrest. Road conditions
deteriorated sharply after the Roman withdrawal and were not to be
of the same quality again for over a thousand years. The invention
of the coach and the turnpike road prompted a revival of interest
in road building, but it was the invention of the steam train and
the expansion of the railways into every byway of England
which allowed mass travel for the first time. It precipitated
a social revolution which encompassed the institution
of the seaside holiday for city dwellers.

TRAVEL & TRANSPORT

FIRST TRACKS

ENGLAND'S ANCIENT ROADS AND TRACKS HAVE CARRIED PEOPLE AND LIVESTOCK FOR CENTURIES. EVIDENCE OF WOODEN PATHWAYS HAS BEEN PRESERVED IN PEAT IN THE SOMERSET LEVELS, AND PREHISTORIC TRACKS SUCH AS THE RIDGEWAY AND THE ICKNIELD WAY ARE STILL VISIBLE IN THE MODERN LANDSCAPE. IRON AGE ROADS USUALLY ACCOMMODATED THE CONTOURS OF THE TERRAIN AND USED LOCAL FEATURES AS LANDMARKS — OR CREATED THEIR OWN, SUCH AS THE UFFINGTON WHITE HORSE. THE ROMAN ROADS, BY CONTRAST, WERE EFFICIENT MILITARY STRUCTURES, FOLLOWING STRAIGHT LINES ACROSS THE LANDSCAPE FROM FORT TO FORT. THEIR NETWORK WAS SUBSEQUENTLY DEVELOPED FOR COMMERCIAL USE, BUT AFTER THE ROMAN WITHDRAWAL ROADS GRADUALLY DETERIORATED. DROVE ROADS AND GREEN LANES WERE USED IN MEDIEVAL TIMES.

I t is impossible to say exactly when the first English trackways came into being. From about 6000 BC, ancient Britons were using fire to burn down the forest and create new grazing land, moving herds of cattle from pasture to pasture along well-defined routes. The prehistoric tracks made in the Somerset Levels, for example, are evidence of ancient land management. Cattle were driven over the peat bogs along pathways woven from coppiced hazel rods between 5,000 and 6,000 years ago.

Neolithic peoples were traders as well as farmers, often travelling long distances to exchange salt for stone

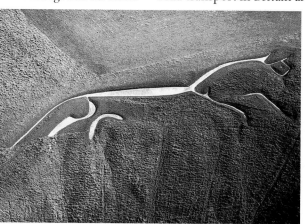

tools. Where river crossings were needed, fords were generally used, although the clapper bridge at Portsbridge in Dartmouth is estimated to be 2,000 years old. It is constructed from slabs of granite 4.5 m (15 ft) in length and supported by two piers of roughly shaped granite in the centre of the stream. Another crossing at Tarr Steps in Somerset is thought to be even older. Seventeen flagstones cover a distance of 55 m (180 ft), but the supporting piers are lower here and the bridge is periodically damaged by the high waters of the River Barle, a tributary of the Exe.

Wherever possible, however, ancient trackways ran along the downs or bare ridges, avoiding the swamp and forest below, which their users lacked the technical knowledge to drain. The Icknield Way, for example, followed the line of the Chiltern Hills, linking the fens of East Anglia – then, as now, a major source of food – with the more populated areas around Avebury and Stonehenge. Chesterton's celebrated comment that 'The rolling English drunkard made the rolling English road' is in reality a little unfair, as the old roads were good enough for some form of wheeled transport and

adapted logically to the native terrain. The Ridgeway, a great prehistoric route running into the heart of Wessex, follows a similar pattern along the Berkshire downs. It climbs the hill at Uffington past the magnificent White Horse cut into the chalk near the summit, 305 m (1,000 ft) above sea level and a prominent landmark at the junction of local roads. The position over the surrounding countryside was so dominant that an Iron Age fort was built there too, defending the Ridgeway from both east and west.

The engineering skill of the Romans transformed road transport in Britain after the invasion of AD 43. The legions, assisted by local conscript labour, constructed a new network across the country, designed primarily for military use and linking forts in a straight line across country for rapid reinforcement. Some, such as the Fosse Way, running from Lincoln to Exeter via Leicester and Bath, formed a provisional frontier. Once the military links were secure, the Romans built commercial roads as well, connecting the major industrial centres – the Nene potteries, the Weald iron industry, the lead mines of the Mendips and the Pennines – with the main ports and regional capitals. In the first 100 years of occupation they built at least 13,000 km (8,000 miles) of road, so many that even the remotest farm or hamlet was never more than 10 or 11 km (6 or 7 miles) from the nearest engineered road.

The roads were constructed of local materials, usually a large bed of stones, then a smaller one, then a surface layer of gravel or flint mixed with earth that would compress in use. They were built to last, and many of them still exist today, their ancient origins long since concealed under acres of concrete. There is no longer anything remotely Roman about Watling Street

PAGES 290, 291
Main picture: The Roman
  Fosse Way which runs from
  Lincoln to Exeter.
Detail: The Ribblehead Viaduct
  on the Settle to Carlisle
  Railway in Yorkshire.

PRECEDING PAGES
1 The ancient landmark of
   the White Horse at
   Uffington is cut into a chalk
   hill along the Ridgeway, a
   major trading route of
   prehistoric Britain.
2 From late Saxon times
   onwards, the boundaries of
   large estates were often
   marked by green lanes. This
   one is near Stow-on-the-
   Wold in Gloucestershire.

1

by St Paul's Cathedral, for example, once the starting point for Shrewsbury. Yet some Roman roads remain instantly recognizable, as at Wheeldale Moor in Yorkshire, or Holtye in Sussex and Blackpool Bridge in the Forest of Dean, where stretches of Roman paving are apparent. Chesters in Northumberland still has the remnants of a Roman bridge, as does Piercebridge in Durham. Other roads have reverted to nature, but are recognizable from the air by chalk outlines in the soil or the straight hedgerows that often grew up alongside.

After the Roman withdrawal in the 5th century, no hard roads were built in England until 18th-century turnpikes. The Romano-British and Saxon peoples simply made do with what the Romans had left behind, without attempting to maintain it. Bridges collapsed, surfaces gradually disintegrated, and the stones were

2

eventually quarried for other purposes. The Saxons, who took over large areas of England in the sixth century, made good use of the remaining Roman network, and even built a few roads of their own, called *straets*. The Vikings did the same, but they built muddy tracks rather than proper stone highways. In the 10th century, Alfred's new *burhs* (fortified towns) sometimes developed new street patterns, but elsewhere, as in London, the Roman paving was simply covered by rough Saxon tracks. It was another thousand years before the English again enjoyed a network as good as the Romans'.

Anglo-Saxon communities still needed mobility to trade, however, particularly in salt – a very valuable commodity, as it could not be produced locally. The inland brine springs at Droitwich are first mentioned in 716, when King Ethelbald gave the rights to Evesham Abbey. By the time of the Domesday Book, 68 manors and estates were entitled to receive Droitwich salt and William the Conqueror personally owned 85 salt pans there. There was another inland centre at Northwich, but most salt came from the sea, or from tidal rivers, the source of a considerable industry in Norman times and beyond. The distribution network stretched across the country, an elaborate system of saltways linking the centres of supply and demand, often following the ancient trackways from place to place. Roads across England are still marked 'Salt Way' today.

Salt was an important preservative, able to prevent meat from going rancid during the long winter months, when most livestock had to be killed because there was no grazing. England was an agrarian economy, carefully attuned to the requirements of the seasons. New live-stock was reared in the spring, then moved to lusher pastures to be fattened up for market. The process was purely local in the early Middle Ages, becoming more sophisticated in later centuries as population distribution patterns changed. For centuries, sheep, cattle and poultry were driven down from the shires to London markets, grazing on short-turfed verges as they went.

The original grassy livestock routes are known today as green lanes. Some are prehistoric, others date from

1 At Buttertubs Pass in the Yorkshire Dales, a modern road follows the same route as an old drove road, used over centuries for driving livestock to market.

2 A few guideposts, precursors of modern signposts, still survive at the intersections of old drove roads. This one is Ralph Cross, in the North York Moors National Park.

3 Glaisedale Rigg on the North York Moors, for thousands of years a busy trading route, is now the province of hikers and ramblers.

3

the years around the Norman Conquest. A good example is Mastiles Lane in the Yorkshire Dales, which links Malham with Kilnsey. It was used regularly in the Middle Ages by the monks of Fountains Abbey, herding their flocks of sheep. Mastiles was also used as a drove road for driving cattle to market. The cattle trade developed from the 16th century onwards; Welsh cattle in particular passed through the Midlands on their way to London and other southern markets. The roads avoided towns and traffic, with stances at regular intervals to pen the cattle in overnight, and sometimes wayside inns for the drovers. The drove roads often passed through deserted countryside, so an elaborate system of guideposts (precursors of modern signposts) was set up to help the drovers identify where they were.

The tracks across Dartmoor were marked by rough granite crosses as early as the 13th century. Crosses appeared in Kent in the 16th century; and at the end of the 17th century Parliament required local officials to erect a standing-post at every crossroads. A few early crosses survive, such as Fat Betty near Rosedale, Lacon Cross near Ripon, and Bennett's Cross on Dartmoor.

THE COACHING ERA

THE POOR QUALITY OF ROADS IN MEDIEVAL ENGLAND MADE TRAVEL A PERILOUS UNDERTAKING. PACKHORSES WERE OFTEN MORE EFFICIENT THAN CARTS OR WAGONS, AS THE PARISHES TECHNICALLY RESPONSIBLE FOR MAINTAINING LOCAL ROADS HAD LITTLE INTEREST IN DOING SO. THE INCOME FROM TOLL BOOTHS BROUGHT A SIGNIFICANT IMPROVEMENT IN THE 18TH CENTURY, AND INCREASING NATIONAL MOBILITY ENCOURAGED LOCAL TOURISM AND RURAL MIGRATION TO TOWNS. AN EXPANDING STAGECOACH NETWORK PROMPTED THE DEVELOPMENT OF COACHING INNS, OF VARIABLE QUALITY, CHARACTERIZED BY WIDE, HIGH ENTRANCES. FURTHER IMPROVEMENTS, INCLUDING THE ADOPTION OF TARMAC, INCREASED THE ROAD USE FURTHER, EVEN AS ROYAL MAIL COACHES STARTED TO TRANSFORM ENGLAND'S COMMUNICATIONS.

Travel in medieval England was a dangerous and often expensive procedure, seldom undertaken unless essential by most of the population. The poor state of the nation's roads limited the development of both trade and the economy; even heavy goods were carried by packhorse trains well into the 17th century, and slow river transport proved more efficient than cart or wagon. Rutted roads, barely adequate for wheeled vehicles in summer, proved virtually impassable in winter, particularly in areas of clay. There was no efficient system of maintenance, so they were left to deteriorate, sinking deeper and deeper into the mire as wagons and pack animals struggled to find a way forward. Main roads were often very wide in places, to ensure at least one route through during winter time: the Salisbury Plain road was 400 m (1312 ft) from side to side. Although ploughs drawn by eight or ten horses sought to level the surface of some main roads in the spring, the traffic of wheels and hoofs over the centuries sometimes gouged out 'hollow ways' several metres in depth. London's Holloway began exactly like that, as a dent in the Great North Road.

A description of the Great North Road in 1621 was typical of the road conditions encountered early in the century: 'By the often and Contynuall drifts and droves of Cattell driven towards the Cittie of London for the serving thereof and by meanes of the frequent passages of Waynes Carts and Carriadges to and from the said Cittie, the roade is made soe fowle, full of holes, sloughes, gulles & gutters that yt is now in the winter tyme made impassable and soe dangerous that noe Coatch Carte nor horse loaded can almost passe that waie.'

Progress was so slow that travellers sometimes only managed 10 km (6 miles) a day during the winter months. There were very few roadside inns to offer them a bed for the night, and those that did exist were of poor quality. Highwaymen were not uncommon, and hold-ups were so frequent that it was routine to carry two purses, one with limited funds to surrender to the robbers. Conditions in more remote regions were so dangerous that travellers were advised to draw up a will before they set out.

Attempts to improve the system during the 17th century met initially with little success. The first milestones since Roman times were erected on the Dover road in 1663, and the Great North Road in 1708. The oldest extant milestone dates from 1727, on the Trumpington road just outside Cambridge. But these were all the result of private enterprise, rather than any official effort. The upkeep of the roads was the responsibility of the local parish, yet all too often the local parishioners had insufficient time or inclination to fulfil their obligations. They were required by law to contribute six days a year of unpaid labour on the roads, but the task was often tackled inefficiently, if at all. They seldom used the main roads themselves and knew little of road repair. In contrast, structures such as bridges had been under church patronage since medieval times, built by the same stonemasons who worked on churches and cathedrals. Small stone chapels on the sides of bridges reveal this past association. Examples remain in Wakefield, Rotherham, St Ives in Cambridgeshire and Derby. The chapel on a bridge at Bradford on Avon (page 233) was rebuilt in the 17th century as the village lock-up.

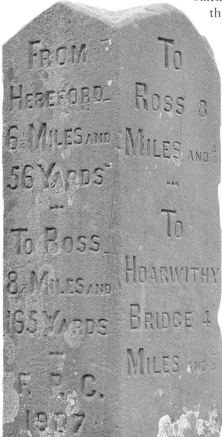

2

1 Reintroduced in the 17th century, milestones made a significant contribution to the improvement of England's inadequate transport system. This one still stands in the churchyard at Fownhope in Herefordshire.

2 An 18th-century cartoon depicting the bustle of activity occasioned by a stage coach arriving at an inn yard. Coaching inns, providing refreshments, accommodation, fresh horses and even vehicles, were established on all the major traffic arteries in the 18th century.

3 England's roads were so bad in the early days of coach travel that travellers were often advised to make a will before setting out. The uneven route across Coverdale in Yorkshire was one of the most notorious.

3

1

As the volume of traffic increased in the 17th century, it was apparent that other resources needed to be found. The obvious answer was to charge road users a toll and use the money for highway repairs. The first experimental turnpike was set up at Wadesmill, on the Great North Road, in 1663, but although it was a modest success, the idea proved slow to catch on. The next turnpike act was not passed until 1695, and in 1705 four days was still considered worthy of boast for a journey from London to York. Only in the middle of the 18th century, when almost 400 road acts were passed in 20 years, did the system really come into its own.

Once it was working, however, the improvement in national communications was considerable. Long-distance journey times were slashed by well over half during the course of the 18th century – from 50 hours to get from Norwich to London in 1700 to only 19 in 1800, for instance, and similarly from Manchester to

London. 'However incredible it may appear,' boasted an advertisement for the Flying Coach in 1754, 'this coach will actually (barring accidents) arrive in London in four days and a half after leaving Manchester'. Fifty years later, the time had been cut by half. More to the point, the system was more reliable as well.

Most turnpike roads were 32 or 48 km (20 or 30 miles) long, with a tollhouse at the entry point where the tollkeeper lived with his family. At least 8,000 tollhouses were eventually built, of which quite a few survive. They were usually situated close by the actual road, with a gate across the highway and windows strategically placed for a good view of approaching traffic. The tollkeeper had a list of charges, generally considered extortionate by those required to pay them. Carriages at Tyburn had to find 10d, horsemen 4d, and drovers 5d for 20 oxen or 2d for 20 pigs. Not surprisingly, the charges were thoroughly unpopular, particularly

A TABLE of the TOLLS payable at this TURNPIKE GATE.
[By the Local Act.]

	s d
FOR every Horse, Mule, Ass, or other Beast (Except Dogs) drawing any Coach, Berlin, Landau, Barouche, Chariot, Chaise, Chair, Hearse, Gig, Curricle, Whiskey, Taxed Cart, Waggon, Wain, Timber frame, Cart frame Dray or other Vehicle of whatsoever description when drawn by more than one Horse or other Beast the Sum of Four pence half-penny	4½
Such Waggon, Wain, Cart, or other such Carriage having Wheels of less breadth than four and a half inches:	
AND when drawn by one Horse or other Beast only the sum of six pence (Waggons, Wains and other such Carriages having Wheels as aforesaid)	6
FOR every Dog drawing any Truck, Barrow or other Carriage for the space of One Hundred Yards or upwards upon any part of the said Roads, the Sum of One Penny	6 1
FOR every Horse, Mule, Ass, or other Beast laden or unladen and not drawing, the Sum of Two-pence	2
FOR every carriage moved or propelled by Steam or Machinery or by any other power than Animal power the Sum of one Shilling for each Wheel thereof	1 0
FOR every Score of Oxen, Cows or neat Cattle, the Sum of Ten-pence and so in Proportion for any greater or less Number	10
FOR every Score of Calves, Sheep, Lambs or Swine the Sum of Five pence and so in proportion for any greater or less Number	5

(By 4. G. 4. C. 95)

2

1 The tollbooth at Putney Bridge in London was typical of thousands built at the height of the turnpike boom. Tollkeepers, widely disliked by the travelling public, would not allow travellers to pass until the toll was paid.

2 A list of charges at the Northchapel tollhouse near Petworth, West Sussex. Wherever possible, drove roads for livestock avoided the turnpike and cut across country instead in order to avoid the toll.

3 As roads improved and coach travel increased, better quality inns were established to cater for the demand. The Feathers Hotel at Ludlow in Shropshire was celebrated in the 18th century for its hospitality. Today, it retains a striking timbered façade.

with humble drovers using the roads to get to market. Attacks on tollkeepers were commonplace, so frequent that they soon became a capital offence. Avoidance of the toll was routine as well – indeed a national sport, as one Yorkshire tollkeeper complained: 'As many as please can go round by Okenshaw (a long and very bad way) and come in at Agbridge turnpike…There are some who ride thro' the Calder at sunset to save their penny, such sordid dogs dwell in this country.'

Even prime ministers were not averse to evading the toll if possible, as illustrated in an incident described by Sir Nathaniel Wraxall in his memoirs of the 1780s: 'Returning by way of frolic, very late at night, on horseback…Lord Thurlow, then Chancellor, Pitt and Dundas, found the Turnpike Gate situate between Tooting and Streatham, thrown open. Being elevated above their usual prudence, and having no Servant near them, they passed through the gate at a brisk pace, without stopping to pay the Toll; regardless of the remonstrances or threats of the Turnpike man, who, running after them, and believing them to belong to some Highwaymen, who had recently committed depredations on that road, discharged the contents of his Blunderbuss at their backs. Happily he did no injury.'

Most people paid up, however, and the turnpikes prospered. The population was rapidly becoming more mobile, drifting away from the land towards the towns and factories. The agriculturalist Arthur Young deplored the new mobility in 1771, complaining that it only encouraged the rural exodus of yeomen and labourers: 'To find fault with good roads would have the appearance of paradox and absurdity; but it is nevertheless a fact that giving the power of expeditious travelling depopulates the Kingdom …A country fellow, one hundred

miles from London, jumps on a coach box in the morning, and for eight or ten shillings gets to town by night.'

People were beginning to travel for pleasure as well, something not contemplated before. The 18th century was the age of the Grand Tour for the upper classes: young men set off for the Continent with a great baggage train following in their wake. Ordinary people were travelling too – if not so grandly – to the nearest town, to see historic sites, or to a provincial spa to take

3

1 *The London to Bristol and Bath Stage Coach*, painted in the early 19th century by Charles Cooper Henderson. Stagecoaches took pride in their journey times, travelling rapidly from inn to inn and sometimes stopping for barely a minute to take on more passengers. Wealthier ones travelled inside and the rest sat on the roof, exposed to the weather.

2 A 19th-century painting of the bustling Plough Inn at Cheltenham – a staging post for Bath and itself an attractive spa resort.

3 The improvement of the roads in the 18th century enabled society to flock to Bath for the season. Splendid public buildings were erected in the town, including the lavish Assembly Rooms, site of the most prestigious social events.

the waters. Cheltenham, for example, a small Cotswold market town, owed its 18th-century prosperity to the discovery of a mineral water spring, coupled with the enthusiasm of a more mobile society to visit it. By the mid-18th century it had become a very attractive spa, complete with hotels, fine public buildings and elaborate private villas faced in stucco or Cotswold stone.

Cheltenham was also a staging post for Bath, an increasingly fashionable health resort distinguished by elegant architecture and a sophisticated social season. The health-giving properties of its waters had been known since Roman times; the sulphurous springs were particularly beneficial for gout, arthritis and gastric disorders. Coaching inns sprang up in every major

town during the 18th century, providing lodgings, refreshment and a change of horses. Many of their typical broad archways survive today, leading into a courtyard behind which the fabric of an earlier building is sometimes retained. The galleried courtyard at the George Hotel in Huntingdon dates in part from the 17th century, although its frontage is Victorian.

Apart from the aristocracy, who owned their own carriages, most long journeys involved the hire of a postchaise and postilions. Changes of horse could be made at coaching inns, or simpler staging inns with large stables that lined the main thoroughfares. The introduction of turnpike roads and more reliable coaches meant that overnight stops could be spaced

3

more widely apart. In the early 18th century, a traveller by coach from London might halt at Stevenage or Baldock, but in later years might reach Biggleswade or even Stamford in Lincolnshire.

The best establishments amounted to highly regarded hotels, a far cry from their origins as monastic hostelries offering simple board and accommodation to pilgrims. The first stagecoach service began in 1657, and by the middle of the next century, stagecoaches were operating on all the important routes. Watling Street, which followed the route of the Roman road, became one of the busiest roads in England. The organization of stage coaches resembled a modern bus service, as the carriages travelled from inn to inn to deposit passengers and pick up new ones. With 40 coaches a day leaving Birmingham alone, and 54 departing for Manchester, any time from three in the morning to nine at night, it was a very brisk trade.

Some of the largest coaching inns were very large indeed. Famous examples such as The George and Blue Boar at Holborn had 40 bedrooms and stabling for 50 horses. The London Inn at Exeter claimed to have 500

horses. They were sophisticated establishments with elegant bedrooms, liveried servants and a well-stocked taproom, catering to a traveller's every need. But many inns were still rudimentary, offering little more than a roof for the night. It was quite normal until well into the 19th century for complete strangers to have to share a room, and sometimes a bed. Celia Fiennes remembered four beds in a room, with three people in each. A German visitor to Windsor in 1782 had to share a room above the taproom. 'The floor shook. Drinking songs were sung … I was hardly able to sleep with such a noise and bustle, and had just dozed off a little when my sleeping-partner arrived, possibly one of those from the taproom, who bumped into my bed. With great difficulty he found his own and threw himself onto it just as he was – clothes, boots and all.'

The extra traffic created further problems for the fabric of the roads. Despite the turnpike tolls, it was still a constant battle to keep them in good condition and they remained for the most part 'loose, rough and perishable, expensive, tedious and dangerous to travel on, and very costly to repair'. The problem lay in their construction, determined chiefly by the character of the local soil. Even as late as 1789 the roads of Herefordshire proved virtually impossible to negotiate after the autumn rains. The answer lay in a complete redesign of the system by the Scots landowner John McAdam. At his own expense, he conducted a series of experiments in the 1790s, first in Scotland and later in Falmouth, where he was an agent for the navy, and arrived at the same idea as the Romans – the construction of roads from broken stone. Properly drained, and impacted over time, they provided a solid foundation, lasting much longer than roads of mud or clay.

McAdam became surveyor-general of the Bristol roads in 1815 and put his theories into practice. By 1823 his system

2

1 Postal services improved remarkably with the introduction of Royal Mail coaches in the 1780s. Post was delivered to coaching inns at first, and later to purpose-built post offices, such as this one at Byfield.

2 The Bell Inn at Stilton was a collection point for local dairy produce, including cheese. Stilton cheese takes its name from the town where it was collected, even though the cheese was produced elsewhere.

3 A feature of the New Inn at Gloucester is the enclosed courtyard and first floor gallery, typical of early coaching inns.

1

was being adopted nationwide, with the later addition of tar to make tarmac (named after McAdam himself). Roads improved dramatically: by 1840 there were 35,000 km (22,000 miles) of good turnpike roads in England. Travel times dropped again, and wheeled transport was redesigned to take advantage of the new conditions. The phaetons, chaises, landaus and curricles of the early 19th century were lighter and faster than their lumbering predecessors – and were pushed to their limits by the daring aristocrats of the Four-in-Hand Club, whose exploits terrified road users. Old haywains and farm wagons were supplemented by wagonettes and pony carts.

The postal service improved as well, with much faster delivery times across the country. For most of the

2

18th century, post had been transported on horseback, and the service proved consequently slow and inefficient. From the 1780s a new system was attempted – a Royal Mail coach, complete with armed guard, carrying no outside passengers and therefore able to clip along at a good 13 or 14 km/h (8 or 9 mph). The trial runs from London to Bristol were so successful that by 1786 the system was extended to the rest of the country, and also to Edinburgh. Mail coaches became a familiar sight across the land: they were much faster than ordinary stagecoaches and were distinguished by impressive crests, warning bugles and liveried drivers. They created an important communications network, transporting letters, parcels and goods across the country with reasonable efficiency. The newly macadamized roads meant that the mail coach could achieve a consistent pace, stopping just long enough to deliver the mail before setting off again, and adhering rigidly to a timetable that at last had some reliability. The contribution of such improved communication to the industrial revolution's success should not be underestimated.

A vivid account of coach travel in its heyday occurs in *Tom Brown's Schooldays*, a largely autobiographical account by Thomas Hughes of his own time at Rugby in the 1830s. The pace of the coaches is remarkable: on his first day at the school, young Tom had just 45 seconds to climb aboard a Tally-ho coach at Islington before it started off again, rattling through the November darkness at 3 am. By dawn, it was halfway to Rugby, doing a brisk 18 km/h (11 mph) and two minutes ahead of schedule as it arrived at a coaching inn for breakfast.

Nevertheless, the coaching era was soon to be consigned to history. The first steam railway opened between Stockton and Darlington in 1825, and others were quick to follow suit. The coaching companies were becoming anachronistic, even if they did not yet realize it, and by the middle of the 19th century most had already gone out of business. By the century's end, none remained. It was not until the advent of motor cars that the surviving coaching inns saw their fortunes revive and prosper once again.

THE RAILWAY REVOLUTION

Originally developed for industrial use, railways were to prove among the most far-reaching of 19th-century innovations. They transformed the pattern of industry and trade in England, enabling goods to be transported further and faster than ever before, and areas of specialist manufacture to be located away from the site of raw materials. Historic ports and cities lost or gained commercial status depending on their relationship to the railway nexus, and new towns were established to cater for its needs. Railways provided a major market for iron, steel and coal. They also transformed architectural concepts and social mobility, and standardized the nation's time.

The first railway was probably constructed in a Nottinghamshire coalmine at the beginning of the 17th century. Using wooden rails and carts drawn by pit ponies, it was the most efficient way of transporting large quantities of coal to the river, where it was loaded on to barges. By the early 1800s, short local railways, made from iron instead of wood, were a familiar sight in coalmines. The oldest surviving piece of track, 3.2 km (2 miles) in length, is thought to be at Belvoir Castle, in Leicestershire. Laid down in 1815 between Muston Gorse wharf on the Grantham canal and a tunnel beneath Belvoir Castle, it reflected the original function of industrial railways, to link gaps between canals (page 334). The canal network continued to be England's major artery of distribution, especially for heavy goods, for more than 20 years.

It was the application of steam power to the railways, however, that really revolutionized the concept. George Stephenson did not invent the steam engine – stationary pumping engines for mining were well estblished by the mid-18th century – but he was the first to make the railway engine commercial. His locomotives had a valuable industrial function, hauling coal to Tyneside quays from 1814 onwards. The Stockton & Darlington Railway did carry the first passengers by steam power (in coal trucks) in 1825, but its primary function was to transport coal from pits near Bishop Auckland to Stockton, and for many years horse power was more consistently employed.

The profile of steam locomotives was significantly raised in 1829, when the directors of the Liverpool & Manchester Railway held a competition for the best railway engine capable of hauling trucks at an average 16 km/h (10 mph) – without blowing up. Stephenson won hands down with his *Rocket* design, heralding the dawn of a new era. As *The Scotsman* reported: 'The experi-ments at Liverpool have established principles which will give a greater impulse to civilization than it has ever received from any single cause since the press first opened the gates of knowledge to the human species.'

The railway boom followed on the *Rocket's* success, driven by two significant periods of investment in 1836–37 and 1844–48. In 1836 alone, 29 railway compa-nies were formed by act of parliament. Ten years later, the figure had risen to 272, all frantically attempting to raise money on the stock exchange to cover the country with railway lines. Their endeavours began to redefine the industrial and commercial map of England as the freight advantages of the new system became apparent. The small town of Middlesborough, for example, was transformed by an extension of the Stockton & Darlington Railway and a new port developed in 1831. As this line opened up the West Durham coalfield, the east coast port of Hartlepool was brought back to com-mercial life with the introduction of a competitive rail-way. A local rival, West Hartlepool, developed across the newly constructed docks, for a period handling more trade than the northeast ports of England combined.

In 1830 the Liverpool to Manchester Railway opened as an entirely steam-driven form of transport for passen-gers and goods. A new accessibility brought train travel to people accustomed to stagecoaches and horse-back, evincing reactions of delight and terror in its early customers. As the network continued to expand, land-owners and rural communities were horrified at its impact. 'It appears to me to be the vulgarest, most indelicate, most inconvenient, most injurious to Health of any mode of conveyance that I have seen in any part of the World!' proclaimed the duke of Wellington, one of many rich landowners who exerted his influence to make sure no railway line crossed his estate or spoiled

1 Opened in 1830, the Liverpool & Manchester Railway was the first in the world to carry passengers on a regular basis. Its carriages echoed the design of stagecoaches, with plush seats for first class passengers and open air carriages for third – the rail equivalent of travelling outside. Luggage was still piled on the roof.

2 An early train arrives at Bagworth in Leicestershire during the inaugural run of the Leicester to Swannington Railway in 1832. The lines aroused hostility and admiration in equal measure. Stations were usually built on the outskirts of town to keep the noise and dirt well away from the town centre.

1 A steam engine crosses the North York Moors at the Hole of Horcum, near Pickering. Steam power, the mainstay of the railways from 1825 to the 1960s, created an important new market for coal, as well as assisting its transport around the country.

2 Ribblehead Viaduct, one of several on the Settle to Carlisle line, is now a Listed building. Its 24 archways reach up to over 50 m (165) feet at the highest point, an astonishing engineering achievement. Viaducts were needed because the earliest trains had difficulty climbing even a slight gradient.

3 Charwelton railway station, Northamptonshire, photographed in 1900. The railway companies became large employers in the 19th centuries, each with their distinctive uniforms and insignia. The social hierarchy of the railways was highly complex, in contrast to more traditional structures prevailing on the farm or the factory floor.

1

his view. Stations were frequently placed on the edges of towns or, as in London, in poorer areas away from the residential neighbours of the influential and affluent. The arrival of a railway line often caused consternation, as a railway engineer discovered at Watford in 1834: 'One or two strange faces appeared in the town, and men in leathern leggings, dragging a long chain ... were remarked as trespassing in the most unwarrantable manner over pasture land, standing crops, copse and cover ... Then would follow another intruder, bearing a telescope set on three legs, which he erected with the most perfect coolness wherever he thought fit, peering through it at a long white staff.'

In response to farmers who ordered the intruders off their land, the railwaymen produced a copy of the act of Parliament authorizing their intrusion. Violence was sometimes threatened, but the legally approved assessments continued unhindered.

Surveyors were followed by the 'navigators', many of whom had been employed on the canals. They did the hard labour of construction, laying the rails, digging cuttings, throwing up embankments and blasting tunnels through solid hillsides for early locomotives that required the lines to be straight and level. The navvies were a numerous and conspicuous group of employees, 'a great army, which in other conditions might have carved out a great empire'. There were about 200,000 of them, living in a state of utter barbarism according to

John Francis, writing in 1851, but an industrial powerhouse, responsible for carrying railway lines to every corner of the kingdom. The navvies' origins were diverse: many were Irish, escaping the famine at home; others were Scots. They also included drainage experts from Lincolnshire and Somerset, agricultural labourers from the Pennines, Cornish tunnellers from redundant tin mines, even a few Belgians. Their drinking was notorious, and pay was allegedly often withheld for weeks to keep them fit for work.

Nevertheless, they were highly productive and the railway boom lasted well into the 1840s. Some 3,200 km (2,000 miles) of track had been laid by 1843, rising to 8,000 km (5,000 miles) by 1848, with another 14,500 km (9,000 miles) authorized by Parliament. By 1850, the United Kingdom contained half of the railway track in the world. Trains went from London to Birmingham, Southampton and Bristol, and also from Birmingham to Leeds, Manchester to Sheffield, and Glasgow to Edinburgh, operating with a precision and regularity orchestrated by 'time-tables'. This novel instrument brought about the standardization of the nation's time in the 1840s, subordinating local diversity to the exigencies of industry and commerce. The expansion brought great prosperity, not only for railway directors and compensated landowners, but also for the thousands of ordinary people who invested in railway shares (so long as they were not duds). Even the navvies themselves were paid almost three times as much as a farm labourer for their services. The railways also offered continuing and relatively prestigious employment for thousands of people in the new industry, a welcome alternative to the farm or the factory floor.

The Great Northern Railway, the Great Eastern and the Great Western were all big employers of labour, as were the Midland, the Lancashire & Yorkshire, and the London, Chatham & Dover Railways. By 1851, these and other railway companies employed at least 65,000 peo-

2

ple as engine drivers, firemen, signal men or other direct railway workers, and thousands more as engineers, mechanics or coach and wagon builders. By 1907 the figure had risen to 250,000. Most companies had elaborate uniforms and peaked caps for the staff, and brass buttons as a badge of rank, echoing the liveries of coaching days. Hierarchies were rigorously maintained, with engine drivers, firemen and station masters enjoying the most status; guards looked down on shunters, and shunters in turn on porters, but even porters saw themselves as superior to working men in other jobs.

There was a novelty and glamour to the railways in the early days that other occupations could not match.

A community spirit was fostered to some extent by railway towns such as Swindon and Crewe. The railway dominated as principal employer, and social life revolved around the railway pubs and clubs. Swindon, formerly a small Wiltshire market town, was transformed by the Great Western Railway works at which most of its engines and rolling stock were produced. Isambard Kingdom Brunel and Matthew Wyatt designed an ordered community of model housing for

1 Although generally known as St Pancras station, this flamboyant Gothic structure is actually the former Midland Grand Hotel; the station is placed behind. The architect, Sir George Gilbert Scott, thought his design was too good for a railway hotel, but the Midland Railway's directors considered it a great showpiece for their growing company.

2 Opened in 1841, the Great Western Railway's Box Tunnel is 3 km (almost 2 miles) long and was a sensation in its day. Isambard Kingdom Brunel designed a triumphal entrance for the tunnel to impress coach travellers on the nearby Bath road.

the workforce: it was rapidly outgrown and more sprawling development merged with the original town.

Established towns were also influenced by the railway's proximity or distance. York became the headquarters of the Northeastern Railway, recovering a regional status lost through the growth of Leeds, Sheffield, Bradford and Hull. Its new role was reflected in a magnificent arched station, making extensive use of iron and glass. Derby also gained new impetus as the headquarters of the Midland Railway, with a station of innovative design by Francis Thomson. Today the station has gone, but the Midland Hotel, dating from 1840, remains, together with housing built for railway workers and part of the great locomotive and carriage works.

Other survivors from the early period include the world's first railway stations at Darlington's North Road and at Manchester's Liverpool Road. The Darlington station is now a museum, displaying among other things *Locomotion*, the original engine from 1825. At Manchester, the original 1830 station, also part of a museum, is still on the Liverpool road. It echoes the design of a Georgian coaching inn from the outside, with an ornate entrance for first-class passengers and a more modest one for the rest. There was no platform: passengers simply climbed aboard the train as they did a coach, and luggage was similarly piled on the roof.

As more and more stations were required, their architects drew on a variety of architectural styles. The pure classical in Huddersfield and Monkwearmouth in Sunderland was balanced by the Tudor Gothic of Brunel's original Temple Meads station and headquarters building at Bristol, Chester's Italianate structure is the largest surviving building designed by Francis Thomson, a great and prolific railway architect, while the splendour of London's stations, created between 1863 and 1886, led a commentator of the time to declare, 'Our metropolitan termini have been the leaders of the art-spirit of our times.' Arguably the leading expression of 19th-century exuberance is London's St Pancras, Gothic in design but clearly Victorian in construction. With Euston's Greek Doric station on one side, and

King's Cross's functional Italianate on the other, St Pancras was the Midland Railway's showpiece station. It opened in 1874 with the Midland Grand Hotel in front and a vast single-span roof behind, covering seven platforms and 10 tracks, and was acclaimed an engineering marvel. The architect was Sir George Gilbert Scott, who also designed the Foreign Office (it would have resembled St Pancras if he had had his way).

Equally dramatic, in a different style, was the work of Isambard Kingdom Brunel. Although responsible for Paddington station, Brunel was primarily an engineer rather than an architect. His railway bridge over the Tamar was radical in its day — an iron suspension bridge with two central spans each 139 m (456 ft) long, the whole construction held steady by trusses linked to rounded tubes overhead. Brunel's Box Tunnel on the Great Western Railway was also a sensation: it took five years to build and is almost 3.2 km (2 miles) long — unheard of in 1841, and rare now. Brunel deliberately

2

1

built the impressive tunnel entrances much larger than necessary, and there is a pleasant tradition that he designed it to enable the early morning sun to shine directly along the tunnel every 9 April – his birthday.

The demands of the railways were to produce some of England's most accomplished architecture, drawing upon both traditional masonry and ironwork for construction. Viaducts and bridges are among the most impressive achievements, utilitarian in concept yet retaining the grandeur of classical aqueducts. Among the most elegant structures are the stone railway

2

viaducts, mostly in the north of England, such as the viaduct at Penistone, built from Coal Measures sandstone for the Yorkshire & Lancashire Railway in 1885. The 24 archways of Ribblehead reached up to an incredible 50.3 m (165 ft) on the way from Settle to Carlisle, a remarkable feat of construction for its time. Viaducts were to become commonplace in the railway age, but the best of them, such as Ribblehead, are recognized now as part of an important industrial heritage.

As railways expanded, they fired the social and commercial imagination of the age. Queen Victoria made her first journey by train in 1842 and travelled regularly by rail thereafter. The railway companies vied with each other in the lavishness of the saloon cars – all plush seats and red velvet – which they provided for her use. By the middle of her reign, rail had become the accepted form of transport over long distances – particularly after the Great Exhibition of 1851, which drew visitors to London for the day by train and returned them home before nightfall.

Such visitors travelled on excursion trains, a peculiarly English phenomenon that enabled people to travel to a particular place for a certain event and then return home. The travelling public took up the idea with great enthusiasm. In 1841, when Thomas Cook arranged a special train to visit a temperance fête at Loughborough, 570 people jumped at the chance, precipitating the entrepreneur into the travel business. Rival companies organized excursions to the Isle of Wight or the Epsom Derby, engendering an entirely new industry of mass market travel.

The influence of rail travel on tourism was immense. Chatsworth, the Duke of Devonshire's country seat, had always enjoyed a steady stream of visitors, but the stream turned to a flood after the arrival of the railway in 1849 – an average 80,000 sightseers every summer. A day out at the seaside became a real possibility for Londoners and urban factory workers. Popular destinations included Brighton, Eastbourne, Ramsgate and Margate in the south, Scarborough and Blackpool in the north. Margate had been a resort since the 18th century, its pier dating from Regency times, but it was the railway network that really drew the crowds. As ports such as Barrow and Grimsby boomed, and the trading fortunes of Southampton were revived by the South Western Railway, the seaside holiday brought new prosperity to other coastal towns. From their humble beginnings as industrial locomotives, the railways of the 19th century had produced nothing less than a social and commercial revolution.

1 Brighton Pavilion, initially a simple structure, was transformed by Beau Nash into an exuberant oriental palace, drawing on Indian and Chinese influences. The town's association with the Prince Regent made it a fashionable resort in the late 18th century, but railways made Brighton and other coastal towns accessible to a wider public.

2 Another south coast town, Eastbourne, owed its prosperity even more directly to the railways. A day trip was now possible for London's office workers, who came in large numbers.

3 Margate on the Kentish coast was one of the most popular resorts. Thousands came to promenade on the pier, as shown in this photograph of 1912.

The industrial revolution of the 18th and 19th centuries
had a profound effect on the landscape and buildings of England.
The economic expansion driven by the demand for goods and fuelled
by the availability of labour and raw materials in turn prompted the
building, in vast numbers, of mines, mills, factories, canals, railways, roads,
ships, bridges, tunnels and warehouses to service extraction, manufacture,
distribution and storage. It was an age of invention, and as mass labour
coalesced in towns and new factories, of political unrest. The growth of
cities to cope with the influx from the countryside saw the creation
of slums and the plight of the urban poor fuelled the emergence
of movements for the reform of housing and health. Rising
prosperity was signalled by visual symbols of civic pride,
as magnificent town halls and public buildings
were erected in every major city.

THE INDUSTRIAL REVOLUTION

FUELLING THE FURNACES

THE INDUSTRIAL EXPANSION OF ENGLAND DURING THE 18TH AND 19TH CENTURIES WAS ESSENTIALLY DEPENDENT UPON IRON, COAL AND, LATER, STEEL — THE CORE INGREDI-ENTS OF NEW INDUSTRIAL PROCESSES. SMALL MINES AND IRONWORKS HAD EXISTED FOR CENTURIES, AND THE REGIONS WHERE THEY WERE LOCATED BECAME FOCAL POINTS OF ECONOMIC EXPANSION. TOGETHER WITH DEVELOPING MANUFACTURING CITIES, THE MINES AND FOUNDRIES OF THE BLACK COUNTRY, TYNESIDE, YORKSHIRE AND DURHAM BECAME MAGNETS FOR A DISPOSSESSED RURAL POPULATION, WHO HELPED TRANSFORM BRITAIN INTO THE LEADING INDUSTRIAL POWER OF THE AGE.

ENGLAND'S REMARKABLE LEVEL of industrial expansion was achieved through a combination of economic circumstances. Not least was the ready availability of coal and mineral supplies; Staffordshire, Warwickshire and Worcestershire, for example, had reserves of both and the small market town of Birmingham had become famous for metal products, such as knives, tools and nails, as early as the 16th century. Coal was well established as an industrial as well as domestic fuel by the 17th century, contribut-ing to metal processing, glass making and the salt and sugar industries. Distribution networks from the major coalfields were also in existence; large quantities of coal from Northumberland and Durham pits, for example, were shipped to London and the east coast via Tyneside and Wearside. Tyneside was also a region of metal processing in the late 17th century. A Quaker metal manufacturer from Stourbridge, Ambrose Crowley, transported iron ore from Swindon to furnaces and forges at Winlanton, south west of Newcastle, where he produced quality nails and specialized iron goods such as hinges, cannon and tools. Crowley also developed model settlements, includ-ing welfare services, for his workforce in an anticipation of Robert Owen's New Lanark and the Yorkshire communities of Akroyden (Copley) and Saltaire.

The Forest of Dean and the Bristol region also con-tained important coal workings associated with metal industries. Two works opened in 1690 on a coalfield east of Bristol to produce copper and brass, and a third was established at Redbrook on the River Wye. In 1702 Abraham Darby, a Quaker from Birmingham, set up a brass foundry just outside Bristol to produce 'hollow ware' – primarily pots and utensils. He later moved to Coalbrookdale in Shropshire, where he modernized an old charcoal furnace and experimented with the use of coke in the smelting process, drawing upon earlier experience in the malting industry. The first successful smelting of iron and coke (coal had too high a sulphur content) took place on the site in 1709, producing coal suitable for basic cooking pots and kitchen ranges. A subsequent stage of conversion to cast iron, able to withstand forging and rolling into shape, was developed by Darby's son in 1750, effectively releasing the industry from its dependence on charcoal. The world's first iron bridge was erected over the River Severn in Coalbrookdale in 1779 by another Abraham Darby, the third generation of innovative ironmasters. It still stands today, continuing to illustrate the elegant poten-tial of cast iron construction and surrounded by an industrial centre. No substantial town developed on the 18th-century site, although the small Shropshire coal-field contributed to tile, pottery and porcelain works at Coalport as well as to the region's iron foundries. Instead, the Black Country region in the West Midlands, supplemented by Yorkshire and Tyneside, was to domi-nate iron production in England in the next century.

In 1758, John Wilkinson opened the Black Country's first large-scale furnace, which was sited at Bilston. It employed coke in the smelting process, according to Coalbrookdale methods, and included a forge plus a steam engine to recycle water as early as 1775. James Watt, already celebrated for his improvements to the Newcomen engine, went into partnership with the industrialist Matthew Boulton who had established the Soho Manufactory in 1761 on the outskirts of Birmingham for the large scale produc-tion of 'toys' – boxes, trinkets, silverware etc. By 1770 the Manufactory was employing c.700 people and had developed the capacity to assemble Watt's new steam

PAGES 314–315
Main picture: Abraham Darby's
cast iron bridge at Iron-
bridge, Shropshire.
Inset: Brunel's *Great Britain* in
dry dock, Bristol.

PRECEDING PAGES
1   Coalbrookdale by Philip de
Louterbourg (1740–1812).
Many artists were fascinated
by the developing industrial
landscape.
2   The Newcomen Engine
House at Elsecar Colliery,
near Barnsley in South
Yorkshire.

engines. Before their full impact was realized in wide-spread mechanization and the railways, steam engines had mostly been used for pumping and drainage purposes – Newcomen's first steam engine was developed to tackle drainage problems in the Cornish tin mines, although it was erected at a colliery in Worcestershire in 1712 – as well as the primary metal industries for hammering, rolling and blowing the molten sheets. Wilkinson introduced a Boulton and Watt steam engine to drive the forge hammer in 1782. By 1800 several hundred of their engines were employed in textile mills, ironworks, coal mines and other industries. Watt's refinement of the Newcomen engine through the use of a separate condenser was probably the greatest single improvement ever made to the efficiency of the steam engine. Further improvements included a centrifugal governor to open and shut the valves to maintain constant speed, a parallel motion system and a system of

rotary gears that translated vertical movement into a circular motion. The latter brought a new flexibility to businesses previously dependent on local water supplies for power. The huge boilers, pistons and wheels of 19th-century engines still impress today as the mechanical motors that drove the industrial age.

The momentum of industrial growth was sustained by a remarkably fertile period of invention in the late 18th and early 19th centuries. In 1784 Henry Cort, a private contractor to the navy, devised a 'puddling' method of refining iron using coal in his small forge at Titchfield near Portsmouth. He used a reverberatory furnace in which the cast iron and coal were in separate chambers, thus keeping the damaging sulphur away from the iron and so avoiding the need for complex refining processes. Cort's technique made wrought-iron production significantly more efficient, enabling it to be made in far greater quantities and used widely in construction, machinery and engineering.

Coal extraction, particularly from seams near the surface and close to rivers and coasts, had contributed to local economies for centuries. The Forest of Dean in Gloucester has a long association with mining activity and collier ships of the 16th century brought substantial amounts of coal to London from Tyneside and Wearside pits. Daniel Defoe, travelling across England in the early 18th century, observed Newcastle's 'prodigious heaps, I might say mountains, of coal', much of which was redistributed across the country by land or water routes. In the northeast, low coal outcrops on coastal cliffs had been gathered by locals since medieval times. Collection of coal from exposed seams under the sea, and of colliery waste deposited at sea and washed ashore, was – and is – common practice in the region.

As industrial demand increased, deeper excavations were made and pits were sunk at sites further inland. Transport became more problematic, leading to the development of the first 'rail-ways' – wooden railed tracks along which horse-drawn wagons could be hauled. The undertaking was vast, and it is estimated that 20,000 horses were employed in Newcastle alone. George Stephenson, himself a Tynesider, mounted experiments in steam locomotion and established a locomotive manufacturing works in Newcastle in 1823. His success with the *Rocket* engine in the Rainhill Trials in 1829 secured a commercial future for the works and laid the foundations for the city's future engineering role.

1 An illustration depicting 19th-century working conditions inside Old Hatton Colliery, South Staffordshire.

2 Collection of coal from the beaches near Tynemouth, Northumberland. So-called 'sea coal' is either washed ashore from fragmented seams out at sea, or the result of colliery waste brought back to land.

3 The County Durham shoreline was extended by over 120 m (400ft) when coal production in the northeast was booming. Coal waste and debris was simply dumped on the beaches in such quantities that the sea is still dark grey.

2

3

1 A photograph of the preserved engine house at Beamish Colliery, Urpeth, County Durham.

2 The mining community of Langley Park, County Durham was typical of many pit villages in the region. It is set in a slight valley with tightly grouped terraced houses. On still days, chimney smoke hangs over the town in a grey pall.

3 Chatterley Whitfield Colliery is the best surviving example in England of a large, early 20th-century colliery, the first to produce one million tonnes of coal a year. Chatterley Whitfield incorporates buildings and machinery from most of the 19th century, and was further developed through to World War II.

1

Opencast or drift mining was widely practised in the northeast, achieving significant output without extensive tunnels underground. Bell pits provided hazardous but effective methods of coal extraction in which narrow shafts were dug down as far as the coal seam, subsequently excavated either side of the shaft to create the bell shape. Both men and coal baskets were raised or lowered by a simple winch mechanism, operated from the surface by colleagues or a horse. The method was also employed in deeper pits where galleries radiated off from the central shaft, 120 m (400 ft) or more in depth. No form of safety shoring was used on either, although in deeper pits columns of coal were left intact at regular intervals to provide natural roof support, a method known as pillar and stall working.

As pits became deeper, the danger of flooding and inflammable gases rose proportionately. The invention of steam-powered pumps enabled deep workings to be kept reasonably clear of water but gases remained a serious threat. A firedamp explosion in Chester-le-Street in 1708 killed about 100 miners, and another in Bensham, also in the north Durham region, killed 80 more. Before mechanized winding gear, lower mine workings were often accessed by unprotected flights of ladders. Women and children hauled coal along the narrow confines of the levels and, laden with coal, made the dangerous ascent. Working conditions were atrocious, yet productivity continued to rise. In 1800 nearly 12 million tons of coal were exported from the Northumbrian coalfields alone, an astonishing feat of non-mechanized labour.

By 1820 all the coalfields were benefiting from steam-powered machinery; those in the West Midlands, Nottinghamshire and Yorkshire were also connected to the national network of canals. Mining technology allowed the sinking of even deeper pits, and stronger pithead winding gear transported people and material more efficiently. George Stephenson had observed that 'the strength of Britain ... lies in her iron and coal beds' and the economy bore this out. Coal production doubled between 1750 and 1800, but it doubled again before 1830 and

2

again, even more remarkably, before 1845. As more pits were opened, purpose-built mining villages were established to accommodate the workers. The new sites were characterized by tightly grouped, parallel terraces, dominated by pithead winding machinery and mounds of colliery waste, in stark contrast to formerly agricultural mining settlements, which in Durham still retained their village greens. Where iron was discovered as well as coal seams, larger towns were developed, providing a focus for previously dispersed metalworking communities. Examples of such mining towns include Consett in the northeast and Barnsley in Yorkshire.

The number of miners in the industry continued to grow, increasing from 216,000 in 1851 to 495,000 some 30 years later. Conditions underground improved marginally; the 1842 Mines Act, for which Lord Ashley (later Shaftesbury) had campaigned so vigorously, prohibited female labour underground, although boys over 10 were not included in its provisions. In 1850 a committee was appointed to oversee the safety of mines, but the work remained highly dangerous, despite the introduction of Sir Humphry Davy's safety lamp at Heburn Colliery at Tyneside in 1816. Explosions continued to be a feature of the mining industry, particularly in deep seam mines,

3

1 Brunel's Royal Albert Rail
Bridge over the Tamar at
Saltash was built in 1859,
one of an increasing number
of civil engineering projects
that became feasible with
better iron production and
the advent of steel.

2 The pit winding gear at
Astley Green Colliery
demonstrates the crucial
role that iron played
in the growth of industries

such as mining, and the
cross-reliance of the iron
industry itself upon coal.

3 The Anderton Boat Lift in
Cheshire made a significant
contribution to the expanding canal network. Opened
in 1875, the mammoth
structure was able to raise
boats a height of 15 m (50ft)
from the Weaver Navigation
to join the Trent and
Mersey Canal.

with 843 such incidents being recorded between 1835 and 1850 with severe loss of life. Seaham Colliery in County Durham was the scene of one such accident on 8 September 1880, made even more poignant by the discovery of a note written by one of the miners before the supply of air ran out following a roof collapse: 'Bless the Lord, we had a jolly prayer meeting, every man ready for glory. Praise the Lord'. There are very few coal mining villages in the main areas of production without at least one memorial to the victims of local pit disasters.

As steam-powered railways transformed distribution in the 19th century, they also created a vast new demand for iron and coal. A more stable political environment, in the wake of the Napoleonic Wars and the suppression of the Chartist movement, encouraged economic confidence and a climate that favoured entrepreneurial investment. The experimentation by Henry Bessemer in

1856 to develop a more efficient process for manufacturing steel led, with subsequent improvements over the next decade, to the emergence of the modern steel industry. It quickly dominated large construction and engineering projects, including winding gear; far-sighted iron manufacturers, such as those on Teeside, changed to become steel producers in the face of a modified market demand.

The traditional process of steel manufacture, such as the crucible method used in Sheffield and developed in the 18th century by Benjamin Huntsman, involved coke in its purification process. Bessemer blasted molten iron with pressurized air to remove impurities, and then supplemented the result with carbon. A durable metal with immense tensile strength, steel became invaluable in the maintenance of machine tools, bridges, ship's hulls and weaponry.

1

The first commercial steam vessel, the *Charlotte Dundas*, was a paddle-wheel steamer launched on the Forth and Clyde canal in Scotland to perform tug duties in 1802. Most of the early breed of steamships did indeed use a combination of paddles and sail, such as Isambard Kingdom Brunel's famous *Great Western*, which was launched in 1837. Equipped with four flue type boilers and two side lever engines, the *Great Western* was 72 m (236 ft) in length. In competition with its rival *Sirius*, built at Liverpool, the ship crossed the Atlantic in 1838, taking 15 days (3 days less than the fastest clipper voyage). But paddle-driven steamships were hampered by heavy seas, when both paddles could not sustain contact with the water simultaneously, causing engine strain and instability. The amount of coal needed for long journeys also reduced cargo space to non-commercial levels.

Brunel's next ship, the *Great Britain*, iron-hulled and driven by a single propeller, was launched in 1843. The largest vessel afloat at the time, its construction had incidentally given rise to the steam hammer, developed by James Nasmyth in response to Brunel's plan, later abandoned, for giant paddles. The *Great Eastern*, the third of Brunel's huge ships, was designed to

1 The River Tyne around Jarrow was one of the principal shipbuilding areas of England during the 19th century, supported by heavy iron and steel industries and abundant supplies of coal.

2 Brunel's *Great Eastern* under construction at Millwall docks on the Thames.

3 Isambard Kingdom Brunel (1806-1859) was arguably the greatest of the pioneering 19th-century engineers. Not only responsible for ship construction, he built 2,570 km (1,600 miles) of railways for the Great Western Railway Company. The photograph shows Brunel in front of the *Great Eastern*'s launch chains.

travel great distances without refuelling; it could accommodate 12,000 tonnes of coal in a double iron hull and featured both a 7-m (24-ft) screw propeller and paddle wheels 18 m (60 ft) in diameter. Despite its impressive proportions, the *Great Eastern* was not commercially successful because it was too big for its time, too large for normal port facilities and too hungry for coal. Charles Parson's steam turbine, developed in 1884, introduced a new breed of efficient steamships that came to dominate naval and commercial fleets.

The change from sail to steam had an architectural impact on England's great naval dockyards, especially Portsmouth and Devonport. New constructions in brick, stone and iron were built to accommodate steamships, replacing the brick and timber structures of the sailing era. At Chatham dockyards, the age of steam produced the Slip of 1837, with its huge timber-roofed shed, and the even larger 'Ship Shop' in 1847, an innovative architectural construction framed in iron.

The impact of steamships became pronounced after the 1860s. Their size proved problematic for the centuries-old London Pool on the Thames; inner London docks declined, to be supplanted in 1855 by the Victoria Dock between Blackwall and Gallions Reach in east London. It was later supplemented by the Albert and George V docks (1880 and 1921 respectively) to create the largest enclosed dock in the world.

Advances in industrial technology were adopted relatively slowly by Britain's naval fleet, which considered the large wheels of paddle-steamed vessels vulnerable in combat. Their presence on the ship's side also restricted the vessel's ability to fire a full broadside. HMS *Warrior*, the world's first successful amoured ocean-going warship, was built by the British engineer John Russell in 1860. Now a floating museum at Portsmouth, it was the largest, fastest and most powerful vessel of the day.

Steamships were also responsible for the gradual relocation of England's shipbuilding industry. Traditionally concentrated in the south where there was a plentiful supply of timber, momentum in the second half of the 19th century swung towards the northeast region with its deep tidal rivers and local supplies of iron and steel. The regions around the Tyne and Wear became associated with a number of prestigious yards, such as those of William Armstrong at Newcastle and Charles Palmer at Jarrow. Proximity to coalfields was another important factor, contributing also to developments in Sunderland and around the River Mersey in the west.

The process of industrial change dominated England by the mid-19th century. Technical advances were seen by contemporaries as a social phenomenon, impacting upon the nation's identity and purpose. Radical structures of iron and steel challenged the established order, a material expression of an evolving world. In 1866 the periodical *Engineering* could boast that its profession 'has done more than war and diplomacy…more than the Church and the Universities…more than abstract philosophy…more than our laws have done…to change society'. The consequences still reverberate today.

2

'DARK SATANIC MILLS'

THE MANUFACTURE OF TEXTILES HAS BEEN AN IMPORTANT INDUSTRY IN ENGLAND SINCE MEDIEVAL TIMES. DIFFERENT FABRICS HAVE LONG BEEN ASSOCIATED WITH INDIVIDUAL REGIONS, WITH LOCAL TOWNS SPECIALIZING IN SPINNING, WEAVING OR KNITTING. THE INDUSTRY WAS EARLY TO ADOPT MACHINERY POWERED BY HAND OR WATER, AND WITH THE APPLICATION OF STEAM POWER TEXTILES BECAME ONE OF THE MOST EFFECTIVE ENGINES OF ECONOMIC GROWTH. A RAPIDLY EXPANDING COTTON INDUSTRY TRANSFORMED THE FORTUNES OF MANCHESTER AND THE NORTHWEST IN THE 18TH AND 19TH CENTURIES, AND TEXTILE TOWNS ACROSS THE COUNTRY DEVELOPED VAST MILLS AND FACTORIES FOR LARGE-SCALE PRODUCTION.

DESPITE ITS LATER DOMINANCE of the textile industry, cotton manufacture in England was very limited before the 18th century. Wool was a more traditional fabric, its processing structured since medieval times around a largely domestic labour force of weavers, spinners and carders (who cleaned and combed the raw wool). Whole families were involved, using hand-powered looms and spinning wheels. They worked independently or under the control of clothiers who organized the commercial aspects. A further element of mechanization existed in the form of fulling mills – ordinary water mills that drove hammers rather than millstones to pound the woven cloth into a more solid fabric. The wealth generated by the industry is reflected in the ornate clothiers' houses at Trowbridge in Wiltshire, dating from the 18th century and richly embellished with columns, cornices and decorative window frames.

Hand-operated looms and knitting frames were also used in the processing of silk, another long-established material. Increasing demand for silk yarn led Thomas Lombe to develop the first textile 'factory', powered by water from the River Derwent, in Derby in 1719.

By the 18th century technological innovation was also taking place in the cotton industry, where Indian calicoes and muslins, imported by the East India Company, had established a fashionable presence. John Kay's flying shuttle, developed in 1733, made the weaving process significantly more efficient, enabling as it did a weaver to move the shuttle across the loom by means of a fly cord, rather than having to transfer it by hand. Cloth could consequently be woven to a wider measure and output more than doubled. This semi-automated process resulted in a need for swifter spinning, to which James Hargreaves' spinning jenny, created in 1764, made effective response. Hargreaves' machine replaced the single horizontal spindle of a conventional wheel by eight vertical ones, but fear of its implications aroused violent hostility among local Lancastrian spinners. Hargreaves' home was attacked in 1768, even as Kay's had been 15 years before, and he relocated to Nottingham, belatedly obtaining a patent for the jenny in 1770.

Full-scale mechanization of cotton production was begun by the entrepreneur Richard Arkwright in the late 18th century. He successfully modified the concept of a spinning machine driven by water power, originally developed 30 years earlier by John Wyatt and Lewis Paul. In 1771, the resulting water frame was installed in England's first cotton factory, located at Cromford in Derbyshire on a small tributary of the River Derwent. A second mill was constructed on the site in 1777 and in 1783 the nearby Masson Mill beside the fast flowing

1

1 Masson Mill, Matlock Bath, Derbyshire, was built by Richard Arkwright in 1783 at the height of his entrepreneurial powers.
2 The bobbin room at Masson Mill is crammed full of all shapes and sizes of bobbin. Each is specifically designed for particular types of thread and machine.

3 Stott Park Bobbin Mill, near Newby Bridge in Cumbria, was built in 1835 to create wooden bobbins, used in huge quantities by spinning and weaving industries in Lancashire. All the machinery was driven by belts from line-shafts.

2

3

1 A colour lithograph of Dean Mills, 1851, showing the doubling room which produced piping cord. The workshop appears clean, but the noise of non-stop machinery was deafening.

2 Skipton, North Yorkshire, is a typical Pennine textile town. It is conveniently located on the Leeds-Liverpool Canal, with mills on both sides of the waterway.

3 A house from North Street in Cromford, Derbyshire, where Richard Arkwright built the first 'model' industrial housing in 1771. The three-storey gritstone houses have one room on each floor. Looms were installed on the top storey.

1

Derwent itself. The façade of the final mill remains today, distinguished by elegant Venetian-style windows. Arkwright also built North Street, the oldest surviving example of 'model' industrial housing, in 1776 for his imported workforce. Three storeys in height, the houses were designed to accommodate handlooms to weave the yarn produced on site. They feature distinctively wide, mullioned windows on the top storey to provide maximum light. The factory functioned continually, although the water power was not sufficient to operate all machinery simultaneously. Spinning took place at night, preparation and carding in the day. Further complexes of mills and associated housing were built down the River Derwent valley, at Belper and Milford by the Strutts and at Darley Abbey by the Evans family.

Water-powered mills were subsequently constructed across the fast flowing Pennine streams of Yorkshire and Lancashire, both established textile regions. Some made use of existing spinning towns – Bury and Rochdale in Lancashire and Yorkshire's Hebden Bridge. Other sites, such as Todmorden on the border, expanded from handweaving villages to thriving towns, structured around a mill driven first by water and then steam, and accommodating canal and railway in swift succession.

2

The Midland counties of Nottinghamshire, Derbyshire and Leicestershire, like Lancashire, experienced considerable labour unrest as technology continued to advance. Samuel Crompton's spinning 'mule', developed in 1775 and repeatedly modified in design until the 1790s, combined aspects of the spinning jenny and Arkwright's water frame to transform the output of spun cotton. It was complemented in 1785 by Edmund Cartwright's power loom, which was to have a radical impact on weaving capacity.

The first steam-driven cotton mill, powered by Boulton and Watt engines, was developed near Nottingham in 1786; the first in Lancashire opened at Warrington the following year. Fast-flowing water was no longer essential, so steam-driven mills were often located by canals to access the inland waterway network. Steam power was not widely used for weaving machinery until the 1820s, when the number of power looms in use rose dramatically (from 14,150 in 1820 to an estimated 100,000 in 1833).

Increasing mechanization and large-scale production methods exacerbated fears among textile workers using the older, hand-operated machines. A sustained campaign of machine-breaking took place, especially in Lancashire, Wiltshire and the Midlands. The first mill in Manchester to install the power loom was burnt to the ground in 1791. Serious rioting occurred in Manchester, Rochdale and other major Lancastrian cities in 1807, after a petition by local handloom weavers for a Minimum Wage Bill, containing 130,000 signatures, was rejected. The government's response to continual 'Luddite' activity (named after Ned Ludd, a historical machine-breaker) was a repressive Frame-Breaking Bill in 1812. It was attacked in the House of Lords by the young Lord Byron, who in a letter to Lord Holland condemned the framebreakers' impoverished circumstances as 'a disgrace to a civilised country'.

Conditions inside many textile factories could have been similarly described. Poor lighting and ventilation, combined with unguarded machinery and deafening noise levels, made them dangerous and oppressive places. Work patterns were rigorous and regimented, with 12- or 14-hour shifts routine, even for the large numbers of children employed in the mills. The young were frequently used for unskilled yet dangerous tasks, such as piecing broken threads or gathering cotton waste without stopping the machines. Many parishes supplied textile mills with children to avoid paying poor relief, a practice often involving despatch to an entirely different part of the country. In 1794 the parishes of St Margaret and St John the Evangelist in Westminster, for example, sent over 50 children to a worsted mill in Nottinghamshire in a single week.

The emotive issue of child labour became a natural focus for reformers campaigning to improve factory conditions overall. In 1801 Robert Southey described a Manchester cotton factory he had visited as resembling Dante's *Inferno*, and Richard Oastler, in a famous letter to the *Leeds Mercury* in 1830, highlighted the contrast between concern for the emancipation of slaves and the apparent disregard for 'British infantile slavery' existing in 'the worsted mills of Bradford'. The 1833 Factory Act prohibited the use of children under 9 in wool and cotton mills, and set a maximum 9-hour day for children between the ages of 9 and 13. This age group was also required to make limited school attendance, and inspectors were appointed to ensure the act's provisions were enforced. Following further pressure, a statutory limit on hours worked by women and young persons aged 13 to 18 was imposed by the Ten Hours Bill in 1847.

Cotton manufacture was the area of most vigorous growth, but technology and new organization also had a major impact on the wool trade. In the 19th century

1

Yorkshire gained economic ascendancy over the west of England as regions adapted to larger scales of production. Textiles manufacture in the western counties declined, and in Bradford-on-Avon the attractive Abbey Mill, built in 1875 with an elegantly designed façade, can be seen as a final flourish of the industry.

Mechanical innovations established themselves more slowly in the wool industry than in cotton, although both the spinning jenny and flying shuttle were used widely by 1770. Carding was mechanized shortly afterwards, and mills for the purpose were often constructed beside traditional fulling mills. Finally, hand-operated jennies and weavers were drawn into sheds close by mill buildings, unifying all stages of production. The first factory to encompass all wool manufacturing processes, and the first in Yorkshire to use steam power, was Bean Ing in Leeds, constructed by Benjamin Gott in 1792.

Bradford, which expanded dramatically in the late 18th century, became Britain's most important manufacturing centre for both wool and worsted. Its status was reflected in its commercial buildings of the Little Germany quarter and in its huge mill complexes, such as Manningham Mills, constructed by Samuel C. Lister in 1873 as an integrated silk mill. It is an impressive building in the style of an Italian palazzo; even the boiler house chimney adopts the architectural theme, assuming the guise of a campanile.

Yorkshire also contains two of the 19th century's best known 'model' communities for textile workers. Saltaire, established by Sir Titus Salt in 1853, is probably the best known, located just outside Bradford in convenient proximity to the River Aire, railway and canal. The high quality housing, with its open-ended streets for light and ventilation, is impressive, as were Salt's social provisions. Allotments, almshouses, a school and a prominent church were also included in Saltaire.

The stone houses of Akroyden near Halifax, founded by the Akroyd family in 1859, challenge the monotony of back-to-back terraces through diverse sizes and attractive Gothic details.

Despite the poor quality of much urban housing, the architecture of many mills and factories expresses an immense pride in industrial achievement. The novelty of the building type meant the most fantastic designs were considered. Temple Mill in Leeds (1838–43) allegedly replicates an Egyptian temple at Edfu; Bliss Tweed Mill in Oxfordshire resembles a Renaissance palace. Manchester, the greatest of the textile cities, was known as 'Cottonopolis', and Disraeli, an admirer of its size and energy, applauded the 'illuminated factories with more windows than Italian palaces and smoking chimneys taller than Italian obelisks'. Such buildings were the secular cathedrals of the dawning industrial age.

2

1 The huge mill at the centre of Sir Titus Salt's 'model' community, Saltaire, near Bradford. Constructed in 1853, it reflects the period's economic prosperity. The Italianate architecture employed on the mill became the accepted regional style and was copied by other manufacturers.

2 An aerial view of the Saltaire complex showing the importance of good transport and communication links to 19th-century industry. Canal, river and railway run within metres of each other on either side of the mill.

3 Silk weavers' cottages in Leek, Staffordshire, occupy the same street as the mill. The distinctive large windows on the upper floor allow the weavers maximum light for their work.

CANALS & THE POTTERIES

THE CANAL NETWORK CONSTRUCTED ACROSS ENGLAND IN THE LATER 18TH CENTURY HAD A RADICAL EFFECT UPON INLAND TRANSPORT. INITIALLY DESIGNED TO LINK MAJOR RIVERS AND IMPROVE THE ROUTES OF EXISTING WATER TRAFFIC, THE NETWORK EXPANDED TO ENCOMPASS PREVIOUSLY LANDLOCKED INDUSTRIAL REGIONS SUCH AS THE POTTERIES IN WEST CENTRAL ENGLAND. NEGOTIATION OF THE LANDSCAPE REQUIRED CONSIDERABLE TECHNICAL INGENUITY AND A DISTINCTIVE ARCHITECTURE OF BRIDGES, AQUEDUCTS, LOCKS AND WHARFS. BY ACTING AS DISTRIBUTION ARTERIES FOR THE MANUFACTURING INDUSTRIES, CANALS ENABLED THE COUNTRY'S SPECTACULAR ECONOMIC GROWTH.

THE NAVIGABLE RIVERS of England have been used commercially for centuries, sustaining the prosperity of towns such as York, Norwich and Ware in Hertfordshire. A series of improvements to inland waterways took place in the late 16th century and the Lighter Canal, built by the Exeter Corporation in 1564–66, introduced the pound lock system into the country, although it was not England's first canal; Roman engineering skill had created the Fossdyke – which joins the rivers Trent and Witham, passing though Lincoln – in AD 120. Poor road conditions meant that water was preferred for the transport of heavy goods, and in the 1750s the short Sankey Brook was created to link St Helens with the Mersey at Warrington. St Helens subsequently became a more substantial town, most notably the site of the Ravenhead glassworks, established in 1773.

Economic motives also determined the development of the famous Bridgewater Canal by Francis Egerton 3rd duke of Bridgewater and engineer James Brindley in 1761. Demand for coal was increasing, both for domestic and industrial purposes, and a fiercely competitive market placed mine owners lacking direct water transport at a serious disadvantage. Egerton encountered such difficulties in shipping coal from the family colliery at Worsley, northwest of Manchester. The nearest river navigation system was controlled by the Mersey & Irwell Navigation Co., which refused to allow the duke to build a short cutting from his mine to the river's nearest access point at Barton. Egerton, who had recently seen the Canal du Languedoc (now the Canal du Midi) in France, while on his grand tour, embarked

with his agent upon a project to bypass the river and build a canal running into Manchester. Permission was granted by an act of Parliament despite strenuous opposition from the navigation company, and the substantial funding achieved through sale and mortgaging of the duke's estates and assets, supplemented by private and commercial loans. Technical challenges were the province of James Brindley, who was responsible for building the 16-km (10-mile) stretch of canal, and the 48-km (30-mile) extension from Manchester to Liverpool, completed in 1776. His experience in building elaborate drainage channels in a Lancashire pit proved valuable for one of the canal's greatest feats – a network of subterranean waterways within the Worsley Colliery itself. The system enabled coal to be hauled to the mine's entrance in flat bottomed boats, capable of holding 12 tons. The boats were then linked in convoys of five or six vessels, and drawn along the canal by horses or mules.

The crossing of the River Irwell, requiring an aqueduct to carry the canal, was also a major achievement. Initially treated with scepticism, the elegant stone bridge spanned the river in three arches. Boats travelling on river and canal crossed one another at right angles, those on the canal 11.5 m (38 ft) above, and the unusual spectacle became a tourist attraction. Over a century later, development of that stretch of the Irwell into the Manchester Ship Canal produced an ingenious example of Victorian engineering. The original aqueduct of the Bridgewater Canal was replaced where it crossed the river by a steel tank, capable of rotation through 90 degrees on a single pier; this enabled larger ships to pass beneath. The tank

PRECEDING PAGES
A textile mill in Bingley, West Yorkshire. The West Riding became the major region of wool manufacture in the 19th century.

1   A memorial erected to Francis Egerton 3rd duke of Bridgewater (1736–1803) on the green at Worsley, where he built England's first industrial canal in 1759. It drew upon the inspiration of the Canal du Languedoc in France which the young duke had visited.

2   The Bridgewater Canal at Barton-on-Irwell, near Manchester, just before its original crossing point over the Irwell on Brindley's celebrated aqueduct.

2

itself carries a 71.6 m (235 ft) section of the Bridgewater Canal and weighs 1,450 tons, including 800 tonnes of water. It remains fully operational today.

Although the duke had been close to bankruptcy several times, his eventual financial success meant that his achievement had considerable implications. His canal

1, 2 The Barton Swing
Aqueduct replaced the first
aqueduct over the Irwell
when the Manchester Ship
Canal was built in 1894. The
canal was created to link the
industrial heart of
Manchester and the port of
Liverpool directly, enabling
easier import and export of
goods by sea. The

Bridgewater Canal was still
important for transporting
coal, so the swing aqueduct
was devised. This allowed
large ships to use the Ship
Canal while keeping the
Bridgewater Canal in
operation.

effectively halved the price of coal in Manchester, enabling steam power to become a viable proposition for expanding industries. The perceived financial and economic benefits of the Bridgewater Canal encouraged proposals for similar schemes throughout the country. Brindley himself sought to create a network of canals in a cross formation, linking five rivers: the Mersey, Severn, Thames, Humber and Trent. His next construction, the Grand Trunk Canal (now the Trent and Mersey Canal), posed a particular problem in the shape of Harecastle Hill in Staffordshire. The canal required a tunnel that was 2,630 m (1½ miles) long. In order to minimize costs Brindley decided to restrict its width, making the tunnel navigable only by narrow-beamed barges. Narrower canals allowed cost reduction across the project, including locks and water requirements, and consequently the narrowboat developed into the standard form of transport throughout the network. Approximately 21 m (70 ft) in length, 2 m (7 ft) wide, and able to bear loads of 35 tonnes, they were often highly decorated. An example is now permanently moored at Gloucester docks, an inland nexus for a network of canals.

A period of major canal construction took place at the end of the 18th century. It began with the Staffordshire and Worcester Canal in 1772 which connected the Mersey and Severn. The new town of Stourport in Worcestershire, founded on the site of the canal's junction with the Severn, anticipated the development of towns near the railway in the 19th century (page 307). Orchestrated around canal basins, designed to anchor craft well away from the Severn's notorious floods, the town reflected the age's prosperity in attractive Georgian warehouses, inns and rows of terraced cottages. As the canal network became established, towns across England boomed or declined according to their proximity, anticipating the impact of the railways.

Bewdley, an ancient river port from which goods arriving on the Severn were transported to Birmingham by road, suffered from the development.

The overall effect on manufacturers, however, was a liberating one. By 1772 the Trent, Mersey and Severn rivers were interlinked by a canal network, allowing more flexibility in distribution for domestic or export markets. Goods from Birmingham and the Black Country, or the Potteries in Staffordshire, could be exported from Liverpool, or Hull, as well as Bristol. The canal network was in part responsible for Liverpool's ascendancy over Bristol in the early 19th century, as the

2

Midlands became more oriented towards the Mersey and cotton manufacture in Lancashire towns boomed. Significantly, the Leeds and Liverpool Canal, begun in 1770, suffered from delays in construction due to the challenging Pennine terrain. It was not completed until 1816, by which time other canals, such as the Rochdale Canal, had claimed much of the regional trade. Even in the 1840s, however, proximity to the canal was seen as important for steam-powered cotton mills, such as the Clocktower Mill at Burnley in Lancashire.

1 The canal 'mania' which swept England during the 1790s created a substantial network of trade routes. Many of them, including the Birmingham and Worcester Canal, still dominate the countryside.

2 The Bingley Five Rise Locks in West Yorkshire are the last in a series which raised the Leeds-Liverpool Canal out of the Aire Valley. Barges were lifted 18 m (60ft) through the Five Rise Locks, after which they had a clear run of 27 km (17 miles) to Skipton.

3 Gloucester developed into one of the most important links between inland manufacturers and their overseas markets, conducted by individual carrying companies. The Severn and Canal Carrying Company offered a service from the factory to the Bristol Channel.

2

1

During a period spanning 13 years, Brindley was responsible for engineering approximately 590 km (365 miles) of canals, and by the time waterborne transport was eclipsed by the railways in the 1830s, a network extending to over 6,440 km (4,000 miles) had been built. Never fully complete, it nevertheless linked developing industrial centres of the north and Midlands to the four main navigable rivers of the Trent, Mersey, Thames and Severn (a new connection between the two last had been created in 1789). Ports on those rivers encouraged the widespread distribution of imported goods, including raw materials such as cotton. They were shipped inland by barges, which were then loaded with manufactured goods on the return journey for distribution around England or export.

The canal 'fever' of construction reached a peak in 1792 when as many as 42 new canals were proposed and speculation in shares was rife. Companies were formed from local landowners, merchants and manufacturers to finance canal developments, but unpredictable construction costs, due to the wide variety of terrain, often led to wildly optimistic projections, and although some investors achieved good returns, many did not. As engineering expertise increased, however, technical problems posed by aqueducts and tunnels became easier

to address. Tunnel length remained a problem, especially in the Pennine region, where the longest could only be negotiated by human propulsion. Bargees were obliged to lie on their backs and 'leg' the barge along against the tunnel wall, to rejoin the horse at the other end.

Locks were also essential to accommodate changes in ground level. The longest flight of locks in Britain was on the Worcester and Birmingham Canal at Tardebigge near Bromsgrove, where boats had to pass through 30 successive locks in one single stretch of water. Canal builders initially followed the landscape, reducing the need for expensive civil engineering works. Locks were grouped together in order to minimize the amount of time spent working through them. Later canal builders, responding to increased commercial pressure to reduce transit times, opted for more direct routes with the consequent need for tunnels, bridges and embankments. Canals were not the exclusive province of business, however; pleasure trips were undertaken and during the Napoleonic wars they shipped large quantities of men and materials to defences on the south coast.

The pottery industry, in need of transport for heavy raw materials and fragile finished goods, benefited greatly from the development of canals. Josiah Wedgwood, whose Staffordshire firm was earning a reputation for creamware by the mid-18th century, was an enthusiastic supporter of the canal venture, assuring Brindley that his works would provide the 'most lasting memorial to his time'. He was a strong influence behind the building of the Grand Trunk Canal, conscious of the costs in moving Cornish china clay and Devon ball clay by road from the nearest port. Such calculations were proved correct; when the canal was completed, a route of sea and inland waterways reduced the financial outlay by as much as 80 per cent.

The first potter to introduce scientific methods of fabric and glaze analysis into commercial pottery production was John Dwight. At his pottery in Fulham from 1671 onwards, he developed the manufacture of stoneware and a partly translucent ceramic similar to porcelain. This early start was developed in a number of places during the 18th century, of which the most important was the Staffordshire region known as the Potteries for its close association with the industry. As

1 The Gladstone Works, Longton, Staffordshire, have been preserved as an industrial museum and provide an invaluable insight into life in the potteries. Each bottle oven was stacked with earthenware, which was then fired for up to three days. The constant belching of smoke from the chimneys created serious environmental problems.

2 Josiah Wedgwood (1730–1795) combined business enterprise with the ability to produce high quality ware using mass production techniques instead of a hand-crafted art. His most famous commission was the 952 piece 'Frog' service for Catherine the Great of Russia.

2

consumption of tea, coffee and chocolate increased, large quantities of Chinese porcelain were brought back as cheap ballast in the giant Indiamen that sustained trade with the East. Sold at low prices, they created in England a new demand and expectation of quality that the Potteries sought to address. The industrial centre was composed of six individual towns, close to sites containing the raw materials of clay, coal and water. In the 17th century local red clay produced excellent quarry tiles, butter pots and other domestic implements for the rich farming area of neighbouring Cheshire. These clays were subsequently augmented, or replaced, by whiter varieties from Cornwall, Devon and Dorset, for a higher quality domestic product. As new pottery styles were created, traditional white salt glazes were succeeded by creamwares, and later by bone china that possessed an oriental-style translucence, produced by the addition of cattle bone ash to the clay mix.

Josiah Wedgwood displayed remarkable commercial acumen, making exclusive items for a limited clientele and adapting them into articles for mass-production. Designated Her Majesty's Potter after completing a tea service for Queen Charlotte in 1765, he was an innovator, continually experimenting with scientific techniques, moulds and designs. His 'Etruria' factory, built alongside the Trent and Mersey Canal, closely resembled Matthew Boulton's engineering works in Birmingham (page 316), and steam beam engines were subsequently introduced to Etruria to improve productivity. Etruria's focus changed in later years from expensive 'ornamental' ceramics to stylish yet affordable earthenware. Mass-market production brought its rewards, and at his death in 1795 Wedgwood was the country's most successful potter, and the industrial revolution in the pottery industry was in full flood.

Longton, one of the Potteries' six towns, became a major centre of bone china production in the 19th century. Dozens of distinctive bottle ovens were crowded together in the city centre, and their haphazard development – juxtaposed with shops, terraced houses and pubs – served to create serious environmental health problems, even by the standards of the time. The six towns were in fact notoriously polluted. In preparation for firing, each bottle oven was stacked high with up to 2,000 saggars (fireproof clay containers in which the ware was fired), each weighing up to 25 kg (56 lb). When fully loaded the ovens were lit, to be stoked up every four hours for up to three days, reaching a maximum temperature of over 1,000°C. When all 2,000 coal fired ovens were lit, the sky was obliterated by smoke and the atmosphere became noxious. Not surprisingly, the average age for adults at death was only 46, and one in four children died in infancy as late as 1900. Today, the ovens have been replaced by smokeless firing plants. However, a complete pottery works, saved from demolition in 1971, has been restored by the Staffordshire Industry Preservation Trust and is featured in the Gladstone Pottery Museum.

Women in the six towns were often employed as paintresses. They applied powdered colours mixed by chemists from metals or metal compounds to produce diverse hues for different firing temperatures. Although a skilled and relatively well-paid job, it carried significant risk of lead poisoning, as did the task of the 'dippers' who placed the ware in liquid glaze before its second firing. Dippers, well paid to run such risks, took epsom salts or drank milk to line their stomachs before each shift. Children were widely employed in the pottery industry, particularly from families that had lost a male breadwinner. In 1861 it was estimated that more than one-third of children in this category and aged between 8 and 12 were at work.

By the end of the Victorian era, the Potteries of North Staffordshire made up 90 per cent of England's output of ceramics. In addition to ornamental and household goods, the industry produced an enormous range of domestic sanitary ware and building products for a rapidly growing market. From the earliest times, when it was made by hand for domestic use, pottery has been a staple product; its contribution to the economic upturn produced by the industrial revolution was to be highly significant.

AN URBAN ENGLAND

THE GROWING INDUSTRIAL CENTRES OF ENGLAND WERE TO TRANSFORM ITS LANDSCAPE AND POLITICAL STRUCTURES DURING THE 19TH CENTURY. NORTHERN MANUFACTURING CITIES BEGAN TO EXPLOIT THEIR ECONOMIC POWER, AND INCREASING MIGRATION FROM AN IMPOVERISHED COUNTRYSIDE SAW THE DECLINE OF A TRADITIONAL WAY OF LIFE. AS THE CENTURY'S TURBULENT EARLY YEARS GAVE WAY TO A MORE STABLE COMMERCIAL ENVIRONMENT, REFORM MOVEMENTS SOUGHT TO ADDRESS THE TERRIBLE LIVING AND WORKING CONDITIONS IN MANY NEW CITIES, ENFORCING LARGE-SCALE IMPROVEMENTS IN HOUSING AND SANITATION. IN TIME, A CONFIDENT URBAN IDENTITY WAS CELEBRATED THROUGH THE MONUMENTAL CIVIC BUILDINGS AND STATUARY THAT DOMINATE ENGLISH CITIES TO THIS DAY.

1

THE DEVELOPMENT OF ENGLAND'S cities in the 19th century was an unprecedented social phenomenon. Industry itself was nothing new to the country – mining, textile manufacture, metalwork and construction, for example, had existed alongside agriculture for centuries, but the scale of mechanized production required radical change. New structures and machinery were needed to compete, drawing long established rural industries, such as brewing, saddlery, weaving and building, into urban environments. The tradition of rural craftsmanship declined across the century, as did many small towns, especially in textile regions. Villages became primarily agricultural

in focus, and consequently more exposed to a volatile agrarian economy. As enclosure of open fields and commons was virtually complete by 1820, most agricultural labourers were unable to supplement low incomes. In 1795, in response to perceived local distress, Berkshire magistrates introduced a minimum level of parish relief to supplement low wages, but this unfortunately served to spread the financial burden on to yeomen farmers while enabling larger farmers to keep wages down. Significantly, there was considerable regional variation; wages of agricultural labourers in the north, where mines and factories provided local competition, were consistently higher than those in southern counties.

1 The Cotswold village of
   Lower Slaughter with its
   water-powered mill would
   have been typical of many
   parts of rural England
   before the population drift
   to urban centres in the 18th
   and 19th centuries.
2 Almshouses at Corsham in
   Wiltshire. Almshouses were
   a common feature of many
   villages, either funded by
   the church, a 'poor rate'
   which was a tax levied on

   individual householders
   or by endowment. Land
   enclosures increased rural
   poverty, and provision for
   the poor became a pressing
   issue during the later 18th
   and 19th centuries.
3 *Leeds from Rope Hill, c.1840.*
   The view captured by
   Alphonse Douseau in his
   lithograph shows the relentless encroachment of cities
   upon the countryside.

High wheat prices caused by European blockades
in the Napoleonic Wars brought immense suffering,
as prices virtually trebled between 1792 and 1812. The
crash that followed ruined many previously successful
farmers, putting further strain on rural communities.
The Corn Laws, introduced in 1815, sought to stabilize
the price of grain at an artificial level to prevent further
bankruptcies, driving unemployed labourers to near
starvation and encouraging a drift to cities or ports. The
eventual repeal of the Corn Laws in 1846 was considered
a major victory for the free-traders of the so-called
'Manchester' contingent. The name acknowledged the
city's symbolic importance in England's economic
development, and the increasing political influence of
the manufacturers with which it was associated.

Rural deprivation substantially increased migration,
and the effect on city populations, particularly in new
manufacturing regions, was dramatic. Birmingham
more than doubled in size between 1800 and 1831, and
Manchester rose from 75,000 to 182,000 in the same period. London also saw its population explode, rising from
900,000 in 1800 to 4.7 million in 1900, significantly bigger
than either Berlin or Paris. Although the health of agriculture still affected the economy, the foundations were
being laid for a predominantly urban England.

2

Social changes in the 19th century also challenged
the structures that had sustained rural communities for
centuries, such as parishes and almshouses. The latter,
often created from private bequests for the support
of the aged poor, were replaced in both town and
country by a harsh workhouse regime. The Poor Law
Amendment Act of 1834, presented to Parliament as a
measure of agricultural relief for beleaguered yeomen
farmers, sought to reduce the escalating costs of poor
relief, which had grown from £2 million in 1784 to
approximately £7 million in 1832. It amalgamated over

3

Leeds, from Rope Hill (circa 1840) From the original Water Colour in the Collection of J. Alex Symington, Newlay.   Alph. Douseau.

1 The Wells Union Work-
house, photographed in
1836, was one of many built
as a consequence of the
Poor Law Amendment Act.
It transferred responsibility
for sustaining the poor away
from individual parishes
into regional Unions.
2 Thurgaton Hundreds Workhouse in Norfolk resembles
a prison rather than a charitable institution. The ethos
behind such places sought

to discourage all except the
absolutely destitute.
3 Living conditions in
England's industrial towns
were often very poor. The
urban population growth
rates were spiralling to
unmanageable proportions
and few infrastructures
were designed to cope.

1

13,000 individual parishes into almost 600 unions, each
possessing workhouses managed by a board of elected
guardians. Conditions were deliberately austere as a
deterrent to anyone other than the destitute, but such
utilitiarian logic in practice created a place of dread for
the urban and rural poor. Workhouses were characterized by solid, functional façades, usually of a basic classical design but sometimes featuring Gothic trimmings.
Many still exist in English villages and towns, converted
for modern use.

Standards within were often little better than those
maintained in grim penal institutions. Families were
spit up, with members classified by their age, sex and
circumstances. The premises themselves were usually
dirty and became very overcrowded in times of acute

economic hardship. In 1848, for example, up to 60,000
children were receiving workhouse relief from the
Lancashire Unions, usually consisting of the bare minimum needed to keep them alive. Sick wards contained
a mixture of patients with no regard for contagion,
although criticism of such practises in the new Bolton
workhouse in 1864 led to the addition of isolation wings.
Not surprisingly, the death rate of children born in the
workhouses' lying-in wards was high.

Edwin Chadwick, one of the compilers of the Royal
Commission Report that resulted in the New Poor Law,
described the system as an administrative 'experiment',
responding to a 'moral plague'. Certainly the condition
of workhouse inhabitants was an unpalatable social
theme; Lord Melbourne, for example, took exception
to Charles Dickens' novel *Oliver Twist*, which made
trenchant criticisms of workhouse management, for
presenting 'a low and debasing view of mankind'.

Even for those outside the workhouse, urban conditions remained extremely poor. In northern cities like
Leeds, Manchester and Sheffield, as well as Birmingham
in the West Midlands, the population was expanding at
an incredible speed. Much of it was accommodated in
notorious 'back-to-back' housing which also dominated
Nottingham and Liverpool. Constructed in tightly
packed terraces, such buildings shared a party wall with
the terrace in the next street, possessing only one external façade. Air and light were consequently extremely
limited, a situation exacerbated by the practice of
enclosing street ends in narrow courtyards of further
housing. In Leeds, addresses from the north and east of
the town, such as Ebenezer Street, George Street and
Union Street, recur with ominous regularity in the burial registers of the nearby cemetery in Beckett Street. As
new industries and mines brought work to previously
undeveloped areas, housing was often provided by
companies without any building control. Occasionally
this had benefits; communities built by more enlight-
ened employers, such as Saltaire and Akroyden, near
Bradford and Halifax respectively (page 330), were of
much higher quality and a more imaginative design.

2

Nevertheless, the majority of housing for the urban poor remained both cramped and insanitary. London, Birmingham and other cities were initially characterized by 'courts', the result of infills and subdivision of existing buildings. Housing reformers were appalled by such claustrophobic yards, entered by narrow passageways from the street and packed with cramped and insubstantial structures. Hygiene, especially in courts, was a major concern, although the full implications of inadequate waste disposal were not at first fully realized.

Water supplies were collected from public standpipes, where a pipe serving 16 houses might be turned on for a few minutes once a week; even purchased water supplies were limited to a few hours a week. The Sanitary Report compiled by Edwin Chadwick, an insatiable campaigner for public health reform, described an incident in Liverpool in which the whole court was 'inundated with fluid filth which had oozed through the walls from two adjoining ash-pits or cesspools, and which had no means of escape'. The court in question

3

was owned by two different landlords, of whom one was prepared to finance half the cost of a drain, while the other refused to coutenance it; the issue, therefore – literally – stagnated.

Even where sanitation nominally existed, it often failed to be of use. A medical officer of the Whitechapel Union in London cited for the Chadwick Report the example of a sewer in the Rosemary Lane region of the district that was not connected to the slum dwellings and consequently irrelevant to the inhabitants. Their landlords were not obliged to pay for the plumbing work, and were refusing to do to.

In London, where water drawn from the Thames for drinking was heavily contaminated with sewage, the situation was particularly severe. A serious outbreak of cholera in 1849 killed 400 people a day, mostly from squalid, severely overcrowded slums. The notorious 'rookery' at St Giles contained 3,000 people in fewer than 100 houses, living in close proximity to overflowing sewage. Even smarter areas of London were not immune; elegant houses in Belgrave, Manchester and Portman Squares were located over leaking and ineffective sewers, threatening some of the leading figures of the day. A series of cholera and typhoid outbreaks in English cities finally confirmed the connection between drainage and water quality, and the Public Health Act of 1848 sought legal enforcement of more hygienic living conditions. Municipal corporations were created with the powers to control building and sanitation, and the Metropolitan Board of Works was established to do the same for London in 1855. Trunk sewers were built to the north and south of the Thames, served by elaborate pumping stations, which contained

1

magnificent steam pumps. Attempts were made to remove the worst urban slums through private organizations such as the Society for Improving the Condition of the Labouring Classes, established in the 1840s and sponsored by Prince Albert, and the Peabody Trust, founded in 1862 by an American philanthropist. The buildings of can still be seen in the capital today. The former, dating from 1849, are found in Streatham Street, Bloomsbury. They are five storeys in height and built in an austere, late Georgian design with a sizeable internal courtyard. Distinctive Peabody estates occur across the capital, again with large courtyards and severe façades, but much praised by contemporaries for their efficient internal layout and good sanitation. The first buildings of the Peabody Trust, still in existence today, were erected in Commercial Street, Spitalfields, between 1862 and 1864. By the end of the century more than 5,000 living 'units' had been constructed, reflecting their founder's desire to produce 'cheap, cleanly, well drained and healthful dwellings for the poor'.

Two later industrialists who would have endorsed such a concept were George Cadbury and William Hesketh Lever. Both established model communities for their workforces at, respectively, Bournville (on the outskirts of Birmingham) and Port Sunlight, a new factory town on Merseyside named after Lever's bestselling brand of soap. Each consisted of individual, two storey houses with spacious private gardens; they were either semi-detached or set in short rows, in contrast to the uniform terraces of most industrial towns. The houses in Port Sunlight are particularly distinctive, with attractive vernacular features and geometrically patterned

1 The reign of Queen Victoria (1837–1901) covered a period of rapid social and economic change. Railways, urban expansion and political reform were among the century's major developments. Expanding colonial possessions overseas also increased the country's economic power and prestige abroad.

2 An engraving of Benjamin Disraeli speaking in the House of Commons. A well known admirer of cities such as Manchester, he presided over a period of dramatic industrial expansion in the last quarter of the 19th century.

2

brickwork. A clear emphasis on green spaces was a consciously rural note in an era where attitudes to the cities were often highly ambivalent.

Many Victorians were repelled by the ugliness of urban development, and the severing of roots with the past which cities seemed to represent. In reaction to the uncontrollable present, artistic and architectural trends reverted to medieval Gothic, a self-conscious historicism taken at times to extremes. Retreat from urbanization was the paradoxical but not uncommon practice of successful industrialists. The paint manufacturer Theodore Mander, for example, designed Wightwich Manor near Wolverhampton in 1887 in the style of an Elizabethan manor house. Tudor beams and period features, including a minstrel's gallery, are combined with fashionable 'modern' conveniences – electric lighting, heating and a Turkish bath. A few years previously, William Armstrong, a shipyard owner and artillery manufacturer, had commissioned Norman Shaw to build an exotic mansion, Cragside, in a remote Northumbrian setting. Armstrong had also lived in Jesmond, a leafy suburb of Newcastle; as with Headingley near Leeds and Edgbaston close to Birmingham, the faint echo of a rural environment ensured such an areas's popularity.

1 Burslem Library in the heart
of the Potteries typifies the
new civic monuments which
celebrated achievements of
prominent residents. The
building was in honour of
Josiah Wedgwood, whose
Brickhouse works once
occupied the site.
2 An illustration showing the
inauguration of the Great
Exhibition at Crystal Palace
in 1851. Largely conceived
by Prince Albert, the Great
Exhibition was the world's
first international trade fair.
3 Leeds Town Hall, built by
Cuthbert Broderick
between 1853 and 1858, was
one of the first great public
buildings to celebrate the
growing civic status of the
northern industrial cities.

1

2

Many eminent Victorians were severe critics of the urban environment, for a variety of reasons. Some viewed cities as dangerous centres of political ferment, particularly at the height of Chartist activity. The incident dubbed 'Peterloo' that occurred at St Peter's Fields near Manchester in 1819, when a peaceful demonstration for reform was charged by the local yeomanry, served to link Manchester even more closely with a tradition of radical protest. The strength in the 1840s of the working-class Chartist movement for electoral reform was of concern to the Peel administration, as it provided a focus for national anxiety about the 'Condition of England'.

Growing disillusionment with the government created some unlikely bedfellows; in 1844 representatives of Manchester commerce invited Benjamin Disraeli and two other members of the Young England group of Tories to address a meeting at the Athenaeum. This piece of political theatre fuelled Disraeli's enthusiasm for Manchester's industrial vigour. He later described it as 'the most wonderful city of modern times'.

The aristocratic feudalism of Young England was dismissed with disdain by Victorian liberals. George Eliot, for example, saw it as no more than 'a sort of idyllic masquerading', irrelevant to the country's contemporary needs. Nevertheless, Disraeli's description of England's 'Two Nations … between whom there is no intercourse and no sympathy' reflected a very real sense of alienation in the newly urban workforce. The reality of the new social fabric was, inevitably, more complex. A middle class existed in varying degrees of prosperity

3

and comfort, and skilled artisans maintained higher standards of living than unskilled workers. The subtle gradations were increasingly reflected in geographic segregation, as distinct areas of the expanding cities were inhabited by different social groups.

Partly to establish a more unified identity, newly empowered civic authorities commissioned monumental public buildings. The best of these, such as St George's Hall in Liverpool, begun in 1838, celebrated a distinctive urban heritage. An elegant neoclassical structure with a highly decorative interior, St George's Hall provided both a cultural venue (the original intention) and a site for the new Crown Court and Civil Court. The *Illustrated London News* applauded its construction, observing that 'this magnificent edifice will be a perennial monument of the energy and public spirit … of the people of Liverpool'. It continues to dominate the town today from its raised plateau.

An even earlier civic building had been created in Birmingham in 1834. Predating the establishment of the city's civic administration (which took place in 1835), it provided an assembly hall and cultural arena in a cool, neoclassical style that was allegedly inspired by the Temple of Castor and Pollux at Rome.

Leeds Town Hall, built between 1853 and 1858, was one of the first great town halls of the industrial north. A vast, frontal colonnade with an ornate steeple-cupola contribute to a design of exuberant English baroque. The building followed St George's Hall in housing both law courts and rooms for cultural venues, and it set a precedent for grand municipal buildings in Halifax (1859–63) and Manchester (1868). The latter, famous for its Great Hall containing Ford Maddox Brown murals, is located on a large central square that shows its elaborate Gothic architecture to full advantage. Another famous

example of Manchester Gothic is the John Rylands Library, designed in 1888 by the architect of Mansfield College, Oxford, following a donation from Ryland's widow.

As the prosperity of individual cities boomed, covered markets became more ornate. Exposed iron-work and glazing were combined with fantastic domes, turrets, cupolas and gables. Borough Market in Halifax, and County Arcade and Kirkgate Market in Leeds are striking monuments to a new consumerism.

The greatest iron and glass structure of the age was, however, Joseph Paxton's Crystal Palace in Hyde Park. Created for the Great Exhibition in 1851, its technical ingenuity reflected the nation's growing industrial sophistication. The completed exhibition hall, named 'Crystal Palace' by the satirical magazine *Punch*, covered a vast 10.5 ha (26 acres), more than six times larger than St Paul's Cathedral. The exhibition itself featured almost 14,000 exhibitors, over half of whom represented Britain or its colonial interests. It was attended by over 6 million visitors, many travelling by railway, and symbolized a mid-Victorian sense of social progress and economic optimism.

The final decades of the century saw major municipal improvements in urban housing, transport and other social amenities. Baths and wash-houses were established, along with public parks, art galleries and museums. Libraries and universities were also erected and maintained by local ratepayers, contributing to a new impetus to intellectual life. Industrial areas were transformed by architectural developments and social reforms into centres for urban living. William Morris' fears that urbanization would mean 'a counting house on top of a cinder heap, with the pleasure of the eyes having gone from the world' had, for many Victorians, been effectively dispelled.

CHAPTER

12

Early antiquarians, fascinated by the material remains
of the past, sought to observe and record monuments and
buildings for posterity. Most people, however, until comparatively
recently, regarded the past and its physical remains with disinterest
or avarice. The stones of Hadrian's wall are embedded in many a local
farmhouse and byre, and the great monasteries of England were used as
building material after the dissolution. Now it is very different; there is a
popular fascination with the past and archaeologists strive to protect
what material and evidence remains. New technology that allows
accurate dating, the scanning of the ground for physical
signs without the need for initial digging and the
micro-scrutiny of objects have revolutionized
our understanding of their function
and place in society

DISCOVERY &
PRESERVATION

DETECTING THE PAST

HUMANS ARE CURIOUS ANIMALS — THE ONLY ONES WHOSE SPECULATION EXTENDS INTO THE PAST AND THE FUTURE. UNLIKE OUR CLOSEST RELATIVES, OTHER PRIMATES, WE ARE AWARE OF OUR INDIVIDUAL MORTALITY AND ABLE TO PONDER OUR ORIGINS. ARCHAEOLOGY ENABLES US TO EXPLORE THE MATERIAL REMAINS OF THE PAST, RANGING FROM MINUTE SAMPLES TO HUGE, MONUMENTAL STRUCTURES. IT IS A FASCINATING AND CONSTANTLY CHANGING PROCESS, AND AS DISCOVERIES ARE RE-INTERPRETED IN THE LIGHT OF NEW SCIENTIFIC TECHNIQUES, IT IS PROVIDING US WITH THOUSANDS OF YEARS OF PREVIOUSLY UNKNOWN HISTORY.

ARCHAEOLOGY RECOGNIZES the proximity of the past to our everyday lives. It seeks to make sense of a historical legacy by systematically studying its physical remains, from the stone circles of Avebury and Stonehenge to microscopic pollen deposits indicating the clearance of ancient woodland. In addition to attempting a reconstruction of the past, archaeologists increasingly use the material remains as a way of understanding ourselves; how we perceive the world and our place in it.

An archaeologist's approach to the past differs from the historian's in focusing upon material remains rather than written documents as the primary source of evidence. One advantage is greater time depth: the earliest hominid remains in Britain, at Boxgrove in Sussex, date from about 500,000 years ago; the earliest written evidence by a first-hand observer is by Julius Caesar, who carefully composed his campaign accounts from his soggy winter quarters in the Morvan forests in eastern Gaul half a century before Christ. Even so, the practice of archaeology — and the interpretation of its findings — has often been directed by the power and authority of the written record: the Bible, Caesar's campaigns or Geoffrey of Monmouth's 12th-century fictional account of Britain's origins.

It is obvious to us in the self-critical 21st century that the written record is not value free; its writers were not neutral observers. Caesar, the campaigning general and fiercely ambitious politician, wrote to influence his Roman audience in a coolly 'objective' third person singular. Geoffrey, a cleric in Oxford, drew on arcane, and possibly non existent, Welsh sources, to legitimate the Norman rulers of England and create a myth of national unity. For Geoffrey the rousing story of Britain could be constructed from a collection of myths, classical sources, tall tales and mysterious monuments such as Stonehenge. It was an imaginative brew, only discredited with the emergence of more objective textual criticism by Renaissance scholars.

Archaeology developed out of that same Renaissance tradition of systematic observation and recording. Apparently a logical and neutral science, its evidence may be manipulated as propaganda or exploited for financial gain. Shortly after

PRECEDING PAGES

Main picture: Aerial view of
the remains of a medieval
village on Hound Tor,
Dartmoor.
Detail: Chancel wall painting
of an Apostle, St Mary's
Church, Kempley, Glos.

1   The consolidation of
Stonehenge trilithons in the
1950s. Several restoration
projects have taken place at

Stonehenge since storm
damage in 1899.
2   Barbury Castle, Wiltshire.
The circular enclosure is a
late prehistoric hillfort. In
the foreground there are
small, late prehistoric/
Romano-British fields, well
preserved on the downland
slopes, which have never
been ploughed. No archaeological features survive on
the scoured arable fields.

2

Geoffrey established Arthur as a national figurehead, for example, Caradoc of Llancarfan identified Glastonbury Abbey as the king's burial site, prompting the earliest recorded excavation in England. Significantly, a fire had destroyed Glastonbury Abbey in 1184, and the precedent of Canterbury Cathedral 10 years earlier, restored by the pilgrim cult of Thomas Becket, revealed the profits of association with historical figures. In 1191 Abbot Henry de Soilly ordered his monks to dig for Arthur's body between 'two pyramids' – a place identified by the recently deceased Henry II, who was given the secret by 'an ancient Welsh bard'. They unearthed a lead cross, inscribed in Latin 'Here lies the renowned King Arthur

in the Isle of Avalon', along with two bodies, said to be those of the king and Guinevere. The discovery not only created a tourist attraction that has lasted for over 800 years, but also crushed any hopes that Arthur might return to lead a British rebellion, thereby strengthening the position of the Anglo-Norman kings.

It seems highly likely that the Glastonbury monks buried two bodies, faked the lead cross and stage-managed the discovery. In a remarkably modern case of spin-doctoring, they even invited a famous, but not too sceptical, Welsh writer, Gerald of Wales, to witness the opening. The successful excavation at Glastonbury had a distinguished precedent in Christendom. Helena, the

1 Wigmore Castle, 1732, one of a series of engravings of castles published in the 1740s. Such recording of the landscape is in effect an early form of archaeology.

2 Silbury Hill, Wiltshire is the largest prehistoric mound in Europe, 39 m (128 ft) high. Its precise purpose is unknown, but it is part of the sacred landscape of Avebury with its huge henge monument, avenues, timber circle and burial mounds.

3 Archaeologists from the Museum of London examine the burial of a young woman found in a lead coffin in a Roman cemetery at Smithfield. DNA studies indicate that the woman probably came from southern Europe, perhaps Spain.

mother of Constantine, the first Christian emperor, carried out a similarly well-targeted piece of research when she dug up the true cross in Jerusalem.

Objects from the past can be imbued with an almost tangible power. Britain's prime minister authorized a medieval artefact in Westminster Abbey to be dismantled in order to return the Stone of Scone to Scotland. Stonehenge, associated by Geoffrey of Monmouth with Merlin, remains a contested landscape, disputed by neo-pagans, environmentalists and leyline hunters. In countries as diverse as Israel, Afghanistan and Serbia, past relics may retain religious and political significance far beyond their academic or intellectual role. This may result in the proud display of Masada (the citadel where, as tradition has it, a group of Jews defied Rome), the recent destruction of the Buddhas of Bamiyan or the re-building of Suleiman's war-ravaged bridge at Mostar.

Since the later 19th century the object of archaeology has been to generate scientific knowledge about the human past using material evidence. To do this we need to know where to look and how to find appropriate evidence to accumulate data, or to test the questions thought to be important. As in all human activities, archaeological fashions change – from treasure hunting to building artefact typologies, from economic reconstruction to consideration of the role of the individual within a society. In recent years archaeologists have moved the focus from specific sites – prehistoric henges or tombs, Roman villas, medieval abbeys and castles – towards mapping the landscape as a whole, and to a considered explanation of change.

Early antiquarians, such as William Stukeley, were attracted to the downlands of southern England or the Yorkshire Wolds. On these largely pastoral uplands they

2

saw the traces of generations of human activity. Iron Age hillforts and their associated field systems overlay Bronze Age barrows and Neolithic causewayed enclosures, all preserved as upstanding earthworks in the grassland of the Downs. The antiquarians assumed that prehistoric people inhabited the dry uplands, avoiding the marshes and forested valleys. In fact, the activities of arable farmers, ploughing continually for over 2,000 years, have long since flattened earthworks in the lowlands. The prolific archaeology of these regions only became obvious with the discovery and recording of crop marks. One particularly observant antiquarian of the 17th century, John Aubrey, noticed that some features hidden below ground, such as Roman roads, could be seen in the right conditions as marks in growing crops. His work was taken up by Steven Stone, who plotted crop marks near Dorchester-on-Thames in the 19th century from the vantage point of horseback. It became far easier to see and record crop markings with the development of aerial photography. Today the National Monuments Record in Swindon contains millions of aerial photographs, revealing huge numbers of archaeological sites. English Heritage's National Mapping Programme documents those within their landscapes. We can now see Stonehenge as part of the sacred complex built up over centuries within a natural amphitheatre, or the Fens of East Anglia as a huge network of Romano-British farming communities. The earthworks preserved on Dartmoor and in the Cheviots and Yorkshire Dales can also be efficiently recorded from the air, although intensification of arable agriculture has meant that massive areas of ancient landscape have been erased.

Some of archaeology's most spectacular finds have occurred in extreme climate conditions. In a temperate climate, such as England's, we would never find a Tutankhamun with his flowers and furniture; such artefacts survive as a result of the dry conditions of Egypt. In the Altai mountains on the Sino-Russian border, freezing has preserved tattooed

3

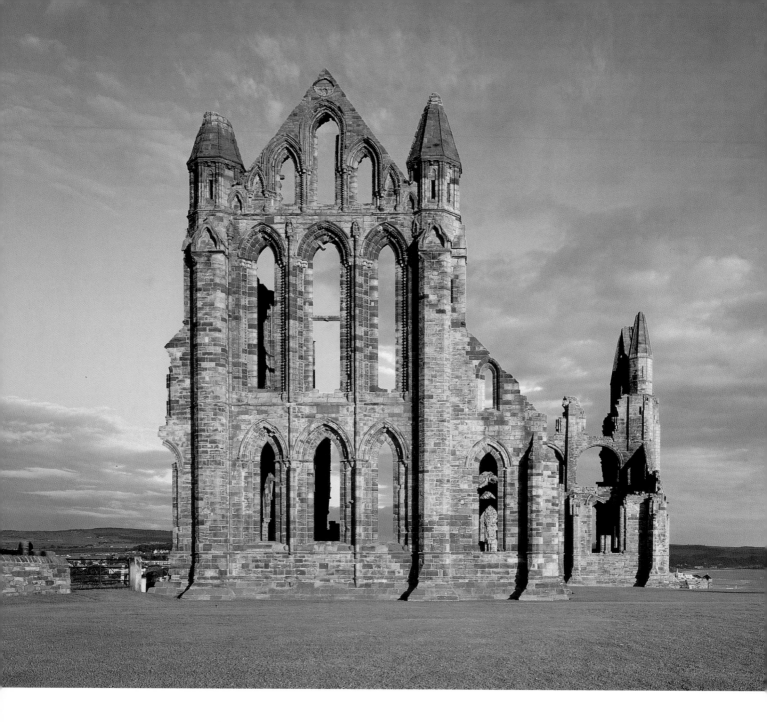

bodies, Chinese carpets, felt hangings and elaborately carved wooden horse harnesses. A prehistoric trans-Alpine traveller, equipped with a remarkable array of gear, was similarly frozen and preserved. In England, paradoxically, we have to rely on the airless, waterlogged conditions of the Fens, northern peat bogs or the Somerset Levels (site of the earliest known Neolithic timber trackways) to preserve material. One of the most vivid of my own archaeological experiences was seeing a thick, organic layer of leaves, twigs and iridescent beetles, 400,000 years old yet perfectly preserved in an ancient channel of the River Thames. In comparison, letters found in the waterlogged rubbish dump of the Roman fort at Vindolanda on Hadrian's Wall (page 361) are almost modern. Inscribed in ink on wood, they form a body of unique evidence that brings us close to the everyday lives of individuals: invitations to parties, complaints about the state of the roads, requests for clothing supplies and foodstuffs, or the condescending attitude to 'the little Brits'.

The preservation and discovery of timbers, such as those of Roman and medieval wharves in London, has enabled archaeologists to fine tune their first priority – dating. For early antiquarians, chronology proved a

3

major stumbling block. In a documented period such as the Roman world – with its inscriptions and coins – dating deposits was possible, but prehistory proved more difficult. Christian Thomsen introduced relative order when, in 1819, he classified museum collections in Copenhagen in terms of the three successive ages: Stone, Bronze and Iron. This provided a sequence for objects but, in the absence of documentary evidence such as the king-lists of Egypt, no dates. Thomsen's system was extended to include the Palaeolithic (Old Stone Age) and the Neolithic (New Stone Age). Archaeologists also developed elaborate studies of style, or the seriation of objects such as stone or bronze axes, pottery and brooches to establish relative chronologies. We use this principle in daily life to assess the age of a car, a pair of shoes or a piece of furniture.

Since the late 1940s archaeologists have seen a revolution in dating technology. The initial development of radiocarbon dating was later refined, thanks to the study of tree-rings (dendrochronology). The timbers of London waterfronts have provided a sequence of tree-rings dating back to the Roman period. Each tree-ring is a signature for a specific year; together they enable the accuracy of radiocarbon dating to be tested. In fact, radiocarbon dates are a bit young, requiring calibration for a more accurate estimate of calendar years. By radiocarbon dating tree-rings of a known age, inaccuracies can be more clearly perceived. It is thus possible to reconstruct, and more accurately date, the sequence of building at Stonehenge, and to reinterpret the pattern of change across whole periods throughout the world. The origins and spread of plant and animal domestication, for example, may be reconsidered.

4

In the countryside many archaeological sites lie very close to the surface. Systematic field walking will reveal scatters of stone and tiles from a Roman building, flint flakes from prehistoric tools or pottery sherds spread during the manuring of fields. Geophysical surveys allow archaeologists to detect walls, ditches, graves, pits or burnt areas below ground. Ground-penetrating radar

1 An aerial view of Fort
Cumberland, built to
protect Portsmouth and its
harbour. It now houses
English Heritage's Centre
for Archaeology and its
science laboratories.
2 A wooden writing tablet,
remarkably preserved in the
waterlogged rubbish dumps
of the Roman fort of
Vindolanda on Hadrian's
Wall. The handwritten

memorandum in Latin,
makes disparaging reference
to the 'Brituntuli' (the
'little Brits').
3 Museum of London
archaeologists excavating
the burial of the rich
Roman woman found in
the Smithfield cemetery.
The markers are being
placed in order to carry out
archaeomagnetic dating.

4 Dendrochronology or tree-
ring dating is the most
precise method of dating
the past. Furniture,
standing buildings and
archaeological remains of
timber can be dated with
this method, provided that
the outermost tree ring
survives and the parent tree
has not grown in
exceptional conditions.

1

can reveal features in deeper
deposits – particularly useful in
towns where archaeological layers
may accumulate to several metres
in depth. Systematic excavations,
carried out before redevelopment
in towns such as Winchester and
Carlisle, have transformed our
knowledge of urban origins and
development – from pre-Roman
tribal centres and Roman towns
to Anglo-Saxon *burhs*. As urban
deposits accumulate quickly,
archaeological evidence can be
remarkably well preserved, be it
Viking workshops in York, Roman
cemeteries in London, or the
lavatorial deposits of Oxford dons
during the Civil War.

These last two are the closest
we can get to people. From
human bones and DNA we can
study the health of past populations, and sometimes their place
of origin. Grave goods help to
establish the relative status of
the individual, his or her social
identity and the significance of age
and gender. In early Anglo-Saxon
communities a woman's tribal
identity was marked by the style of
dress and jewellery with which
she was buried (and probably wore
in life). A 6th-century West Saxon
woman in her mid-20s, excavated
at Lechlade, Gloucester, wore a
string of amber beads and a gilded
saucer brooch decorated with sun
symbols (page 359). Both were
probably protective amulets
reflecting pagan beliefs, links with

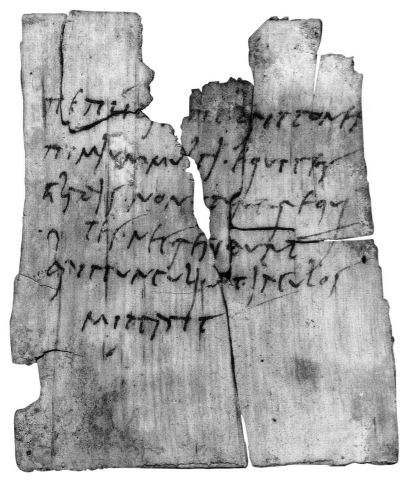

3

the Baltic region, and her status as a mature woman and keeper of a household. A century later, the great granddaughters of such a woman had changed their style of dress. Jewellery was less bold and they wore a wimple around the head, pinned beneath the chin. Higher status women were adorned with gold, available through new trade links via Kent to Merovingian Gaul. Their pendants were set with garnets, traded from the Indian subcontinent through Europe, and amber had disappeared. No longer belonging to West Saxon pagan tribal society, the women dressed like their wealthy English cousins in Kent or East Anglia, part of a new, Christian generation. The most important women carried objects that indicated their role in the wealth-generating textile industry or as 'wise women' protecting the health of the community.

Archaeology is often associated with excavation, but its techniques can equally be applied above ground, in analyses of buildings as varied as Whitby Abbey and a Yorkshire textile mill. Archaeology can open up windows into our deep past, but it also sheds light on contemporary history. A recent English Heritage book considers 'the Archaeology of Rocketry' and deals with monuments of the Cold War. Perhaps nothing will better reflect the nature of the 20th century.

2

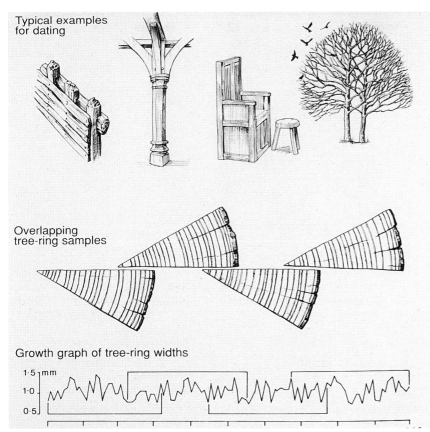

4

Typical examples
for dating

Overlapping
tree-ring samples

Growth graph of tree-ring widths

THE LIVING LANDSCAPE

MODERN ARCHAEOLOGICAL PRACTICE INCREASINGLY FOCUSES ON THE MAPPING AND INTERPRETATION OF THE LANDSCAPE AS A WHOLE, RATHER THAN A PARTICULAR BUILDING. NEW TECHNOLOGY, SUCH AS GROUND-PENETRATING RADAR AND GEOPHYSICAL SURVEYS, ENABLE ARCHAEOLOGISTS TO TRACE THE HISTORY OF AN INDIVIDUAL STRETCH OF GROUND OVER CENTURIES, AND TO CONSIDER ITS STRUCTURES AND FEATURES IN THIS BROADER CONTEXT. WE NOW KNOW THAT FIELD BORDERS AND BOUNDARIES ARE OFTEN EXTREMELY ANCIENT AND PROVIDE NEW EVIDENCE OF CONTINUITY IN FARMING THE LAND OVER CENTURIES. DESPITE ITS RESILIENCE, THE LANDSCAPE IS A COMPLEX INHERITANCE WHICH MUST BE MANAGED IF IT IS TO BE PRESERVED FOR FUTURE GENERATIONS.

THE EVIDENCE OF THE PAST in the English landscape fascinated people since long before the advent of television or *Time Team*. Excavation in the mid-19th century was more like a field sport than a scientific activity. Dean Merriweather may have set an unfortunate precedent when, in 1849, he bagged 35 barrows on the Marlborough Downs in 28 days. Only five years earlier in Canterbury, the British Archaeological Association had held the first-ever archaeological conference, involving the unwrapping of an Egyptian mummy followed by tomb raiding on Breach Down. An audience of 200 watched the action from their carriages. Not everyone approved; some protested at the desecration of 'time-hallowed monuments for no better purpose than the indulgence of craving acquisitiveness and the adorning of ill-understood relics'.

Unfortunately, the craving for relics has not disappeared, although archaeological objects ripped untimely from their context have little value beyond the financial. Since the meticulous excavations of General Pitt-Rivers (1827–1900), Britain's first inspector of ancient monuments, archaeologists have sought to record not only the eye-catching but the everyday — animal bone fragments, plant debris, broken pot shards. Yet archaeologists still generally record what they consider important; carbonized seeds and fish bones, for example, will usually only be recovered by sieving. If we do not look, we will not find.

Archaeology is not simply about detailed, objective recording, but an appreciation of human response to the world, today and in the past. People have always sought to change the landscape, for example, perhaps through simple tools such as the polished stone axe which lies on my desk. Explanations for polished axes, a tool characteristic of the Neolithic era, were until recently functional and utilitarian. Such axes belonged to the period when farming developed. There was a need for clearings in the forest to provide open spaces for domesticated plants and animals. The polished stone axe was more efficient than its flaked predecessors, more hard wearing and capable of being resharpened without excessive waste.

Now archaeologists can ask questions beyond the merely functional. Objects have complex lives: they may be made and used by people of different ages, gender or social affiliation; they may have particular powers – stone, for example, is often used for amulets, or seen as powerful and precious. We are now able to characterize material scientifically; geological techniques allow us to establish the source of the stone. The axe is made from a greenish grey tuff which is found high on the crags of Great Langdale in the Lake District. This place is remarkably inaccessible and raises complex questions. Why transport the greenstone axe 270 km (170 miles) to this part of present-day Oxfordshire when there is a perfectly good supply of flint less than a day's walk

PLATE I

Excavation of a barrow, 1844
(*Gentleman's Magazine*, 1852).
(See p. 7.)

1

1 'Barrow digging men' slicing into a Bronze Age round barrow in 1844. Hundreds of barrows were cut open in such an unscientific manner in the mid-19th century in the search for antiquities to add to personal and museum collections.

2 Belas Knap, Gloucestershire is a Neolithic chambered tomb of the 4th millennium BC. One of England's earliest monuments, it was built to house the dead, whose bones were collected and placed inside the chamber. The forecourt was probably used for ceremonies and feasting by the community who built the tomb to dominate the Cotswold skyline and emphasize their ancestral right to the land.

2

1 An aerial photograph of Foxley Farm, near Eynsham, Oxfordshire. Prehistoric barrows on the fertile gravel terraces of the Thames Valley have long since been ploughed flat. They appear from the air as a complex pattern of crop marks, in barley and wheat fields. The circular marks or ring-ditches indicate the ditches around Bronze Age burials.

2 The late 1st-century Romano-British landscape at Claydon Pike, Lechlade, Gloucestershire, is shown in this plan constructed from aerial photographs and excavation evidence. Pastoral fields surround the central settlement, which includes a temple at the crossroads, and two large hay barns, probably under military control.

3 An aerial photograph of the late prehistoric/ Romano-British settlement at Claydon Pike. The parallel lines (lower left and upper right) indicate the side ditches of a Roman road; it bends in a dog-leg across the marshy area indicated by the branching pale areas. Claydon Pike is the site of one of the largest rescue excavations funded by English Heritage in the 1980s before gravel digging began in the area.

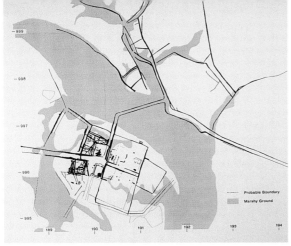

2

away? Why go to the trouble of polishing it all over? Is the shape significant? To my eye its smooth curves resemble those of Neolithic burial mounds on the hills above Stanton Harcourt.

Polishing, in fact, not only sharpens the axe but reveals the quality, colour and character of the stone. Recent research on Neolithic tombs and stone circles suggests that the people who built these monuments particularly valued exotic stone – the bluestones at Stonehenge, hauled and shipped from the Preseli Mountains of Pembrokeshire, are the best examples of the efforts that prehistoric people made to obtain the right material. The greenstone axe may be more than a functional tool. It may possess a link to a distant high place, a highly symbolic object to the person who disposed of it at Stanton Harcourt. And names, like the materials of the landscape, can tell us something of a place's history. Harcourt was the family of Norman lords to whom this land was given by William the Conqueror. 'Stanton' is an older element – 'the settlement of stones' in Anglo-Saxon. The stones were erected in the Neolithic period about 5,000 years ago as part of a henge monument that the later Christian villagers called The Devil's Quoits. They were not conservationists, and when they laid out the strip fields of the village most of the stones were pushed over and buried. We know that polished stone axes are not found inside henges, but they were often deliberately buried in pits outside, or placed in rivers and bogs. The axe then links us to a wider cultural landscape, to high places far away, to sacred enclosures and places that are suitable for offerings and burials in the earth or in water. It may also tell us of political links 5,000 years ago, when many of the Great Langdale axes were transported eastwards into Yorkshire. In the Stanton Harcourt area other unusual objects found in burials, such as jet belt fittings, provide links to eastern

3

Yorkshire. Should we see these areas as associated politically, bonded through gift-exchange, marriages and alliances? In response to such questions archaeologists have to think on a wider scale, exploring the whole landscape in the context of ideas on prehistoric social structures, beliefs and perceptions.

The landscape is a place of constant change. Aerial photography reveals the palimpsest of crop marks where successive generations have altered, destroyed or re-used their ancestors' construction (opposite). In the uppermost part of the Thames Valley, between Lechlade and Fairford in Gloucestershire, aerial photographs show a detailed pattern of Iron Age and Roman features – dating between 300 BC and AD 400. This low-lying marshy area was interspersed by a drier inland region of gravel. In the 1980s most of it was dug away for building material, but not until a team from the Oxford Archaeological Unit had carried out their research.

Evident crop marks were first carefully mapped. Geophysical surveys added detail and phosphate analysis

1 Rievaulx Abbey, one of the finest medieval ruins in Europe. Cistercian monks, 650 of them in the early years, built the abbey and farmed their estates from 1132. The spectacular architectural development was directed by Abbot Aelred (1147–67). Following the dissolution of the monasteries, Rievaulx survived as a romantic ruin because of its relatively isolated position in the North York Moors. In more densely populated areas, such as Oxford, buildings of similar size completely disappeared as they were quarried for stone.

2 The ruins of the abbey church are just the tip of an archaeological iceberg. A detailed survey in the park land around the ruins reveals an amazing complex of medieval and later features still surviving as faint earthworks.

3 The ruins of Jervaulx Abbey in the Ure Valley are in private ownership. Like an alpine rockery, they come alive with colour in spring and summer.

1

showed, for example, where animals had gathered. Streams and relict watercourses divided the whole area. For the archaeologists, this revealed that waterlogged organic deposits were plentiful and the watercourses defined drier settlement and pastoral areas.

This low-lying, wet area was potentially valuable farmland if it could be managed, and about 300 BC farmers dug a system of drainage ditches. Between them there was a scatter of timber-and-thatch round houses occupied by the farmers themselves – small family groups that looked after herds of cattle and sheep. They also wove cloth on the site and brought salt from Droitwich, across the Cotswolds, to cure meat and hides. Cattle and sheep grazed the land year-round, reducing pasture in places to bare, muddy patches. Dung beetles were the most prolific inhabitants of this open, rather prairie-like landscape.

In the late first century AD an enormous change took place: new fields on either side of a carefully constructed metalled road; a nucleated settlement at a cross-roads. A temple at the crossroads itself, where the cone of an umbrella pine (*Pinus pinea*), symbol of the god Attis, was placed in a pit. Beside the temple a fortified gateway protected two enormous barns. Farmworkers lived in simple rectangular houses across the road. This new house form changed the lives of people who had lived in round houses for generations. The dung beetles were gone. Instead of being overgrazed, fields – for the first time in British history – grew hay and were protected from animals by hedges.

Inside the protected enclosure with the barns there was also a rectangular timber building of a construction found in Roman forts. Finds from the area included Roman cavalry harness, an unusually large quantity of coins, glass and Spanish and Italian amphorae, large vessels that held wine and oil. There was also a Roman officer's ring with an imperial eagle cut into an intaglio. It seems likely that this valuable Thames-side pasture, into which the locals had put 300 years of effort, was taken over from the 'little Brits' and exploited by the cavalry regiment based 16 km (10 miles) to the west at Corinium, present-day Cirencester.

In this area conquest meant a transformation of the landscape, new plants and animals, new roads and the erasure of old settlements. Roman rule was not only enforced by the military but legitimated by the new religious structure at the crossroads. The British lived in new-style houses and ate new foodstuffs, including Mediterranean herbs – coriander, cumin and poppy

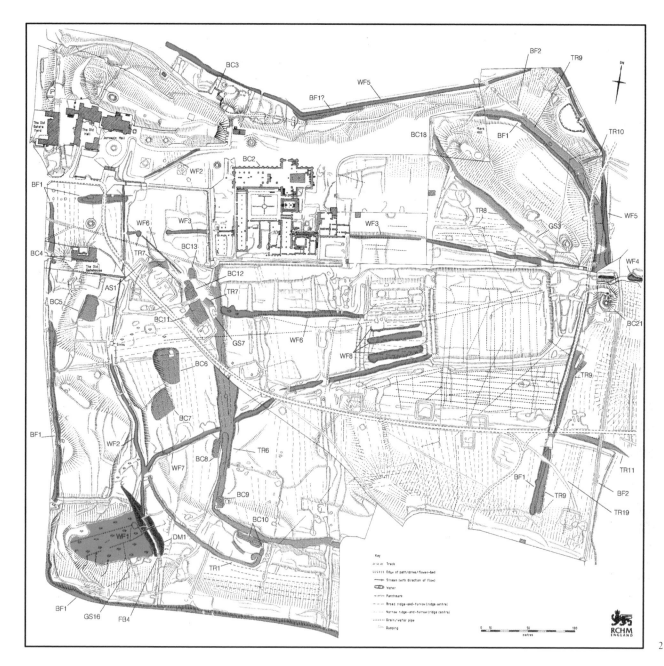

2

seeds. The countryside was a complex place, not just an economic shop-floor but a contested area that was charged with meaning, dispute and symbolism.

Every landscape is different, and they vary in the ease with which their history can be read. Claydon Pike, for example, before it was quarried away and became a lake, was relatively flat and featureless. Other landscapes reveal the past without excavation or aerial photography.

Some of England's most evocative monuments are the ruins of Yorkshire abbeys such as Fountains, Rievaulx or Jervaulx. They were originally established in remote well-watered valleys by monks seeking both solitude and

3

room for agricultural expansion. In the populous and intensively farmed Thames Valley, most archaeological sites have been reduced to below-ground deposits, or even dug away completely in gravel pits. The preservation of ancient structures in remote areas is often better as there are far fewer pressures to flatten, plough and rob the stone.

Yorkshire's abbeys had the life torn out of them at the dissolution of the monasteries, yet many of the ruins are surprisingly intact. Archaeologists used to focus on the main buildings, architectural fragments of the formal framework for those who lived, worked and prayed there for centuries. But for a deeper understanding of the monks' lives, their impact on neighbouring communities and the landscape, we need to move beyond the ruins. The detailed survey around Jervaulx Abbey (page 367) has revealed a remarkable complex of watercourses, gardens and enclosures, visible to the naked eye of the careful observer. But as with crop marks, not all these features are of a single period; some belong to the later, landscaped park and others are the legacy of munitions dumps from World War II. The landscape is a complex document, one whose messages are often coded, like the greenstone axe. It is also a far richer place for the archaeologist than is often assumed, not something that can be simply translated or determined by geography. In recent years new environments have revealed their potential. England's river valleys contain layers of flood silt, or alluvium, now known to have built up in the late prehistoric, Roman or medieval periods. This is the result of tree clearance and intensive arable farming which generate run-off of water and soil erosion. Beneath the alluvium lie some of the best preserved sites in the country, protected from ploughing and often airless and waterlogged. In the Nene Valley in Northamptonshire a Roman watermill collapsed, to be rapidly covered by flood silts and preserved in a remarkable condition up to its eaves. At Dorney in Buckinghamshire Bronze Age

1, 2 The Holme timber circle
in Norfolk is usually called
'Seahenge' though it is not
strictly speaking a henge,
nor was it built in the sea.
The circle of oak timbers,
with an inverted oak bole at
the centre, is dated to
2049 BC. The timber circle
was excavated by the
Norfolk Archaeological
Unit (above) because the
wood was being rapidly
destroyed, both through
coastal erosion and wood-
boring snails.
3 Hoo Fort, near Chatham,
Kent, was built after 1860
as part of the Victorian
defence system of the
Thames and Medway. The
fort itself is defended from
coastal erosion by the hulks
of old ships that have been
drawn up along the
seashore.

timber bridges survived across abandoned meanders of the Thames, with ritually placed deposits of pots, a plough and human remains on nearby sandbanks.

Britain has the longest coast in Europe, much of it subject to increased erosion. As the north Norfolk coast is washed away, sites such as the unique timber circle at Holme are emerging. Inside the continuous palisade of logs there was an inverted oak stump. The timbers died in 2050 and 2049 BC, but because their surfaces have been protected by the fine silt into which they were embedded, we can see that 38 similar axes cut and trimmed the timbers. This suggests that this relatively small monument was constructed rapidly by a communal group. They worked together to build a structure of social and religious significance – a symbolic world tree linking the heavens and the underworld – for the first time using axes that were not stone, but made of a remarkable new, gleaming material, transformed from the earth by fire and brought across the sea.

Along the coast there are prehistoric, Roman, medieval and early modern fortifications, often slipping into the sea. In the Norfolk survey the most common features were World War II defences. Wrecks of ships in the sea can form a time capsule, but many remain to be located. Even landscape survives below the sea, including Doggerland, the land bridge to the continent. Before the Channel formed 8,000 years ago, generations of hunters followed herds of mammoth, horse and reindeer along this route, leaving their footprints on what is now the seabed. Archaeologists have yet to learn to explore such environments.

3

AN URBAN HERITAGE

ENGLAND'S TOWNS AND CITIES ARE REMARKABLY RICH IN ARCHAEOLOGICAL INTEREST, PARTLY BECAUSE OF THEIR INTENSIVE USE OF LAND. MANY URBAN CENTRES POSSESS ROMAN ORIGINS, AND THE EVIDENCE OF SUBSEQUENT OCCUPATION APPEARS IN LAYERS OF HISTORY IN BUILDINGS, PAVEMENTS AND FOUNDATIONS. THE URBAN LANDSCAPE IS CONTINUALLY CHANGING AND MANY EXCAVATIONS HAVE BEEN TAKEN IN A 'RESCUE' CONTEXT BEFORE FURTHER DEVELOPMENT, BUT THE IMPORTANCE OF ENGLAND'S INDUSTRIAL HERITAGE IS NOW FULLY RECOGNIZED. THE PRESERVATION OF AREAS SUCH AS BIRMINGHAM'S JEWELLERY CENTRE UNDERLINES THE IMPORTANCE FOR THE FUTURE OF THIS ASPECT OF ENGLAND'S PAST.

ENGLAND IS ONE OF THE MOST urbanized countries in the world and the first in modern times to change from 'the life of the fields to the life of the city'. But this is still a recent development. Even in the early 17th century the Venetian Girolamo Lando could report that England 'does not possess many large towns, a small number for its size, but has very frequent and populous villages and small towns'.

Over the next two centuries the character of much of England was to change. Daniel Defoe's *Tour through the Whole Island of Great Britain* (1724–76) noted the burgeoning English enthusiasm for towns and making things, 'this whole Kingdom, as well as the people on the land, and even the sea, in every part of it, are employed to furnish something, and I may add, the best of every-

thing'. In his travels Defoe reported on the metal trades of Birmingham, the cutlery of Sheffield, the goldsmiths, pewterers and hatters of London, the clothiers of Halifax, the crowded looms of Norwich and the salt-works of South Shields.

To discover the origins of the very first towns we have to rely on archaeological evidence. Before the Roman Conquest new British trading, religious and political centres appeared, usually at the junction of routeways. Archaeologists call these large defended enclosures, such as Dyke Hills on the Thames near Dorchester or at Camulodunum (Colchester), *oppida*, after the Latin word for towns. But the native *oppida* still contained big open spaces for grazing and collections of thatched round houses, at variance with our stereotype of urban life. At Number 1 Poultry, in the City of London, archaeologists have revealed the origins of one of the first truly urban sites in Britain, buried deep beneath the streets. A timber drain under the earliest Roman street has been dated by dendrochronology to AD 47 – the most precise date yet obtained for the origin of London. Because of the marvellous preservation at No 1 Poultry, it is possible to reconstruct the character of this part of early London: streets packed with residential and commercial buildings; granaries, bakeries and mills by the River Walbrook confirming the historian Tacitus' description that London 'abounded with dealers and was celebrated for suppliers'. Urban archaeology has been one of the success stories of recent years. In towns such as Winchester, Oxford, Lincoln and York the debris of generations of town dwellers has piled up, relatively undisturbed until the appearance of powerful modern mechanical excavators. In the centre of Oxford the earliest streets of the Anglo-Saxon town, defended against the Danes, now lie 3 m (10 ft) or more under the modern surface. In York timber buildings of the same period survive in the boggy ground.

Urban life was not always sweet. Archaeologists thrive on the filth of our ancestors as much as the rats, bugs and kites that shared the medieval towns with their human occupants. Only with the improvement of

3

1 Excavations by Museum of London archaeologists during the construction of the new building at No 1 Poultry in the City. The deep deposits were some of the best preserved to have been found in London.

2 Reconstruction of part of early Roman London based on the excavations undertaken at No 1 Poultry.

3 The Vaughton Gothic Works in the Birmingham Jewellery Quarter, built in 1902. The factory, recently listed Grade II, specialized in the production of metals, badges and civic jewellery.

4 The power press room at 94 Vyre Street in the Birmingham Jewellery Quarter. It is a unique urban area under pressure from redevelopment and the decline of some of its traditional industries.

4

1

The excavation in London of the vaults of Christ Church, Spitalfields was a remarkable archaeological project. Vaults under the church had been used for burials from 1729, when the church was consecrated, until 1852. It offered an opportunity to obtain a great deal of information about the environment of Spitalfields and the living conditions of its inhabitants. Health and safety were major issues, as well as the sensitivity of excavating recent burials. Many of the Spitalfields bodies were not just dusty bones, and health risks were posed by the possible presence of live bacteria.

Nearly 1,000 bodies were excavated in total, and 387 were of known age and sex. This 'named sample' provided reliability checks for international methods used by anthropologists and forensic scientists to establish age, sex, genetic traits, occupational and environmental indicators, and motherhood. A range of ageing methods was tested on the named sample, and proved to be remarkably inaccurate, even in such broad categories as young (below 35), middle-aged (35–50) or old (51+). Only 39 per cent were correct, invaluable knowledge for forensic pathologists and anthropologists.

The named sample were identified mostly through coffin plates or other direct evidence, backed up by historical research. This sought to give each a biography, covering personal and family information as well as occupation and economic status. Of these individuals, 28 died after civil registration began in 1837, and 26 death certificates were traced. Only one of the group showed skeletal evidence of cause of death – William Leschallas, who committed suicide by shooting himself in the head. Other causes registered on the death certificates ranged from 'decay of nature' (in the cases of the old) to 'debility and convulsions' in the case of Jane

drains, sewers and water supply did the urban death rate fall sufficiently to enable the population to reproduce itself, rather than relying on immigration from the countryside.

But archaeologists are not only interested in the cities beneath our feet. The standing buildings of towns encapsulate their history and character, although they are too often unappreciated. The Birmingham Jewellery Quarter is a fascinating urban area, a unique mix of residential and manufacturing structures that has been preserved from development. It forms the centre for the jewellery-making and metal working businesses which thrived from the 18th century, and the recent survey of its buildings and workshops has sought to widen knowledge of its character and significance.

Stephens, aged 22 days. Few 'causes of death' as registered mean much to us today, though William Pulley, who died at 61 from disease of the spine, after five years of certified paraplegia, appeared to have entirely normal legs; perhaps 'paraplegia' meant something else in 1847.

The suicide William Leschallas had an extremely expensive denture fitted, consisting of a small gold base with four porcelain teeth on gold pins, which fitted so closely that it could not be removed. Other skeletons had dentures, some held by springs and others by silk ties; a few had undergone dental work. Most bodies showed evidence of tooth decay; of a sample of 100 skulls that had 12 teeth present, 87 per cent had teeth with caries, including all of those aged 26–35.

Many of the Spitalfields bodies were Huguenots, French Protestant refugees from religious persecution who had become involved in the English silk industry. One of the Ogier family, Louisa, married Samuel Courtauld in 1749. She lost four of her first five children in infancy, then had a further three who survived, one of whom, George, founded the Courtauld textile industry. Louisa herself was widowed at the age of 36, but

1

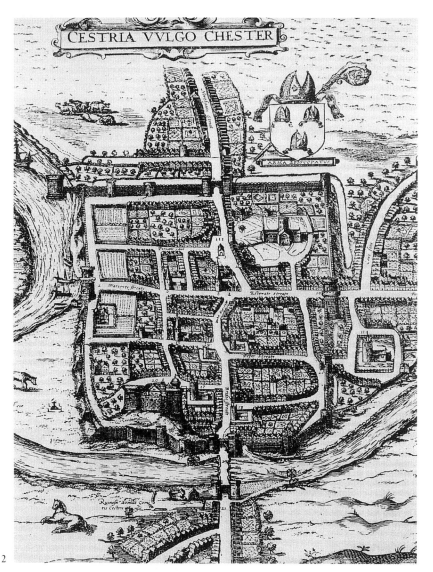

2

Louisa Courtauld next to paintings of them alive. It is also sad to reflect that, when the vaults were in use for burial, the death rate for those under 21 was a consistent 50 per cent. Child survival rates were extremely variable: Sarah Hurlin, an illiterate weaver's wife, raised nine of her ten children to adulthood, while Martha Lazabet, a member of the wealthy Mesman dynasty, lost all six in infancy. Over 100 of the children buried in the vaults of Christ Church were aged under five. The body of Ann Lemaistre, who died in 1763 aged 3 months and 14 days, was buried clothed in bonnet and dress in a coffin lined with delicately edged fabric.

Archaeological projects may often seem concerned with people whose lives and deaths are impossibly remote. Spitalfields, in contrast, was not only an invaluable archaeological and anthropological project, but also about the real, tangible people who lived in our past.

All towns are different, with individual historical legacies – sometimes due to periods of relative stagnation. Chester's rectangular plan and grid of streets, for example, still reflects its Roman origins. Visitors now congregate there because they appreciate the charm, robust enough not to be twee, of its half-timbered buildings, particularly The Rows. Some of these buildings were given a face-lift by the Victorians, but detailed surveys reveal their medieval core. The Rows actually date from the time of medieval campaigns against the Welsh in the mid-13th century when, as in the Roman period for the same reason, Chester thrived. Economic decline meant

lived to the ripe old age of 77 and chose to be buried in Spitalfields, where she had spent her youth, rather than with her husband and infant children in Chelsea.

Such evidence almost literally clothes the skeletons whose identity we know. It is a little macabre to be able to place photographs of the skulls of Peter Ogier and

1 A cutaway reconstruction drawing of the medieval Eastern House from Booth Mansion, Watergate Street in Chester. Booth Mansion is one of many medieval buildings that still exist in the city.

2 Part of Brown's map of Chester, dating from *c*.1580. It shows the basic grid plan of the Roman town, which still survives in the modern street layout.

3 St Nicholas' Church in Sevenoaks before archaeological investigation in advance of new construction beneath the floor.

4 The interior was excavated and recorded by the Oxford Archaeological Unit. The original 11th-century church expanded as the town of Sevenoaks grew in size and prosperity.

3

that town structure and architecture changed little, even as nearby Liverpool and Manchester flourished.

The growth and transformation of a town can be reflected in a single building, particularly significant ones like the parish church. St Nicholas's Church in Sevenoaks encapsulates the history of its community. It was a prosperous town on an important route into London, with a growing population from the 11th century. Excavations have shown how St Nicholas's Church expanded in response. The medieval graveyard lay outside the small church, but as the church grew, it spread across the graves of its early parishioners.

Sevenoaks attracted a varied population. Huguenots from the Continent, who prospered in the textile trades as at Spitalfields, combined with the aristocracy and wealthy middle classes, attracted by the proximity to London. They competed in death, as in life, for position and status. Their crypts and lead-lined coffins clamoured for position in the nave of the church and close to the altar, almost undermining the foundations of the church itself. In the late 20th century priorities were different. The nave and aisles of St Nicholas's Church were excavated to provide a suite of below-ground rooms, such as a nursery, kitchen and meeting halls. The difference reflects the needs of a parish community more concerned about their activities in this life than their position on the starting grid for the next.

4

STRATEGIES FOR CONSERVATION

ATTITUDES TOWARDS THE HISTORIC ENVIRONMENT — WHAT TO PRESERVE AND HOW BEST TO PRESERVE IT — HAVE HAD TO CHANGE RADICALLY IN RECENT YEARS. TECHNOLOGICAL ADVANCES HAVE TRANSFORMED BOTH URBAN AND RURAL ENVIRONMENTS, AND THE RATE OF LOSS HAS NEVER BEEN HIGHER. THE PRESERVATION AND CONSERVATION OF WHAT WE VALUE FROM THE PAST IS UNDERPINNED BY STATUTORY PROTECTIONS. WE ALSO INCREASINGLY RECOGNIZE THAT A GENERAL EVALUATION OF THE ENTIRE HISTORIC ENVIRONMENT IS VITAL IF WE ARE TO PRESERVE THE SENSE OF PLACE AND BELONGING THAT LINKS PEOPLE TO THEIR PAST HISTORY AND PRESENT SURROUNDINGS.

THE PACE OF CHANGE HAS NEVER been so rapid as in the modern world. Our towns and countryside are transformed by the demands of new technology, transport and housing, and since the war an entire motorway system has come into being. England has developed new shopping and entertainment centres and supports large-scale farming technology with an emphasis on production. The effect on the landscape has been dramatic.

The historic environment is consequently under constant pressure, with farming the single most destructive agency. English Heritage's Monuments At Risk Survey (MARS) shows that at least 22,500 monuments have been completely destroyed since 1945 – just over one per day. About one-third of all monuments are in arable cultivation, many of them designated as Scheduled Ancient Monuments. In the days of animal

traction – or even small tractors – the plough would glance over the surface of buried deposits such as the remains of Roman buildings. Now powerful agricultural equipment can simply cut into these layers, eroding them away gradually, or, in the case of deep ploughing, cutting through them in one season. At Dorchester-on-Thames the tines of a deep plough pulled a complete

Roman coffin to the surface. In the Fens the earthworks of entire networks of Roman villages and farmsteads have disappeared since World War II.

In wetlands, such as the Somerset Levels and river valleys like that of the Thames, drainage schemes desiccate the organic deposits that contain thousands of years of biological information – the beetles, plants, seeds and pollen that tell us how it was that the English landscape developed.

The sea is constantly eroding the land, particularly along the geologically soft margin of eastern England, and the process is happening more rapidly with global warming, rising sea levels and increased storminess. The Bronze Age timber circle at Holme, Norfolk, known as Seahenge, is just one of hundreds exposed by the sea. In one day on Humberside archaeological surveyors recorded 17 new sites, all made of timber. The soft cliffs at Whitby Abbey are falling into the sea, taking with them the evidence of Roman and Anglo-Saxon occupation that preceded the abbey buildings. In this era of rapid change it is fortunate that the value of ancient monuments such as Whitby is generally appreciated. The times are long gone since John Aubrey, the antiquarian who wrote the engagingly gossipy *Brief Lives*, could bemoan 'This searching after Antiquities is a wearisome task …For nobody else hereabouts hardly cares for it, but rather makes scorn of it.' In a poll conducted for English Heritage's recent publication *Power of Place*, 96 per cent of people said that the historic environment is important to teach them about the past.

Official recognition of the importance of monuments came in 1882 with The Act for the Better Protection of Ancient Monuments. Attached to the act was a schedule

1, 2 Wigmore Castle, Herefordshire, was founded in 1068, shortly after the Norman Conquest as the seat of the Mortimers, the archetypal marcher barons. The hilltop castle with two smaller earthwork fortifications, probably remnants of a siege of 1155, dominated the Welsh border for centuries. Its walls were slighted in the Civil War, and the castle left to crumble. In 1995 Wigmore Castle was given to the nation and English Heritage carried out a £1 million restoration programme. Rather than stripping the site to its bare stones, its rich plant life was protected and Wigmore's romantic and picturesque character maintained.

2

1   A detail of the silk wall covering in the South Hall of Brodsworth Hall before its restoration. Brodsworth Hall, built and furnished between 1861 and 1863, is one of the most intact Victorian country houses in England.

2   The kitchen at Brodsworth Hall as it appeared in 1995, following a major conservation programme which sought to preserve

the atmosphere of the site. Though it was abandoned in 1919, the kitchen still contains an intriguing range of utensils, including copper and iron pans.

3   Sculptures are carefully positioned among the elegant columns of the South Hall.

1

of some 68 monuments in England, Wales, Scotland and Ireland – hence the term Scheduled Monument. These included such notable, and clearly upstanding, sites as Stonehenge and the Rollright Stones. Castles and abbeys were clear candidates for protection. Many of these came into government guardianship – sites all too often distinguished by a rather sterile, Ministry of Works appearance, like a pristine golf course. Approaches to conservation change. At Wigmore Castle, illustrated on pages 376–7, English Heritage's strategy is now to maintain the ruin in a stable but picturesque state, encouraging plants and wildlife.

At Brodsworth Hall the aim is not just to present a grand country house as a shell, but also to capture the idiosyncratic and complex life of all its inhabitants. Brodsworth is a genuine time-capsule. The Thellusson family, like many of the inhabitants of Sevenoaks, were Huguenots who fled France in the mid-16th century. Peter Thellusson came to London in 1760 where he established a banking business in Philpot Lane in the City. Like a good English gentleman, he bought himself a country estate, at Brodsworth. The present house was built between 1861 and 1863 to an Italianate style – designed by 'Chevaliere Casentini' of Lucca for the classically named Charles

2   Sabine Augustus Thellusson. The

identification with the Roman empire continued through the decoration of the house, with Pompeiian colours, painted marble effects and a collection of white marble statues. These somewhat insipid, sentimental figures, may not appeal to modern taste but they provide a rare opportunity to see how a wealthy member of the English upper class chose to present himself. Nor are other members of the Brodsworth family and the working community invisible. A kitchen with all its equipment has been left untouched since 1919. And for such a lavish house there is a distinct lack of plumbing, lavatory and washing facilities. Brodsworth does not compare well, in the comfort stakes, with the centrally heated villas of 4th century Britain.

As at Wigmore, the conservation approach is light-handed and forensic. The aim is not to reduce the building and its contents to a pristine cleanliness, but rather to retain the patina of time and the archaeological evidence of change, use and personality.

The original schedule of 68 monuments reflected the biases of the time towards well known prehistoric stone circles and medieval ruins. Today English Heritage's Monuments Protection Programme ensures that a more representative sample is selected for protection. Regional biases are being tackled, and the enormously complex landscapes around the more visible stone monuments, which provide their context and history, are now scheduled.

The non-archaeological historic environment is also protected through statute and planning regulations. Some 450,000 buildings of historic importance are listed, 43 battlefield sites and nearly 1,500 historic gardens are contained in Registers which form part of the planning process, and our most important buildings, monuments and landscapes are protected by international law as World Heritage Sites.

Sites and buildings are at their most vulnerable shortly after they fall out of use. This is why textile mills, steel works, cinemas, the explosives industry, World War II defences and Cold War monuments are now the subject of detailed surveys. Not everything can or should be preserved, but sensible management, reuse or even demolition needs to be based on understanding. And it should encompass an understanding of what is important to local communities, not solely to academics and curators.

The legislation provides statutory controls. However, the emphasis is increasingly being placed on the characterization of town and country. The Victorian schedule had something of the collector's mentality which filled Brodsworth Hall with stuffed animals in glass cases, or of the 'barrow-digging men' who collected artefacts. The historic environment is all around us, in the streets of Birmingham, the fields of Hampshire or the moorland of the Pennines. Rather than simply picking out important sites for scheduling or buildings for listing, characterization helps us to appreciate the human landscape as a whole. Change is inevitable and often desirable, but it needs to be undertaken on the basis of knowledge, partnership and co-operation. When a road or a supermarket is proposed today, the route or site is always

1

2

1 St Paul and the Viper, a
   12th-century mural from
   St Anselm's Chapel in
   Canterbury Cathedral.
2 The city of York under flood
   water. In low-lying riverside
   towns, such as York, London
   and Oxford, archaeological
   deposits accumulate to considerable depth. In the airless
   conditions organic remains
   are often well preserved.

3 These half-timbered houses
   in Elstow, Bedfordshire are
   typical of the vernacular
   architecture of the southeast of England. They are
   protected by listing because
   of their age and their contribution to the the character
   of the local environment.

4 The abandoned remains
   of Cold War defences at
   Greenham Common,
   as well as those of the
   two World Wars, are now
   being surveyed by English
   Heritage. Buildings and
   sites are often at their most
   vulnerable when they first
   fall out of use.

environmentally assessed. If archaeological remains are identified, changes may be made to exactly how and where the new structure will be built. If excavation is needed, as at No. 1 Poultry, the developer will normally pay for it. As a result enormous excavations have taken place, for example in advance of the Channel Tunnel Rail Link, revealing prehistoric settlements and Roman villas on an unprecedented scale.

The 'rescue' excavation of sites is not always the right solution, however. In towns we need to learn to appreciate the richness of the historic fabric, its potential for reuse, for creating a sense of identity and being economically viable. We all want fantastic new buildings in the 21st century, such as the Jubilee Line stations in London (the sites of which were meticulously investigated by archaeologists before they were built on) or the new art galley in Walsall. However, old buildings have potential for imaginative reuse, such as Tate Modern's Bankside power station or the Magna Science Adventure Centre near Rotherham, a former steelworks. Places as diverse as the Birmingham Jewellery Quarter, Liverpool's warehouse district or Chester's elevated shopping streets can retain their unique identities. The English countryside does not have to be the factory floor of a farming industry blinkered to the historic landscape. With co-operation, knowledge and flexibility we should be able to live with the past for the benefit of the present and future.

4

The past does not speak for itself, however; it requires interpretation. Archaeologists themselves have a world view, a cultural perspective that influences their thinking – from Pitt-Rivers, a disciplined Victorian gentlemen with a developed Darwinian idea of progress, to the New Archaeologists of the 60s, influenced by the wonders of number-crunching IBM computers and the success of the space programme. In reaction, contemporary archaeological thought is less mechanistic, more self-aware and profoundly conscious that 'the past is a foreign country' in the famous phrase of L P Hartley. To attempt to interpret material from the past, we need to acknowledge our own world view and that of the society which produced, or used and disposed of the object. How did they see their world and how do we see ours?

In his stimulating book, *Archaeology: The Basics*, Clive Gamble, a professor of archaeology at Southampton University, summed up history's enduring significance. 'The past is not a neutral subject … something like trainspotting that is only of interest to hobbyists in anoraks … It cannot be ignored because, as the history of Europe alone has shown over the past 70 years, it will come and drive you from your home, your land and your country'. The past remains intimately connected to our experience of the present, whether we are considering architecture, political concepts, social developments or archaeological sites. Its complex legacy is disregarded at our peril.

3

CHAPTER

13

Despite, or perhaps because of, our technological
progress, the past continues to exert a fascination for us.
The traditional perception of history as endless facts, dates and
figures, largely relating to monarchs, battles or distant political
events, has been complemented by a new emphasis on the
more intimate history of the people who came before us in our
houses, streets and cities. The details of their daily lives, and their
attitudes towards family, religion, culture, morality, are the
social realities which stir the imagination. They lead us not
just to visit the remains of past lives, but to seek to
recreate the past, to join in with it and to
understand it as much as we can.

LIVING THE PAST

PERSPECTIVES ON THE PAST

THE URGE TO UNDERSTAND HOW PEOPLE LIVED IN THE PAST IS VERY STRONG. HOWEVER, ANY REAL APPRECIATION MUST TAKE ACCOUNT OF THE MANIFOLD DIFFERENCES BETWEEN LIVES THEN AND NOW. EXISTENCE WAS MORE PRECARIOUS AND UNPREDICTABLE; POLITICAL AND ECONOMIC STORMS COULD SWEEP AWAY WHOLE COMMUNITIES. RELIGION WAS CENTRAL TO EVERYONE'S EXISTENCE AND EDUCATION WAS AVAILABLE ONLY TO THE FEW. TO LOOK BACK FROM THE 21ST CENTURY TO THE PRE-TECHNOLOGICAL ERA IS TO LOOK ACROSS AN UNCROSSABLE GULF. WE SEEK TO UNDERSTAND, AND FEEL KINSHIP WITH, THE PEOPLE OF THE PAST WHO INHABITED THE PLACES WHERE WE NOW LIVE. BUT WE MUST ALSO ACKNOWLEDGE THAT ITS REALITIES WILL ALWAYS REMAIN DISTANT AND INTANGIBLE.

'The poetry of history lies in the quasi-miraculous fact that once, on this earth, on this familiar spot of ground, walked other men and women, as actual as we are today, swayed by their own passions, but now all gone, vanishing one after another, gone as utterly as we ourselves shall be gone like ghosts at cockcrow ...'

THESE FAMOUS WORDS by G. M. Trevelyan sum up the fascination of the past, the hold that history has on us all. People like us once lived in our houses, in our town. Our personal past, our family past, our country's past, how our home town developed ... all are enthralling and all important, not just because our roots help us to understand who we are, but because we perceive those who inhabited the past as a mixture of people like us and distant strangers. 'The past is a foreign country', indeed; but it is also another planet, another world. How can we, who have seen men walk on the moon, understand the panic and dread caused in the past by a solar eclipse? Time travel is an enduring fantasy, and we look back on the past with insatiable curiosity.

But how easy – and indeed how valid – is it for us to believe that we can look back at the past with any understanding? How can ears that have heard Mozart listen to Monteverdi and even begin to understand how his music must have sounded during his lifetime? We dismiss as philistines Van Gogh's contemporaries who failed to recognize his genius, but may not those who

today mock the conceptual art of the Turner Prize be similarly derided by the art critics of the 2050s?

The cultural assumptions of the past were as different as were their modes of conduct. For the aristocracy of medieval Europe, the courtly pastimes of music, hunting and elegant dalliance were the height of sophistication. In the 18th century, classical ideals influenced language and architecture, partly a consequence of the Grand Tour undertaken by leisured young gentlemen. Some idiosyncrasies of the past may appear to us a mere indulgence, but their creators considered them innovative. The ostentatious display of wealth is not a recent phenomenon, but has left us intriguing memorials to inspirations of another age.

We need to recognize how different our expectations and standards are on the domestic front. How can we, in our 24/7 world, imagine rising at dawn and going to bed as dusk falls on a pre-electric hovel? In the West we now take for granted the fact that our homes will have bathrooms, running water, central heating and electricity, and we expect to keep them clean and well maintained ourselves. Yet many of us live still in houses that were built without bathrooms and with provision for at least one servant. How can we imagine what people who lived 100 years ago smelled like? Or how grindingly hard and dirty it was to keep the coal fires burning so that food could be cooked and rooms kept warm? The recent television experiences of

PRECEDING PAGES

Main picture: Young re-enactors wearing the uniforms of drummer boys in the 33rd Foot as it was during the Napoleonic Wars.

Detail: Food is cooked in cauldrons over open fires as in the past.

1 A picturesque garden and fine timber-framed house provide appropriate background for this medieval scene. Elaborate patterns of conduct and conversation formed part of a sophisticated flirtation.

2 The juxtaposition of 'Lord Burlington' and one of his servants at Chiswick House in west London highlights the gulf between the rich and most of the population.

3 The Temple of Worthies at Stowe: familiarity with the classical past, allegories, symbols – all formed part of a cultured man's armoury.

2

1 The Angel Gabriel in the Chapter House at Westminster Abbey.
2 The magnificent nave in Ely Cathedral. The scale and magnificence of these buildings is still impressive today, but must have been far more so when they dwarfed all that surrounded them – a clear indication of the centrality of worship to daily life.

3 Grand tombs indicated status, belief in eternal life and the apparent permanence of family, lineage, wealth and reputation. *Sic transit gloria mundi*, as epitomized here by the tomb in Holy Trinity Church, Long Melford, of Sir William Cordell. Master of the Rolls under Queen Elizabeth I, he died in 1581.

modern volunteer families in houses of 1900 and 1940 have revealed a multitude of practical problems – carbolic soap, corsets, food that had to be prepared from scratch and cooked on an open fire. Yet, even while they were living within the domestic realities of 60 or 100 years ago, their minds were those of 21st-century people. However much they adapted to the clothes, food and routines of daily life in that environment, they cannot possibly have truly experienced how people who really lived then thought or felt. In the days before women had the vote, or a right to own property, we do not know whether most resented male dominance, or accepted it as part of the natural social balance. Nor do we know the basis of their relationships, or whether their concept of 'love' differed from our definition today. Was the chambermaid, required to turn her face to the wall when her mistress passed, raging at the indignity of her position? Did the lady of the house truly believe it was demeaning to look her servants in the face?

Fascinated we may be, but the reality is that everything is foreign to us: belief, understanding, knowledge, social behaviour, physical health and hygiene, attitudes towards animals, towards women, towards foreigners. The past is a mixture of received ideas and cliché, nostalgia and horror, even as we try to understand. Many of television's historical dramas are rigorously researched, with elaborately constructed sets and costumes, and authentic language and mannerisms. But those of us who read *Pride and Prejudice* with 21st-century views on equality between the sexes, on the death of deference, on the viciousness of prejudice, can find it hard to believe that the feisty Elizabeth Bennett could ever have found the cold, contemptuous Mr Darcy attractive. When Darcy was urged by Mr Bingley to dance

with Elizabeth, his response was: 'She is tolerable; but not handsome enough to tempt *me*; and I am in no humour at present to give consequence to young ladies who are slighted by other men.' Young men today might think in similar terms, but they would be risking severe physical damage if they actually expressed this thought, as Darcy does, within Elizabeth's hearing.

In previous centuries religion dominated all aspects of people's lives. At a time when our cities and towns are architecturally enriched by mosques, synagogues and Hindu temples, and our understanding and tolerance of different faiths is growing, a world in which the Christian religion was totally at the centre of English daily life is unimaginable, even to practising Christians. Bishops and archbishops still sit in the House of Lords,

2

but the days are long gone when the princes of the church were as powerful, as rich and as warlike as the secular lords. We still have some convents and monasteries, despite the Reformation, but entering the church is no longer the obvious career for a younger son, or a convent the natural refuge of an elderly widow. The ruins of medieval abbeys no longer speak to us of their vast wealth or their importance within the community. Cathedrals, parish churches and nonconformist chapels often still dominate their environment, and are mostly still used for their original purpose, but they are no longer the spiritual and physical home of the whole parish: they are places that many of us enter only when we are christened, married and buried. In medieval times the building, the people who ran it and the religion it fostered were as important to parishioners as their own families and dwellings. Like today, churches were a vehicle for the display of wealth and piety, for both the living at worship and the dead in their elaborately carved tombs; but unlike today, most parishioners were personally involved.

3

To see the cathedrals of Canterbury and Ely, Durham and Lincoln today is still to marvel at their beauty, size and the skills of those who built them. Each continues to dominate the city around, despite intrusive modern additions. But imagine how high and how vast they must have seemed when first built, in contrast to the few low buildings around them. Imagine the expense of these huge constructions, the effort expended in acquiring the materials, the skill of the architect, the craftsmanship of the masons, the stone-carvers, the carpenters, the stained glass artists, all in the days before lorries, hard-surfaced roads, concrete mixers, and all the advantages of modern building tech-

nology. We still build cathedrals and churches today, of course, but their scale is in tune with the rest of our buildings. The great medieval cathedrals were monuments not only to the people who built them, but to the tenor of the times, the binding importance to the whole community of the worship of God.

For centuries, religious faith and teaching were the basis of life in society. The church provided moral precepts that governed all behaviour, and was the source of both understanding and superstition. When the world beyond your village was a frightening enigma, the church and Christianity provided a haven, both by its

1

2

physical presence and the certainties of its teachings. It could also inspire immense terror: wall paintings depicted the violent torments of the damned, and excommunication was a very real, irrevocable promise of eternal suffering. Natural disasters, plagues and famine were explained as divine retribution, and even sophisticated minds such as Samuel Johnson's could be gripped by the fear of torment after death.

Despite these manifold differences, as Trevelyan says, the people of the past were like us. The similarities emerge in sometimes unexpected ways: the face of the Angel Gabriel, for example, on a medieval carving in the Chapter House in Westminster Abbey, looks a bit like the actress Kate Winslet. Adam and Eve, as painted by Van Eyck in the great altarpiece of Ghent, reveal the faces of a modern man and woman. As modern visitors we might struggle with the language of the past, the food would be unpalatable, and we would be disoriented by sharp social contrasts – but we would nevertheless recognize the people as fellow humans, who might smile at us, or be afraid of us, or attack us.

The idea of attack may seem unexpected, but we have no way of understanding, in these days of relative security, how precarious life was in the past. Death was

1 Castles, such as this one at Carlisle, were the visible sign of a local lord's dominance. The portcullis could exclude as well as protect, and many castles also had prisons within their walls.

2 With enclosure, the ownership and management of agriculture became concentrated in fewer hands. This idyllic landscape near Chartham Hatch, Kent, probably had its origins in dispossession.

3 Life in previous centuries was precarious; people could only hope that warfare would pass them by, that armies would not pillage their winter stores and that their menfolk would not be taken off to serve in the feudal levy. Military power served to subjugate most of the population.

an ever-present reality and surviving childhood was a lottery: the cemetery at the deserted medieval village of Wharram Percy in Yorkshire has more graves of children in it than any others. In an era before good medical care, women were all too likely to die in childbirth, and infants were even more vulnerable. Large families were the norm, not the exception, in part to cope with the inevitable wastage. The psychological consequences of such experience are hard for us to imagine. Did parents love their children less, or bond with them less closely, in order to counter the inevitable grief? If death is a much more immediate part of everyday life, do we adjust more quickly, or mourn less?

The notion of controlling one's life through choices and decisions is in many ways a very contemporary one. Regal and feudal powers were absolute – medieval castles were not ruins, but ever-present indicators of an arbitrary, dominant authority that might impose its will at any moment. Most people lived in the hope that the tempests of invasion, war, political unrest, famine and plague would pass them by. Imagine a life lived entirely in one place, knowing little about the world beyond your village. Imagine the situation of a woman whose husband is conscripted by his local lord to go and fight the king's war in France. When he fails to return, she has no way of knowing whether he is alive or dead; whether he will ever come back; even whether the king won or lost the battle. The recently excavated grave of some of the dead of the bloody battle of Towton yielded men who had been taken prisoner and tortured before being executed. Modern technology was able to re-create the face of one of them, and revealed that he had survived a previous disfiguring wound to his face. Had he previously returned to his wife and children with his dreadful wound, only to be called up again and this time not return? Did they ever find out what happened to him?

Even more traumatic for the communities involved were upheavals caused by social movements, such as the industrial revolution. Poverty was widespread and

there was no effective social security. We cannot begin to envisage how people coped with the harshness of legislation in place as recently as the beginning of the 19th century, aimed at protecting property against the desperation of the dispossessed, rootless masses. The theft of anything valued at over five shillings – the price of a particularly nice silk handkerchief – was punishable by hanging, with transportation to the penal colonies the more lenient alternative. Men, women and children were hanged or transported in their thousands, and the records of their trials and punishments survive in our Public Records Offices as tiny rectangles of paper with a couple of sentences in Latin describing the crime and the sentence. Often the abbreviation 'susp' – 'hanged' – is added in one corner, concluding a miserably brief record of one brief and miserable life.

3

INTERACTION WITH THE PAST

RE-ENACTMENT EVENTS ARE IMPORTANT AND POPULAR WAYS OF ENGAGING WITH THE PAST. METICULOUS RESEARCH IS CARRIED OUT INTO EVERY DETAIL — FROM THE WEAVE OF THE CLOTH, TO THE EXACT DESIGN OF THE HELMET, TO THE RECIPE FOR THE SOUP... THE EVENTS THEMSELVES ARE ALSO HISTORICALLY ACCURATE: THIS WAS DUKE WILLIAM'S POSITION AT THIS POINT IN THE BATTLE OF HASTINGS; THAT WAS WHERE RICHARD III WAS KILLED AT BOSWORTH; THIS WAS HOW ROMANS CONTROLLED THEIR HORSES WITHOUT STIRRUPS, AND HOW THE FOOT SOLDIERS MARCHED AND WHEELED. THE PAGEANTRY AND SPLENDOUR OF THE PAST ARE GLORIOUSLY RE-CREATED THROUGH THESE THEATRICAL EVENTS.

THE PAST is all around us, continuing to impact upon our daily lives. Stonehenge is still there, 5,000 years after it was built, to tantalize us with fruitless speculation as to its purpose. Many of the great medieval cathedrals, castles and palaces remain: those still used for their original purpose are home to the ceremony and ritual that in part define our roots and offer a reassuring, and perhaps comforting, link backwards in time. As the great industries have become obsolete, the buildings that housed them remind us of the huge fortunes made by the owners, the social changes caused by this new wealth, the worldwide empires built on the new technologies, and the hopeless poverty of the workforce. 'Workers of the world, unite. You have nothing to lose but your chains.' Now even the trade unions may seem to be part of a receding industrial past.

Yet to those who lived in the past, whether recent or more distant — 'men and women, as actual as we are today' — their lives were just what they were. Difficult though it might be, we must not impose on them our 21st-century morals and value judgements. Alexander the Great would have listened with total incomprehension to anyone preaching the evils of war and conquest — someone metaphorically twisting flowers round his soldiers' sarissas, in place of poking them down the barrels of 1960s guns. Certain precepts were established as an immutable part of the nature of things, whatever we may think now: public executions were an entertainment: animals were there to be worked and eaten; women were only second-class citizens; Africans were there to be enslaved.

Recognition of such contemporary assumptions is an important step in engaging with the past. So is a frank

acknowledgement of our own limitations. Despite social progress, we are deficient in many skills that our ancestors would have thought essential: most of us could not begin to be as self-sufficient as people had to be in the past. We may now undertake our own decorating, and do our own cleaning and cooking without the benefit of servants, but we rely on handymen for repair work and buy our meat from the butcher rather than keeping animals and slaughtering them ourselves. We no longer make our own clothes unless we choose to do so, but in the past many of us would have had to make our own shoes or go barefoot.

Until recently, England was an agricultural country and the seasonal round of activity continued relatively unchanged for generations. Our modern urbanized lifestyle is a recent phenomenon and a different way of living is still very much within living memory. We can approach even a remote past by learning and understanding how people dressed; what their houses were like; how they cooked, cleaned, gardened and farmed; what they ate; what rituals governed their lives. Archaeological and historical research can contribute a good deal about daily life, especially useful in societies where little was written down. Animal bones with butchery marks, along with the residues in cooking pots, tell us about diet; the pots themselves tell us about cooking and storage methods. Brooches and pins allow us to re-create styles of dress; the textile fragments that are sometimes caught in them tell us about fabrics, patterns and weaving methods. Ancient tools and weapons are valuable sources of information not only about methods of farming and warfare, but also about the technological skills of the period.

1, 2 In the agricultural community, everything was made or done by hand. Cloth was woven (shown here by a 'resident' at West Stow village), houses were built and thatched. Food was grown, animals killed and leather was tanned by hand. The weather, crop diseases, harvest failures were powerful enemies, resulting in a very real prospect of starvation.

3 Pagan gods associated with nature and the seasons were integral to an agricultural nation. Their veneration survived Christianity, and figures such as the Green Man featured in the design of churches and cathedrals, both inside and out. The Green Man below is carved on the porch of St Botolph's Church, Boston in Lincolnshire.

2

3

1

Some seemingly mundane archaeological finds offer spine-tinglingly immediate glimpses of daily routine. A scatter of flints in the Fens, for example, represents in a very direct way the visit of a travelling flint knapper, who arrived within a small community, plied his trade according to their needs, and moved on – leaving behind him, in the residue of his work, evidence to be found in the 20th century of a few days in his life several thousand years ago.

Unlike flint knapping, thatching is a traditional skill that has survived because it is still needed. Stripped to its rafters, a medieval thatched cottage can offer all sorts of evidence for life in the past: old thatch is sometimes the only source of plants and weeds which were once common; burn marks on timbers indicate the frequent fires of the past, the result of the constant need for flames for cooking and warmth. The roof was often the repository of magic talismans against the frightening and the unknown – a cat's skeleton, or a charm against witches. Superstitions tell us a lot about the precariousness of life, the fear of the unknown and ignorance of the great wide world that would have been so much part of existence. A community dependent on the land

2

was always at the mercy of a good harvest – hence the veneration of powerful natural forces such as the ubiquitous Green Man. Urbanized we may be, but some of this instinct is still with us. How many of us look frantically round for a piece of wood to touch when we are tempting fate?

The evidence of all-pervading religious faith through the centuries is perhaps most accessible, because it still exists and is still in use. A small country church may continue to exude the musty ambience it has held for generations. Its historical legacy is there for all to see – from the tomb of a medieval lord, through the worn inscriptions on Victorian graves in the floor of the nave, to a memorial to the village dead of the two world wars in the 20th century. Those who worship there now might well feel close to those who used the church 1,000 years ago; indeed, even the religiously uncommitted may wish to christen their children at the village font – perhaps for the vague feeling of kinship and continuity with the families of the past. The great cathedrals resonate with the atmosphere of history, especially when the organ starts to play or – even better – the choir to practice. It really is touching the past

1 Many re-enactors make their own tools, weapons, jewellery and clothes, using traditional methods and materials. Others buy them, perhaps from this stall at the 'History in Action' festival, held at Kirby Hall in August each year.

2, 3 West Stow Saxon village provides an immediate and tangible experience of the past. The construction details of a Saxon hut's wall and roof become significant through being used, as they would once have been, to store weapons and armour. In the Weald and Downland Museum in Sussex (below), jettied buildings have been saved from demolition, conserved and re-erected as part of living history displays.

to touch the tomb of Mary Queen of Scots in Westminster Abbey, and realize that her body lies only centimetres away, with its head severed.

We know a lot more about the upper classes than about those further down the social scale, because their houses and possessions have survived better, and because they were the stuff of history as reported by historians and novelists. Yet many facts about their lives remain obscure. The banquets given by Tudor kings, for example, are recorded in all their glory, and we know a lot about the rituals with which they were served. But we are less often told about the techniques of cooking, or about the vast distances between the kitchen and banqueting hall along which food had to be carried, so that it was eaten lukewarm and congealed. The grand rooms in our great mansions are there for us to marvel at, theatres that we can people with the lords and ladies of the past; but perhaps more evocative is the kitchen, where a wooden surface is worn into a series of holes – the surviving evidence of decades of breadmaking. No wonder the enamel of their teeth eroded, with all the wood they ate along with their daily bread!

Illness and pain were much more part of daily life for the population in the past and early death was much more common, at all levels of society. We can deduce general standards of health, life expectancy and the efficacy of medical treatments from skeletons and other evidence. We can, as with the man from Towton, recreate faces. We can deduce the life-changing effects of a broken bone, and we can find out what diseases they suffered

from, even sometimes how they died. The grave of Robert the Bruce, who died in the 14th century, was found in the early 19th century in Dunfermline Abbey and resealed, but not before a cast was made of his skull, which revealed to a 20th-century scientist that he had died of leprosy. The 'madness' of George III is now explained as the result of the rare genetic disease, porphyria. We know from an analysis of the teeth of

3

1, 2, 3 Armies of re-enactors
are out every weekend in
summer, sometimes just
marching and parading,
sometimes engaging in real
battles. Here, a Civil War
contingent of pikemen and
musketeers charges,
Highlanders of the 42nd
Regiment leave for the
Napoleonic Wars, and
members of the 1st-
century Roman Imperial
Army stride along
Hadrian's Wall.

1

those buried in the vaults of Christ Church, Spitalfields,
(page 372) in the 18th and 19th centuries, that most
people must have suffered a constant toothache.

Research and re-creation can help us to understand
the differences between then and now. Henry VIII, having been a slim, athletic young man, became fat. But his
huge bulk, as seen in his portraits, is exacerbated by the
thick fur linings of his coats, the method used by Tudor
aristocrats to keep warm in draughty halls. Modern re-
enactors of the Tudor period make authentic clothes
and, by wearing them, discover how they worked.

On the subject of bulk, our modern homage to
anorexic slimness would have been bewildering to rich
people of the past. For much of his life Henry VIII
would have been regarded as a fine figure of a man. The
folds of voluptuous flesh on Rubens' women were the
height of beauty. Being fat meant that you could afford
to eat, and eat well; it meant that you did not have to do
hard manual labour to earn a crust. The Victorians
thought nothing, even at a small dinner for six given in
1861 by people of modest means, of serving 13 courses
plus dessert. Nor was this the only meal of the day, but

the end of an eating odyssey that
would have started with the potted
meat and fish, cold meats, varieties
of pies, chops and steaks, kidneys,
sausages, bacon and eggs, muffins
and toast which made up breakfast.
The growing popularity of sugar
in the 16th century, most of which
was consumed by the aristocracy,
triggered tooth decay, a curse that
is still with us. Queen Elizabeth I,
enthroned in all her splendour,
displayed to her courtiers black,
decayed teeth, and decreed that
her portraits should show her with
her mouth closed.

Re-enactments help us to probe
more deeply beneath the surface of
faceless research. Modern enthusi-
asts learn to ride as the Romans did, without stirrups.
They make their own chain mail; weave and dye their
own cloth; produce tools, weapons, surgical instruments and pots. They make *garum*, the Roman fish
sauce, and they cook with it and eat the results. And
they eat without a fork, an implement that made its
debut only in the 16th century. Their experiences show
the rest of us, too, how things were done. 'Doctors' re-
enact amputations and pulling teeth without the benefit of anaesthetic; trepanning to remove evil humours
from the brain; the application of leeches to thin the
blood. 'Medieval knights' clothe themselves and their
horses in full armour and perform jousts. Fake hangings prove too lifelike for some spectators. Musicians
make their own medieval instruments and play tunes.

And then there are the battles. Military re-enactors
regularly gather in their thousands to re-create the set-
piece battles of the past — great military clashes that
shaped the historical landscape. The battle of Hastings is
re-fought on 14 October every few years on the field
where it happened. The forces of King and Parliament
regularly do battle again at Marston Moor and Naseby,

2

with strict adherence to the strategy and tactics of the time, and in accordance with events as they really unrolled. The Scots and English, and adherents of the White and Red Roses, fight again at Flodden and Culloden, Tewkesbury and Bosworth. Roman armies drill and march. Napoleonic regiments combine horsemanship with guns. The battles of the American Civil War and World War II are re-created, with all their blood and slaughter.

But, of course, there is no blood. The swords are blunt, the bullets are blanks, and the 'dead' will get up and go home. There may be hard labour, huge effort, sweat, smoke, the yelling of insults and orders; but there is no death and no pain, and without them none of the terror that must have been almost tangible.

However authentic the methods and materials used, however much the re-enactors study the evidence of what really happened, the fact remains that at the end of the day the actuality of combat proves elusive. No one now knows what it was like to stand in line with your pike or your bow, probably not knowing why you were there, facing hours of sweaty, smelly, bloody, confused struggle, with a vicious, painful death a strong possibility. The reality of a pitched battle, even a battle fought within living memory– the Somme, Arnhem, or Goose Green – is unimaginable to someone who has not participated in it. The weight of chain mail is bearable for a day, perhaps, but its modern wearer does not have to put it on again tomorrow. The man who dangles on a fake gibbet may well have caused screams and

3

1 Life, at least for those in the West, is generally more secure in the 21st century. Impregnable fortresses, such as Orford Castle shown here, are no longer essential protection for a community, nor are thick walls with defensive gates considered necessary for urban survival.

2 Invasion is unlikely in the Napoleonic sense, and the re-enactor, firing his 'modern' weapon over the back of that age-old fundamental of battles, the cavalry charger, is only pretending. But many still alive can remember the fear of invasion in 1940, and the devastating threat of nuclear war is still fresh in the memory. In adapting to our modern anxieties, we can appreciate more about fears of the past.

faints – and may have felt, in the sudden plunge, some of the terror of extinction at the rope's end – but he, too, will be lowered to the ground for a reviving cup of tea.

The realism of films can get us a little closer. The opening scenes in *Gladiator*, showing Marcus Aurelius' army facing the Germanic barbarians, seek to convey the noise, the mud and the fear of combat. Modern cinema shows the horror and chaos that accompanies battle – but when we leave the cinema, have we really come closer to understanding how those men felt?

Soldiers on the winning side of England's ancient battles might be euphoric for a time, and might be fêted and rewarded; but they might also be wounded and in pain – and certainly completely exhausted, faced with meagre rations and a hard bed, and conscious that many of their companions had not made it through the day. For the survivors on the other side, the reality was to be hunted down as fugitives and, if caught and depending on the politics behind the conflict, summarily executed or imprisoned. Even if they escaped, they were probably far from home, facing weeks of exhausted and impoverished travel before finding their families again, and possibly facing the knowledge that their participation in the conflict could have repercussions for themselves and their kin.

Whatever the realities, we are still fascinated. Thousands of people join re-enactment societies and spend weekends living in the past. Thousands more visit re-enactments. 'History in Action', put on every year by English Heritage at Kirby Hall, is probably the largest festival of its kind in the world, and features historical re-enactments of periods from the Roman incursion to D-Day. The past is alien, but it is paradoxically an enduring part of our present and future. We seek to anchor ourselves – to be part of the future's past. 'Kilroy was here'; or, more immediately, 'Z… H… born in this room June 1975', scratched into the window of a small 18th-century cottage – a permanent memorial to a transient moment. That is what history seeks to explore.

We may think ourselves civilized and fortunate to live today – in some ways we certainly are. But consider the genocide of the last century, the murderous territorial, tribal, or religious wars that continue to occur, the horror of floods in Bangladesh and earthquakes in Turkey, and recognize that we are not immune from the fear of the unexpected or the unknown. We lived with the constant fear of a nuclear holocaust in the days of the Cold War, a much larger cataclysm than our forebears had to face. Will our descendants look back on our times and regard us as impenetrable strangers? Almost certainly! So perhaps, despite the manifold differences, we are not so far distant from the past after all.

2

CONCLUSION
AN EVOLVING HERITAGE

FOR NATIONS AS FOR INDIVIDUALS, the past shapes their present and future. History is no neat progression of self-contained epochs but a complex continuum, symbolized by the legacy of structures and landscapes from a much earlier age. The new century is no exception to this, although perceiving it in a historical context is difficult. It may appear to us an exciting time of technological innovation, but we cannot begin to guess how we will be viewed by those living in 2101, still less 2501 and 3001. In all probability, especially given the increasingly rapid pace of change, the people of the future – provided humans survive at all – will regard us with the same curiosity and sympathy as we do our forebears.

Historians of the future will seek to evaluate our lives from what they will see as 21st-century heritage, even as we interpret the buildings and artefacts of the past. Their judgements will be influenced by prevailing social attitudes, something subject to continual change. Contemporary British views are different from those held before World War II or in the 19th century, in part through advances in communication. As our perspective becomes more global, we can no longer, literally or metaphorically, inhabit isolated villages. Our horizons are in many ways broader than in the past, and an increasingly secular outlook has redefined our perceptions of the material world. Britain has become a more multicultural society, aware not only of the value of such diversity, but also of its contribution to the heritage of the future. A vibrant, modern nation is emerging through the interaction of different cultures, not just those of European white Christians. England's history and heritage did not come to a standstill in 1914. What we perceive as the present will in turn become the future's past – its heritage.

So rapid was the pace of change in the 20th century that many of us have witnessed such a transition in our

1

own lives. Anyone aged over 50 in 2001 – born before, during or just after World War II – can vividly remember the days before supermarkets, when biscuits were bought by the pound from display tins, the only vegetables available in the greengrocer's were potatoes, carrots and spring greens (none of your lemon grass!) and a roast chicken was a Christmas treat. Social expectations were very different: wives stayed at home with the children, few families owned a television, still fewer a washing machine or a fridge. To the young amongst us, those days are already a part of our heritage.

So are many examples of modern technology – perhaps the greatest indicator of accelerating social change. Early manifestations of the computer and internet age now appear as cumbersome historical artefacts. The first 'personal' computers are displayed in the Science Museum in London, and brick-like mobile phones are period pieces compared with the streamlined gadgets of today. People throughout history have had to adapt to new, imposed circumstances, but the sheer speed and volume of modern innovation is beginning to challenge the versatility of our species.

In a society driven by technological development, it is more important than ever to maintain our relationship with the past. We do not exist in a vacuum but in a country defined by centuries of learning, conflict, worship and trade, to name but a few influences. Our modern era continues to demonstrate – often through wars, migration or political violence – the human desire for historical and geographical roots: an atavistic sense of belonging to a particular place for centuries. Such an awareness has enhanced our respect for the legacy of the past which previous centuries, with more limited resources, viewed as a source of plunder. Ruined Roman forts and medieval abbeys provided accessible building materials. Power and politics overcame localities: whole towns were razed to make way for new castles, those symbols

1 Antony Gormley's statue, *Sound II*, in the crypt of Winchester Cathedral, is intended to stand in or near water, symbolizing contemplation and the depths of the soul. Water floods naturally into the crypt in winter, reflecting the differing colours of the lead statue as well as the Norman arches. It forms a powerful symbol of the present encompassed by the past.

2 Gateshead's famous new Millennium Bridge, the first to rotate to allow ships to pass underneath, joins a series of outstanding bridges crossing the Tyne. A magnificent piece of modern architecture, it complements its older neighbours in the historic environment.

3 The ruins of Dunstanburgh Castle, built to protect the English against Scottish border raids, dominate a wild expanse of the Northumbrian coast. Its defensive capacities, long since unnecessary, are reinforced today by a flock of indomitable sheep.

of conquest and might. Medieval ways of life were swept aside by the 18th-century requirements for enclosed fields and livestock-rearing. Modern decisions to protect and conserve the artefacts of the past would have been inconceivable to 18th-century soldiers, politicians and entrepreneurs, if not to scholars and intellectuals. Even to them, it would not have seemed sensible to protect an apparently useless piece of the past at the cost of fashion, convenience and potential profit.

We feel differently now. It is not just great medieval religious and military buildings, chocolate-box thatched cottages, magnificent stately homes and venerable stone circles that are protected by statute. Organizations such as English Heritage have responsibilities for structures which some might consider ugly and redundant. Vast textile mills and coal mines are visible symbols of England's great industrial past, but for others they are all too immediate memorials to exploited labour and hardships. Housing estates and tower blocks, built within living memory, may be seen as symbols of the death of local communities, although they replaced slums. Modern bridges, schools and churches, still too new, in some eyes, to have proved themselves, are also now subject to protection. The legislation can seem restrictive. The owners of the marvellous Willis Corroon

building in Ipswich, designed in the 1970s by Norman Foster and listed Grade I, had to seek Listed Building consent for internal alterations, something few owners of modern buildings have to consider. But such concern will enable not only buildings of different ages, but gardens, bridges, industrial artefacts and other important features of today's landscape to be valued by our descendants and preserved for their children.

In addition, as a nation we increasingly recognize the scope of the historic environment. The local corner shop, the cobbled side alley, the Victorian coalholes let into the pavement, are all part of the everyday environment that gives people a sense of place and of belonging, an essential understanding of how they fit into the broader picture. Physical features are part of the lives of an area's inhabitants, even if not consciously noticed. Their significance is indicated in major local protests about the demolition of a much-loved neighbourhood landmark, or even the felling of a tree — protests which often now win the point!

The current conservation practices of organizations such as English Heritage understand all this. They list

modern buildings and encourage good modern architecture, both within the historic environment and on new sites. And alongside this, most people recognize that the past cannot be preserved in aspic. It must change and develop in order to be relevant to today and to the future. Only through such awareness can we decide what we — and our descendants — can afford to lose. A growing understanding of the importance of the past to the present and the future, enables us to make those judgements intelligently and evaluate more clearly what we want to pass on.

2

3

ENGLISH HERITAGE

ENGLISH HERITAGE IS THE INDEPENDENT BUT GOVERNMENT-SPONSORED BODY RESPONSIBLE FOR THE HISTORIC ENVIRONMENT OF ENGLAND. ITS AIM IS TO PROTECT ENGLAND'S UNIQUE ARCHITECTURAL AND ARCHAEOLOGICAL HERITAGE FOR THE BENEFIT AND ENJOYMENT OF PRESENT AND FUTURE GENERATIONS.

THE MOST VISIBLE aspect of its work is the 400 sites and monuments that are in its care, most of which are open to the public and many of which are free of charge. They range from Stonehenge and parts of Hadrian's Wall, both of which are World Heritage Sites, through grand houses like Audley End, Osborne House and Brodsworth Hall in Yorkshire, to the ruins of great medieval abbeys like Rievaulx and Cleeve, and megaliths and ruined chapels in the middle of fields. English Heritage not only protects and conserves these major monuments of past civilizations but also opens them to the public, runs events in them and offers shops and catering facilities. Some, like Warkworth and Dunstanburgh Castles in Northumberland, are ruins – still dominant, brooding and huge, but no longer habitable; others, like Eltham Palace in southeast London, or Down House in Kent, were, until recently, homes. Eltham is truly amazing: a combination of the magnificent 15th-century Great Hall, built for Edward IV, with the 1930s Art Deco home of Stephen and Virginia Courtauld, all surrounded by luscious gardens. Down House, in itself an unremarkable building, is revered as the home of Charles Darwin, the revolutionary Victorian scientist who spent both his happiest and his most productive years there. It was at Down House that he worked on his theory of evolution; in the study, still much as it was when he used it, he wrote *On the Origin of Species by means of Natural Selection*; the sandwalk in the garden was his 'thinking path'.

But English Heritage's work is much broader than its properties. It is England's principal centre of expertise on the historic environment. It advises the government on the listing of buildings of historic importance – including wide categories of post-World War II buildings, which are so important architecturally that they are regarded as the heritage of the future – and the scheduling of monuments – including the monuments of the industrial age and the conflicts of the 20th century. It also advises on the designation of conservation areas, which range from the glorious Georgian terraces of Bath and Stamford, through picturesque villages, to urban streets of Victorian and Edwardian houses. It supports archaeological investigations of all kinds, from traditional excavation through geophysical survey of buried remains to the detailed analyses of standing buildings. There are 43 known and researched historic battlefields on the Battlefields Register, and some 15,000 historic gardens on the Parks and Gardens Register, both important planning tools. The archaeological scientists do ground-breaking research in dating methods, artefact conservation and the study of environmental remains such as human and animal bones, pollen and seeds. The Collections and Building Conservation teams carry out wide ranges of research and practical conservation work, for example into easel and wall paintings. The National Monuments Record in Swindon contains over 11 million items. The Education Service is internationally renowned for the work it does with schools and colleges at all levels of formal education.

There are currently around 470,000 members, people who support English Heritage because they believe the membership fees are a tangible and direct way of supporting the work English Heritage does as well as enabling them to enter sites and events free of charge. Membership offers a quarterly magazine, special events for members (including an annual season of lectures and 'behind-the-scenes' activities) and an annual handbook listing all the sites with details of opening hours. Information about all the benefits membership brings, plus the costs of the various membership categories, can be obtained from English Heritage Membership Department, PO Box 570, Swindon, SN2 2UR; telephone 0870 333 1181; e-mail members@english-heritage.org.uk

The lists below of places to visit do not give opening hours, charges, or directions, because these details are subject to change. What they do provide is a glimpse of the many fascinating things you can see at English Heritage's sites; those mentioned below are only some of the 400-plus properties for which it cares, most of them open free of charge. They have been arranged according to the subject matter of the book's chapters, in the hope of tantalizing you with some of the less well-known sideshows at the sites, as well as offering a range of high-profile and interesting things to see and do.

WHO ARE 'THE ENGLISH'?
How better to begin to think about this than by visiting Stonehenge and the sites around it: Avebury, West Kennet Long Barrow, Silbury Hill – who built them and why? The whole of the landscape in this part of Wiltshire is dotted with barrows; one cannot fail to wonder about the builders and their lives, and what use they made of the results of their mammoth efforts. The Rollright Stones, too, and Castlerigg – stone circles built with huge labour by people long gone – what for, why?

QUINTESSENTIAL ENGLAND
This, as it says, is the essence of our heritage, good and bad: Wharram Percy, a deserted medieval village, redolent of the poverty and uncertainty of medieval life, with its graveyard full of children; Nunney Castle, an

exquisite small castle standing within its moat in a picturesque Somerset village – it looms gently at you over the roofs of the cottages, now peaceful, but once a possible refuge in times of war; the Uffington White Horse, almost a symbol of Englishness – how did its ancient builders get the perspective so right? Leigh Court Barn, a magnificent structure built for the monks of Pershore, a reminder in its sheer size of the wealth and power of medieval monasteries; Clifford's Tower, symbol of Norman military strength but also poignant memorial to the 13th-century Jews massacred within its walls, said to exude blood in memory; and perhaps most evocative of all, Tintagel, legendary birthplace of King Arthur, the quintessential Englishman, in myth at least. The recent discovery of a stone incised with an Arthur-line name has only added to the mystery of this ancient legend.

INVASION, CONQUEST AND WAR
So many sites could be listed under this heading, since many of them are the castles that presided over the medieval landscape; they continue to dominate in their ruined state today. Think soberly of Richmond Castle, where a number of conscientious objectors to World War I were incarcerated, initially under sentence of death – their poignant graffiti are still there; or fondly, if you are a member of the Richard III society and don't subscribe to his Shakespearean persona, of Middleham Castle, his childhood home; or romantically of Boscobel, where Charles II took refuge in the oak tree after losing the battle of Worcester. On a winter's day, the forts on Hadrian's Wall vividly evoke their shivering Roman guards; their domestic arrangements are there to see, too, in the multi-seater lavatory at Housesteads. Dover Castle perhaps crowns them all, with its 2,000 years of military history from the pre-Roman hillfort on its site, through its importance to the Romans who built a lighthouse there, and on to William I and Henry II who recognized the strategic value of the site and built the magnificent castle. Medieval and Napoleonic tunnels in the cliffs were still hugely important during World War II, and were later adapted as Cold War bunkers.

A MARITIME NATION
The forts all around the coast underpin the vital part the sea and the coast played in England's history, not only as the entrance points for invasion and immigration, but also as the centre of English sea power, the basis of its imperial and colonial success. Henry VIII's forts, forming a defensive chain around the south coast, possess a distinctive clover-leaf design: Deal Castle is still in good shape, with roofs and internal structures in place, but Walmer Castle, just along the coast, is now a comfortable home as well as a castle – transformed by its renaissance as the official residence of the Lord Warden of the Cinque Ports. The duke of Wellington died there during his tenure of that office, the real-life

inspiration for Lord Marchmain in Evelyn Waugh's *Brideshead Revisited* lived there at the time of World War I. Further round the coast, Portchester Castle, like Dover, can boast 2,000 years of history; and further on still, Dartmouth Castle, on its magnificent site overlooking the River Dart, was the first castle to be built with artillery in mind, while Pendennis and St Mawes, again built by Henry VIII, face each other across the estuary of the River Fal. By contrast, at Whitby Abbey, you may like to look down from the abbey ruins at the scene of the arrival of the ship carrying Dracula – only a Bram Stoker story, of course…!

IN FEAR AND PRAISE
Canterbury has always been one of the major centres of Christianity in England; its archbishop is the leader of the English church and its cathedral dominates the city. But also to be seen there are the ruins of St Augustine's Abbey, founded by the emissary of Pope Gregory who landed on the Kent coast in AD 697 to reconvert the English to Christianity. English Heritage has many ruined abbeys in its care, but only one cathedral; its ruins can be seen within the ramparts of Old Sarum, Wiltshire, whose inhabitants decamped down the valley in the 13th century to build a new cathedral at Salisbury. Two churches maintained by English Heritage have magnificent wall paintings: St Mary's, Kempley is a Norman church with splendid decorations dating back to somewhere between the 12th and the 14th centuries; in contrast, St Mary's, Studley Royal, part of the Fountains Abbey estate, was magnificently ornamented in the Victorian era.

PILLARS OF WISDOM
Many of England's centres of learning are, of course, still used for their original purpose. The medieval origins of Oxford and Cambridge colleges, for example. have been extended through the centuries; along with the castle in Durham, they are living, working universities, full of students and academics. Think instead, therefore, of how things were in the past when education was the privilege of the few and mostly to be found in the institutions of the church. Abbeys such as Rievaulx and Byland, Furness and Cleeve were the homes of monks who scripted and decorated books, themselves teachers and scholars; at Mount Grace Priory, Carthusian monks worked and studied in their own small cells – one has been reconstructed there. Whitby Abbey exemplifies the importance to the early church of educated women; its formidable abbess, Hilda, a woman of great wisdom and learning, hosted the Synod of Whitby there in AD 664.

DEATH AND REMEMBRANCE
It is the fate of us all to end up as 'human jam', as Thomas Hardy so memorably put it, and monuments to the dead are legion. At Belas Knapp Neolithic Long

Barrow in Gloucestershire, the remains of 31 people were found – presumably the more privileged dead who merited a place within the barrow. Farleigh Hungerford Castle is a magnificent ruin; do not miss the tiny chapel with an array of almost collapsed lead coffins, some those of children placed on top of, possibly, their mothers. The Eleanor Cross at Geddington is one of only three remaining originals from the great sequence built at the behest of Edward I to mark the resting places of his wife's body on its way to London – a poignant reminder that even great kings, known for their brutality, could experience love and loss. As could great queens: the Albert Memorial in London's Hyde Park, recently fully restored by English Heritage to its original glory, was Queen Victoria's monument to her husband, for whom she never ceased to mourn.

LAW, CRIME AND PUNISHMENT

Carisbrooke Castle, on the Isle of Wight, was the prison of Charles I, who tried to escape twice; prisoners of lesser importance were made to tread the waterwheel, until the introduction in the 17th century of donkeys, who are still there today. All castles were centres of administration and lawmaking, as well as defence, and many still have dungeons: Goodrich Castle, in Herefordshire, has a nasty little dungeon, airless and lightless, though it is not as cramped as Warwick Castle's truly horrible oubliette. Carlisle Castle has a small cell with engravings probably made by the prisoners of Richard of Gloucester in about 1480, and also held Mary Queen of Scots at one time, as well as the remnants of Bonnie Prince Charlie's army in 1746.

A PLACE IN THE COUNTRY

Of course, there are the major stately homes: Audley End, Osborne House, Brodsworth Hall. But do not forget others such as Aydon Castle, in Northumberland, one of England's finest examples of a 13th-century manor house, later fortified, and later still converted into a farmhouse that remained at the centre of a working farm until 1966. Or consider Stokesay Castle in Shropshire, not a real castle but another 13th-century fortified manor house, with a magnificent timber-framed Jacobean gateway. Prudhoe Castle features a Georgian manor house built where the medieval residential cross-range used to be; it now finds itself in the middle of an industrial estate. Similarly, Bolsover now towers over a motorway in a former mining area, but was built in the 17th century for elegant living.

TRAVEL AND TRANSPORT

Wall Roman site, in Staffordshire, was an important Roman staging post, situated on the crossroads of two major Roman roads. In later times, castles were built on important strategic routes, controlling traffic and commercial travel as well as to protect and defend. Beeston Castle, in Cheshire, commands probably the most stunning views of any castle in the country, but was built to control the roads and the countryside around.

THE INDUSTRIAL REVOLUTION

The Iron Bridge, built by the local ironmaster, Abraham Darby, over the River Severn in 1779, was the world's first iron bridge; it is now one of Britain's best known industrial monuments and a World Heritage Site. Less spectacular, but still redolent of the vast changes wrought by the industrial revolution, is Stott Park Bobbin Mill in Cumbria. Built in 1835 to make the bobbins vital for the Lancashire spinning and weaving industries, it worked continuously until 1971. Other mills include Saxtead Green Post Mill, used for milling corn and still in working order; Berney Arms Windmill, one of the best and largest remaining marsh mills in Norfolk; Sibsey Trader Windmill, an impressive tower mill built in 1877; and Mortimer's Cross Water Mill, still in working order. And then, if you want to consider the industries of the more distant past, there is Grimes Graves in Norfolk, where the 'moon landscape' with its saucer-shaped depressions conceals the shafts dug 4,000 years ago to mine flint to make tools and weapons. One shaft has been fully excavated and can be visited.

DISCOVERY AND PRESERVATION

All English Heritage sites show aspects of its work in investigating, discovering and conserving evidence for the past. One particular site is perhaps diagnostic of the ways in which the examination of past monuments and methods of presenting them have changed radically in recent years. Sites used to be displayed in a sanitized way, with smooth mown lawns and all debris cleared away; indeed, many of them are still like that. But Wigmore Castle illustrates a new approach. Once one of the main fortresses of the Welsh Marches, the castle was abandoned in the 17th century and left to collapse. It became totally overgrown with greenery, which helped to preserve the fragile masonry. When English Heritage took it over in 1995, it was decided not to strip the greenery all away, but to remove it carefully, conserve what needed work underneath, and replace it. The castle therefore appears still as a 'romantic ruin', and remains a haven for plants and wildlife. Entry is free, but its lack of landscaping and facilities makes it quite a challenge for visitors.

LIVING THE PAST

All English Heritage's sites offer a taste of history, and many of them host the thousands of events run each year, which help to bring the past vividly to life. Kirby Hall has the biggest and best: 'History in Action' in August is probably the largest in the world, with over 2,500 performers re-enacting all periods of history from the Romans to World War II.

FURTHER READING

AILTON, Andrew & Bignamini, Ilaria, *Grand Tour: The Lure of Italy in the Eighteenth Century*, Tate Gallery, London, 1996.

ARNOLD, Dana, *The Georgian Country House: Architecture, Landscape and Society*, Sutton Publishing, Stroud, Gloucestershire, 1998

BABINGTON, Caroline, Manning, Tracy & Stewart, Sophie, *Our Painted Past, Wall paintings of English Heritage*, English Heritage, London, 1999.

BAKER, D., *Potworks: Industrial Architecture of the Staffordshire Potteries*, Royal Commission on the Historical Monuments of England, London, 1991.

BLACK, Jeremy, *A New History of England*, Sutton Publishing, Stroud, 2000.

BOLD, John, *Greenwich: an Architectural History of the Royal Hospital for Seamen and the Queen's House*, Yale University Press in association with English Heritage, London, 2001.

BOWDEN, Mark (ed) *Unravelling the Landscape: an Inquisitive Approach to Archaeology*, Tempus, Gloucestershire, 1999.

BRIGGS, Asa, *A Social History of England*, Weidenfeld & Nicolson, London, 1994.

BRODIE, Allan, Croom, Jane & O Davies, James, *Behind Bars: the Hidden Architecture of England's Prisons*, English Heritage, London, 2000.

BROOKS, Chris (ed), *The Albert Memorial*, Yale University Press, London, 2000.

BROWN, Andrew (ed), *The Rows of Chester*, English Heritage, London, 1999.

BROWN, Sarah, *Sumptuous and Richly Adorn'd: the Decoration of Salisbury Cathedral*, Royal Commission on the Historical Monuments of England with The Stationery Office, London, 1999.

CATTELL, John & Falconer, Keith, *Swindon: the Legacy of a Railway Town*, English Heritage, London, 2000.

CATTELL, John & Hawkins, Bob, *The Birmingham Jewellery Quarter: an Introduction and Guide*, English Heritage, London, 2000.

CHADWICK, H., *The Early Church*, Penguin, London, 1967.

CLIFTON-TAYLOR, Alec, *English Parish Churches as Works of Art*, Batsford, London, 1974.

CLIFTON-TAYLOR, Alec, & Ireson, A.S., *English Stone Building*, Victor Gollancz Limited in association with Peter Crawley, London, 1994.

COCROFT, Wayne, *Dangerous Energy: The Archaeology of Gunpowder and Military Explosives Manufacture*, English Heritage, London, 2000.

COOPER, Nicholas, *Houses of the Gentry 1480–1680*, Yale University Press with English Heritage, 1999.

CORMACK, Patrick, *English Cathedrals*, Weidenfeld & Nicolson, London, 1984.

COSSONS, Neil, *The BP Book of Industrial Archaeology*, David & Charles, London, 1993.

COSSONS, Sir Neil (ed), *Perspectives on Industrial Archaeology*, Science Museum, London, 2000.

COWARD, Barry, *The Stuart Age*, Longman, Harlow, 1980.

COX, Margaret, *Life and Death in Spitalfields 1700 to 1850*, Council for British Archaeology, 1996.

DARVILL, Timothy, *Prehistoric Britain*, Routledge, London 1995.

DAVEY, Peter, *Arts and Crafts Architecture: The Search for Earthly Paradise*, Architectural Press, London, 1980.

DAVIES, Norman, *The Isles: A History*, Macmillan Press, London, 2000.

DAVISON, Brian, *Picturing the Past*, English Heritage Gatekeeper series, 1997.

FALCONER, K., *Guide to England's Industrial Heritage*, Batsford, London, 1980.

FLETCHER, Richard, *The Conversion of Europe: From Paganism to Christianity 371–1386 AD*, HarperCollins, London, 1997.

FORD, Boris (ed), *The Cambridge Guide to the Arts in Britain: The Middle Ages*, Cambridge University Press, Cambridge, 1988.

FORSHAW, Alec & Bergstrom, Theo, *Markets of London*, Penguin, London, 1983.

FRANKLIN, Jill, *The Gentleman's Country House and its Plan 1835–1914*, Routledge and Kegan Paul; London, 1981.

GAMBLE, Clive, *Archaeology: the Basics*, Routledge, London, 2001.

GINGER, Andrew, *Country Houses of England, Scotland and Wales, A Guide and Gazeteer*, George Philip Limited, London, 1991.

GIROUARD, Mark, *Life in the English Country House*, Yale University Press, London, 1978.

——, *The English Town*, Yale University Press, London, 1990.

GUEST, Ken & Denise, *British Battles*, HarperCollins in association with English Heritage, London, 1996.

GUILLERY, Peter & Kendall, Derek, *The City of London Churches*, Collins & Brown, London, 1998.

HARDYMENT, Christina, *Behind the Scenes: Domestic Arrangements in Historic Houses*, The National Trust, London 1992, 1997.

HARRIS, John, Orgel, Stephen & Strong, Roy, *The King's Arcadia: Inigo Jones and the Stuart Court*, The Arts Council, London, 1973.

HIBBERT, Christopher, *The English: A Social History 1066–1945*, Grafton Books, London, 1987.

——, *The Story of England*, Phaidon Press, London, 1992.

——, *London: the Biography of a City*, Penguin, London, 1980.

HILLS, Catherine, *Blood of the British*, George Philip in association with Channel 4 Television Company Limited, London, 1986.

HOSKINS, W.G., *The Making of the English Landscape*, Pelican Books, London, 1970.

JACKSON-STOPS, Gervase & Pipkin, James, *The English Country House, A Grand Tour*, Weidenfeld & Nicolson/The National Trust, London, 1984.

JENKINS, Simon, *England's Thousand Best Churches*, Penguin, London, 2000.

JENNER, Michael, *Victorian Britain*, Weidenfeld & Nicolson, London, 1999.

JOHNSON, Paul, *Castles of England, Scotland and Wales*, Weidenfeld & Nicolson, London, 1989.

LAING, Lloyd & Jennifer, *Medieval Britain: The Age of Chivalry*, Herbert Press, London, 1996.

LASDUN, Susan, *The English Park*, André Deutsch, London, 1991.

LLOYD, David W., *The Making of English Towns*, Victor Gollancz Limited in association with Peter Crawley, London, 1998.

LLOYD, Nathaniel, *A History of the English House*, Architectural Press, London, 1931.

McALEAVY, Tony, *Life in a Medieval Abbey*, English Heritage Gatekeeper series, 1996.

——, *Life in a Medieval Castle*, English Heritage Gatekeeper series, 1998.

——, *Life in Roman Britain*, English Heritage Gatekeeper series, 1999.

MORRISON, Kathryn, *The Workhouse: a Study of Poor-law Buildings in England*, English Heritage, London, 1999.

MOWLL, Timothy, *Elizabethan and Jacobean Style*, Phaidon Press, London, 1993.

MUSGRAVE, Toby & Will, *An Empire of Plants*, Cassell & Co, London, 2000.

PLANEL, Philippe, *Locks and Lavatories: the Architecture of Privacy*, English Heritage Gatekeeper series, 2000.

POTTER, T.W., *Roman Britain*, British Museum Press, London, 1997.

RANDALL, *Church Furnishing & Decoration*, Batsford, London, 1980.

RICHARDSON, Harriet (ed), *English Hospitals 1660–1948: A Survey of their Architecture and Design*, Royal Commission on the Historical Monuments of England, London, 1998.

RICHARDSON, John, *The Annals of London*, Cassell & Co, London, 2000.

RIDLEY, Jasper, *The Tudor Age*, Constable & Co Limited, London, 1988.

ROBERTS, J.M., *The History of the World*, Hutchinson, London, 1992.

SAUL, Nigel (ed), *Historical Atlas of Britain: Prehistoric and Medieval*, Sutton Publishing, Stroud, 1994.

SCHAMA, Simon, *A History of Britain, 3000 BC to AD 1603*, BBC Books, London, 2000.

STRATTON, Michael, & Trinder, Barrie, *Industrial England*, Batsford in association with English Heritage, London 1997.

Survey of London: Knightsbridge, English Heritage in association with Athlone Press, 2000.

TREVELYAN, G. M., *English Social History* (illustrated edition), Longman Group Limited, London, 1978; Penguin, London 1986.

——, *History of England*, Longman Green & Co Limited, London, 1952 (revised edition).

WATERSON, Merlin, *The Servants Hall: A Domestic History of Erddig*, Routledge and Kegan Paul. 1980.

WATKIN, David, *English Architcture*, Thames & Hudson, London, 2001.

WOOD, Eric S., *Historical Britain*, Harvill Press, London, 1995.

WOOD, Margaret, *The English Medieval House*, Studio Editions, London, 1994.

WOOD, Michael, *In Search of England: Journeys into the English Past*, Penguin, London, 2000.

——, *In Search of the Dark Ages*, BBC Books, London, 1983.

WOODCOCK, Thomas & Martin Robinson, John, *The Oxford Guide to Heraldry*, Oxford University Press , Oxford, 1990.

YOUNG, P. & Adair J., *Hastings to Culloden*, Sutton Publishers, Stroud, 1996.

GLOSSARY

ARCADE A covered passageway produced by a series of arches, supported by columns or piers along one or both sides.

ASHLAR A form of masonry which uses large blocks of stone, worked to a smooth surface with close joints.

BAROQUE A 17th-century Italian style of architecture and decorative art, distinguished by lavish ornamentation.

BARROW/LONG BARROW A prehistoric earth mound, thrown up to cover a burial site. The earliest versions, dating as far back as 5000–4000 BC, were elongated. From c.4000 BC to approximately the 10th century AD, circular barrows were also built.

BAY A division of a building, either inside or out, created by supporting walls, columns or buttresses.

BLIND ARCADING A series of arches and columns featured solely for decorative effect, usually an actual part of the wall.

CHANTRY A chapel or altar within a church, endowed for the singing of masses for the founder's soul.

CLERESTORY A series of windows placed above the nave, choir and transepts of a large church.

COLONNADE A row of evenly spaced columns supporting a roof, entablature or arches.

COPPICING The technique of managing small, fast growing trees or bushes by cutting them back regularly. Hazel and willow are the species most commonly coppiced, traditionally for flexible poles or firewood. *See also Withies.*

CORINTHIAN An architectural style frequently applied to columns with distinctive, bell-shaped capital and decorative carvings based on acanthus leaves. The Corinthian style originated in ancient Greece and is one of architecture's five classical orders.

CRENELLATE Literally, to erect battlements on the wall of a building. In a broader context, it means making a building capable of withstanding siege. From the French *créneler*.

FLUSHWORK A combination of flint and dressed stone on a flat surface, used to create decorative patterns.

GEODESIC DOME A lightweight, rigid structure made from polygonal or triangular shapes. It is able to cover large areas without braces or supports.

GEORGIAN The adjective applied to art, architecture, furniture etc. from the period spanning the reigns of the Hanoverian monarchs (between 1714 and 1837).

HENGE A Neolithic monument surrounded by a bank and ditch and often encompassing a circle of stones. Their exact purpose is unknown, but may have involved a ceremonial function.

JACOBEAN A blend of Gothic and classical styles of architecture associated with the reign of James I (1603–25).

LANCET A slender window with a pointed arch (known as a lancet arch). In elongated form, lancets are a feature of Early English cathedral architecture.

LIERNE An architectural term used with particular reference to Gothic vaulting. It identifies the short secondary rib that connects the bosses and intersections of the principal (long) ribs.

LODEN A short-piled, substantial woollen cloth. Thick and waterproof, it was traditionally used for making coats.

NEOCLASSICAL An architectural and artistic style of the late 18th and 19th centuries, based upon a revival of classical aesthetics and precepts (such as harmony, proportion and balance).

OOLITIC A form of Jurassic limestone formed from small corals, or spherical grains, known as ooliths. It has a distinctive textured surface, although ooliths vary in prominence in different types.

QUOINS Dressed stones placed at the external angle of a building or opening, often alternately large and small for aesthetic effect.

ROOD SCREEN The wood or stone screen which divides the nave and choir in a church. It traditionally supported a crucifix ('rood').

SAMIAN WARE A form of fine earthenware pottery, reddish-brown or black in colour and also known as Arretine ware and *terra sigillata*. Made in Gaul between the 1st and 4th centuries AD, Samian ware is found in large quantities on Romano-British sites.

SARSEN A boulder composed of silicified sandstone, many of which feature in Neolithic monuments.

SURCOAT The outer coat worn over a coat of armour by warriors of rank to display their heraldic arms.

TORC (also TORQUE) A piece of jewellery, usually in the form of a necklace or armband, worn by Celtic tribes across Europe. They were made from solid lengths of metal, usually gold or electrum; the ends were secured by decorative bosses.

TRACERY The decorative interlacing of stonework at the head of a Gothic-style window.

TRANSEPT Either of the north/south arms in a cruciform church.

TRILITHON A standing stone structure consisting of two upright stones and a lintel placed across the top, as at Stonehenge.

WITHIES (sing. WITHE) Long, flexible twigs, especially of willow, used for tying, binding or plaiting into simple but strong rope.

DETAILS OF PHOTOMONTAGE PAGES

COTTAGES *Page 60:* (*left to right and top to bottom*) Walderton, West Sussex*; Aldeburgh, Suffolk; Clare, Suffolk; Watersfield, West Sussex*; Pulham Market, Norfolk; Hatfield Broad Oak, Essex; Lulworth, Dorset; Pulham Market, Norfolk; Elstow, Bedfordshire; Cromford, Derbyshire; Horsham, West Sussex*; Titchfield, Hampshire*. *Page 61:* Market Bosworth, Leicestershire. (Those marked * were kindly lent by Weald & Downland Museum, Singleton, Chichester, West Sussex.)

CASTLES *Page 110:* Bodiam Castle, East Sussex. *Page 111 (left-hand side, top to bottom)* Pevensey Castle, East Sussex; Dover Castle, Kent; Clifford's Tower, York; Dunstanburgh Castle, nr Craster, Northumberland; Bamburgh Castle, Northumberland; Castle Rising, Norfolk; Framlingham Castle, Suffolk; Burgh Castle, Norfolk. (*right-hand side, top to bottom*) Martello Tower, Aldeburgh, Suffolk; Tattershall Castle, Lincolnshire; Portchester Castle, Hampshire; Bamburgh Castle, Northumberland; Conisbrough Castle, South Yorkshire; Orford Castle, Suffolk; Warkworth Castle, Northumberland.

CATHEDRALS *Page 174: Bristol. Page 175 (left to right and top to bottom)* Canterbury; Lincoln; Norwich; Winchester; Peterborough; Exeter; Rochester; Canterbury; Lincoln; Exeter ; Durham; Peterborough; Lichfield; Wells; St Albans; York Minster.

GREAT HOUSES *Page 278:* Kenwood, London. *Page 279 (left to right and top to bottom)* Athelhampton, Dorset; Stowe, Buckinghamshire; Audley End, Essex; Chatsworth, Derbyshire; Little Moreton Hall, Cheshire; Stokesay Castle, Shropshire; Ickworth House, Suffolk; Kirby Muxloe Castle, Leicestershire; Markenfield Hall, North Yorkshire; Oxburgh Hall, Norfolk; Baddesley Clinton, Warwickshire; Audley End, Essex.

BRIDGES AND VIADUCTS *Page 312 (left to right and top to bottom)* Ribblehead Viaduct, North Yorkshire; Newby Bridge, Cumbria; Stowe, Buckinghamshire; Tower Bridge, London; Bridge of Sighs, Oxford; Sadgill Bridge, Cumbria; Cookham, Berkshire; Albert Bridge, London; Ribblehead Viaduct, North Yorkshire; Stockley Bridge, Cumbria; Slater's Bridge, Cumbria; Tyne Bridges, Newcastle-upon-Tyne. *Page 313:* Ironbridge, Shropshire.

LIVING THE PAST *Pages 396–397:* All photographs were taken in August 2000 at English Heritage's 'History in Action', at Kirby Hall, Northamptonshire. Grateful thanks to all those featured!

INDEX

References in italic refer to illustrations.

ACKNOWLEDGEMENTS

AUTHOR'S ACKNOWLEDGEMENTS
Through the medium of this book I would like to offer my personal thanks to all those who care for the environment and countless historic buildings contained within it. This includes organizations such as the Weald and Down Museum and the Landmark Trust, who both salvage and preserve priceless vernacular buildings and English Heritage, whose work extends far beyond those sites open to the public.

The compilation and production of England's Heritage has been a team effort of vast proportions and I would firstly like to thank David Miles, Chief Archaeologist at English Heritage and Val Horsler, head of their Publications Department for contributing Chapters 12 and 13. I would also like to thank Oliver Pearcey, Director of Conservation at English Heritage for his valuable advice and suggestions.

My own photographs have been augmented by archive material from the National Monument Record in Swindon, among others. I am very grateful for the perseverance of Alyson Rogers, who extracted the images from a collection totalling millions. Both Celia Sterne from the English Heritage Photographic Library and picture researcher Cecilia Weston-Baker have provided an excellent selection of architectural and fine art pictures.

A heavily illustrated book relies on the skill of its designers to collate all the elements successfully. The book's designer, Ken Wilson, and Austin Taylor, Art Editor at Cassell & Co, have created a work of visual delight that does full justice to both illustrations and text.

Finally, I must offer my sincere thanks to two very special people who have kept both me and this book on the straight and narrow – my wife Madeline for endless coffee, bananas and patience during months of writing, and my editor Catherine Bradley, who not only contributed so much to the planning of the book but whose guidance, dedication and commitment have also carried it through to a successful conclusion.

The publishers gratefully acknowledge the assistance of the following in the preparation of this book:
Slaney Begley, Nicholas Best, Pete Cawston, Kathy Gill, Molly Perham, Christopher Westhorp, the Oxford Archaeological Unit and all those who contributed time, effort and inspiration at the National Monuments Records at Swindon and English Heritage in London.

The publisher would like to thank the following people, museums and photographic libraries for permission to reproduce their material. Every care has been taken to trace copyright holders. However, if we have omitted anyone we apologise and will, if informed, make corrections in any future edition.

All photographs are © Derry Brabbs with the exception of the following:

Reproduced by permission of English Heritage
Pages 12 EH/Alan Sorrell; 15 top, EH/Terry Ball; 17 top; 18 top right and bottom; 22 bottom; 88; 94 bottom left and right; EH/Peter Dunn; 98 top EH/Peter Dunn; 106 EH/Peter Dunn; 108 top; 112; 112-113; 122; 123; 124; 125 top and bottom, EH/Alan Sorrell; 126; 129 top and bottom; 137; 148; 162 bottom; 190; 215 bottom; 217 top EH/Peter Dunn; 237 bottom; 241 top and bottom; 253 top and bottom; 254 top and bottom; 255 top and bottom; 257; 262 bottom; 266 top; 267; 274 top and bottom; 278; 280; 281; 282; 283 top and bottom; 284; 285 top and bottom; 323 bottom; 325 bottom; 327 bottom; 356; 358 top and bottom; 361 bottom; 362; 365 top and bottom; 367 top; 369; 371 top and bottom; 372; 374 top and bottom; 373; 378 bottom; 381 top and bottom; 386; 400.

Reproduced with permission of English Heritage/Skyscan
Pages 17 bottom; 19; 91; 100; 363; 366

Reproduced with permission of English Heritage (from the National Monument Record at Swindon)
Pages 13; 16; 30–31; 32 bottom; 38 bottom; 40 bottom; 44 bottom; 45; 46 top; 52 top and bottom; 57; 58 top; 69 top and bottom; 71 top and bottom; 78 top; 84 top; 87 bottom; 98 bottom; 127; 136 bottom; 144; 167; 178 top; 189 bottom; 194 top; 205; 206; 207 bottom; 209; 216; 231; 234 bottom; 237 top; 243 bottom; 246; 248 bottom; 252; 259; 261 bottom; 273; 276; 286; 287; 289 bottom; 291; 292; 298; 302 top; 303; 307 bottom; 309; 313; 317; 319 top; 320; 321 bottom; 322; 323 top; 324 bottom; 330 bottom; 331; 337; 338 bottom; 339; 343 top; 344; 345; 349 bottom; 351; 353; 355; 360; 364, 369.

Reproduced with permission of English Heritage Special Events Department
Pages 384; 385 top; 389; 394; 395 top and bottom; 399.

© Bridgeman Art Library
Pages 11 BAL/British Library (BL); 18 top left BAL/Private Collection; 24 BAL/BL; 25 BAL/BL; 27 BAL/Private Collection; 73

BAL/Victoria & Albert Museum; 75 BAL/Museum of London; 82 BAL/Biblioteque National, Paris (Fr4276 f.6); 83 BAL/BL; 84 bottom BAL/Wallace Collection, London; 85 BAL/National Portrait Gallery, London; 86 BAL/Maidstone Museum & Art Gallery; 90 BAL/Museo e Gallerie National de Capolinato, Naples; 96–97 bottom BAL/Museum de la Tappisserie, Caen; 103 bottom BAL/Alecto Historical Editions. London; 105 BAL/BL; 108 bottom BAL/Christie's Images, London; 114 BAL/PRO; 120 BAL/Private Collection; 131 BAL/Musee de la Marine, Paris; 134 BAL/Woburn Abbey; 139 top BAL/Private Collection; 141 bottom BAL/Private Collection; 151 BAL/BL; 189 top BAL/Royal Academy of Arts Library; 201 bottom BAL/Private Collection; 216–217 BAL/Private Collection; 224 BAL/Private Collection; 233 top BAL/Private Collection; 236 BAL/Philip Mould Historical Portraits; 238 BAL/Private Collection; 245 BAL/Towner Art Gallery, Eastbourne; 249 BAL/Private Collection; 264 BAL/Private Collection (bottom); 268 BAL/Private Collection; 297 top BAL/Guildhall Library, London; 300 BAL/Christie's Images; 301 bottom BAL/Cheltenham Art Gallery and Museum; 305 BAL/New Walk Museum, Leicester City Museum Service; 316 BAL/Science Museum; 318 BAL/Ironbridge Gorge Museum; 325 BAL/Private Collection; 328 BAL/Private Collection; 343 bottom BAL/Leeds Museum & Art Gallery; 347 BAL/Private Collection; 349 top BAL/Private Collection.

© Christ Church, Spitalfields Archaeological Project
Pages 372; 373.

© The Hulton Getty
Pages 201 top; 203; 242; 354.

© Museum of London Picture Library
Pages 357 bottom; 361 top right; 370.

© National Maritime Museum, London
Pages 133 bottom; 135 bottom; 136 top; 138 top; 138–39 bottom.

© Norfolk Archaeological Unit
Page 368 top and bottom.

© North News
Page 401 top.

© Oxford Archaeological Unit, Oxford
Pages 359 top and bottom; 361 top left; 375.

© The Mary Rose Trust
Page 133 top.